On the Origin of the Right to Copy

Taking as its point of departure the lapse of the Licensing Act 1662 in 1695, this book examines the lead up to the passage of the Statute of Anne 1709 and charts the movement of copyright law throughout the eighteenth century, culminating in the House of Lords decision of *Donaldson v Becket* (1774). The established reading of copyright's development throughout this period, from the 1709 Act to the pronouncement in *Donaldson*, is one that bears witness to its singular transformation from publisher's right to author's right. That is, legislation initially designed to regulate the marketplace of the bookseller and publisher evolves into an instrument that functions to recognise the proprietary inevitability of an author's intellectual labours. The historical narrative which unfolds within this book presents a challenge to that accepted orthodoxy. The traditional analysis of the development of copyright in eighteenth century Britain is revealed as exhibiting the character of long-standing myth, and the centrality of the modern proprietary author as the raison d'être of the copyright regime is displaced.

On the Origin of the Right to Copy

Charting the Movement of Copyright Law in Eighteenth-Century Britain (1695–1775)

RONAN DEAZLEY

OXFORD AND PORTLAND OREGON
2004

Published in North America (US and Canada) by
Hart Publishing
c/o International Specialized Book Services
5804 NE Hassalo Street
Portland, Oregon
97213-3644
USA

Hart Publishing is a specialist legal publisher based in Oxford, England. To order further copies of this book or to request a list of other publications please write to:

Hart Publishing, Salters Boatyard, Folly Bridge, Abingdon Rd, Oxford, OX1 4LB Telephone: +44 (0)1865 245533
Fax: +44 (0)1865 794882
email: mail@hartpub.co.uk
WEBSITE: http//:www.hartpub.co.uk

British Library Cataloguing in Publication Data
Data Available

ISBN 1-84113-375-2 (hardback)

Olympus Infotech Pvt Ltd, India, in Palatino 10/12 pt
Printed and bound in Great Britain by
MPG Books Ltd, Bodmin, Cornwall

Contents

One fine winter's day when Piglet was brushing away the snow in front of his house, he happened to look up, and there was Winnie-the-Pooh. Pooh was walking round and round in a circle, thinking of something else, and when Piglet called to him, he just went on walking.

'Hallo!' said Piglet. 'What are *you* doing?'
'Hunting,' said Pooh.
'Hunting what?'
'Tracking something,' said Winnie-the-Pooh very mysteriously.
'Tracking what?' said Piglet, coming closer.
'That's just what I ask myself. I ask myself, What?'
'What do you think you'll answer?'
'I shall have to wait until I catch up with it,' said Winnie-the-Pooh.

AA Milne, *Winnie-the-Pooh* (1926)

Table of Cases

Table of Statutes

Introduction
The History of Copyright; Evolutionary Strains

> The individual sense of wrong stimulates the moral growth of society at large; and in due course of time, after a strenuous struggle with those who profit by the denial of justice, there comes a calm at last, and ethics crystallize into law. In more modern periods of development, the recognition of new forms of property generally passes through three stages. First, there is a mere moral right, asserted by the individual and admitted by most other individuals, but not acknowledged by society as a whole. Second, there is a desire on the part of those in authority to find some means of protection for this admitted moral right, and the action in equity is allowed — this being the effort to command the conscience of those whom the ordinary policeman is incompetent to deal with. And thirdly, in the fullness of time, there is declared a law setting forth clearly the privileges of the producer and the means whereby he can defend his property and recover damages for an attack on it … As it happens, this growth of a self-asserted claim into a legally protected interest can be traced with unusual ease in the evolution of copyright, because copyright itself is a comparatively new thing.[1]

These words, penned by Brander Matthews in *Books and Playbooks*, were first published in 1895, two hundred years after the collapse of the prepublication licensing system in England. Matthews, a qualified lawyer, accomplished novelist and poet, and Professor of Dramatic Literature at Columbia University, in a chapter entitled "The Evolution of Copyright", details how, in fifteenth century Venice, the printer-publisher, who "stood for the author and was exactly in his position", prompted the legal recognition of printing rights "less than a score of years after the invention of printing had made … injury possible". Such acts, he continues, "established a precedent — a precedent which has broadened down the centuries until now, four hundred years later, any book published in Venice is, by international conventions, protected from pillage for a period of at

[1] B Matthews, *Books and Playbooks* (London, Osgood, McIlvaine & Co, 1895) 4–5.

least fifty years, through a territory which includes almost every important country of continental Europe".[2]

His examination of the English experience provided further evidence in support of this notionally organic unfurling of copyright law. What began in England as a "privilege granted at the caprice of the officials" blossomed into "a legal right, to be obtained by the author by observing the simple formalities of registration and deposit". Matthews was, of course, making reference to the passing of the *Statute of Anne* 1709. He proceeds:

> Besides the broadening of a capricious privilege into a legal right, and besides the lengthening of time during which this right is enforced, a steady progress of the idea that the literary labourer is worthy of his hire is to be seen in newer and subsidiary developments. With the evolution of copyright, the author can now reserve certain secondary rights of abridgment, of adaptation, and of translation.[3]

From the single seed of the printer's privilege grows the author's legal right to print his work for a certain length of time. From this author's right emerge a number of secondary rights, the term of protection lengthens, the right is extended to other "authors" (such as dramatists) operating within the realm of cultural production, and finally, this vibrant, slowly blooming flower outgrows the very country in which it first took root. "[T]he next step in the process of evolution" is that the author's right extend "beyond the boundaries of the country of which he is a citizen". At the time of writing, the development of international copyright protection was still in its infancy, and Matthews conceded as much, recognising that "[t]his great and needful improvement ... is still far from complete". Nevertheless he concluded, "year by year it advances farther and farther".[4]

There are of course many cultural manifestations of the authorial ego to be traced in the centuries prior to the Hanoverian reign in Britain;[5] indeed, that the figure of the author had been socially and culturally reified to such a significant extent as to have an identifiable market presence by the beginning of the eighteenth century was of central importance in securing the *Statute of Anne*.[6] However, few today would uncritically adopt Matthews' assertion that that particular legislation

[2] *Ibid*, 9–10.
[3] *Ibid*, 23.
[4] *Ibid*, 17, 27.
[5] See for example J Loewenstein, *The Author's Due: Printing and the Prehistory of Copyright* (Chicago, Il, University of Chicago Press, 2002); J Loewenstein, *Ben Jonson and Possessive Authorship* (Cambridge, CUP, 2002).
[6] See ch 2, The Statute of Anne; A Miserable Havock.

had anything to do with acknowledging the moral claim that authors might have for protecting such work as they produce. In its place, a more sophisticated and subtle narrative has been adopted concerning the development of copyright during this period wherein the coalition of author as cultural persona and author as proprietary rights holder is not realised with the inception of the 1709 Act but is instead deferred until later in the century. One of the more recent and succinct restatements of this alternate but now orthodox history can be found in a report prepared for the UK Commission on Intellectual Property Rights by Zorina Khan from the US National Bureau of Economic Research. Examining copyright's early development in England, Khan recounts how it "began as a monopoly grant to benefit and regulate the printers' guilds, and as a form of surveillance and censorship over public opinion on behalf of the Crown". Following this "[t]he English system of privileges was replaced in 1710 by a copyright statute [which] was intended to restrain the publishing industry and destroy its monopoly power". This Act was not concerned to secure rights of property to the author, but to regulate the marketplace of the bookseller and publisher. Thereafter, "[s]ubsequent litigation and judicial interpretation added a new and fundamentally different dimension to copyright". By the end of the eighteenth century, the House of Lords in *Donaldson v Becket* (1774),[7] reinvestigating the nature and significance of the earlier legislative provision, adjudged "that authors had a common law right in their unpublished works, but on publication that right was extinguished by the statute, whose provisions determined the nature and scope of any copyright claims". In short, the story of copyright during this period is one of "transition from publishers' rights to statutory authors' rights".[8]

The work of two legal historians, Harry Ransom and Lyman Ray Patterson, provides foundational support for this reading. Their combined examination of the movement of the law at this time departs from the history presented by Matthews and underpins the more contemporary realisation as captured by Khan. Nevertheless, their work, and that of others who have contributed to this alternate story, shares a common bond with that of Matthews, in that it too exhibit traces of the same leitmotif of organicism and inevitable progression. Ransom, writing in 1956, divided the history of copyright into two distinct periods: from 1476 to 1710 and from 1710 to the present. His work, *The First Copyright Statute*,[9] examines

[7] (1774) 4 Burr 2408.

[8] BZ Khan, *Intellectual Property and Economic Development: Lessons from American and European History* (London, Commission on Intellectual Property Rights, 2002) 33–34.

[9] H Ransom, *The First Copyright Statute: An Essay on An Act for the Encouragement of Learning, 1710* (Austin, Texas, University of Texas, 1956).

the first of these two periods, from the establishment of Caxton's press to the passing of the *Statute of Anne*. Early in his work, Ransom declares it impossible "to trace a steadily progressive development of copyright in England"; there are, he considers, "too many stopping places and too many points at which theory and practice revert to earlier concepts and procedures". However, much of his ensuing argument and commentary operates to undercut this basic assertion. Throughout Ransom's work there exists a tension between the denial of this "steadily progressive development", and a use of language and idiom that endorses the very notion he seeks to disavow. He writes of the "many years" that "went into the making of early English theories of copyright", the "process by which the Crown established a central authority over the press" as being a "gradual one", the "[r]egulations which reflect the changing attitudes of ruling minds towards the press" which showed "the growing concept of ownership of printed words", the decrees of the Star Chamber which "formalized basic concepts of literary property", the Stationers' Company who, despite the fact that their "insistence on their particular rights did confuse and delay the progress of statutory copyright law", nevertheless exerted "a tremendous individual and collective influence of the growth of copyright", all of which lead to the passing of the *Statute of Anne*, which for Ransom, "marks a middle ground, where early regulation was summarized and where a new law concerning literature began". He seems unable to escape the very conclusion he seeks to dismiss, that "[t]he historical meaning of the statute depend[s] upon the long and sometimes obscure development of literary property from the time of Caxton to the end of the seventeenth century".[10] The *Statute of Anne* stands defined by its prehistory.

Patterson's history of copyright law begins in similar territory to Ransom's with the incorporation of the Stationers' Company in 1557, but continues through the seventeenth century, past the *Statute of Anne*, through to the establishment of the American copyright tradition with the Supreme Court decision of *Wheaton v Peters* (1834)[11] in the nineteenth century, and beyond.[12] Patterson is conscious of the way in which previous treatments had figured the history of modern copyright as beginning with the *Statute of Anne*; he considers that, in overlooking earlier developments, these accounts were infused with a fundamental confusion about the nature of copyright as being an author's right. To ignore the prehistory to the 1709 Act was to ignore the fact that "copyright began as a publisher's right, a right which functioned in the interest of the

[10] *Ibid*, 4–14.

[11] *Wheaton v Peters* (1834) 33 US 591.

[12] LR Patterson, *Copyright in Historical Perspective* (Nashville, Vanderbilt University Press, 1968).

publisher, with no concern for the author". For Patterson "[t]he Statute of Anne can be understood only when it is related to the history of events which preceded its enactment"; only by placing the Act in its historical context could it be properly interpreted. In the exposition of this thesis however, Patterson's commentary, like Ransom's, necessarily implies that the 150 years preceding the *Statute of Anne* culminated in the passing of that Act. "The mechanics for obtaining the statutory copyright" he explains "were substantially the same as for obtaining the stationer's copyright". Copyright "was a product of censorship, guild monopoly, trade-regulation statutes, and misunderstanding". To this extent "[t]he Statute of Anne was not primarily a copyright statute", but was instead, "basically a trade-regulation statute ... designed to insure order in the book trade while at the same time preventing monopoly".[13] Imbued with the desire to drive home the importance of the statute's prehistory, Patterson unfolds his history in a manner that invariably leads to, and so must necessarily inform our understanding of, the *Statute of Anne*.[14]

The transformation of copyright as publishers' right to copyright as authors' right takes place in the years following the 1709 Act culminating in the decision of *Donaldson* and, as Kathy Bowrey points out, this history is one that "has been written from the perspective of lawyers, printers, authors, literary theorists, Marxist theorists, post-modern writers and post-industrial critics".[15] Jane Gaines, in her examination of 'celebrity' within American intellectual property law notes the "structural similarities between legal and literary discourse" in this area, both of which posit "the bourgeois subject in their notion of what constitutes an author". Both discourses inform each other, she continues, because "they share the same cultural root buried deep in the seventeenth century".[16] This structural synthesis of these literary and legal manifestations of the authorial ego figures in Patterson's reading as well as the work of numerous other commentators. For Alvin Kernan, the figure of

[13] *Ibid*, 8–19.
[14] Louise Goebel has recently sought to question Patterson's account of the development of the law prior to the *Statute of Anne* writing that "it is hard to accept in full the argument that the stationers" copyright emerged as an "economic" concept without "any interference from the courts or the legislature". She suggests that "there might be a case for rethinking the history of copyright in the century and a half leading up to the 1710 Statute of Anne alongside shifting political and economic 'interests' in the civil sphere. The evolution of concepts of public and private interests ... might shed some further light on the relationship between the publishers and civil authorities in the regulation of 'print' and 'copyright'"; L Goebel, "The role of history in copyright dilemmas" (1998) 9 *Journal of Law and Information Science* 22.
[15] K Bowrey, "Who's Writing Copyright History?" (1996) 6 *EIPR* 322. See also K Bowrey, "Who's Painting Copyright's History?" in D McClean and K Schubert (eds), *Dear Images: Art, Copyright and Culture* (London, Institute of Contemporary Arts, 2002) 256.
[16] JM Gaines, *Contested Culture: The Image, the Voice, and the Law* (London, BFI Publishing, 1992) 23.

Samuel Johnson stands out as of particular importance in this process. "When the printing business turned literary art into property by getting Parliament to pass a copyright law", he suggests that "Johnson extended the idea to the point where he argued that the author has 'a stronger right of property than that by occupancy; a metaphysical right, a right as it were of creation, which should from its nature be perpetual'". "Copyright" he remarks "encouraged Johnson to think of the writer as the *author* of his work in the fullest and most explicit sense of that word". The movement leading to this realisation is, for Kernan, "long, complex and roundabout" but one in which the author, in the end, "stands out sharply real against the social background, as a creator and as a valuable and cooperative member of a society".[17]

Perhaps the most engaging of writers in this area is Mark Rose who, in *Of Authors and Owners*, explores the process in which the legal development of literary property combined with the emergence of the romantic concept of the author. Rose, focusing on the decision in *Donaldson*, considers that "the representation of the author as a creator who is entitled to profit from his intellectual labour came into being through a blending of literary and legal discourses in the context of the contest over perpetual copyright".[18] Rosemary Coombe, in her review of his work, assesses the way in which Rose details how the relationship between the author and the text "developed conceptually over an extended period of time, flowering most fully in the aesthetic theories of Romanticism".[19] For Rose, copyright, while "not a transcendent moral idea", is a "specifically modern formation produced by printing technology, marketplace economics, and the classic liberal culture of possessive individualism".[20] As to *Donaldson* itself, he comments that, while the House of Lords rejected the

[17] A Kernan, *Samuel Johnson and the Impact of Print* (Princeton, NJ, Princeton University Press, 1987) 18, 101–2. Other writers make similar observations about this period. For example, Martha Woodmansee examining the emergence of "the professional writer" in Germany in the late eighteenth century, comments that the professional author appeared later than in England primarily because "the requisite legal, economic, and political arrangements and institutions were not yet in place to support the large number of writers who came forward". The tension between authors and publishers, and between publishers and literary pirates she remarks, "triggered an intense debate in which all manner of questions concerning the "Book" were disputed … an interesting interplay between legal, economic, and social questions on the one hand and philosophical and esthetic [sic] ones on the other". She continues that "it is precisely in the interplay of the two levels that critical concepts and principles as that of authorship achieved their modern form"; M Woodmansee, "The Genius and the Copyright: Economic and Legal Conditions of the Emergence of the 'Author'" (1983–84) 17 *Eighteenth Century Studies* 425.

[18] M Rose, *Authors and Owners The Invention of Copyright* (London, Harvard University Press, 1993) 30.

[19] RJ Coombe, "Challenging Paternity: Histories of Copyright" (1994) 6 *Yale Journal of Law and the Humanities* 397, 400.

[20] Rose, *Of Authors and Owners*, n 18 above, 142.

London booksellers' claims to a perpetual copyright, this did not involve a rejection of "the powerful representation of authorship on which that claim was based".[21] To coin a phrase from Joseph Loewenstein's work, *The Author's Due*, the result of the decision in *Donaldson* was to facilitate a form of historical "back-reading" in which that which was originally designed as a mechanism for regulating the book trade was re-branded as an instrument that functions to recognise the proprietary inevitability of an author's intellectual labours.[22]

Thus stand the two parameters between which copyright shifts throughout the eighteenth century, the *Statute of Anne* and the decision of the House of Lords in *Donaldson v Becket*, encapsulating the twin concerns of publisher and author alike. The nature of this inexorable evolution, and its representation, has however drawn criticism from, amongst others, David Saunders. He considers such commentaries to be flawed, as having been written "as if there was a final form of authorship that history already had in store and towards which all earlier forms were directed, whether they knew it or not". In these accounts of the emergent modern authorial form, he complains, "the law of copyright loses its positivity and becomes the pliant tool of a general movement of consciousness". For Saunders the central question is whether we can do without:

> [A] historicism which treats a definite historical arrangement like copyright merely as a stage toward a more final form, and which thus all too neatly arranges diverse circumstances and historical contingencies into a fundamental movement toward the point where the law becomes at last transparent to the nature of aesthetic creation?

Arguing instead that we should recognise that "the historical overlap of the legal personality of the copyright holder and the aesthetic persona of the romantic author was circumstantial", he advocates an acceptance of the fact that "the law does not work for some ultimate philosophical end such as the fulfilment of human potentiality through culture".[23] Rejecting the notion of a "natural authorial right existing continuously ... across quite different legal-cultural contexts, and standing as the necessary goal or destiny of law on literary and artistic rights", Saunders contends that "[s]omething more sensitive than the notion of a single general historical axis is needed if we are to reconstruct the actual forms taken by literary and artistic cultures in their legal existence". The problem, he considers, lies in:

[21] *Ibid*, 107.
[22] Loewenstein, *The Author's Due*, n 5 above.
[23] D Saunders, "Approaches to the Historical Relations of the Legal and the Aesthetic" (1992) 23 *New Literary History* 505.

> [T]reating culture as *directed*, as involving a prehistory and a destiny aligned along a single axis: a prehistory during which a recalcitrant or merely inadequate law fails to recognise the authorial nature of literary production and musters only incomplete forms of recognition such as the privilege and the *honorarium*, while at the point of destiny the law becomes transparent to authorship and in effect historically conscious of aesthetic value.[24]

Although Saunders' own work in this area has not been without its critics,[25] his basic message, the call for a positivist analysis of the history of copyright law, is worth pursuing.

This book represents a response to Saunders' criticism and attempts to provide an accurate, empirical account that charts the movement of copyright law, in Britain, throughout the eighteenth century. As such it contributes to an already rich tradition of copyright historiography established by Ransom, Patterson, Kaplan,[26] Feather,[27] Rose and many more. The narrative presented here takes in the lead up to, and passage of, the *Statute of Anne* 1709, as well as the numerous attempts to legislate, some successful, some not, that followed; in addition, it considers every case that came before the Court of Chancery, the Scottish Court of Session, and the English courts of common law, concerning the question of literary property, up to the House of Lords' decision in *Donaldson*. What distinguishes this work from previous accounts is an attention to relevant and revelatory material that others have overlooked. At this early stage, one example might suffice. A key moment in the movement of the law throughout this period occurred when the London booksellers, following the expiration of the terms of copyright protection provided by the *Statute of Anne*, attempted to secure additional legislation

[24] *Ibid.* In a similar vein Martin Kayman warns against the acceptance of "a compatible and collaborative relationship between law and literature in the constitution of the unitary human subject". What "rights we have over our words" he observes "are not constant, universal 'human rights'". Rather, "they vary over time and are the result of positive law, constituted in different ways at different times in different jurisdictions"; MA Kayman, "Lawful Writing: Common Law, Statute and the Properties of Literature" (1996) 27 *New Literary History* 761, 765–66.

[25] See for example the stinging review of his book, *Authorship and Copyright*, by Coombe, "Challenging Paternity: Histories of Copyright" (1994) 6 *Yale Journal of Law and the Humanities* 397, 400.

[26] B Kaplan, *An Unhurried View of Copyright* (New York, NY, Columbia University Press, 1967).

[27] J Feather, *A History of British Publishing* (London, Routledge, 1988); J Feather, *Publishing, Piracy and Politics: An Historical Study of Copyright in Britain* (London, Mansell, 1994); J Feather, "The Book Trade in Politics: The Making of the Copyright Act of 1710" (1980) 8 *Publishing History* 19; J Feather, "The English Book Trade and the Law 1695–1799" (1982) 12 *Publishing History* 51; J Feather, "From Censorship to Copyright: Aspects of the Government's Role in the English Book Trade 1695–1775" in KE Carpenter (ed), *Books and Society in History* (New York, NY, Bowker, 1983).

to once again bolster their market position. Four Bills were brought before Parliament, in 1735, 1737, 1738 and 1739. Of these only the last received the Royal Assent,[28] and this addressed the rather narrow issue of regulating the importation of foreign reprints of books first published in Britain. Following this lack of success, the booksellers instead took to the courts, so beginning a legal contest, concerning the fundamental nature of copyright itself, which would last over thirty years and culminate in the *Donaldson* decision. Certainly that is the way in which Patterson and others read this sequence of events: "[a]fter failing in Parliament in their quest for perpetual copyright, the booksellers turned to the courts".[29] However, the straightforwardness of this explanation for the transition in the booksellers' focus from legislature to the judiciary fails adequately to account for two significant considerations: that the mood and focus of the first two Bills that were drafted for Parliament's consideration had become increasingly antagonistic to the interests of the booksellers, as well as the timing and significance of *Baller v Watson* (1737),[30] a decision before the Court of Chancery, in which an eight year litigation culminated in Lord Talbot granting the estate of John Gay a perpetual injunction to prevent the reproduction of his works. Both factors combined to indicate to the London monopolists that a moment of tactical redirection was appropriate. Shifting the locale of their argument to the courts does not simply testify to a lack of success before Parliament, but rather, reflects the most strategically advantageous position the southern booksellers might have adopted at that particular time and under those particular circumstances.[31]

Such disclosures are of a certain interest in and of themselves. More significant however than the individual historical insights such details provide, is the fact that the orthodox story of copyright's singular transformation and development throughout this period begins to buckle under the weight of numerous identifiable but disparate threads of influence and understanding. Laddie, Prescott and Vitoria, in their opening discussion of the modern law of copyright observe that "an outline account of its origins is surely not without general interest" and while they concede that "[a] detailed historical treatment would be inapposite in what is a practitioners' textbook," they continue that such work "is more fittingly the task of academic workers, who have yet to publish, perhaps, the final word in this field".[32] Academics and practitioners have

[28] *An Act for the Prohibiting the Importation of Books reprinted abroad and first composed or written and printed in Great Britain and for limiting the Prices of Books* 1739, 12 Geo II, c 36.
[29] Patterson, *Copyright in Historical Perspective*, n 12 above, 158.
[30] Ch 3. The Statute of Anne, Polly, and the Perpetual Injunction.
[31] Ch 4.
[32] H Laddie, et al, *The Modern Law of Copyright and Designs*, 3rd edn, (London, Butterworths, 2000) vol 1, 51.

been writing the history of copyright for over 150 years and it is unlikely that there will or indeed can ever be such a thing as a final word. In 1840 John Lowndes published *An Historical Sketch of the Law of Copyright*.[33] In the *Preface* to his work Lowndes wrote:

> The object of the following treatise is to give a succinct account of the origin of the property known as 'Copyright', and of the modifications and alterations it has subsequently undergone down to the present time. The notice in laying it before the public, is to attempt to remove any misapprehensions which prevail with regard to this species of property ... I feel sensibly that more time and study than have been in my power to bestow, are necessary to do justice to this subject; but if, by the perusal of the following pages, the reader is convinced that such a right as that known by the name of Copyright did formerly exist at common law, and was only taken away by a mistaken interpretation of the effect of the statute of Anne ... I shall not consider the few leisure hours I have appropriated to their composition from the severer duties of my profession as either misspent or unprofitably employed.[34]

This first account of the development of copyright law within Britain sought to establish in the mind of the reader that copyright "did formerly exist at common law", that copyright was and is the inevitable preserve of the author. Since that time we can trace an ever-expanding history of tales concerning the history of copyright. The story that unfolds in this latest instalment operates to invert the claim made by Lowdnes. The traditional analysis of the development of copyright in eighteenth century Britain, culminating in *Donaldson*, is found to exhibit the character of long-standing myth, and the centrality of the modern proprietary author as the *raison d'être* of the copyright regime is displaced.

[33] JJ Lowndes, *An Historical Sketch of the Law of Copyright* (London, Sanders and Benning, 1840). Previous treatises had included some comment upon the history and development of copyright within a larger exposition of the law on literary property. Most notable of these was R Maugham, *A Treatise on the Laws of Literary Property* (London, Longman, 1828).

[34] Lowndes, *An Historical Sketch of the Law of Copyright*, n 33 above, Preface.

1

Politics, Propaganda and Profanity; Not Property

AN END TO CENSORSHIP; JOHN LOCKE AND EDWARD CLARKE; THE WHIG "COLLEGE"; TWO BILLS

IN MAY 1695, with the close of the last session of William III's second parliament, the *Licensing Act* 1662 expired and pre-publication censorship of the English press came to an end. In November 1694, a time when the government was dominated by the Whig Junto,[1] a committee had been appointed in the House of Commons to inspect what laws are "lately expired and expiring which are fit to be revived and continued". This committee, in January 1695, resolved to renew, amongst others, the 1662 Act, which suggestion was rejected by the House of Commons on 11 February 1695 without division.[2] When the *Continuation Bill* reached the upper house, absent the *Licensing Act*, the Lords amended the Bill, to re-include the 1662 Act, and returned it to the Commons. In response, the lower house appointed a committee to prepare a set of reasons for disagreeing to the amendment. Edward Clarke, MP for Taunton, reported that the committee had prepared a number of objections and presented them to the house whereupon it was ordered that "a Message be sent to the Lords, to desire a Conference upon the subject-matter of the amendments made by them to the said Bill" and that Clarke carry that message forward.[3] The following day, 18 April 1695, the House of Lords agreed to

[1] Charles Talbot, the Earl of Shrewsbury held the office of Secretary of State, Edward Russell was the First Lord of the Admiralty, and Charles Montagu was the Chancellor of the Exchequer. For commentaries upon the political situation of this time, see generally: G Holmes, *The Making of a Great Power, Late Stuart and Early Georgian Britain, 1660–1722* (London, Longman, 1993) 195–211, 322–33, 334–49; D Hayton, *The House of Commons 1690–1715* (Cambridge, CUP, 2002) vol 1; M Kishlansky, *A Monarchy Transformed, Britain 1603–1714* (London, Penguin, 1997) 287–312; and JP Kenyon, *Stuart England* (London, Penguin, 1978) 268–97.

[2] For an account of the House of Common's rejection of the 1662 Act see R Astbury, "The Renewal of the Licensing Act in 1693 and its Lapse in 1695" (1978) 33 *The Library* 1978, 296. See also M Treadwell, "The stationers and the printing acts at the end of the seventeenth century", in J Barnard and D F McKenzie (eds.), *The Cambridge History of the Book in Britain, Volume IV 1557–1695* (Cambridge, CUP, 2002).

[3] Journal of the House of Commons (CJ) 11:305–6.

allow the Bill to proceed without the clause restoring the 1662 Act. In doing so, the Lords' decision heralded an end to a relationship that had developed throughout the sixteenth and seventeenth centuries between the state and the Company of Stationers, a mutually beneficial association which provided the monarch and the government of the day with an effective means to monitor and censor the press, and the stationers with a statutory protection securing the reproduction of their copies, their property.[4] It also marked the beginning of a transitional period in which parliament and the party system had to renegotiate its attitudes to, and relationship with, an embryonic, independent fourth estate. On no account was the removal of a system of pre-publication licensing unconditionally embraced. Indeed, over the next ten years, there would be no fewer than twelve additional attempts to re-introduce some form of statutory regulation of the press. Of these, only one would succeed, and that was directed not at the press writ large, but towards the specific suppression of blasphemous notions by "writing, printing, teaching or advised speaking".[5] Of the other Bills, each and every one was ultimately rejected by the parliament of the day.

Much of the substance of the Commons' position on the *Licensing Act* had its genesis in the life-long friendship that existed between Edward Clarke and the philosopher John Locke, and the opinions on that legislation which both men had shared. In 1675 Clarke, then a barrister of the Inner Temple, married Locke's cousin Mary Jepp, and in February 1682 a correspondence between the two men began, which would last the rest of

[4] This relationship between the state and the stationers began in 1557 when the Stationers' Company received its charter from Philip and Mary, for the purpose of providing the monarchy with a method of controlling the printing of (what they considered to be) seditious and heretical material. Following this, there were three Star Chamber decrees of 1566, 1586, and 1637, as well as three Ordinances during the Interregnum, in 1643, 1647 and 1649, all directed towards the regulation and censuring of the press, in return for which the stationers were guaranteed protection for their works. Finally there came the *Licensing Act* 1662, continuing in the same tradition, which, while it was initially enacted for a period of two years only, remained in force until May 1695 (except for the period between March 1679 and June 1685 during which it had been allowed to lapse). Examining all of these enactments, Patterson writes that "[t]hese acts of censorship, sustaining the Stationers' Company's copyrights, became the main support of the company's monopoly; and the final lapse in 1694 of the Licensing Act of 1662, the last of the censorship acts, meant more than the end of censorship: it meant also the end of legal sanctions for the stationer's copyright"; LR Patterson, *Copyright in Historical Perspective* (Nashville, Vanderbilt University Press, 1968) 6. See also: H Ransom, *The First Copyright Statute* (Austin, Texas, University of Texas, 1956); M Rose, *Authors and Owners: The Invention of Copyright* (London, Harvard University Press, 1993); J Loewenstein, *The Author's Due: Printing and the Prehistory of Copyright* (Chicago, Il, University of Chicago Press, 2002); T Crist, "Government Control of the Press After the Expiration of the Printing Act in 1679" (1979) 5 *Publishing History* 49; and, Astbury, "The Renewal of the Licensing Act", and Treadwell, "The stationers and the printing acts at the end of the seventeenth century".

[5] *An Act for the more effectual suppressing of Blasphemy and Prophaneness* 1698, 9 & 10 Will III, c 32, s 1.

Locke's life.[6] Benjamin Rand notes that "[i]t was chiefly to carry on to the better advantage such deliberations of measures before Parliament that Locke, [John] Freke, and Clarke later formed the 'College.'"[7] The "College", headed by John Freke,[8] represented an intimate group of friends (principally Freke, "the Bachelor", Locke, "the Castle", and Clarke, the "Grave Squire") who shared opinions on contemporary political events and aimed to promote various legislative measures in parliament, mainly through the agency of Clarke.[9]

Locke had first written to Clarke about the 1662 Act, when it was decided that it should be renewed in 1693, counselling him to "have some care of book-buyers as well as all of booksellers". He complained about the monopoly which the stationers exercised over the "ancient Latin authors", the poor quality and high cost of their publications, and the deleterious impact this was having upon the work of scholars.[10] Much of his criticism was picked up and expanded in a highly critical commentary on the 1662 Act and its impact on the printing trade in England which he wrote in 1694. In this commentary Locke did make reference to the importance of securing the "liberty to print",[11] however, as with the earlier correspondence with Clarke, most of his vitriol was reserved for the "lazy, ignorant Company of Stationers", those "dull wretches" who abused the registration process for their own gain, and whose "monopoly of all the Clasick Authers" resulted in the production of books which were "scandalously ill printed both for letter paper and correctness", for which they charged "excessive rates". Rejecting the idea that anyone should have a

[6] See generally: B Rand, *The Correspondence of John Locke and Edward Clarke* (Oxford, Clarendon Press, 1927); E Cruickshanks, S Handley and DW Hayton (eds), *The House of Commons 1690–1715* (Cambridge, CUP, 2002) vol III, 576–98.

[7] Rand, *The Correspondence of John Locke*, n 6 above, 38.

[8] John Freke, a barrister and well known Whig, was a friend to both Clarke and Locke. Of these three men Rand writes: "The friendship existing between [them] was always of the most intimate kind"; *ibid*, 21. See also ES De Beer (ed), *The Correspondence of John Locke, in Eight Volumes* (Oxford, Clarendon Press, 1978); M Cranston, *John Locke, a Biography* (London, Longmans, Green & Co, 1957).

[9] The most important legislative measure with which they were concerned was the Coinage Act; Rand, *The Correspondence of John Locke*, n 6 above, 41. Cruickshanks, Handley and Hayton note that Clarke "became the philosopher's mouthpiece in the Commons and consequently the most important member of Locke's 'college', a policy making and parliamentary pressure-group that was particularly active in the mid-1690s"; Cruickshanks et al (eds), *The House of Commons 1690–1715*, n 6 above, 577. De Beer writes that the College was "vigorous politically" from the end of 1694 until early 1697, after which it became less active, being mentioned in Locke's correspondence for the last time in 1701. Throughout this time Locke wrote letters both to Clarke and the College. The letters addressed to Locke were written generally by Freke, and signed by him and Clarke, or by him alone. See De Beer, *The Correspondence of John Locke*, n 8 above, vol V, 199.

[10] Rand, *The Correspondence of John Locke*, n 6 above, 366.

[11] In this regard, he rejected the need for the 1662 Act arguing that, in any case, any man printing seditious material would be answerable for it at common law.

right to print any book in perpetuity as being "very unreasonable and injurious to learning", Locke continued:

> [T]is very absurd and ridiculous that any one now liveing should pretend to have a propriety in, or a power to dispose of the proprietie of any copys or writeings of authors who lived before printing was known or used in Europe.

Rather he suggested that, for those purchasing copies from authors, "it may be reasonable to limit their property to a certein number of years after the death of the Author, or the first printing of a book, as, suppose, 50 or 70 years."[12]

The parallels between Locke's commentary and those reasons presented by the Commons to the Lords for refusing to renew the 1662 Act are striking. While the committee's report on the *Licensing Act* did acknowledge the unwelcome prospect of a "great Oppression" re-emerging with the appointment of a new licensor, their arguments, like Locke's, had little to do with freedom of speech and the liberty of the press.[13] After beginning with the observations that the 1662 Act "in no wise answered the end for which it was made", and that the writers of "treasonable and seditious" books might, in any case, be left to punishment at common law, the Commons' committee preferred instead to focus on the more practical and commercial implications of re-enactment. These concerned the restraint to trade that the Act represented, the Company of Stationers' abuse of their position, and the monopolistic control they exercised over work by "Classick Authors".[14]

[12] J Locke, "Memorandum on the 1662 Act" in DeBeer, *The Correspondence of John Locke*, n 8 above, vol V, 785–95. For a slightly different version, see Lord King, *The Life of John Locke, with Extracts from his Correspondence, Journals and Common Place Books* (London, Henry Colburn & Richard Bently, 1830) vol 1.

[13] G Holmes and WA Speck, *The Divided Society: Party Conflict in England 1694–1716* (London, Edward Arnold, 1967) 67. Kenyon writes that: "The Act was renewed in 1685 and 1690, but objections to the monopoly it conferred on the Stationers' Company and the university presses (rather than any abstract love of press freedom) caused it to be abandoned for good in 1695"; Kenyon, *Stuart England*, n 1 above, 350.

[14] Whatever impression such arguments made upon the upper house, it is more likely that the real reason for the failure of the Lords to secure the return of the *Licensing Act* lay in a more fundamental conflict of constitutional authority between the two chambers. On 9 April Clarke wrote to Locke with the observation that: "[T]he Commons will not agree to the amendment for many reasons and particularly because they allow not the Lords to begin a Bill in which there is any pecuniary penalty that being a sort of raising money which the Commons says belongs solely to them"; De Beer, *The Correspondence of John Locke*, n 8 above, vol V, 326. Robert Harley, holding office as Speaker of the House of Commons, echoed these sentiments in his letter of 8 January 1702, to the Archbishop of Canterbury who was proposing to introduce a Bill for the Better Regulation of Printers and Printing Presses in the Lords in 1702. Harley wrote to the Archbishop: "[T]his caution is necessary that it have not any pecuniary penalty when sent down to the Commons". Lambeth Palace Library, Todd MS, 930 (25), below n 95 and accompanying text. Thomas, writing on the legislative process in the eighteenth century, notes that, "[b]ills could be introduced first into either the House of

While the *Licensing Act* was allowed to expire, the radical transition to a print culture free of statutory regulation was ameliorated by two significant considerations. In the first place, the earlier assessment by Locke that the restoration of the *Licensing Act* was unnecessary, as there existed sufficient authority within the common law to control the dissemination of seditious publications, would prove uncannily prescient. In May 1695, barely a month after the 1662 Act had lapsed, the Lord Justices declared that the offences of criminal and seditious libel were, when detected, still punishable at common law.[15] As Laurence Hanson states:

> [They] decided in short that the Licensing Act had been declarative of the common law, that it had vested in the Secretaries no powers of which they had not before possessed, and that its expiration meant no diminution of their prerogatives.[16]

In one sense then, nothing had really changed. True, the official office of licensor no longer existed, but instead, his functions were to be taken up by the then Secretaries of State; it became "the recognized practice of the Secretaries to issue warrants for the arrest of all those suspected of crimes against the State".[17] Second, parliament itself had various methods at its disposal by which to check the political press. It was, at that time, still considered a breach of parliamentary privilege, to report in print the proceedings of either house or even to mention the names of members of parliament in the press. For such an offence, when sufficiently outraged, either chamber could summon before it the printer guilty of this breach of privilege, and, depending on the gravity of the offence, could commit the printer to the custody of the Sergeant at Arms until the end of the parliamentary session or until payment of certain fines.[18] Furthermore, on rare

Commons or the House of Lords, except for certain categories of bills: all finance measures necessarily originated in the House of Commons; and it was the privilege of the Lords that all acts of grace should begin in their House"; PDG Thomas, *The House of Commons in the Eighteenth Century* (Oxford, Clarendon Press, 1971) 47.

[15] Criminal libel was understood to incorporate the publication of any material with the deliberate intention of causing a breach of the peace; seditious libel was defined as publishing any material likely to bring into hatred or contempt, or exciting disaffection against, the King, the government, ministers, either House of Parliament and the administration of justice, as well as material inciting changes in Church or State by other than lawful means.

[16] L Hanson, *Government and the Press 1695–1763* (Oxford, Clarendon Press, 1932) 30.

[17] *Ibid*, 29. During the seventeenth century the office of Secretary of State was divided into two departments, Northern and Southern, which carried the responsibility of looking after English affairs in northern and southern Europe respectively. These two ministers, in addition to conducting foreign policy, instructing English diplomats abroad, and negotiating with foreign diplomats in London, had overall responsibility for the state of the press. Holmes, *The Making of a Great Power*, n 1 above, 94–95.

[18] On the various privileges of Parliament, see C Wittke, *The History of Parliamentary Privilege* (New York, NY, Da Capo Press, 1970) 21–54.

occasions, as, for example, with the trial of Dr Sacheverell in 1710, either house was deemed capable of addressing *any* political libel, not simply those works relating to their own proceedings or members, and impeaching the author or printer in question.[19] More often than not however, parliament was satisfied in condemning the publication at hand, ordering that it be burned at the hands of the common hangman, and directing the Attorney-General to prosecute the author at common law.[20]

Nevertheless, the availability of these twin censorial strategies did not mean that there would be no further legislative attempts to bring the press to heel. As previously indicated, throughout the next ten years there were to be no less than twelve further attempts to introduce some measure of statutory regulation. In the years following the repeal of the *Licensing Act*, it remained uncertain just how far the common law was adequate to deal with an emerging and increasingly unruly press. Indeed, over the next fifteen years there was to be little governmental action, despite the declaration by the Lord Justices; in general "[o]nly when Parliament pressed for action, or when particularly ill-willed or continued criticism was published, did the executive venture to act."[21] Moreover the exponential proliferation of newspapers provided, in the minds of some, a sufficient impetus for continuing to press for the renewal of a system of regulation. As Feather comments:

> A completely different situation was created by the lapse of the *Licensing Act*, for even the Messenger of the Press, Robert Stephens, could not keep track of all publications, especially when the multiplication of newspapers increased the flow to a flood.[22]

[19] Dr Henry Sacheverell, an Anglican parson and Tory zealot, preached a sermon, on 5 November 1709, in St Paul's Cathedral warning against "The Perils of False Brethren", castigating low churchmen and occasional conformists as "athiests", "bloodsuckers" and a "brood of vipers". Soon after Sachervell had delivered his sermon, more than 100,000 copies of it were in print. The Whig ministry of the time sought to impeach him, in February and March 1710, for "high crimes and misdemeanours" against the State. On 20 March, by a vote of 69 to 52 in the House of Lords, Sacheverell was found guilty of the crimes alleged. Despite the conviction however, the Whig ministry were not to emerge victorious. Sensing Queen Anne's dissatisfaction, they compromised upon the punishment Sacheverell should receive, and it was proposed to the House that he be debarred from preaching for only seven years, that he was to be prevented from receiving any additional ecclesiastical preferment other than that which he already enjoyed, that he be imprisoned for three months, and, finally that his sermons were to be burnt by the Common Hangman. In the debate that followed, there was a Tory rout, and only the proposal that Sacheverell's sermons be burnt survived. For an in depth account of Sacheverell's trial see G Holmes, *The Trial of Doctor Sacheverell* (London, Eyre Methuen, 1973).

[20] Hanson, *Government and the Press*, n 16 above, 7–35.

[21] *Ibid*, 60. See generally, *ibid*, 36–83.

[22] J Feather, "From Censorship to Copyright: Aspects of the Government's Role in the English Book Trade 1695–1775" in KE Carpenter (ed), *Books and Society in History* (New York, NY, Bowker, 1983) 187.

The first of these twelve additional legislative proposals began on 11 February 1695, the very same day that the Commons had rejected the suggested renewal of the *Licensing Act*. Instead, a committee was appointed in the lower chamber, again, led by Edward Clarke, to prepare and bring in a *Bill for the Better Regulating of Printing and Printing Presses*.[23] The stated purpose of this new Bill, first presented to the house in March 1695, was for "preventing the mischiefs that may happen in church or State for want of a due regulation of printing and printing presses".[24] As it was, this new Bill did not represent too radical a departure from the old Act.[25] Rather than abandon the earlier commitment to pre-publication licensing, this Bill simply narrowed the range of material that would require the prior sanction of a suitable licensor before publication: books relating to divinity, the laws of England or the affairs of state and history of the realm, were to be first licensed by the Archbishop of Canterbury, the Lord Chancellor or Lord Keeper, or one of the secretaries of state, respectively (clause 3), and nothing contrary to the laws of the realm or the Christian religion was to be printed (clause 4). In this respect the Bill was certainly more moderate in tone than the 1662 Act which had provided a much more extensive list of prescribed works including any work of philosophy, science or art.[26] However, the freedom that had been gained as regards those areas of publication no longer subject to the scrutiny of the licensor was to be accompanied by an increased emphasis upon making the authors, printers, publishers and sellers of books more easily identifiable, and so accountable for their works. Whereas the 1662 Act had only required that the printer of every work set his name to it, and be prepared to declare who the author of the work was, should the Licensor so require,[27] now, with the prospect of a free press, a more effective

[23] Thomas comments of this initial stage that "it was by no means a formal one, and debates often arose" as a result of which "more than half the bills taken to a vote at this stage were defeated". Should the motion for leave to bring in the Bill be approved then "the practice was to appoint a Select Committee to draw up the Bill"; Thomas, *The House of Commons*, n 14 above, 48.

[24] For a transcript of the Bill, taken from a manuscript copy sent from John Freke to John Locke, see De Beer, *The Correspondence of John Locke*, n 8 above, vol V, 791–95.

[25] A number of clauses can be traced directly to the 1662 Act, for example: the requirement to reserve three copies of every new book and book printed with additions for the use of the King's library and the two universities (clause 9); the power to enter, search for and seize any works that were "treasonable, seditious, atheistical or heretical" (clause 10); the time limit for bringing prosecutions under the legislation (clause 12); the provision detailing a limited time-span for the Bill itself (clause 13).

[26] The 1662 Act had also required that books relating to heraldry, titles of honour and arms, and physick be subject to the scrutiny of the Licensor. John Freke, in correspondence with John Locke, described the Bill in this regard as "very unlike the old"; John Freke and Edward Clarke to Locke, 28 February 1695, in De Beer, *The Correspondence of John Locke*, n 8 above, vol V, 278–79.

[27] *Licensing Act* 1662, s 7.

means of discovery and punishment of those writing seditious or libellous material came to the fore. Locke, earlier, had written that:

> To prevent mens being undiscovered for what they print you may Prohibit any book to be printed published or Sold without the printers or booksellers name under great penalties whatever be in it. And then let the printer or bookseller whose name is to it be answerable for whatever is against law in it as if he were the author unlesse he can produce the person he had it from which is all the restraint ought to be upon printing.[28]

To this end the Bill directed that: notice be given of any press being erected within the country; the name of the printer and the place of printing had to appear on all works; anyone who put their name to a work would be accountable as the author of the work (along with the author); there was to be no sale of a work without a name printed on the work; and finally, that no-one was allowed to use another's name without authority (clauses 1–2, 5–8).

Four days after the House of Commons was given leave to prepare and bring in the new Bill, the Master of the Stationers' Company, John Sims, called an extraordinary meeting of the Court of Assistants.[29] It was agreed to petition the house, and the company treasurer was authorised to satisfy whatever costs were entailed in the process.[30] This was the first of two petitions received by the house relating to the Bill,[31] representing two separate interests of the book trade: the masters (the printers and booksellers) who were concerned with protecting their investment in books (copies), and the journeymen (the masters' employees) interested in protecting their particular place within the publishing hierarchy.[32] What were the stationers so concerned about, and why were they disposed to act so quickly? The proposed Bill, unlike the 1662 Act, made no provision to protect any property in books. Understandably, this omission greatly alarmed the stationers, resulting in the preparation of the petition from the "Master, Wardens

[28] John Locke, "Memorandum on the 1662 Act" in DeBeer, *The Correspondence of John Locke*, n 8 above, vol V, 786.

[29] The Court of Assistants was a body of members within the Stationers' Company responsible for administering the business of the Company. Blagden describes that "[t]he business of the Court was the 'better Ordering' of the Company, the correction of abuses and the admission of apprentices and freemen"; C Blagden, *The Stationers' Company, A History, 1403–1959* (London, George Allen & Unwin, 1960) 155.

[30] J Feather, "The Book Trade in Politics: The Making of the Copyright Act of 1710" (1980) 8 *Publishing History* 19, 23.

[31] The first was from the Stationers' Company; the second was from "several free Workmen and Printers".

[32] Feather, "The Book Trade in Politics", n 30 above, 19.

and Commonalty of the Art or Mystery of Stationers" in which they made clear to the Commons that:

> [I]f their property should not be provided for by the said Bill, not only the petitioners but many widows and others, whose livelihood depends upon the petitioners property, will be utterly ruined.[33]

In this regard, it was not just the stationers who had misgivings about the Bill. Clarke, along with Freke, wrote to Locke on 14 March complaining that "the Court the Bishops and the Stationers Company take great exceptions to it for they all agree to say that it is wanting as to the Securing of property". He continued:

> [W]hen they are asked what they mean thereby they can none of them give any good answer and if they would all speak out they (every party) mean differently. The Court means that it would be allowed the power of granting patents. The Stationers mean that they would have the regulation of property and disposal of it by making their Register the standard of it … The Bishops mean I know not what but they Chime in with the other two because they think property a very popular word, which Licensor is not.[34]

In response Locke suggested that they might secure the "Author's property in his copy" by either including some provision that would allow a right to reprint those works which bore the name of the author or publisher upon them, or by issuing a "receit" upon delivery of three copies of any printed work for the use of the King's library and the two universities which would "vest a priviledg in the Author of the said book his executors administrators and assignes of solely reprinting and publishing the said book for ____ years from the first edition thereof".[35] The philosopher's attitude to and understanding of the nature of literary property, however, ran contrary to the opinion of the other members of "the College". In their opinion, addressed to Locke on 21 March:

> [T]here needs no new care to be taken about property for tis a rule in Law that where ever there is damnum and injuria it may be recompensed in damages in an action on the case and who ever prints my Coppy injures me and endammages me so that I have the same security for this property that anyone has for any other.[36]

[33] CJ 11:288.
[34] John Freke and Edward Clarke to Locke, 14 March 1695, in De Beer, *The Correspondence of John Locke*, n 8 above, vol V, 291.
[35] *Ibid*, 795–96.
[36] *Ibid*, 294–95.

In this brief exchange, two conflicting positions were adumbrated that would resonate throughout the next eighty years. For Locke, as was also evidenced by his previous comments as to the absurd notion of a property existing in the work of "Clasick Authers", what property existed in a book was to be statutorily defined as well as temporally limited in extent. For Clarke and Freke, both members of the legal profession, appropriate remedies for the unauthorised publication of books already existed at common law. At this point in time, the latter opinion was apparently not sufficient to allay the fears of the book trade, for while there were other objections raised in the Commons against the Bill,[37] the most problematic aspect, and the principal reason for its failure, certainly seems to have been the absence of a legislative protection for the property in books. Without this, the booksellers argued, they would "be utterly ruined" and as a consequence, at the end of the parliamentary session, the Bill remained in committee.

A GENERAL ELECTION; THE TRIENNIAL PARLIAMENT; AN INFLUENTIAL ELECTORATE; THE EMERGENCE OF THE POLITICAL PRESS; ROBERT HARLEY; TWO NEW ATTEMPTS TO LEGISLATE

There followed a general election and the formation of the first parliament under the new terms of the *Triennial Act* 1694.[38] This Act, which required the Crown to dissolve parliament at least every three years, provided the catalyst that sparked a number of significant changes to the face of British politics throughout the next twenty years.[39] Between 1695 and 1715 there were to be no less than ten general elections.[40] This Act, in Holmes' opinion, "ushered in the true 'golden age' of the unreformed English electorate"; he comments that:

> [T]he English electorate emerged in the 1690s and remained for two decades a force genuinely, if crudely, representative of the will of the politically-conscious classes in the country. As such, it showed itself regularly capable of swaying the fortunes of parties and even at times of influencing the composition of governments.[41]

[37] Other objections concerned the fact that the Bill provided the liberty to set up a press in any town in England, as well as the freedom to print and disseminate new "Notions in Physick". See John Freke and Edward Clarke to Locke, 14 March 1695; *ibid*, 291–92.
[38] 1694 6 & 7 Will. & Mar, c 2.
[39] The *Triennial Act* 1694 was repealed and replaced by the *Septennial Act* 1715.
[40] There were elections held in the following years: 1695, 1698, 1701, 1701–2, 1702, 1705, 1708, 1710, 1713, 1715; the first six took place in England, the next four, following the Act of Union 1707, took place in Great Britain. For information on these various elections see generally: Hayton, *The House of Commons 1690–1715*, n 1 above, vol 1, 217–47; Holmes, *The Making of a Great Power*, n 1 above, 422–24.
[41] *Ibid*, 325–26.

More than any other factor, this legislation not only heralded the emergence of a vital and influential electorate, but also contributed significantly to what Plumb referred to as "the rage of the party".[42] During this twenty-year period, political activity in Britain came to be characterised along definable party lines and, by 1701, the emergence of the two party system of Whig and Tory was essentially complete, in which election results were easily identifiable victories for one or other of the two parties.[43] These two parties were divided over "matters of outlook, principle and instinct"; Kishlansky writes that:

> Tories ... represented Anglicanism, the country landed interest, and a xenophobic view of England's destiny. Their intellectual heritage derived from loyalty to the Stuart monarchy ... [while] Whigs ... stood for dissent, the urban monied interest and an internationalism that had once been at the heart of the Protestant cause. Their intellectual heritage derived from the defence of liberties ...[44]

Just as party lines came to dominate proceedings within the two houses, this was similarly reflected in political life outside parliament, where there evolved Whig and Tory coffee-houses, taverns, social clubs, theatres, race-tracks, and even Whig and Tory hospitals and doctors.[45] Perhaps most importantly, however, in terms of the history of the development of copyright, this post-regulatory regime witnessed the emergence of the political press proper.

Immediately prior to the lapse of the *Licensing Act* there existed only one (official) newspaper, the government's *London Gazette*. Following the demise of the 1662 Act with the end of the parliamentary session, between May and October 1695, three tri-weekly newspapers appeared: George Ridpath's *Flying Post*, Abel Roper's *Post Boy* and John Fonvive's *Post Man*, all three of which were still in circulation in 1710. A provincial press began to develop in 1701 with the publication of the *Norwich Post*. Elizabeth Mallett launched the first daily, the *Daily Courant*, in March 1702, which, within weeks, passed into the hands of Samuel Buckley; the first evening paper, the *Evening Post*, was started in August 1706. In 1704 there were at least nine separate newspapers servicing London;[46] by 1709 this figure had doubled.[47] Not surprisingly, most of these

[42] JH Plumb, *England in the Eighteenth Century* (London, Penguin, 1950).
[43] Holmes, *The Making of a Great Power*, n 1 above, 322–33.
[44] Kishlansky, *A Monarchy Transformed*, n 1 above, 318.
[45] Holmes, *The Making of a Great Power*, n 1 above, 334–49.
[46] JR Sutherland, "The Circulation of Newspapers and Literary Periodicals, 1700–30" (1934–35) 15 *The Library* 110. The nine newspapers listed by Sutherland are as follows: *Daily Courant, London Post, English Post, London Gazette, Post Man, Post Boy, Flying Post, Review*, and the *Observator*.
[47] G Holmes and D Szechi, *The Age of Oligarchy: Pre-Industrial Britain 1722–1783* (London, Longman, 1993) 195.

papers had a strong party bias: the Whigs were represented by the *Flying Post* and the *Daily Courant*, the Tories by the *Post Boy* and the *Evening Post*. Fonvive's *Post Man*, and the government's *London Gazette* proved the exception to the rule, by managing to maintain a reasonably non-partisan stance on the matters of the day.[48] Alongside the papers, there also appeared various similarly politicised journals: the *Observator*, Daniel Defoe's *Review*, Addison and Steele's daily *Spectator*, and Jonathan Swift's *Examiner*, to name but a few.[49]

The establishment of a triennial parliamentary system, the development of clearly definable party lines, and a vital and influential electorate, ensured an ever-increasing demand for political information, information that could be supplied selectively to support, or attack, party lines on any given topic of the day. From 1695, with the lapse of the *Licensing Act*, politicians began to realise the value of an efficient and effective propaganda machine, in reaching and influencing not only those within parliament, but also, more importantly, the electorate. No one realised this more, perhaps, than Robert Harley. Harley, the Earl of Oxford, served as the Speaker of the Commons from 1701 to 1705, Secretary of State for the Northern Department from 1704 to 1708, and as head of the Treasury from 1710 to 1714. When the war over the Spanish succession (the Nine Years War) ended in 1697 with the signing of the Peace of Ryswick, a controversy arose over the retention of a standing army during times of peace — an expense that many landowners (and so taxpayers) were more than willing to dispense with. A protracted debate elicited a number of printed opinions on the matter; the effectiveness of the press campaign to disband the army, supported by Harley, resulted in a substantial victory for the opposition pamphleteers, and defeat for William III.[50] The potential of a properly marshalled press was apparent to Harley and others. Within a few years, with the publication of Daniel Defoe's *A Review of the Affairs of France*, Harley would realise the inception of a ministerial propaganda machine, the first government organ of its kind, specifically designed to influence and tap public opinion and support.[51]

Against this developing background, there was, once again, an attempt to revive the *Licensing Act*, as well as to secure a new *Printing Bill*; this time however their introduction into the House of Commons was chronologically reversed. On 26 November 1695, Harley and Clarke were asked to prepare and bring in a *Bill for the Regulating of Printing and Printing*

[48] HL Snyder, "The Circulation of Newspapers in the Reign of Queen Anne" (1968) 23 *The Library* 206, 211.
[49] *Ibid.*
[50] The Commons eventually voted to disband all those forces that had been raised since 1680.
[51] See generally: JA Downie, *Robert Harley and the Press: Propaganda and Public Opinion in the Age of Swift and Defoe* (Cambridge, CUP, 1979) 1–79; GA Cranfield, *The Press and Society: From Caxton to Northcliffe* (London, Longman, 1978) 31–57.

Presses; like the previous Bill, this would also remain in committee until the end of the session.[52] On 16 January 1696 a committee was appointed to investigate which laws were expiring, and in March a Mr Brotherton reported that it was the opinion of the committee that the 1662 Act be revived. A question was put to the Commons as to whether or not they agreed to this proposal and the suggestion was rejected.[53] This was to be the last time that either chamber would try to secure the return of the 1662 Act in its extant form.

No doubt the Commons' reasons for rejecting the revival of the *Licensing Act* remained largely the same as they had been in the previous session, however the fledgling press added a new dimension for consideration, and a new reason to resist the return of an official licensor. Parliament and the electorate were becoming hungry for political information and opinion. Freke writing to Locke at this time informed him that "the young members" of the Commons were "possesst with a sufficient prejudice against the Old Act".[54] He chose not to elaborate upon the source of this prejudice, but it is likely that the explanation lay along the same lines as the observations of Federic Bonet, the resident envoy of the Court of Brandenburg in London at the time. Bonet wrote that the Bill had been rejected due to concerns that the *Gazette* would simply report news in a manner endorsed (or controlled) by the Secretary of State, as a result of which certain news and information might be "hidden, played down, or indeed exaggerated".[55] In short, the young members had developed the taste for uncensored news and information, which they would be hard-pressed to concede.

As for the new *Printing Bill*, it essentially represented a re-working of its immediate predecessor, but one that endeavoured to accommodate the various objections that had earlier been raised.[56] For example, the previous

[52] CJ 11:340, 341, 343, 345.
[53] CJ 11:393, 523.
[54] John Freke to Locke, 5 December 1695, De Beer, *The Correspondence of John Locke*, n 8 above, vol V, 475–76.
[55] Bonet wrote as follows:

> De plusiers lois expirees, qu'un committee estoit d'avis qu'on renouvellast, les commutes ont precisement rejette celle qui parois-soit la plus necessaire et qui estoit pour empescher qu'on ne put rien imprimer sans la permission des personnes deputees pour cet effet par les secretaires d'etat. Le motif, qu'ils ont eu, a ete pour conserver deux gazettes sans aveu, quiparaissant 3 fois la semaine ou tous les jours de poste pour l'Angleterre, et dont les auteurs disent a tort et a travers tout ce qui vient a leur connoissance, au lieu que le gazettier, qui travaille sous le secretaire d'etat, est plus reserve. Ils se defient qu'on ne leur cache des nouvelles ou qu'on n'en etenue ou exagere d'autres'.

Quoted in L Von Ranke, *A History of England* (Oxford, Clarendon Press, 1875) vol 5, 105.
[56] There exist two drafts of this Bill, one housed in the University Library at Cambridge, the second in the Lambeth Palace Library.

Bill had allowed for presses to be set up anywhere in England subject to adequate notice being given to the statutorily designated authorities. In March a second petition had been entered to the Commons, this time from the "Free Workman Printers", the journeymen of the book trade. Alarmed that the Bill allowed printers to "set up in any town in England" which would "leave the said Trade open to all Persons" they had asked the house to cap the numbers of those able to practice their art, as had been the case under the 1662 Act, in order to secure work for those currently exercising their trade.[57] In response, the new Bill set out that presses could be erected only within London, Westminster (and their suburbs), Oxford, Cambridge, York, Bristol and Norwich, as well as, in a later draft of the Bill, Exeter.[58] Apart from this, and some other minor changes,[59] there were two major departures in the substance of the November Bill. First, the licensing provisions became more complicated and robust, signalling a return to the earlier categories of the 1662 Act,[60] but now subject to the concession that:

> Nevertheless it shall be and is hereby declared and enacted to be lawful to print any books not containing anything therein contrary to the laws of God or laws of this Realm without any such licence so as the rules hereinafter proscribed by this Act be pursued followed and performed by the printers thereof.

While this must have seemed like a retrograde step to those advocating reform, it was accompanied by an additional and entirely new provision detailing an alternative to the old system of seeking licence (clause 4). The Bill set out that, instead of securing a licence prior to publication, so long as the printer sent the relevant licensor a copy of their work "sheet by sheet as the same is printed off, And with the first sheet thereof a note of the name of the printer by whom and place where the same is printed" then he was free to publish the work. Free to publish that is, subject to the obvious proviso that, should any of that published material contravene

[57] CJ 11:289. In a letter from John Freke and Edward Clarke to Locke 14 March 1695, Freke comments that, aside from the question of the protection of the property in books "there are many other objections against this Bill as that it leaves the printers at Liberty to set up in any Town in England"; De Beer, *The Correspondence of John Locke*, n 8 above, vol V, 291.

[58] The Bill further provided that no press was to be erected anywhere else within England, Wales or Berwick-upon-Tweed without a special licence from the King or the Bishop of the diocese.

[59] See for example clauses 5–10, 15–16 which represent variations upon provisions from the March Bill.

[60] Books concerning the common law, the history and affairs of the state, and heraldry, honour and arms all had specific licensors, and "all other books … whether of Divinity, Physick, Philosophy or whatsoever other Science or Art" were to be licensed by the Archbishop of Canterbury, the Lord Bishop of London and the Chancellors and Vice-Chancellors of either of the universities.

"the Laws of God, or Laws of this Realm", then he would of course face prosecution. In reality then, this innovation amounted to a removal of the pre-publication censorial eye and allowed for, in theory, a fully free press albeit one that was subject to post-publication legal proceedings.

Second, two clauses in the new Bill made specific allowance for the "preserving of propertyes in the copys of Books". The first of these (clause 13) declared that:

> [W]hosoever shall print any book, pamphlet, portraiture or paper which has been before printed and the property thereof lawfully vested in any other person or persons, without the licence of him or them in whom the lawful property is or shall be lawfully vested shall incur the penalty and forfeit the sum of ____ to the person in whom the property or sole right of printing the same is or shall at that time be vested.

The drafters had obviously learned the lessons of the previous session well. About this provision, there are two things to note, the first of which is that the "lawful property" being protected was no more than a reproduction right, the "sole right of printing". Secondly, the vesting of such a right was made conditional upon first publication; that is, it was to be the act of printing the work that vested the property in the copy of the book with the owner. Having "preserved the property" in such works however, the Bill then proceeded to set a temporal limit on the extent of that protection. The following clause provided, somewhat definitively, that:

> [N]o person ... hath or shall have any sole property or sole right of printing any book, pamphlet, portraiture or paper, for any further or longer time than ____ years to be accounted from and next ensuing the first printing of the same by such proprietor ... any law, statute, ordinance or custom to the contrary notwithstanding.[61]

It was now evident, by contrast with Clarke and Freke's earlier position, that, what property was in a book was not indeed the same as any other form of personalty; rather it was to be determined by statute alone.

Following the Bill's committal, Freke and Clarke wrote to Locke, detailing a number of issues with which various factions of the Commons had taken umbrage. Among these, Freke noted that "[t]he Universitys are also Alarmd and rail at the Bill but make noe other objection but that there is

[61] The earliest version of this Bill continued with the provision that: "Provided always ... that any person ... who now have propriety in any coppys or the sole right of printing any books ... shall have and enjoy the same to them and their assigns for the terms and space of ____ years only to be accounted from and next ensuing the last day of this session of Parliament and no longer". This passage, however, was subsequently dropped from the later draft.

noe saving of their privileges as was in the old Act". He continued, "for that I believe it will be allowed them that it shall be added in the words of the Act by a saving without words of confirmation of their privileges."[62] Freke's observation that the universities would get their way, proved correct. In the later draft of the Bill, one additional clause was introduced which was, in fact, a simple restatement of s.18 of the 1662 Act:

> [N]othing in this Act contained shall be construed to extend to the prejudice of infringing of any the just rights and privileges of either of the two Universities of this Realm touching and concerning the Lycencing or printing of Books in either of those Universities.

Anxiety about the universities' printing privileges, however, provided only one of a number of protestations raised against the proposed legislation. On 5 December 1695 Freke wrote that "though all the objections against the last are cured [the new Bill] raises now more Clamour than was raised on that subject last Sessions".[63] He explained the nature of this "Clamour" in a later letter to Locke. The list of those "Alarmd" was a long one indeed. The Bishops felt "that more care might be taken of the Church", while the Dissenters sought an audience with the "Grave Squire" to voice concerns about the Bill. Amongst a "hundred petty objections" outlined by the government, its most pressing concern was the "fear of losing the prerogative of granting other mens Labours and making mony by Giving a sole power to some to impose a kind of tax on others that is by enabling them to set what prices they please on books they can purchase a patent for the sole printing of". The King's printers were similarly worried at the prospective loss of their prerogative grants. Finally, not surprisingly, "the Booksellers and Stationers and especially the Company" objected that "their property is like to be limited to certain number of years."[64] Evidently, addressing the interests of the universities alone was not sufficient to carry the Bill; as the parliamentary session drew to a close, it remained and so faltered in committee.

[62] John Freke and Edward Clarke to Locke, 14 December 1695, De Beer, *The Correspondence of John Locke*, n 8 above, vol V, 483. There is in fact a document in the Lambeth Palace Library collection, dated 2 December 1695, from Oxford University, setting out several aspects to the Bill as it then stood, which they considered problematic: *Oxf: obj: ag: scheme of Printing Act 1694–95*. In relation to the "Universitys in particular" they argued that it was "requisite that there be (as in several Acts of Parliament)" a proviso ensuring that nothing in the Bill would be interpreted to prejudice the rights and privileges enjoyed by both universities, so that they could "peaceably enjoy ... their ancient rights ... and the several grants of His Majesty, his Progenitors and Predecessors"; Lambeth Palace Library, Todd MS, 939:10.

[63] John Freke to Locke, 5 December 1695, De Beer, *The Correspondence of John Locke*, n 8 above, vol V, 475–76.

[64] John Freke and Edward Clarke to Locke, 14 December 1695, *ibid*, 481–84. The complaints of the "Common Printers" and the stationers were, as with the March 95 Bill, set out in two individual petitions laid before the Commons. On 5 December 1695, the house took note of a petition presented by "several Printers and Booksellers in and about the Cities of London

A NEW SESSION; A NEW PRINTING BILL; JOHN SALUSBURY, PRINTER OF THE *FLYING POST*; AN ATTEMPT TO REGULATE THE NEWS FAILS; ANOTHER PRINTING BILL; THE LORDS ORDER A BILL WHICH IS NEVER BROUGHT; AN ACT CONCERNED WITH BLASPHEMY AND PROFANITY IS PASSED

On 28 October 1696 the Commons were presented with a pamphlet entitled *An Account of the Proceedings in the House of Commons, in Relation to the Re-coyning of the Clipp'd Money, and falling the Price of Guineas*. The house considered it a breach of parliamentary privilege and ordered that it be burnt, and that a committee be appointed to examine and discover the "author, printer, publishers, and dispersers" of the same.[65] James Dover was subsequently discovered to be the printer of the pamphlet and, on 30 November, was ordered to be taken into the custody of the Sergeant at Arms attending the house.[66] One week prior to this order being made, the new partnership of Harley and Edmund Waller was given leave to prepare and bring in a *Bill for the Regulating of Printing and Printing Presses*. In fact, this Bill was presented to the house neither by Harley or Waller but instead by Thomas Bere, on 2 February 1697, and once again would remain in committee until the end of the session.[67]

Whereas, in relation to the previous two *Printing Bills*, the different faces of the book trade had separately petitioned the Commons, the stationers on the one hand seeking protection of their copies, their property, the journeymen on the other trying to ensure some level of guaranteed employment, now both interests came together in a joint document that, in effect, advocated the reinstatement of the *Licensing Act*.[68] Without such

and Westminster", and referred it to the committee then considering the Bill. A second petition was received on the same day from "several of the free Workmen Printers" in which they set out essentially the same arguments as they had when petitioning the Commons in relation to the March 95 Bill. Their arguments related to the proposal to open up the printing trade to all, the lack of work to support all printers currently operating, and the consequence of this state of affairs in occasioning "many scandalous and seditious libels ... which some have been forced to print for the Support of their families"; CJ 11:354.

[65] CJ 11:572.

[66] The same day, a Royal Proclamation was issued for the apprehension of a Mr Grascomb, the author of the pamphlet. CJ 11:602.

[67] CJ 11:567, 685, 704. Feather incorrectly suggests that the Bill ordered to be prepared in October 1696, and the Bill presented by Bere in February 1697 were two different Bills; Feather, "The Book Trade in Politics", n 30 above. The order in October that a Bill be prepared and brought before the House, was the only one made in this Parliamentary session to pre-date the February Bill. See also Hoppitt who, in his study of legislation which failed in Parliament, during the period of 1660–1800, lists these Bills as one and the same; J Hoppitt (ed), *Failed Legislation 1660–1800: Extracted from the Commons and Lords Journals* (London, The Hambledon Press, 1997) 212.

[68] CJ 11:706. See *Reasons humbly offer'd to the Consideration of the Honourable House of Commons, shewing the great necessity of having a Bill for the Regulating of Printing and Printing-Presses*, Lincoln's Inn Library, MP, 102 Fol 311, British Library, 1887.b.58.(7). Although this document

a Bill they argued, "neither the Government, in CHURCH or STATE, nor PROPERTY, can be well secured." In relation to their property, the "Owners of Copies" referred to the argument that "the Bookseller hath the same Remedy against the Invader of his Property, that other Subjects have". Such argument they suggested "carries no solid weight with it", for the following reasons:

> [F]or those that will Invade their Rights, may wage Law with them out of the profits of their Own Books so pyrated upon them; and though they should lose the Cause, yet may be considerable Gainers by the Bargain, whilst in the meantime the Proprietor may be ruin'd; it being no easy matter for him to prove out of a stol'n Impression of a Thousand Books (or perhaps more, especially if dispersed in the country by Haberdashers etc.) that One hundred of them have been sold; and besides, if this should happen to be prov'd, yet even Then they cannot expect suitable Costs and Damages.

Their consternation, unlike previously, was not simply directed towards providing for their property in the Bill, but rather in securing an effective method of protecting such property in preventing and punishing piracy.

Towards the end of this session, on 1 April 1697, while the *Printing Bill* was still in committee, the House of Commons also gave leave for a *Bill to prevent the Writing, Printing, and Publishing any News without Licence* to be prepared. Directed at the burgeoning newspaper market in particular, rather than the book trade in general, it was given its first reading two days later, but rejected upon its second reading the same day.[69] It was the activities of John Salusbury, the printer of the *Flying Post*, which provided the immediate catalyst for the promotion of this Bill. Salusbury had been summoned before the Lords, two days previously,[70] and before the Commons, on the day the house ordered the Bill be prepared,[71] to answer for comments that had been made in the *Flying Post*. Having written an article reflecting on the "Credit and Currency of the Exchequer Bills" which contained, in the opinion of the lower chamber, "a malicious Insinuation", it was ordered that Salusbury "be sent for in Custody of the Sergeant at Arms ... for printing and publishing the said paper."[72] On 5 April Salusbury petitioned the house, acknowledging his offence,

is dated "1698?" it makes specific reference to "the late Wicked and Scandalous Libel" concerning clipped money and so can more accurately be dated to this time.

[69] CJ 11:765.
[70] On 29 March, upon being informed that Salusbury had printed material in the *Flying Post* "relating to his Grace the Duke of Bolton, which is false and scandalous", it was ordered that he be brought before the house. The next day both John Salusbury, and John Combs were brought before the house and reprimanded; Journal of the House of Lords (LJ), 16:138–39.
[71] CJ 11:765.
[72] *Ibid*.

begging pardon for the same, and requesting that he be released from custody.[73] Three days later the Commons ordered that he be discharged.[74] Despite the undoubted element of tokenism connected with, and reactionary nature of, the clamour for the bringing of this *News Bill*, in this parliamentary vignette there emerges a nascent indication that the "content" and physical "context" of printed material, need not receive coterminous legislative attention. True, the Bill in March 1695 had simply provided for regulation of the press, but the main reason for its failure was its inability to secure the property in such publications. Here however, the possibility that one could divorce these two aspects of the text, and legislate to control the content of such work, regardless of the property in the work itself, was explored for the first time.

A new parliamentary session saw another attempt to legislate when Sir William Ashurst and John Pocklington, a practising barrister, were asked to prepare and bring in a *Bill for Regulating Printing And Printing Presses*. Called for on 7 December 1697, their Bill was not presented until 12 February 1698 and did not receive its first reading until 16 February whereupon a motion was made that it be read a second time. The Bill was rejected.[75] Here then for the first time a *Printing Bill* did not even proceed to the committee stage. The failure of this Bill and of the previous *News Bill* to attract any sustained support in the Commons provides a good indication of the changing nature of the members' attitudes towards the press and the place it had in disseminating information and news as well as influencing contemporary debate and public opinion. In *A Letter to a Member of Parliament, showing that a restraint on the Press is inconsistant with the Protestant religion, and dangerous to the liberties of the nation*, printed in 1697, the author of the piece set out a strident argument in favour of a free press:

> The greatest enjoyment that rational and sociable creatures are capable of is to employ their thoughts on what subject they please, and to communicate them to one another as freely as they think them; and herein consists the dignity and freedom of human nature, without which no other liberty can be secure.[76]

For Holmes this publication provides evidence enough to support the contention that by now, in contrast to the arguments raised by the Commons in April 1695 for rejecting the revival of the *Licensing Act*,

[73] CJ 11:768.
[74] At the same time as the order for his release was made, the Commons also instructed the Attorney-General to prosecute Salusbury "for publishing false news" in the *Flying Post*; CJ 11:774. See also Feather, "The Book Trade in Politics", n 30 above, 25.
[75] CJ 12:3, 99, 104.
[76] Holmes and Speck, *The Divided Society*, n 13 above, 69.

the "House was genuinely concerned with the freedom of the press".[77] It was becoming apparent that the Commons, rather than legislate in a manner contrary to the general ethos of a free press, was happier to allow the print trade to continue uninhibited, while prosecuting when individual cases demanded. Not for another six years would there be any attempt to introduce another regulatory measure in the lower chamber, and that would come as a result of a change in the monarchy, the appointment of a Tory dominated government and a highly charged controversy over the issue of occasional conformity. However, it took little more than a week for the Lords to take on the mantle that the Commons had so recently shed. William III, upon the opening of this parliamentary session (less than three months previously) had taken the opportunity in the King's Speech to set out a number of objectives for the forthcoming year. He commented: "I esteem it one of the great advantages of the Peace[78] that I shall now have leisure to rectify such Corruptions or Abuses as may have crept into any Part of the Administration during the War, and effectually to discourage Profaneness and Immorality".[79] Whether spurred on by the King's request, by an increasing intolerance with the Commons' inability to secure a *Printing Bill*, by an increasingly adventurous and controversial press,[80] or indeed a combination of all three, the lords were, for the first time, moved to act.

On 24 February 1698, only eight days after the lower house had rejected Ashurst and Pocklington's *Printing Bill*, the House of Lords formally requested that Powell J, with the assistance of the other judges, prepare a *Bill to Restrain the Licentiousness of the Press*, a Bill that was never brought before the House.[81] On the same day, indeed, immediately prior to the ordering of the *Licentiousness Bill*, another *Bill for the more effectual suppressing of Atheism, Blasphemy and Prophaneness*, was presented and read for the first time by the house. Two days later, this *Atheism Bill* was passed in the Lords;[82] on the same day, the Commons gave leave to bring in a "Bill, or Bills, for the more effectual suppressing of Profaneness, Immorality and Debauchery".[83] In the lower chamber, the Lords' *Atheism Bill* was committed to, and would languish in, a committee of the whole house,[84] headed by Sir John Philips, who, along with Edward Harley, had

[77] *Ibid* 66.
[78] William III was referring to the end of the Nine Years War.
[79] LJ 16:175.
[80] On four occasions in the previous twelve months (January 1697 to January 1698) the Commons considered it necessary to address various publications for breach of privilege, or their libelous content. This compares with only two occasions in 1696, and none in 1695.
[81] LJ 16:217.
[82] LJ 16:217, 218, 220.
[83] CJ 12:132.
[84] CJ 12:134, 138, 142.

also been charged with the task of preparing and bringing in the Commons' *Blasphemy Bill*. This *Bill for the more effectual suppressing Blasphemy and Profaneness* was not to suffer the same fate. Presented to the Commons for the first time on 7 March, and despite the bare majorities relied upon to carry it,[85] the Bill proceeded through all the stages of the house, was passed and brought before the Lords by Philips. The Lords considered it for the first time on 2 April, subsequently amended it, and carried it back to the Commons. On 18 May the Commons took the Lords' amendments into consideration, and objecting to the first of them, drew up a committee to prepare reasons for the Lords as to why they disagreed. A conference was convened, the result of which was that that the Lords chose not to insist upon their amendment to the Bill. At the end of the parliamentary session *An Act for the more effectual suppressing of Blasphemy and Profaneness* received the Royal Assent.[86]

A GENERAL ELECTION; THE COMMONS REJECT A PRINTING BILL FROM THE LORDS; A FURTHER TWO ELECTIONS; WILLIAM FULLER AND MRS BALDWIN; A PRINTING BILL FAILS IN THE LORDS; THE DEATH OF WILLIAM III; ANNE SUCCEEDS THE THRONE; A FOURTH GENERAL ELECTION AND A TORY LANDSLIDE; JOHN TUTCHIN AND *THE OBSERVATOR*; THE COMMONS INTRODUCE ONE FINAL BILL; DANIEL DEFOE WRITES AN ESSAY ON THE REGULATION OF THE PRESS

Following another general election, a new parliamentary session brought renewed agitation for a Bill on printing. Despite the passing of the *Blasphemy Act*, William III evidently still retained reservations about the state of the press. Once again, upon the opening of the new session, 9 December 1698, he requested that parliament take issue with this increasingly licentious press, suggesting that they "employ their thoughts about some good Bills ... for the further discouraging of Vice and Profaneness [which] being of common concern, I cannot but hope for Unanimity and Dispatch".[87] Less than a month later, the *Bill for the Better Regulation of Printing and Printing Presses* received its first reading in the House of Lords. Its preamble detailed the manifold mischiefs which it was designed to eradicate, a modest list incorporating "treason, sedition, blasphemy, heresy, atheism, profanity, irreligious behaviour and the

[85] On its second reading the Bill was carried by a vote of 98 to 84. Upon its third reading, when a motion was made that the debate on the Bill be postponed, this was rejected by the slenderest of majorities: 117 to 113.

[86] CJ 12:147, 151, 154, 155, 183, 258, 269, 276, 280, 295; LJ 16:255, 262, 267, 271, 274, 296, 298, 306.

[87] LJ 16:351–52.

liberty and licentiousness of evil-minded persons". In form, the initial draft of the Bill represented an amalgam of various provisions from the 1662 Act and the *Printing Bills* from 1695. In substance, the basic approach of the Lords was to allow for a free press, subject to certain measures designed to accommodate more effective post-publication surveillance of printed material as well as increasing the accountability of the producers of the same. Substantially amended in committee, the Bill as carried to the Commons was only five clauses in length.[88] The first allowed from presses to be erected anywhere in the country but required that they be registered. The second clause detailed that no book be published without the name and address of the publisher and owner of the press and continued that should the printer not divulge who the author of any particular work was, when questioned, then he was to be liable for punishment as if he were the author; the third set out the various penalties that were to apply for contravention of these requirements.[89] In addition, clause four also set out that should anyone *sell* any book that did not carry the name of the publisher upon it, then he would be liable to penalty by way of forfeiting his stock. Finally, as had been the case in the *Licensing Act*, and all the *Printing Bills* to date, three copies of every published work were to be reserved for the use of the King's library and the two universities. On 1 February, after only its first reading in the Commons, the Lords' Bill was rejected.[90] In the run-up to the 1698 general election, the value of propaganda, and the importance of courting public opinion, had become more and more evident.[91] That the first Bill since the *Licensing Act* to successfully proceed through one of the parliamentary chambers should be so quickly dispatched in the lower house, only serves to re-emphasise the increasingly intolerant attitude on the part of the Commons towards any suggestions concerning the legislative censoring of the press.

After a further two elections, the first in January 1701 and the second in December the same year, with the Tories now in the ascendancy, there came a second attempt in the Lords to introduce their *Printing Bill*.[92]

[88] LJ 16:358, 359, 360–61, 363, 364, 368.

[89] For a first offence the printer was to forfeit his press, letters and utensils and be imprisoned for three months; for a second, he would forfeit his press, letters and utensils and be imprisoned for six months; for a third, he would forfeit his press, letters and utensils, be disabled from practising his profession for three years. Interestingly, the earlier draft of the Bill also included the provision that should anyone be found guilty of a third offence then the judiciary should be free to impose "such further punishment by fine and imprisonment" as they saw fit. By the time that the Bill was received in the Commons however this latter provision had been dropped. No doubt the Lords had learned their lesson of April 1695 in choosing not to incorporate any pecuniary penalties at all in the revised Bill. Above n 14.

[90] CJ 12:466, 468.

[91] See Downie, *Robert Harley and the Press*, n 51 above, 19–40.

[92] This Bill was essentially a replica of the Bill previously dismissed by the Commons three years earlier. See Downie, *Robert Harley and the Press*, n 51 above, 41–56.

The impetus for this legislative action, as was the case with the *News Bill* introduced into the Commons in April 1697, was directly related to a number of contemporary publications with which the house was expressly concerned. Two books had recently been published and printed by a William Fuller and Mrs Baldwin which generated considerable consternation in the upper chamber: *Original Letters of the late King's and others to his greatest Friends in England*, and *Twenty-Six Depositions of Persons of Quality and Worth, with letters of the late Queen*. Fuller was brought before the house, examined and interrogated about the two works over a period of nearly two weeks in early January 1702, whereupon the Lords declared that the books contained "divers false, malicious and scandalous Matters, reflecting upon several Members of both Houses of Parliament, which is of dangerous Consequence to the Government". A warrant was issued to retain Fuller in the Fleet Prison and the Attorney-General was ordered to prosecute Fuller and Baldwin, along with the printer Peter Buck, at common law, for the printing and publishing of seditious libels.[93] Only four days later, on 22 January, the Lords reintroduced their *Bill for the Better Regulation of Printers and Printing Presses*. The Archbishop of Canterbury, present during every day of Fuller's examination, bar one, had contacted Robert Harley at the start of the affair, sending him a draft of the Bill. Harley, then Speaker of the House of Commons, was less than enthusiastic in his response. While replying, with some diplomacy, that the Bill "contains very good methods to have a printer or author answerable for everything which is published", he nevertheless suggested that he had "no doubt but there are sufficient authoritys given by the Laws in being for suppressing such enormitys, whenever it shall be thought fit to put those laws in execution", even proffering that the Bill was in some respects too lenient with such libellers and that a severer course could often be taken "which present laws are sufficient for".[94] That Harley should have taken such an indifferent line to the prospect of this latest attempt to regulate the press is hardly surprising. Such indifference had, by this stage, clearly begun to manifest within the upper chamber as well. The Bill was rejected after its second reading.[95]

It is apparent, of course, that neither of the Lords' Bills had made any attempt to address the issue of property in books. At this time, foreshadowed in part by the Commons' attempt to introduce a *News Bill*, any mutual interest that had been shared through the twinning of the book trade, in the guise of the stationers, and the monarch and government of the day, had now become severed. The notion of a licensed press was

[93] LJ 17:12, 13, 14, 15, 16, 18, 19.

[94] *A Letter to the Archbishop of Canterbury from Mr Harley*, Lambeth Palace Library, Todd MS, 930:25. See also Downie, *Robert Harley and the Press*, n 51 above, 55.

[95] LJ 17:22, 23.

fast becoming a redundant one. The stationers no longer represented the only effective way to control or even monitor the press, and as such there was no need to secure their compliance through the provision of statutory protections. What parliamentary concerns existed about the content of any individual book, pamphlet or paper could be addressed post-publication by parliament, or by the Attorney-General, and had by now essentially become divorced from any consideration surrounding the issue of the booksellers' property in their copies. Six weeks after the second of the Lords' Bills failed, William's reign came to an end. He died on 8 March 1702.

William was succeeded by Anne and, in July, a third general election was held in the space of three years. Buoyed at the polls with the accession to the throne of an Anglican Stuart who was firmly committed to the Church, the election proved to be a landslide victory for the Tory Party. On the convening of Queen Anne's first parliament, several of the High Tory leaders were appointed to the cabinet in a government dominated by Tory personalities.[96] On 27 February 1703, when Anne prorogued parliament at the end of the first session during her reign, she addressed the House, as William III had done before her, on the issue of the press. She remarked:

> [I]t might have been for the public service to have had some further laws, for restraining the great license, which is assumed of publishing and spreading scandalous pamphlets and libels; but as far as the present Laws will extend, I hope you will all do your duty in your respective stations, to prevent and punish such pernicious practices.[97]

Anne would have to wait little more than a month into the next session until the Commons were to make their last assault on the freedom of the press prior to the passing of the *Statute of Anne* 1709. However, the impetus for this final legislative effort almost certainly had less to do with the monarch's closing observations from the previous session, than it had to do with the High Tory Ministry's sensibilities over the issue of occasional conformity, an issue which, for Holmes, became "the most bitterly contested of all the battlegrounds of the political parties in the years between 1702 and 1705."[98]

In the first session of Anne's new parliament, the Tories, seeking to reassert the dominance of the Anglican Church, had introduced a Bill

[96] The Earl of Rochester was appointed Lord Lieutenant of Ireland; the Earl of Nottingham Secretary of State; and Sir Edward Seymour, Comptroller of the Household and Cabinet Minister; Holmes, *The Making of A Great Power*, n 1 above, 201. See also Kishlansky, *A Monarchy Transformed*, n 1 above, 316–20.
[97] LJ 17:322.
[98] G Holmes, *British Politics in the Age of Anne* (London, MacMillan, 1967) 99. On the question of occasional conformity in general, *ibid*, 97–108.

addressing the practice of occasional conformity, in which they proposed to levy large fines against those who took the Anglican sacrament in order to qualify for municipal and national office,[99] but afterwards attended the services of dissenting churches. The Bill passed the Commons but was defeated in the Lords. When the new parliamentary session began, the Tories once again sought to secure the passage of the *Occasional Conformity Bill*, and were once again defeated in the Lords. Against this background, on 15 December 1703, a complaint was read to the House of Commons concerning comments made by John Tutchin in an issue of *The Observator* "on Occasional Conformity";[100] almost immediately afterwards it was ordered that leave be given to bring in a *Bill to Restrain the Licentiousness of the Press*, nearly six years after the same was ordered in the House of Lords. A committee, appointed to inquire as to who the author, the printer and the publisher of the paper were, reported on 3 January 1704 that Tutchin was the author, John How the printer,[101] and Benjamin Bragg the publisher. All three were ordered into the custody of the Sergeant of Arms of the house for printing a seditious libel.[102] Ten days later, the *Licentiousness Bill* was presented, by the Solicitor-General, to the Commons. Receiving its second reading on 18 January, it was committed to the whole house, however, the committee's final report was repeatedly delayed, and as a consequence was never brought before the house. The life of this Bill had ended.[103]

On 19 February 1704, a day when the committee were reporting to the Commons that they had gone through the *Licentiousness Bill* and had made several amendments thereto, Daniel Defoe published the first issue of his influential journal, *A Weekly Review of the Affairs of France*. Defoe, having been recently released from a six-month sentence in Newgate, was now working in the service of Harley as a political writer and propagandist.[104] Although Defoe would later use the *Review* to mount a sustained press

[99] This was required to meet the demands of the *Corporation Act* 1661 and *Test Act* 1673; *ibid*, 100.

[100] *The Observator*, 8–11 December 1703.

[101] This was not John How's first brush with authority. He had, on a number of occasions in the 1680s and 1690s been accused of printing libelous and seditious materials See D-J Dugas, "The London Book Trade in 1709 (Part Two)" (2001) 95 *Papers of the Bibliographical Society of America* 157, 159–63.

[102] CJ 14:269–70. For more information on the Tutchin affair, see Feather, "The Book Trade in Politics", n 30 above, 28, and Downie, *Robert Harley and the Press*, n 51 above, 67.

[103] Clarke wrote to Locke about this Bill in a post-script to a letter dated 13 January 1704 commenting that "A Byll to Restrayn the Liberty of the Presse was this day brought in, Read, and ordered a Second reading upon Tuesday next, when I hope it will be thrown out againe" De Beer, *The Correspondence of John Locke*, n 8 above, vol VIII, 162–63.

[104] Defoe's tract, "The Shortest way with the Dissenters", written in December 1702, had angered High Tories everywhere by satirically advocating the hanging of Dissenting preachers After its publication he went into hiding. The work was condemned in February 1703, in his absence, as a seditious libel, and in May 1703 he was finally apprehended and committed to Newgate. It was Harley who managed to secure Defoe's release from Newgate, as a

campaign, in advance of the passing of the *Statute of Anne*, to highlight the iniquitous situation in which "scandalous and unjust Invasions of Property" were allowed to be perpetrated upon the writers of the day,[105] of more immediate significance was the fact that, just prior to the launch of his periodical, but between the time that the *Licentiousness Bill* had been ordered to be prepared, and its first reading, Defoe also published his tract *An Essay on the Regulation of the Press.*[106] In this essay, the increasing importance of maintaining a free press, in view of the now dominant party system, proved of fundamental concern to Defoe. He proffered the following scenario:

> [S]uppose this or that Licensor, a Partyman that is, one put in and upheld by a Party; suppose him of any Party, which you please, and a Man of the opposite Kidney, brings him a Book, he views the character of the Man, O, says he, 'I know the Author, he is a damn'd Whig, or a rank Jacobite, I'll license none of his Writings'.

Defoe asked "who will Study, who will breed up their children to Letters, when all the Fruits of their Labours are liable to the Blast of the Arbitrary Breath of Mercenary Men"?, and suggested that, with the return of the Licensor "a book could be damn'd for the Author, not the Author for the book." Like Locke before him, he advocated a free press subject to an increased emphasis on post-publication accountability and prosecution, proposing that "a Law be made to make the last Seller the Author, unless the name of the Author, Printer or Bookseller, be affix'd to the Book". In this way, he continued, "no Book can be published, but there will be somebody to answer for it".[107]

While the Tory sponsored bill clearly advocated a return to a system of pre-publication licensing, against which Defoe vigorously proselytised, whether or not it also provided some form of security for the property in books remains open to conjecture. On balance, there is sufficient evidence to suggest that it did. The evidence for this derives from the fact that, of the petitions received from the book trade concerning the Bill, none of them came from the quarter of the master stationers. This section of the trade apparently considered their properties satisfactorily secured.[108]

consequence of which Defoe was persuaded to use his considerable talents on Harley's behalf. For an in depth examination on the relationship between Harley and Defoe at this time, see Downie, *Robert Harley and the Press*, n 51 above, 57–79.

[105] D Defoe, *A Review*, 3 December 1709.

[106] D Defoe, "An Essay on the Regulation of the Press" reprinted by the Luttrell Society (Oxford, Blackwell, 1958).

[107] *Ibid.*

[108] Given that all the Bills which began in the House of Commons, with the exception of the earliest, the March 1695 Bill, had made some provision for the booksellers, there is no reason to suspect that, in this regard, this Bill was any different.

Of the two main petitions laid before the Commons, one simply re-rehearsed the arguments of the journeymen printers for re-introducing parliamentary regulation of the numbers of people allowed to practice their art of printing.[109] The other signalled a return to those concerns that Locke had expounded upon in his earlier criticisms of the 1662 Act. Submitted on behalf of the "Booksellers and Printers of London", it complained, not about the lack of property in their copies, but about the letters patent that existed "for the sole printing all Books whatsoever, relating to the common Law of the land", which monopoly, they continued was "a thing very Odious in the Eye of the Law". The petitioners protested about the excessive price of books relating to the law,[110] and about having to give an author £200–300 for his manuscript and then "near half as much as more to the patentees, for the Liberty to publish it to the world". Asserting that the old justifications for the Crown's grant of such patents no longer held true given the increase in the numbers of law books, presses and printing houses, they concluded that, in general, the patents represented "a great prejudice to the improvement of Knowledge, the useful art of Printing, and the trade of those who have no other method to get a living".[111] This consternation over the various positions of monopoly held by certain of the stationers was not a new or a recent development. Time and again, throughout the sixteenth and seventeenth centuries, trouble had manifest concerning the excesses and abuses of monopolistic practices within the trade. In the 1580s, for example, John Wolfe had lead an attack on the existing system of printing privileges that resulted in the established patentees of the time gifting some of their less valuable stock to the Company for the benefit of it's more disaffected members.[112] Such internal tensions had existed for almost as long as the practice of printing had been carried on, and that they resurfaced at this time of is no surprise. As we shall see however, to assert, as many do,[113] that the *Statute of Anne*, when finally secured, was essentially designed to

[109] *The Case of the Free Workmen-Printers, Relating to the Bill For Preventing the Licentiousness of the Press*, Lincoln's Inn Library, MP 102, Fol 307.

[110] It is interesting to note that before this time there had never been a clause in any Act or Bill that granted a power to any authority to limit the price of Books. It may be that in this petition lies the origin of the clause for controlling the prices of Books in the 1709 Act. See also the later petition in relation to the 1707 Bill.

[111] *The Case of the Booksellers and Printers, Relating to the Patentees for the sole Printing all Books of Common Law*, Lincoln's Inn Library, MP 102, Fol. 308. A third petition was laid before the Commons which simply provided a counter to the challenge against the patentees as well as a defence of the King's Prerogative. CJ 14:339.

[112] See Loewenstein, *The Author's Due*, n 4 above; Patterson, *Copyright in Historical Perspective*, n 4 above; Ransom, *The First Copyright Statute*, n 4 above; and Rose, *Of Authors and Owners*, n 4 above.

[113] Lowenstein, Patterson and Rose, for example, share the opinion that the primary focus of the 1709 act was that of trade regulation. *Ibid.*

restore some modicum of order to the book trade while at the same time addressing and regulating these past mercantile inequities, is to overstate the case, and to overlook a more fundamental purpose lying at the legislation's core.

Whether or not the *Licentiousness Bill* did in fact make provision for the booksellers' copy, it is of note that it did proceed beyond a second reading in the Commons, when the previous three Bills had failed to gain any ground whatsoever. Why was this the case, and why did it stumble? This can only be understood in light of the particular position of the Tory party at the time. As has been noted, during the first few years of Anne's reign, the Tories held a favoured position in government, as well as dominating parliament. As a consequence, this Bill, brought in response to Tutchin's Whiggish attack on occasional conformity, had the support of some of the most influential men of the political moment: Sir Edward Seymour, the Earl of Jersey, and both Secretaries of State, the Earl of Nottingham and Sir Charles Hedges. Soon after they gained office, however, the Tories' position began to weaken. The Earl of Rochester, Queen Anne's uncle, resigned from the government in February 1703. Through the spring of the following year Tory majorities increasingly diminished. Alongside the damage to their authority over the occasional conformity Bills, a number of other key Bills which they tabled were defeated through the collaboration of the Whigs and some of the more moderate Tories. The Queen began to withdraw her support for the current ministry, and in April 1704, it collapsed when Nottingham's offer of resignation was accepted by Anne, and both Seymour and Jersey were dismissed from office, having persistently obstructed the policies of Godolphin, the Lord Treasurer, and Marlborough, the Captain-General, concerning England's position in the Spanish Succession War.[114] With the main promoters of the *Licentiousness Bill* now out of office, the impetus for the Bill waned, it lost its support in the Commons, and was never to re-appear from committee. Parliament was prorogued on 3 April until 19 July, and then again until 19 October, while Robert Harley was appointed to the new ministry as Secretary of State for the Northern Department. With Harley as Secretary of State, it is hardly surprising that there would be no further legislative attempts to proscribe the press. As Feather observes: "It was this change in the ministry which signalled the end of the attempts to revive the old licensing system".[115]

This concluded the thirteenth attempt in just under ten years to provide some form of statutory regulation for the press following the lapse in

[114] On this period in general see, Holmes, *British Politics in the Age of Anne*, n 98 above; Holmes, *The Making of a Great Power*, n 1 above; Kishlanksky, *A Monarchy Transformed*, n 1 above; and Feather, "The Book Trade in Politics", n 30 above.
[115] Feather, "The Book Trade in Politics", n 30 above, 28.

May 1695 of the *Licensing Act* 1662. Thirteen attempts during a period in politics unlike any other that had preceded it, or indeed any that was to follow. This was a period in which the triennial parliamentary system, the development of clearly definable party lines, and the emergence of an influential and vital electorate, operated to establish the conditions necessary to allow for the birth of a popular political press, and the concomitant realisation of the value and importance of political propaganda in currying popular opinion, both within and without the Houses of Parliament. While the first attempts at regulation during this period may genuinely have been born out of the nervousness of the new state absent a familiar system of licensing, the nature of later legislative efforts became increasingly two-dimensional and reactionary, spawned, in the main, by individually contentious publications such as those of Tutchin, and Fuller and Baldwin. Parliament was becoming more and more intoxicated with the free press, and increasingly intolerant of each passing legislative bid, with the exception, perhaps, of the final *Licentiousness Bill*. Moreover, it was becoming evident that the control and censorship of the book trade, if it was required at all, could be effectively addressed as an issue, separately from any need to provide for the property in such books. The notion of regulation of the content of a book became increasingly detached from questions surrounding the physical context of the book. Had the parliament of the day been pre-disposed to renew the provisions of the 1662 Act, or any of the subsequently proposed measures, this would have had profound implications for the development of a separate and distinct property law providing protection for the reproduction of books. As it was, for reasons concerned with the variously intertwined aspects of politics, personality and propaganda, only one of these Bills succeeded. The booksellers' courtship with the censorial state definitively came to a close. These "owners of copies" realised that a change in approach would be necessary if they were to secure any measure of protection for their property and so avoid being "utterly ruined".

2

The Statute of Anne; A Miserable Havock

WHEN DEFOE WROTE his *Essay on the Regulation of the Press* at the beginning of 1704, while reserving the most of his tract to lambast the "Arbitrary Breath of Mercenary men", he also, not surprisingly, took the opportunity to champion that the law should prevent "a certain sort of Thieving which is now in full practice in England ... Press-piracy". This, he considered, was an abuse upon authors "every jot as unjust as lying with their wives, and breaking up their Houses."[1] Should a law be passed to regulate the press, it could, at the same time, effectively suppress:

> [T]his most villanous Practice, for every author being oblig'd to set his name to the book he writes has by this law an undoubted exclusive right to the property of it. The clause in the law is a patent to the author and settles the propriety of the work wholly in himself, or in such to whom he shall assign it.[2]

The proposed legislation to which Defoe was referring was of course the failed *Licentiousness Bill* 1704. This was not to be the only time, however, that he would address the subject of "press-piracy". While other writers, such as Joseph Addison,[3] did broach the question of literary property, it was Defoe, through his periodical *A Review of the Affairs of France*, first published in February 1704, who most consistently invoked the issue of the writer's property in his work.[4] Defoe, in the years following the collapse of the *Licentiousness Bill*, continually positioned the matter plainly in

[1] D Defoe, "An Essay on the Regulation of the Press", reprinted by the Luttrell Society (Oxford, Blackwell, 1958) 27.
[2] *Ibid.*
[3] *The Tatler*, 1 December 1709.
[4] On the periodical press at this time see: HL Snyder, "The Circulation of Newspapers in the Reign of Queen Anne" (1968) 23 *The Library* 206; JR Sutherland, "The Circulation of Newspapers and Literary periodicals, 1700–1730" (1934–35) 15 *The Library* 110; GA Cranfield, *The Development of the Provincial Newspaper, 1700–1760* (Oxford, Clarendon Press, 1962); J Black, *The English Press in the Eighteenth Century* (London, Croom Helm, 1987).

public view. Writing on 8 November 1705, he set out the problem with the press as it currently stood:

> Books are Printed by no body, and Wrote by every body; one Man Prints another Man's Works, and calls them his own; again, another Man Prints his own, and calls them another Man's ... continual Roberies, Piracies, and Invasions of Property, range among the Occupation. One Man Studies Seven Year, to bring a finish'd Peice into the World, and a Pyrate Printer, Reprints his Copy immediately, and Sells it for a quarter of the Price.

He continued that "[t]hese things call for an Act of Parliament, and that so loud as I hope will not be deny'd, that so Property of Copies may be secur'd to Laborious Students, to the Encouragement of Letters and all useful Studies".[5] Unlike the stationers and booksellers before him, whose petitions had focused on a jealous guarding of their copies and their trade, Defoe proffered an alternate justification as to why the authors of works should be entitled to reap the benefit of their labours. For the first time in this debate, he drew an explicit link between the benefit to society as a whole that comes with the encouragement of learning, and the provision of some form of statutory protection for books as a way to achieve this end. The influence of his argument is easily traced in the emerging discourse and the calls for legislation that were to follow, as the booksellers adopted this new rhetoric when petitioning Parliament. In the words of Mark Rose, it was "Defoe's agitation on behalf of authorial rights" that provided the London stationers with "a new strategy for pursuing their own interests".[6] More than this however, it was in these early writings on the problem of "press-piracy", that Defoe sowed the first seeds of the social contract that would take centre stage in the *Statute of Anne*.

The first manifestation of a change in the booksellers' approach comes in a pamphlet from 1706 entitled *Reasons humbly Offer'd for a Bill for the Encouragement of Learning, and the Improvement of Printing*. This was, most probably, penned and printed by none other than John How, one of the three men responsible for the tract on occasional conformity that had provided the impetus for the Tory government's attempts to secure the *Licentiousness Bill*.[7] In it he suggested that:

> It seems to be very reasonable, that when a Gentleman has spent the greatest Part of his Time and Fortune in a Liberal Education, he should have all

[5] D Defoe, *A Review of the Affairs of France*, 8 November 1705.

[6] M Rose, *Authors and Owners: The Invention of Copyright* (London, Harvard University Press, 1993) 35.

[7] Lincoln's Inn Library, MP 102, Fol 312. The reason for suggesting that How was the bookseller behind this pamphlet lies in the fact that, in a later pamphlet published on 28 November 1709, How makes reference to the fact that he had "for many Years last spent

> the Advantages that may possibly be allow'd him for his Writings, one of which Advantages is the sole and undoubted Right to the Copy of his own Book, as being the Product of his own Labour.[8]

Without protecting the author's copy (and by extension, protecting those persons that give authors "Mony or other valuable Considerations" for such copies), How predicted that "[l]earned men will be wholly discouraged from Propagating the most useful Parts of Knowledge and Literature, Purity of Print will be Destroy'd, and the Bookseller Undone."[9] When thirteen of the most influential "Booksellers and Printers in and about the city of London"[10] laid a petition before the House of Commons on 26 February 1707, they made similar claims.

> [M]any learned Men have spent much Time, and been at great Charges in composing Books, who used to dispose of their Copies upon valuable Considerations, to be printed by the Purchasers ... but of late Years such Properties have been much invaded by other Persons printing the same Books, either here in England, or beyond the Seas ... to the great Discouragement of Persons from writing Matters, that might be of great Use to the Publick, and to the great Damage of the Proprietors; And praying, that Leave may be given to bring in a Bill for the securing of Property in such Books, as have been, or shall be, purchased from or reserved to, the Authors thereof.[11]

No longer did the trade choose to focus the sympathies of the lower house solely on the plight of their precarious livelihood and the numerous stationers' widows facing utter ruin. Rather, the deserving nature of the author's work and the public utility in legislating in such a manner was foremost in their reasoning. On the same day as the petition was presented, it was ordered that leave be given to prepare such a Bill and, two days later, the *Bill for the Better Securing the Rights of Copies of Printed Books*

his Time and Money to secure Property, as [the] Proposals Printed in 1706, to be produc'd upon Occasion, will shew"; J How, *Some Thoughts on the Present State of Printing and Bookselling* (London, How, 1709) BM 11901.A.2(3).

[8] Lincoln's Inn Library, MP 102, Fol 312. *Reasons humbly Offer'd*, (London, How, 1706). BM 11901.A.2(3).

[9] *Ibid.*

[10] The signatories of this petition were as follows: Edward Brewster, Daniel Browne, Richard Chiswell, Robert Clavell, Freeman Collins, Timothy Goodwin, Charles Harper, Henry Mortlock, William Rogers, Samuel Roycroft, Jacob Tonson, Benjamin Tooke and John Walthoe. Of these thirteen, six were former or future Masters of the Stationers' Company, and ten were former or future Wardens of the Company. For more information on the influential position which this cabal of booksellers enjoyed amongst the London book trade, see J Feather, *Publishing, Piracy and Politics: An Historical Study of Copyright in Britain* (London, Mansell, 1994) 56–58.

[11] CJ 15:313.

received its first reading. Like so many of the Bills from the previous ten years however, this too would remain in committee until the end of that parliamentary session.[12] Feather, commenting on the demise of this Bill, speculates that a possible reason for its failure may have been that a licensing clause was "tacked" to the Bill during the committee stage.[13] Defoe, at the time, put forward an alternative and more convincing rationale. Writing in 1709 on "the Subject of regulating the Press" he asked: "[W]ho they were who dropt the last Bill in the House, I mean, who privately declin'd it, and so procured it to be dropt"?, before proposing one of two likely sources for the miscarriage of the Bill: either the "High Party" (presumably *because* the Bill contained no censorial dimension, such as they had pressed for in 1704), or "some Persons concern'd in Patents and limitted Properties, who the Act being but Temporary, thought their Property would at the End of the Term be laid more open than it was before".[14]

Two years later Defoe took up his pen to speak out about "the Shame and Scandal of the present Time", the "daily invasions of Property equal in Villany to robbing a House, or plundering an Hospital", by which practice, a man:

> [H]as his Labour destroy'd, his Expences lost, and his Copy re-printed by sham and pyratical Booksellers and Printers, who eat the Gain of the poor Man's Labour, destroy and spoil the Work itself, cheat the Buyer by performing it imperfect, and ruin the laborious Author.[15]

[12] CJ 15:321, 322, 346. Unfortunately no copy of the Bill appears to have survived. As was the case with the *Licentiousness Bill* 1704 this Bill prompted a petition attacking the profits made by those "Mercenary, and Self-ended Men, [who] engross the chief Branches, of the Whole Trade into their Hands by way of Patents". As to the Bill before the house the author argued that "the Inconveniences it prevents are but trifling to those that it may cause. There are but few instances, if any, of any considerable damage done to any person in their private property", and continued that "there is too much Reason to fear the End of this Bill is to enable the Patentees, and Others, to Extort what they please for their Books." The preoccupation with the price of books provided the mainstay of the pamphlet's commentary, with, not surprisingly, the patentees receiving the most vitriolic criticism. To remedy this situation the petition requested "that a clause be added to the Bill" to cap the price of patentees' books. The next Bill to come before the Commons was the *Statute of Anne* which of course did contain such a clause. *Reasons Humbly Offered to the Consideration of the Honourable House of Commons, Relating to the Bill, For Securing Property in Books*, Lincoln's Inn Library, MP 102 Fol 102, dated 1709 (that this petition relates to a Bill already before the Commons, and does not refer to it as, "For the encouragement of Learning and for Securing the Property of Copies of Books to the Rightful Owners thereof" (ie the 1710 Bill), suggests that this document, while dated 1709, does in fact relate to this earlier 1707 Bill).

[13] J Feather, "The Book Trade in Politics: The Making of the Copyright Act of 1710" (1980) 8 *Publishing History* 19 n 59.

[14] D Defoe, *A Review*, 3 November 1709. Had a licensing clause been incorporated within the Bill, it seems unlikely that Defoe should have written to Harley on 25 March 1707, in the following terms: "I hear that the Bill for Securing the Right of printed Coppyes is stopt. I beg of you Sir in your respect to [the] Encouragement of Letters and Dilligence in Learning to give it your help"; GH Healey, *The Letters of Daniel Defoe* (Oxford, Clarendon Press, 1955) 212.

[15] Defoe, *A Review*, 3 November 1709.

On 26 November, in a manner that echoed his earlier *Essay*, he appealed to both Whig and Tory parties, to put aside their differences and "joyn together, to obtain a Law in the present Parliament for due and just Restraints to the Press ... for the punishing Blasphemies and Errors already printed ... and for the Encouragement of Learning, Arts, and Industry, by securing the Property of Books to the Authors or Editors of them".[16] His plea was, once again, taken up by the bookseller John How. Two days after Defoe had re-opened the debate, How published *Some Thoughts on the Present State of Printing and Bookselling* in which he urged that Parliament might "think fit to secure *Property* in *Books* by a Law".[17] Both men reflected upon the deleterious consequences flowing from the current state of the press, and the way in which "scandalous and unjust Invasions of Property" operated as a "great Discouragement ... to Learning and Industry, by which Means already the best Writers of this Age have laid down and despair'd".[18] Defoe even proffered the wording for what he considered would be a suitable Act. Writing on 6 December 1709, in a passage that requires to be set out in full, he commented that:

> To print another Man's Copy, is much worse than robbing him on the Highway; for the Thief takes only what he finds about him, but the Pyrate Printer takes away his inheritance — An elaborate Work, a long studied Treatise, a painfully collected History; it both is and ought to be the Due, not of the Author only, but of his Family and Children — And this is all ravag'd by the Re-printing Pyrate ...
>
> To say we know not how to prevent this, is saying what is very foolish — This, and the printing seditious or heretical Books, is easily suppress'd by an Act of Parliament of but two Clauses.
>
> 1. That no Man shall presume to print, or sell when printed, any Book that has been printed before, without the consent or agreement of the Author or Proprietor of the said Book — under a Penalty of 5*l*, per sheet for the said Copy, to be paid Half to the Queen, Half to the person injur'd, by the Printer or Publisher of the said Book —
>
>   To make this effectual, it should be enacted,
>
>   1. That every Printer shall be oblig'd to set his name to every Book he prints, and the name of the Person he prints it for, That no Bookseller may be deceiv'd — And that every Bookseller, who shall

[16] Defoe, *A Review*, 26 November 1709.

[17] How, *Some Thoughts on the Present State of Printing and Bookselling*, n 7 above.

[18] D Defoe, *A Review*, 3 December 1709. How considered that, as a result of this "great Discouragement to Learning", authors were inclined to spend less time on their works "which causes our Books to be the more contemptible, to the Scandal of the Nation". Rather he suggested that "if the Booksellers were secure in the Properties of their Copies ... the Author having better Pay, might afford more Pains, and the Publick, by consequence, have more valuable Books".

sell or vend any pyrated Copy, not having the Printer's Name to it, shall be esteem'd the Publisher in the sense of the Act.

2. That the Author or Proprietor of any Copy so pyrated, shall have his private Action of Damages against every Seller or Publisher of such Copy, as well as against the Printer; wherein if he cast the said Publisher, he shall recover for every Book so vended or sold by them, 5*l*, with treble Costs.

2. For the Publick Part. That every Author, who causes anything he writes to be printed or publish'd, shall be oblig'd to cause his Name to be printed in the Frontpiece of the Book, and to give a note under his hand to the Printer of the said Book, sign'd by two Witnesses, acknowledging and owning himself to be the Author of the said Book, and authorising him the said Printer to print and publish the same — Which Note and Acknowledgement shall be allow'd to discharge the said Printer in Law — and shall, on the Printers producing it upon Oath, together with the Oaths of the Witnesses, be sufficient to convict the said Author.[19]

After this month of sustained media attention, and only three days after Defoe had detailed his legislative mission statement, the booksellers, as was the case with the 1707 Bill, provided a renewed impetus for legislative action. On 12 December 1709, they submitted a petition to the Commons setting out that it had been the "constant usage" for authors to sell their copies to booksellers who held such copies "as their property"; they complained, in a fashion by now all too familiar, that:

> [D]ivers Persons have of late invaded the Properties of others, by reprinting several Books, without the Consent, and to the great Injury, of the Proprietors, even to their utter Ruin, and the Discouragement of all Writers in any useful Part of Learning.[20]

Mr Wortley, Mr Compton and Mr Peyton were given leave to bring in a Bill "for securing to [the petitioners] the Property in Books" and, on 11 January 1710, Wortley presented their *Bill for the Encouragement of Learning, and for the Securing the Property of Copies of Books to the Rightful Owners thereof*.[21] Less than three months later, on 5 April 1710, the world's first copyright statute, *An Act for the Encouragement of Learning by vesting*

[19] D Defoe, *A Review*, 6 December 1709.

[20] CJ 16:240. The signatories of this petition included seven of the thirteen booksellers who had petitioned in 1707, namely, Henry Mortlock, Richard Chiswell, William Rogers, Daniel Brown, Jacob Tonson, Timothy Goodwin and Benjamin Tooke, as well as, Thomas Horne, Benjamin Walford, Richard Sare, James Knapton, Robert Knaplock, Timothy Childe, Richard Mount, Daniel Midwinter, and John Sprint. For evidence of the Stationers' Company presence in the Commons during the passage of the Bill, see Feather, *Publishing, Piracy and Politics*, n 10 above, 58.

[21] CJ 16:300, 338, 369, 394–95; LJ 19:19:109, 123, 134, 138, 140, 143.

the Copies of printed Books in the Authors or Purchasers of such Copies, during the Times therein mentioned, was passed.[22]

During this period the Journal of the Commons makes reference to the receipt of only one petition, submitted on 2 February, on behalf of "the poor distressed Printers, and Bookbinders ... and the rest of the same Trades, in and about the Cities of London and Westminster".[23] In this the book trade's journeymen supported the protection of the booksellers' copies as an end to piracies, and so an increase in work for their members. There were, however, five additional pamphlets produced at the time, each contributing something to the debate concerning the Bill,[24] not least the introduction of the term "Copy-Right" to Westminster Hall.[25] While these may not have been formally presented before the Commons, a well placed five-shilling piece to the doorkeeper of the house would ensure that all the MPs entering "would have a copy pressed into their hands".[26] Most of these tracts invoked a general right to reprint works in perpetuity according to common law, while decrying the unsatisfactory nature of their means of redress under the same, and so highlighting the need for statutory intervention.[27] The booksellers' rights were variously defended

[22] For a transcript of the Act, see Appendix I.

[23] CJ 16:291.

[24] *The Booksellers humble address to the Honourable House of Commons In behalf of a Bill for the Encouragement of Learning*, Bod Fol w, 666(227); *A Letter from Holland, concerning the Right which Booksellers have in the Copies, or Sole Power of Printing their respective Books, in that Nation*, Lincoln's Inn Library, MP 102, Fol 104; *More Reasons Humbly Offer'd to the Honourable House of Commons for the Bill for Encouraging Learning and Securing the Property of Copies in Books*, Lincoln's Inn Library, MP 102, Fol 101; *Reasons Humbly Offer'd for the Bill for the Encouragement of Learning and for Securing the Property of Copies of Books to the Rightful Owners thereof*, Lincoln's Inn Library, MP 102, Fol 100; *The Case of the Booksellers Right to their Copies, or sole Power of Printing their respective Books, represented to the Parliament*, Lincoln's Inn Library, MP 102, Fol 103 and BL 1887.b.58(3).

[25] See *Reasons Humbly Offer'd for the Bill*. The use of this phrase at the time was not an isolated event. Defoe, in 1711, commenting upon renewed suggestions of censuring the press propounded that such a prohibition would have a disastrous effect upon "the Livelyhoods, and the Employments of Families and Trades Innumerable, whose dependance and whose Estates lie in several parts of the Printing trade". He continued that "[a]mong these are to be reckoned Patents and Properties in Copies of smaller Books, such as Almanacks, Catechisms, Psalms, little Manuals of many sorts, Religious and Moral; the Copy-Right to which are Estates to many Families, and to preserve which Right from Pyracy and Invasion, a very Just and Necessary Law was made last Parliament, the Advantage of which is happily found in many Cases since"; D Defoe, *A Review*, 29 March 1711. The phrase "copy right" had been used as early as 31 May 1701 in the Stationers' Register, when Timothy Childe, entering himself as proprietor of the work *A New Ecclesiastical History*, records: "Mr Awnsham Churchill is and shall be entitled to one moiety of this book & copy right"; Rose, *Authors and Owners*, n 6 above, 58, n 4. See also Patterson who details two uses of the term in the Stationers' Register in 1701; L R Patterson, *Copyright in Historical Perspective*, (Nashville, Vanderbilt University Press, 1968) 4.

[26] J Brewer, *The Sinews of Power: War, Money and the English State, 1688–1783* (London, Unwin Hyman, 1989) 241.

[27] For example, the author of *More Reasons* writes: "The Subject of our Request is, That You would be pleased to strengthen the Common Law, in our Case, as preceding Parliaments

as having been "enjoined by Common Law above 150 years", as necessary given that the bookseller "takes the risque" of publishing the first edition, and as wholly natural since the author "has the original indisputable Right of Publishing" his work, especially given the investment, both in time and money, he may have made in the preparation of the work. Comparisons were made with other forms of property which, when acquired, subsisted in the purchaser forever, as well as other jurisdictions, in particular Holland, which, it was suggested, provided similar protections for authors and publishers.[28] In *A Letter from Holland*, the unnamed author set out that "[t]he Property of Copies is as Valid here as in any Part of Europe".[29] The way in which Dutch books were protected however was simply by way of a privilege, "a Patent Granted by the States", which vested in the petitioner "the sole Right (exclusive of all others) of Printing the said Book in whatever language or volume he pleases, for the term of the Fifteen next following years".[30] In addition to these various arguments, the potential social impact of failing to legislate was highlighted. The detrimental consequences to the trade were emphasised, as well as the implications the lack of protection had for the "instruction of mankind". Moreover, it was suggested that an effective statutory protection would act as a guarantor for cheaper editions, as well as securing and safeguarding the "purity of printing".

While the Bill was to undergo some considerable transformation during its passage through Parliament, in its earliest incarnation it was only six clauses in length.[31] Drawing upon the *Licensing Act* it forbade

have, in very many others, at divers times For Whereas, by Common Law, we can recover no more Costs, than we can prove Damage; and the Damage we sustain, being always vastly more than we can prove; We desire you will assign such Punishment upon Delinquents, as in Your Great Wisdom You shall think fit."

[28] In *The Case of the Booksellers Right to their Copies*, it was argued that: "This custom of Impropriation of Copies is observ'd in all Nations where Printing is Exercis'd, and we cannot doubt that the Common Law protects it everywhere, since we see it nowhere invaded, and know very well that Copies are sold and convey'd as property in all Countries".

[29] See in particular, *A Letter from Holland, concerning the Right which Booksellers have in the Copies, or Sole Power of Printing their respective Books, in that Nation.*

[30] Note that the author of *The Case of the Booksellers Right to their Copies*, acknowledged that privileges were given in Holland "for a term of years" but continued that "since we see the same Family possess the copy uninvaded even after the Expiration of the Patent, we may justly suppose that the Right is continued by common Law; and if it be asked why then is the Patent granted it may be answered and we believe with great truth, that it serves only to ascertain the Penalty and Summarily to punish Delinquents". This explanation, however, conflicts with the evidence of the author of *A Letter*. About these privileges, he commented: "What makes them more necessary here is, that each of the Seven Provinces being a separate Sovereignty, tho' I should have the Privilege in the Province of Holland, it would not hinder any Bookseller in the Province of Utrecht from printing my Book, and Selling it there; but it will hinder effectually that Bookseller, or any other, importing it into this Province, from thence, any other Province, or any Foreign Country".

[31] This Bill is housed in the Lincoln's Inn Library; it is possible to state with accuracy that this is in fact the Bill that received a first reading in the House of Commons, as the Lambeth Palace

the printing, reprinting or importing of any book which "any author shall hereafter compose or write" (or which any bookseller or printer purchased or acquired from the same) subject to financial penalties,[32] required that all such works be registered with the Company of Stationers prior to publication,[33] and retained the library deposit provisions for the King's Library, as well as those at Oxford and Cambridge.[34] The Bill also introduced a system for controlling the cost of books published at "too high or unreasonable" a price,[35] provided that the defendant in any action taken under the proposed legislation could plead the "General Issue",[36] and proposed to allow anyone to freely import and sell "any of the Classicks [or] any other Book or Books printed Originally beyond the Seas".[37]

A number of these provisions were amended, in relatively minor ways, as the Bill travelled through the Commons: the registration requirement was altered to include an obligation upon the Stationers' Company clerk to issue a certificate verifying registration as and when required; deposit copies were also to be provided for the benefit of Sion College and the

Library contains a document entitled, *An Abstract of the Bill for the Encouragement of Learning and for Securing the Property of Books to the Rightful Owners thereof* which recounts the six provisions of the Lincoln's Inn Bill along with the comment that it was "[a]ppointed to be read a Second time upon Thursday morning the 9th", which corresponds with the Journal records for the proceedings in the House of Commons. It is possible to produce an accurate rendering of the Bill at its first reading, at its third reading, when it was sent to the Lords, after it had been amended by the Lords, and finally of course, the actual Act itself. Of the other changes that were implemented during the Bill's passage through Parliament it remains impossible to determine whether they occurred while the Bill was in committee or at the report stage.

[32] Clause 1.
[33] Clause 2.
[34] Clause 4.
[35] Clause 3.
[36] Clause 6. Blackstone, in his *Commentaries*, in a section on "Pleadings", explained what was meant by pleading the "General Issue" in the following way:

> Pleas that totally deny the cause of complaint are either the *general* issue, or a *special* plea, in bar. … The *general* issue, or general plea, is what traverses thwarts and denies at once the whole declaration; without offering any special matter whereby to evade it. As in trespass either *vi et armis*, or on the case, *non culpabilis*, not guilty; in debt upon contract, *nil debet*, he owes nothing; in debt in bond, *non est factum*, it is not his deed; on an *assumpsit, non assumpsit*, he made no such promise. Or in real actions, *nul tort*, no wrong done; *nul disseisin*, no disseisin; and in a writ of right, that the tenant has more right to hold than the demandant has to demand. These pleas are called the general issue, because, by importing an absolute and general denial of what is alleged in the declaration, they amount at once to an issue; by which we mean a fact affirmed on one side and denied on the other.

W Blackstone, *Commentaries on the Laws of England, Book the Third* (Oxford, Clarendon Press, 1768) 305.
[37] Clause 5.

Faculty of Advocates in Edinburgh;[38] the free importation clause was modified to incorporate not "Classicks" but rather "any Books in Greek, Latin or any other foreign Language printed beyond the Seas".[39] As well as these changes, further provisions were introduced. The operation of the legislation was extended to allow the recovery of penalties before the Court of Sessions in Scotland,[40] and any actions taken had to be commenced within three months from the commission of the offence "or else the same shall be void and of none effect".[41] In addition, as had been the case in the *Licensing Act*, the universities and those holding printing patents had their privileges confirmed, although there was now more than a touch of ambiguity about the phrasing of this saving clause.[42]

Of more obvious consequence were the revisions to the Bill's preamble and first section. The whole emphasis of the Bill as initially drafted lay behind the presumption that the "Copy of a Book" was a clearly recognisable form of property, equal in stature as with any other tangible or estate.

[38] This was further extended in the Lords to include the "Libraries of the four Universities of Scotland", thus tripling the previous legal deposit requirement in the 1662 Act. In addition, the Commons also introduced a provision that should the "WareHouse-Keeper" of the company, or the proprietor of the relevant copy, fail to produce the books for the named libraries, then they were to forfeit "the Sum of Five Pounds for every Copy not so delivered" as well as "the value of the said printed Copy".

[39] It is interesting to consider this section in light of earlier attitudes to importing works printed abroad. The 1662 section governing imported works was designed to reflect the dual aspects of the *Licensing Act*, that of the encouragement and regulation of the printing trade, as well as the detection and censoring of treasonous and seditious works (see ss 5, 6, 9 and 20). When parliament came to legislate in the 1690s, they did so with the primary issue of the control of the press uppermost in their minds. This being the case, the Bill in November 1695 simply declared that the importer of any "treasonable, seditious, atheistical or heretical matter" was to "be deemed and taken as author or printer of the same and shall be answerable and punishable as such" (see clauses 11 and 12). Now, in contrast to what had gone before, the colour of the legislation was neither restrictive nor censorial, nor was it specifically designed to improve the security of the London booksellers. Instead, it actively encouraged importing those books that were taken to be beneficial to the promotion and advancement of study, remaining true to the stated purpose of the Act, the "encouragement of learning". In this attempt to liberate such learned texts from the controls of the indigenous market, one can perhaps trace influences of Locke's earlier commentary upon the state of the trade and its relationship with the dissemination of and access to significant scholarly materials. J Locke, "Memorandum on the 1662 Act" in E S DeBeer, *The Correspondence of John Locke*, vol V (Oxford, Clarendon Press, 1978), 785–95. See ch 1, n 12 and accompanying text.

[40] S 6. This was added at the report stage in the House of Commons.

[41] S 10. This provision had its genesis in the *Printing Bill* of November 1695.

[42] The *Licensing Act* 1662 provided in s 18 "[t]hat nothing in this Act contained, shall be construed to extend to the Prejudice or infringing of any just Rights and Privileges of either of the two Universities of this Realm, touching and concerning the Licensing or Printing of Books in either of the said Universities"; similarly s 22 set out that nothing in the Act would operate to "prejudice the just Rights and Privileges granted by His Majesty, or any of His Royal Predecessors, to any Person or Persons, under His Majesty's Great Seal, or otherwise; but that such Person or Persons may exercise and use such Rights and Privileges as aforesaid, according to their respective Grants; any Thing in this Act to the contrary notwithstanding". By comparison, the Commons now stipulated that nothing in the new Act was to prejudice "or confirm" any right which the universities or the patentees might have "or claim to have"; s 9.

However, what began as a Bill "for Securing the Property of Copies in Books" became an Act "for the Encouragement of Learning, by Vesting the Copies of printed Books in the Authors or Purchasers of such Copies",[43] calling to mind the provisions included in the Bill of November 1695 which "vested" the "property or sole right of printing" for a limited time only in the printer of the work. The preamble to the Bill had begun with a statement about the "[l]iberty frequently taken of late" in printing, without consent, the work of an author:

> [I]n whom the undoubted Property of such Books and Writings, as the Product of their Learning and Labour, remains; or of such Persons, to whom such Authors, for good Considerations, have lawfully Transferred their Right and Title therein, is not only a great Discouragement to Learning in general, which in all Civilised Nations ought to receive the greatest Countenance and Encouragement, but is also a Notorious Invasion of the Property of the Rightful Proprietors of such Books and Writings ... For preventing therefore such Unjust and Pernicious Practices for the future, ... and for the Preservation of the Property of the Rightful Owner thereof ...

The property in books and writings was apparently incontestable. Moreover, the original Bill had in no way sought to limit the term of protection of such property. However, all of this rhetoric and self-evident justification concerning the "undoubted property" of authors in their works was subsequently abandoned. As with the Act's title, the preamble was reduced in length and significance confining itself to the prevention of piracy and the "Encouragement of learned Men to compose and write useful Books". In exchange for the continued production of "useful Books", what was being offered was the "sole right and liberty of printing" such works, that is, a reproduction right. In addition, the notion of any rights existing in perpetuity, guaranteed under the *Licensing Act*, and implicit in the original draft of the Bill, was jettisoned. Favouring a temporally finite twin track approach, the lower house chose to limit the lifetime of this printing right for "the Term of One and Twenty Years" for existing works already printed "and no longer", and, for works that had been written but were not yet "printed and published", as well as works that had yet to be composed, "for the Term of Fourteen Years, to commence from the day of first publishing the same, and no longer".[44]

[43] CJ 16:369.

[44] S 1. In *Reasons Humbly Offer'd*, some comment was made on this proposition that the protection provided be limited in years, propounding that such a course would be the "Ruin of many Families, there being above 6000 People whose whole Dependence and Subsistence is upon the Trade of Printing". The writer of the *More Reasons* tract suggested two further reasons as to why the introduction of the finite term was problematic. On the one hand he argued that the rationale behind the limited term, that ten or fourteen years was a sufficient time to compensate the proprietor for the expense of printing the work, was fallacious given

This was not a legislative endorsement of a pre-existing property right, but instead, the striking of a bargain designed for the benefit of author, bookseller and the reading public.

Also significant, and likewise anathema to the booksellers, was the fact that, for the first time since the incorporation of the Stationers' Company in 1557, not just the booksellers, but also the author, and indeed anyone else who was sufficiently inclined, was entitled to own and deal in the copies of works. The preamble referred generically to the "Author or Proprietors" of books, while the first section made it clear that the author, the bookseller, the printer, or any "other person or persons" who had "purchased or acquired the copy or copies of any book or books" would be entitled to receive the time-limited protections of the statute. Moreover, the Commons were sufficiently astute to introduce an alternative to registration should the Stationers' Company try to reassert a position of dominance within the trade, by simply refusing to register people's works in the company register book.[45] The last section of the Act, supplied this time by the House of Lords, was equally in keeping with these provisions that operated to displace and unsettle existing structures and relationships within the book trade. Section 11 provided that, following the expiration of the fourteen year protection set out earlier, "the sole Right of printing or disposing of Copies shall return to the Authors thereof, if they are then living, for another Term of Fourteen years." On the Lords use of this bifurcated term, Rose comments:

> Most likely [they] felt that the single fourteen-year term was too short … and yet they were reluctant in the light of the Jacobean Statute of Monopolies' provision against any monopoly terms longer than fourteen years simply to declare a longer term.[46]

While he makes a convincing case for the fact that the Commons had taken its cue from the *Statute of Monopolies* in settling upon the 14- and 21-year terms,[47] it is clear that these were not necessarily inevitable choices. Both drafts of the *Printing Bill* in 1695 had left the matter undetermined; alternatively, ten years had been suggested as a possible term for new works,[48] while John Locke had proffered a period of either

that very often works do not achieve the recognition they deserve for ten or even twenty years after first publication. On the other hand, he submitted, somewhat obliquely, that: "[I]f we have a Right for Ten years, we have a Right for Ever, A Man's having possess'd a property for Ten or Twenty Years, is in no other Instance allow'd, a Reason for another to take it from him; and we hope it will not be in Ours".

[45] S 3.
[46] Rose, *Authors and Owners*, n 6 above, 47.
[47] *Ibid*, 44–45.
[48] Lincoln's Inn Library, MP 102, Fol 104; *More Reasons Humbly Offer'd to the Honourable House of Commons for the Bill for Encouraging Learning and Securing the Property of Copies in Books*, Lincoln's Inn Library, MP 102, Fol 101.

50 or 70 years.[49] To suggest that the Lords settled upon their final construction only because they felt constrained by the earlier statute is perhaps to miss the real motivation behind the amendment they made. Had they simply chosen to introduce a longer term, this would, in practice, have meant control of the work remaining with the booksellers. Rather, the use of the divided term, albeit reminiscent of the earlier statute, was designed to ensure that the control of the work would in fact return to the author if still alive. Given that this was the only section within the final Act to make reference solely to the author, it seems likely that the upper chamber intended to benefit the author and only the author.

Although this was the last section of the Act, discussion of the legislation cannot end here. There is an important historical footnote, often disregarded when considering the 1709 Act, in the guise of the 1711 statute for *Laying Down several Duties upon all Sope and Paper made in Great Britain or imported into the same* (the *Stamp Act*).[50] This legislation set out a number of taxes relevant to the book trade: paper, books, prints and maps imported from abroad were to be charged at 30 pounds for every 100 pounds imported,[51] and paper manufactured within Great Britain was to be taxed at variable rates depending on its quality and size.[52] It operated to complement the *Statute of Anne* in two respects. In relation to the duty payable on paper, it provided a general exemption; on the grounds of being "for the Encouragement of Learning" the Act set out that:

> [S]o much Money as shall from Time to Time be paid for the Duties granted by this Act, for any Quantities of Paper, which ... shall be used in the printing any Books in the Latin, Greek, Oriental or Northern Languages, within the two Universities of Oxford and Cambridge ... shall and may be drawn back and repaid ...[53]

Secondly, the Act also raised a duty "for and upon all Books and Papers commonly called Pamphlets, and for and upon all Newspapers or Papers containing publick News, Intelligence or Occurances", and continued in s 112 that:

> [I]f any such Pamphlet containing more than One Sheet of Paper [shall during the next 32 years] be printed or published, and the Duty hereby charged thereon shall not be duly paid ... then the Author, Printer and Publisher of,

[49] See ch 1, n 12 and accompanying text.
[50] 10 Anne c 19, 1711. On the reasons behind the introduction of the *Stamp Act*, and its immediate effect upon the press, see, J A Downie, *Robert Harley and the Press: Propaganda and Public Opinion in the Age of Swift and Defoe,* (Cambridge, CUP, 1979) 149–61, and FS Siebert, *Freedom of the Press in England, 1476–1776* (Urbana, Il, University of Illinois Press, 1965) 305–22.
[51] S 32.
[52] S 38. For a full account of the various charges involved, see J Feather, "The English Book Trade and the Law 1695–1799" (1982) 12 *Publishing History* 51.
[53] S 63.

> and all other Persons concerned in or about the Printing or Publishing of such Pamphlet, shall lose all Property therein, and in every copy thereof, although the Title thereto were registered in the Book of Stationers in London, according to the late Act of Parliament in that Behalf, so as any Person (notwithstanding the said Act) may freely print and publish the same ... without being liable to any Action, Prosecution or Penalty for so doing; anything in the said Act of Parliament for vesting the Copies of printed Books in the Authors of Purchasers of such Copies, or in any By Law contained, or any Custom or other thing to the contrary notwithstanding.[54]

In 1743 it was made a criminal offence to "sell, hawk, carry about, utter or expose to Sale any News Paper, Book, Pamphlet or Paper, deemed or construed to be a News Paper" upon unstamped paper,[55] and the various duties and penalties detailed in the 1711 Act were further extended until the 24 June 1760. By 1760 the duty on newspapers had been specifically addressed and increased by an Act of 1757,[56] while the duty on pamphlets was allowed to lapse. This meant however, that for the 50 years following the passing of the *Statute of Anne*, Parliament had declared that any person could "freely print and publish" any pamphlet for which duty had not been duly paid, as the author, printer or publisher of the same was considered to have lost their property in the work. The Commons were clearly of the opinion that if they could provide these pamphleteers with a statutory protection for their work, they could just as easily take such "property" away. Moreover, if the stationers were uncertain about the impact or significance of the *Statute of Anne*, the inclusion of the reference to "any By Law ... or any Custom" in the *Stamp Act*, sent out a clear signal that, however the booksellers might regulate their own affairs, the legislature was to have the final, authoritative word.

To a certain extent then, the *Act for the Encouragement of Learning* had inherited much of what had gone before, in the guise of the 1662 Act, and the numerous Bills brought before Parliament in the years prior to the 1709 legislation. The limited lifespan of the protection provided, the need for registration of the works, the libraries deposit privilege, and the proviso for the universities, all had a genesis in some previous source. That said however, this Act was as much marked by the new as by the old. It had elements of a largely original endeavour that addressed issues

[54] Moreover, every such person involved in the same was to forfeit £20 with full costs of suit.

[55] S 5. Note that in 1772 it was made a transportable offence (12 George III, c 48) and by 1782 the selling of such unstamped materials was punishable by death (29 George III, c 50).

[56] *An Act for granting to His Majesty several Rates and Duties upon Indentures, Leases, Bonds and other Deeds; and upon News Papers, Advertisements and Almanacks*, 30 Geo II, c 19. Siebert suggests that newspapers were specifically targeted because the government reasoned that "in time of war [the Seven Years' War] an anxious public was willing to pay an increased subscription price for news of the military and naval engagements"; Siebert, *Freedom of the Press in England*, n 50 above, 320.

concerning the encouragement of learning, the position of the author, and the nature of the book trade in general. The end result was not, as Feather suggests, designed to ensure "the control of production by a few wealthy capitalists ... [and] the continued dominance of English publishing by a few London firms".[57] Nor indeed was it an Act that particularly favoured the London booksellers writ large.[58] In his account of the developments at this time, Feather's analysis does not take sufficient account of those features within the new legislation that conflicted with the interests of the established trade. Given that foreign language works made up around ten per cent of the output of the London trade in 1709,[59] the exception allowing the importing of such works printed abroad, and not just those printed "originally beyond the seas", represented a potentially substantial invasion of an otherwise lucrative market.[60] In relation to the rest of that market there was also the introduction of an external control upon the price of books and the fact that three times as many books as before had to be supplied under the new library deposit provision. Should anyone bring an action alleging infringement of his publication right, he now had to do so within three months of the offence; moreover, this was subject to the risk of providing "full costs" should the defendant win, or should the plaintiff simply become "non-suited or discontinue his action". Add to all of this the fact that the Act sought to open up the marketplace to anyone who wished to embrace it, author included, and it must have been abundantly clear that what measure of protection the booksellers had secured, had come at a certain cost.

To propound, however, that the Act was simply "a trade-regulation statute directed to the problem of monopoly in various forms",[61] as Patterson does, is too reductionist an analysis. In concentrating on a copyright Act with "a direct lineage that goes back to a Star Chamber

[57] Feather, "The Book Trade in Politics", n 13 above, 37.

[58] While conceding that "[t]he trade had not won on every point" Feather elsewhere suggests that "[n]evertheless, in general this was a very satisfactory outcome for the book trade in several respects. Most importantly it had gained recognition of rights in copies, and a means of legal redress against the pirates"; Feather, *Publishing, Piracy and Politics*, n 10 above, 62.

[59] These figures are based upon data presented in D-J Dugas, "The Book Trade in London in 1709 (Part One)" 95 (2001) *Papers of the Bibliographical Society of America* 31. Of the 1019 texts printed and published in London in 1709 Dugas identifies 782 as being attributable to a specific printer or publisher. Of these 782 publications, 77 were works in a foreign language.

[60] One consequence of this was that publishers, booksellers and authors often sought a royal licence to protect their foreign language works instead. For information on the various licences that were granted before and after the 1709 Act see S Rogers, "The Use of Royal Licences for Printing in England, 1695–760: A Bibliography" (2000) I *The Library* 133. Alternatively publishers might petition Parliament for protection; see for example, the *Act for granting to Samuel Buckley, Citizen and Stationer of London, the sole Liberty of printing and reprinting the Histories of Thuanus, with Additions and Improvements, during the Time therein limited*, 7 Geo II, c 24, 1734.

[61] Patterson, *Copyright in Historical Perspective*, n 25 above, 150.

Decree of 1586",[62] Patterson focuses too closely on the relationship between the book trade and the state that had developed in the 150 years prior to the passing of the *Statute of Anne*. As a result, while many of these new legislative aspects can be read and understood as anti-monopoly measures, designed to address previous inequities in the book trade in general,[63] this is to overlook the other important, and indeed, central feature of the 1709 Act. Behind Parliament's endorsement of the new legislation lay a more immediate, novel and compelling rationale. This Act was not primarily concerned with securing the position of the booksellers, nor with the guarding against their monopolistic control of the press, although it provided an opportunity for addressing both of these issues. Instead, this Act was primarily concerned with the continued production of books. Regardless of the fact that the booksellers might have made much of the rights and deserving nature of the author in their arguments for protection, Parliament focused upon the social contribution the author could make in the encouragement and advancement of learning. It made good sense to make some provision for writers, and inevitably booksellers, to ensure a continued production of intelligible literature. The central plank of the 1709 Act was then, and remains, a cultural *quid pro quo*. Parliament, to encourage "learned Men (*sic*) to compose and write useful Books", provided a guaranteed, if finite, right to print and reprint those works so composed. The legislators were not concerned with the recognition of any pre-existing authorial right, nor were they solely interested in the regulation of the booksellers' market. Rather, they secured the continued production of useful books through the striking of a culturally significant societal bargain, a trade-off involving, not the bookseller and censorial state, but the author, the bookseller and the reading public. It was the free market of ideas, not the marketplace of the bookseller, which provided the central focus for the *Statute of Anne*.

Where the Act falls down, however, is not in the comprehensibility of its general intent, but in its method of implementation, in the details, the drafting. Augustine Birrell, commenting that the whole issue of perpetual copyright in England "was complicated, and indeed, butchered by an Act of Parliament — the first copyright statute anywhere to be found — the 8th of Good Queen Anne", regarded the Act as a "perfidious measure, rigged with curses dark" and passed by "an ignorant Legislature".[64] For Birrell the *Statute of Anne* was both ill-conceived and badly executed. Ransom on the contrary suggests that, at the time it was passed, its intention and import "seemed quite clear". However, he continues that

[62] *Ibid*, 222–23.
[63] *Ibid*, 144–45.
[64] A Birrell, *Copyright in Books* (London, Cassell & Co, 1899) 19, 22.

"great arguments were to arise from apparently innocent clauses."[65] In Ransom's consideration, what faults there were lay not in the language and drafting of the legislation itself, but in the pecuniary inadequacy of its penalties, the circumvention of the deposit requirements, and its failure to extend in scope to Ireland.[66] Loewenstein, like Ransom, would seek to absolve the drafters suggesting that, if the Act now seems "more irresolute and opaque than it is", this has more to do with the way in which it was subsequently treated in the litigation that followed rather than misunderstandings on the part of the legislators.[67] Rigged with curses dark?, or exuding innocent clarity while subject to subsequent obfuscation? The reality of the legislation falls somewhere between these two poles. While the central import of the Act is readily perceptible, the simple fact remains that it was a poorly drafted piece of legislation.

One obvious example of the poor quality of drafting involved lies in the provision introduced by the Commons to ensure that the stationers could not abuse the registration requirements within the Act by simply refusing to register someone's work upon the company's books.[68] The section set out that "such Person and Persons so refusing" to register the work "shall have the like benefit as if such Entry ... had been duly made and given",[69] in addition to which, the "Clerks so refusing" would be liable, to the proprietor seeking registration, for the sum of twenty pounds. This, of course, reads to make perfect nonsense. While the intention was clearly to afford the person who was *refused* by the company clerk with a form of redress, in actual fact the legislation supplied the clerk (who did the *refusing*) and nobody else with the remedy. Taking the whole of the provision literally, this meant that the clerk of the company might refuse to register any given work, and then, by advertising his refusal, gain for himself the right to print that work under the terms of the Act (subject perhaps to a twenty pound fine). More alarming, perhaps, is the fact that this clause was the subject of some examination, debate, and amendment in the lower house. On the third reading of the Bill the Journal of the Commons details that:

> An amendment was proposed to be made to the Bill; to leave out "refused", and, instead thereof, to insert "refusing" ... [a]nd the same was, upon the Question put thereupon, agreed unto by the House.[70]

[65] H Ransom, *The First Copyright Statute* (Austin, Texas, University of Texas, 1956) 99.
[66] *Ibid*, 105.
[67] J Loewenstein, *The Author's Due: Printing and the Prehistory of Copyright* (London, University of Chicago Press, 2002) 249.
[68] S 3.
[69] This was subject to advertising in the *London Gazette* that they had been refused registration.
[70] CJ 16:369.

Such amendment can only be read in one of two ways. Either, the original draft did in fact give the person who "was refused" the remedy, but that this was then altered in a way that makes no sense (by giving it to the company clerk).[71] Alternatively, it might have been the case that neither part of the section, as originally drafted, made sense, in that the clerk was provided with the remedy upon refusal, while the person applying to register the work was made liable for the twenty pound fine.[72] Upon this reading it becomes obvious that the clause was intelligently amended, but only partially. While the first of these two scenarios seems the more likely, either way, this vignette is instructive about the nature of the parliamentary scrutiny to which the Act was being subjected.[73] Neither was this the only example of the legislators less than meticulous attention to detail. The protections guaranteed by the Act, and the library deposit requirement, had been amended to run from 10 April 1710, while the provision concerning the control of book prices was left to run, as it had initially

[71] In this case the original draft of the Act would have run as follows:

> Provided nevertheless that if the Clerk of the said Company of Stationers for the Time being, shall refuse or neglect to register, or make such Entry or Entries, or to give such Certificate, being thereunto required by the Author or Proprietor of such Copy or Copies, in the presence of two or more credible Witnesses, that then such Person and Persons ***so refused***, Notice being first duly given of such Refusal, by an Advertisement in the *Gazette*, shall have the like benefit as if such Entry or Entries, Certificate or Certificates had been duly made and given; and that the Clerks ***so refusing*** shall, for every such Offence, forfeit to the Proprietor of such Copy or Copies the Sum of Twenty Pounds, to be recovered in any of His Majesty's Courts of Record at Westminster, by Action of debt, Bill, Plaint, or Information, in which no Wager of Law, Essoign, Privilege or Protection, or more than One Imparlance shall be allowed.

[72] In this case the section as originally drafted would have been as follows:

> Provided nevertheless that if the Clerk of the said Company of Stationers for the Time being, shall refuse or neglect to register, or make such Entry or Entries, or to give such Certificate, being thereunto required by the Author or Proprietor of such Copy or Copies, in the presence of two or more credible Witnesses, that then such Person and Persons ***so refusing***, Notice being first duly given of such Refusal, by an Advertisement in the *Gazette*, shall have the like benefit as if such Entry or Entries, Certificate or Certificates had been duly made and given; and that the Clerks ***so refused*** shall, for every such Offence, forfeit to the Proprietor of such Copy or Copies the Sum of Twenty Pounds, to be recovered in any of His Majesty's Courts of Record at Westminster, by Action of debt, Bill, Plaint, or Information, in which no Wager of Law, Essoign, Privilege or Protection, or more than One Imparlance shall be allowed.

[73] In subsequent attempts to legislate, the later drafters did recognise and try to correct this flaw in the original Act; on 26 March 1735, when the *Bill for making more effectual an Act, passed in the Eight Year of the Reign of her late Majesty Queen Anne* (ie the 1709 Act), was presented to the Commons (CJ 22:431), it had modified the original Act to provide that "the author or proprietor of such copy" could advertise in the *Gazette* to secure the protection of the Act. This Bill however was never enacted (see ch 4) and the imperfect, incoherent drafting remained on the statute book for over 130 years when the *Statute of Anne* was repealed and replaced by the *Copyright Act* 1842.

been drafted, from 25 March. The first section bore inconsistencies in vesting the "sole right and Liberty of printing" old works, while providing for the "sole Liberty of printing *and reprinting*" new works. Finally, although the title and preamble to the legislation had been altered to emphasise that the Act was vesting certain rights in the author, and not securing any pre-existing rights, the preamble to the second section still spoke in terms of the "Property in every such Book" being "secured to the Proprietor or Proprietors thereof".

Such flaws, as they are, do not, however, represent the most problematic aspect of the statute. This is more general in nature, and lies in the lack of any attempt to define those concepts central to the Act. The legislation refers, not always consistently, to: "vesting the Copies of printed Books"; "the Author of any Book or Books"; the transfer of "the Copy or Copies of such Book or Books"; "the sole Liberty of printing such Book and Books"; "the sole Liberty of printing and reprinting such Book and Books"; "the Property in every such Book"; the registration of "the Title of the Copy of such Book or Books"; "the Author or Proprietor of such Copy or Copies"; "Nine Copies of each Book or Books"; the right "to the printing or reprinting any Book or Copy"; and finally, "the sole Right of printing or disposing of Copies". Moreover, the run up to the passing of this Act had thrown up various other ill-defined phrases, such as the "Property of Copies",[74] the "undoubted Right to the Copy of [the] Book",[75] "Securing Property in Books",[76] "the Author and Proprietor of any Copy",[77] "Securing the Property of Copies of Books",[78] "the original indisputable Right of Publishing",[79] "the undoubted property [of] books and Writings",[80] and "the sole property of copies of printed books",[81] to name but a few. While the fundamental rationale for securing the legislation is identifiable and comprehensible, this does not necessarily mean that, at the time, there existed any clear idea or appreciation as to what was meant by the concept of actually having a property in books. Defoe, writing in his *Review*, at one point made reference to "the miserable Havock that is made in this Nation, with the Property of the Subject, with Relation to Books".[82] He penned these words a week in advance of the *Statute of Anne* receiving its second reading before the House of Commons.

[74] D Defoe, *A Review*, 8 November 1705.
[75] *Reasons humbly Offer'd* (1706).
[76] *Reasons Humbly Offer'd* (1709).
[77] D Defoe, *A Review*, 6 December 1709.
[78] See the first draft of the 1710 Bill.
[79] *The Case of the Booksellers Right to their Copies, or sole Power of Printing their respective Books, represented to the Parliament*, Lincoln's Inn Library, MP 102, Fol 103 and BL 1887.b.58(3).
[80] Preamble to the first draft of the 1710 Bill.
[81] CJ 16:394.
[82] D Defoe, *A Review*, 2 February 1710.

He might equally well have reserved his caustic observation to critique the final form of the Act that, though well intentioned, would spawn more than half a century of controversy, and secure a legacy of misunderstanding. A miserable havock indeed.

3

Scraps of Proceedings[1]

THE *STATUTE OF ANNE* IN CHANCERY

IN THE THREE decades following the passing of the *Statute of Anne* those litigants seeking to rely upon the statute to protect their property did so before the Court of Chancery. Such actions were begun by submitting a bill of complaint to the court, setting out the facts of the case and praying for some form of relief, ordinarily by way of injunction.[2] Following this, the defendant was required to appear and respond to the charge, generally by the submission of an answer to the plaintiff's bill.[3] Once an answer had been entered, if at all, the plaintiff could raise objections to it, on grounds that it was insufficient in some manner or that it contained "scandalous" material. If the defendant made no objection to the complaint, the matter would be referred to a Master of the Court to adjudge; should he find the answer inadequate, then the defendant would be required to resubmit a revised answer. This bill and answer were referred to collectively as "the pleadings"[4] and, more often than not, cases failed to proceed beyond this stage.[5] Those that did, advanced to a

[1] This is taken from a document prepared for Hamilton and Balfour, on 13 December 1744, by J Graham: "[I]t is easy to produce Scraps of Proceedings depending in a Court, which can serve no purpose whatever, unless the whole Proceedings were fairly laid open, and instructed by authentick Documents"; 4.

[2] For a guide to Chancery proceedings during the eighteenth century see H Horwitz, *Chancery Equity Records and Proceedings 1600–1800: A Guide to Documents in the Public Records Office* (London, HMSO, 1995) 1–26.

[3] Alternatively the defendant might enter a demurrer to the bill. Horwitz explains that the demurrer "sought to evade the force of the complaint by admitting the truth of the complainant's factual allegations but then going on to argue that they did not present any cause for which the defendant might reasonably be expected to answer"; *ibid*, 14.

[4] *Ibid*, 2–3. Fortunately what pleadings exist from this period are housed in the Public Records Office (PRO), Kew, London. The documents relating to actions taken throughout the first half of the eighteenth century are gathered together in 2793 separate boxes, known as the c 11 boxes.

[5] Horwitz notes that "many did not pursue their suits very far. For over one-quarter of the suits in the period, there survive only bills of complaint, and in most of these instances there is no evidence that an answer was ever made", *ibid*, 11. Less than 25% of the cases that came before the Court of Chancery during this period proceeded beyond this pleadings stage.

hearing before the Lord Chancellor, or, in his absence, the Master of the Rolls, who, after reviewing the evidence submitted to the court, and hearing the various arguments of the litigating counsel, would give out his decision.[6] As to the cases taken before the court during this period, they spun off in numerous and variegated directions. Different themes and arguments flew out from the epicentre of the Act like so many ribbons of the maypole. It was these disparate legal threads, which would be picked up by so many booksellers, lawyers and judges throughout the next half-century. They engaged one another, mingling, plaiting and weaving these manifold strands, so that the *Statute of Anne*, by the end of the dance, would stand spectacularly transformed.

THE *STATUTE OF ANNE* AND THE PATENT CASES

Four years after the 1709 Act was secured, John Nutt brought a case before the Court of Chancery petitioning for relief, by way of injunction, against John Basket, John Williams, Edmund Powell, John Matthews and Robert Whitledge, for printing a book by Dr Edward Gibson, *The Statutes, Constitutions, Cannons, Rubricks and Articles of the Church of England*. Their edition, Nutt argued, was printed in contravention of the letters patent he held to print "all manner of Law books whatsoever they be which in any manner of wise touch or concern the concord of statute Laws of the Realm of England".[7] As part of his complaint, Nutt referred to the fact that Dr Gibson:

> [D]id and doth pretend a right to the printing and publishing of the said Book as having been the author of the same and doth likewise pretend that by vertue of an Act of Parliament made in the Eighth Year of her present Majesty … The author or authors of any books not before that time printed should have the sole liberty of printing and reprinting the same by the space of fourteen years to commence from the day of the first publishing the same.[8]

This was the first time that the 1709 Act was referred to in any action before the courts. Gibson was claiming the protection of the legislation

[6] Verbatim transcripts of all the orders and decrees handed down, as well as details of the hearings, re-hearings, and the parties' various petitions and motions before the court, are recorded in the Court's official record, the c 33 books of orders, housed in the PRO, Kew, London. For more information about these records, as well as information on searching for materials in the PRO, see Horwitz, *Chancery Equity Records*, n 2 above, 45–71.

[7] *Nutt v Gibson* (28 January 1714) c 11 1965/21. Queen Anne had granted the patent to Edward Sayer in the first year of her reign, who had subsequently sold it to Edward Jones and John Nutt; Edward Jones had since died.

[8] *Ibid*.

as the author of the work in question. The plaintiff however continued that the defendants were well aware of the "provisor" that nothing in the Act would prejudice any previously existing rights to print books.[9] Nutt insisted that letters patent granted by the monarch were "fully saved by the said provision" and continued that by virtue of the same: "Your Orator is in the same case *as if the said Act had never been passed*".[10] Over the next decade there would be no less than a further 54 petitions for injunctions to prevent the printing of works protected by such patent grants,[11] brought either on behalf of the Company of Stationers, or John Basket who, from 1715, was the King's Printer.[12] It would appear that Nutt's assessment of the impact of the 1709 Act upon the existing letters patent (or rather the lack thereof) was an accurate one, as in none of these subsequent cases would there be any further reference to the *Statute of Anne*; all, that is, except for *Stationers' Company v White* (1716).[13]

On 10 October 1716, the Stationers' Company petitioned Lord Chancellor Dowper to prevent a Mr White, in collusion with John How and Henry Parsons, from printing *A New Version of the Psalms of David*. Given that, since *Nutt*, a further thirteen other bills had been submitted for the court's consideration prior to *White*,[14] the plaintiffs could uncontroversially set out that:

> [A]s often as it hath happened that any person [has] clandestinely printed any book being the legal property of any other person, the said [offender] have, on application made to this Honourable court, been always by injunction debarred and restrained from vending and exposing the same to sale.

Nevertheless, they continued by remarking that, as they had failed to register the work "in the Register Book belonging to the said Company pursuant to the law articles and pursuant to a late Act of Parliament", they

[9] *Statute of Anne* 1709, s 9.
[10] C 11 1965/21; emphasis added.
[11] The types of works protected by such grants were as follows: speeches of the monarch, royal proclamations, statute books, acts of parliament, libels, law books, bibles, the new testament, books of common prayer, psalters, psalms, primers, school books, almanacks, prognostications, predictions. In general the Crown claimed a prerogative right to control the printing of any material relating to the monarchy, the state, the government and parliament, the law, and the established religion.
[12] For a complete list, see RJ Goulden, *Some Chancery Lawsuits 1714–1758: An Analytical List* (British Library, x 205/1260, 1982).
[13] *Stationers v White* (1716) c 11 749/6, 751/16.
[14] 1714: *Stationers Company v Howard, Stationers Company v Spiller, Stationers Company v Phillpott, Stationers Company v Norris.* 1715: *Baskett v Beardswell, Baskett v Whitledge, Baskett v Berrington 1716: Baskett v Baker, Baskett v Brotherton, Baskett v How, Stationers Company v Florence, Stationers Company v Bliss, Stationers Company v Cordery*. For the PRO references for each of these cases, see Table of Cases.

were unable to rely upon the benefit or protection of the 1709 Act. It was because of this omission, they later explained, that they:

> [C]an have no benefit of the said Act, nor otherwise than by the aid and assistance of this Honourable Court in restraining the printing and vending any such books without the consent of the proprietors.[15]

The first answer, from How and Parsons, was received by the court on 8 November 1716. The defendants raised two main issues. First, re-emphasising the plaintiffs' own admission, they pointed out that the stationers "neglected to enter the copy of the said [book] in the Register Book". Second, they highlighted that it was not clear from the initial bill who, in fact, the authors of the work were, and, without identifying the authors, they argued that no one was able to claim under them "to obtain a restraint of any person … from printing or selling the said Version". That being the case, they disputed that "the said plaintiffs have any such property in the said version as to intitle them to have the aid of this Honourable Court".[16] The second answer, from White, was submitted some time in January 1717, by which time the court had granted the plaintiffs an injunction.[17] White admitted that he did in fact print an edition of the Psalms about four years previously, but qualified this by insisting on the benefit of the statute:

> [W]hereby it is enacted amongst other things that all actions … for any offence committed against the said Act shall be brought within 3 months after such offence is committed or else the same shall be void.

White did concede that he had printed a further impression of the work about two months previously, however, in relation to this edition, he proffered that he had sold it at a reasonable price, making only a moderate profit, "whereas the plaintiffs by Enhancing the price of the said Book … doth make an exhorbitant profit thereby". Moreover, he continued that his recent work was, in any case:

> [A] more correct and valuable Book than that printed by the Company … and purged from several errors and doth contain half a sheet more paper and of a larger and better letter.[18]

The behaviour of the Company in this matter, he suggested, was both a hindrance to the trade and an abuse upon the public and he entreated the

[15] C 11 749/6.
[16] *Ibid.*
[17] The defendant set out that he did not "know that any person by the Injunction of this Honourable Court was restrained from printing the said version until the Injunction granted in this present suit"; c 11 751/16.
[18] *Ibid.*

Lord Chancellor to "redress the said abuse and compel the said plaintiffs to sell the same at a moderate price", no doubt drawing upon section 4 of the recently passed *Statute of Anne.* [19] In relation to both of his printed editions White made a further point relating to the registration (or lack thereof) of the plaintiffs work:

> [B]y their Bill confessing that by their not registering the said new version according to the Act that they are remediless at common law, this defendant hopes the said plaintiffs shall not have any aid or assistance of this Court, the said plaintiffs by their careless or wilful neglect to register the same having through Ignorance surprized this defendant into a Suite and thereby put this defendant to great charge and expense which might have been prevented by the said plaintiffs registering their title.[20]

Here then, the failure to register the book, in contradistinction to its being the main reason for the plaintiffs' appeal to this court, was being submitted as good reason for the court not to support the action.[21]

Considering the position that had been expounded in *Nutt*, and apparently taken up in all the patent cases that followed, the reason for the unnecessary involvement of the *Statute of Anne* in this action is, at first glance, somewhat difficult to comprehend. Difficult, that is, unless the counsel acting on behalf of the stationers merely misunderstood the relevance, or rather the irrelevance, of the newly passed legislation to works secured by patent grants. This is in fact the most likely explanation for the misplaced rhetoric of *White*. In their seven petitions before *White*, and in the sixteen that followed, the Stationers' Company had engaged William Peere Williams as their counsel in the preparation of their bills of complaint.[22] Williams had been co-counsel, along with "Nic Hooper" in *Nutt v Gibson* and, following the reference to the 1709 Act in *Nutt*, made no mention of the Act in any of the subsequent actions he prepared for the stationers. The reason that the *Statute of Anne* is drawn into *White* is that this bill, and only this bill, for whatever reason, was prepared by a "Knightly D'Anvais" who misinterpreted and misused the recent legislation. This was to be the only case from this period, concerning patent grants that tried to make use of the 1709 Act. D'Anvais had failed to realise the proper relationship that the legislation bore to such works. Just because an action involved a printed book, did not necessarily mean that it had anything to do with the *Statute of Anne*. Hooper and Williams were right; it was as if the Act had never been passed.

[19] *Ibid.* The Lord Chancellor was one of a number of persons authorised to enquire into the price of any published work, if asked to do so, under s 4 of the 1709 Act.
[20] *Ibid.*
[21] The action was not taken any further.
[22] This was the same Peere Williams who collected a set of Chancery Reports from 1695–1735 (24 ER).

THE *STATUTE OF ANNE* AND AN OBSCENE TRANSLATION

Burnet v Chetwood (1721)[23] was the first case to come before the courts, following the *Statute of Anne*, which did not involve a work protected by letters patent. Rather, it concerned an English edition of Dr Thomas Burnet's latin treatise *Archaeologia Philosophica*, first published in 1692.[24] The author's brother, and executor, had petitioned for, and secured, an injunction to prevent William Chetwood and Richard Franklin printing the work. Merivale, reporting the case nearly one hundred years after it first came to Court, notes that the defendants had propounded that "a translation of a book was not within the intent of" the statute:

> [W]hich being intended to encourage learning by giving the advantage of the book to the author, could be intended only to restrain the mechanical art of printing ... but not to hinder a translation of the book into another language, which in some respects may be called a different book, and the translator may be said to be the author, in as much as some skill in language is requisite thereto, and not barely a mechanic art, as in the case of reprinting in the same language; that the translator dresses it up and clothes the sense in his own style and expressions, and at least puts it into a different form from the original ... and therfore should rather seem to be within the encouragement than the prohibition of the act.[25]

Sympathetic to this argument that a translation of a work may be fairly called a different book on the grounds that a translator "has bestowed his care and pains upon it", Lord Chancellor Macclesfield considered that such endeavours should not fall within the penalties of the 1709 Act. He continued, however, that this was a book that contained "strange notions" and as such should not be made available in the "vulgar" tongue. Rather, it should remain in latin only, "in which language it could not do much hurt, the learned being better able to judge" the work. Asserting that the court had "a superintendency over all books, and might in a summary way restrain the printing or publishing any that contained reflections on religion or morality", he granted the plaintiff his injunction.

Despite this, the defendants subsequently advertised in *The Daily Journal* that they intended to sell their translation of *Archaeologia Philosophica*, as well as a translation of another of Burnet's works, *De statu mortuorum et resurgentium*.[26] The plaintiff once again turned to

[23] *Burnet v Chetwood* (10 October 1721) c 11 242/45; c 33 335/323, 350; 2 Mer 441. For a commentary upon the case see D Saunders, "Copyright, Obscenity and Literary History" (1990) 57 *Journal of English Literary History* 431.

[24] As a result it fell within the terms of the twenty-one year term set out in s 2 of the 1709 Act.

[25] 2 Mer 441.

[26] With regard to this second work, the plaintiff sets out in his bill that Dr Burnet did during his lifetime print a few review copies of *De statu* for himself. The printer however, while

the court.[27] In their answer to this second action, Chetwood and Franklin set out that their work was not the same as *Archaeologia Philosophica* "but a translation of the said book into English", and that whereas the plaintiff was founding his action on the 1709 Act, "yet the said statute doth nowhere prohibit or forbid the translating of such books into any other language and the printing and publishing such translation".[28] They continued that if the works were understood to be the same, then they sought to demurr to so much of the plaintiff's bill as required them to deliver up what copies of the work they had printed, in that to do so would make themselves liable to the penalties prescribed by the Act. This was the case, despite that the plaintiff had offered to "waive any advantage of the penalties"; this, they suggested, the plaintiff was in no position to do, given that one half of those penalties were to be paid to the crown. As to the second work, Chetwood and Franklin simply denied that they had procured any copy of the said book.[29] Their arguments were to no avail as Burnet was granted an injunction to prevent the translating and printing of both works.[30]

THE *STATUTE OF ANNE* AND THE CHANCERY INJUNCTIONS

As has been seen in *Burnet*, and the patent cases, injunctions were readily granted by the Court of Chancery to prevent the printing of the works in question. The patent cases however had little, if anything, to do with the 1709 Act, while the decision in *Burnet* was more concerned with questions of censorship and obscenity, rather than with the property in books. The first case to fall squarely within the rubric of the 1709 Act was *Knaplock v Curl* (1722) [31] in which Edmund Curl was accused of pirating Dr Prideaux's work *Directions to Church Wardens*. On 22 February 1722, Knaplock

printing the works for Dr Burnet, also ran off a copy for himself. This "surriptitious copy" had come into the possession of "a learned and worthy person who had an esteem for Dr Burnet [and] did order ten or twelve copies and no more of the book to be printed ... which he presented to friends with an obligation that neither they nor any person into whose hands the said Book should fall should permit it to be copied or printed." It was one of these printed copies which Chetwood and Franklin had procurred. c 11 242/45.

[27] It is clear from the entry in the Book of Records that the defendants had printed and advertised their intentions to make both works available after the initial injunction had been granted for, as part of the decision, the defendants were ordered to "show good cause unto this court ... why they should not stand committed to the prison of the fleet for their said offence of contempt". c 33 335/350.

[28] C 11 242/45.

[29] *Ibid.*

[30] C 33 335/350.

[31] *Knaplock v Curl* (9 November 1722) c 11 690/5; c 33 337/117, 337/196, 337/203, 337/206, 337/261, 339/12.

petitioned the Court of Chancery [32] and, four days later, was granted an interlocutory injunction.[33] Curl submitted his answer to the cause on 2 March,[34] and the case came before Lord Chancellor Macclesfield on 9 November 1722, when he ordered that an injunction be awarded to prevent the defendant from printing "any edition of the said book for the future, or selling any of the said books by him already printed".[35] The only printed report of the case runs as follows:

> Bill ... for a perpetual Injunction against the Defendant ... The Plaintiffs claim the sole right of printing by grant of the copy from the Author. The Defendant claims a title under the original Printer of the book, to whom the Author first delivered the copy to be printed. And per, Macclesfield, C., the bare delivery of the Copy, by the Author to be printed, doth not devest the Right of the Copy out of the Author, but is only an Authority to the Printer to print that edition, and the Author may afterwards grant the right of the copy to another Person. A perpetual injunction was granted against the Defendant not to print and publish the said book.[36]

Curl however, had not alleged that whoever first printed a work had the right to print subsequent editions, but that Prideaux did in fact formerly "absolutely give and grant to [the first printer] the copy of the book and the sole right of printing the same and of all future editions thereof". The issue was not whether the first printer of a work had the right to print all subsequent editions, regardless of the printer's agreement with the author, as is suggested by the printed report. Rather, it turned upon a factual dispute as to whether or not the author had assigned the work to the printer of the first edition. Curl submitted that there had been a sale of the work, prior to the one to the plaintiffs, and that "no subsequent agreement or conveyance can defeat or take away a prior right and property". This was then an evidentiary issue, and it is most likely that the decisive factor was that the plaintiffs had registered their title in accordance with the 1709 Act, whereas the first printer had failed to do so.

As to the claim for a perpetual injunction, William Blackstone, in the later case of *Tonson v Collins* (1762), would argue that the injunction granted in *Knaplock* "for the future" was evidence of a right anterior to the *Statute of Anne*. Noting that "a perpetual injunction was awarded", he continued that it was clear that Macclesfield LC, who had sat in Parliament during the passage of the 1709 Act, "did not look upon the right to depend merely on the [statute]; for then he would have ordered a

[32] C 11 690/5.
[33] C 33 337/117.
[34] C 11 690/5.
[35] C 33 339/12.
[36] (1722) 2 Eq Ca Abr 523–24.

temporary, not a perpetual injunction".[37] Blackstone's reading however is misguided. The plaintiffs only ever sought such protection as was laid down in the 1709 Act.[38] They argued that, by virtue of the sale of the work to them by Prideaux, "and of the Act of Parliament", they were:

> [I]ntitled to the said copy of the said book and to the sole and separate right and liberty of printing and selling all future editions thereof during the term of 21 years commencing upon 10 April 1710.[39]

The Lord Chancellor's turn of phrase was probably suggested to him by the plaintiffs themselves. They had set out in their bill that Prideaux, "being the sole proprietor" of the work, had sold "the sole right and benefit of printing and disposing of the same *for the future*" to them.[40] That Lord Chancellor Macclesfield considered himself to be operating within the remit of the statute is further confirmed by the fact that he also ordered that the books remaining within the defendant's custody be brought before Mr Edwards, the Master of the Court, and that he "do see the same Damasked" in accordance with the terms of the legislation.[41]

Shortly after *Knaplock* was decided, Lord Macclesfield presided over *Tonson v Clifton* (1722) [42] which concerned a pirate copy of Richard Steele's *The Conscious Lovers*. While similar to *Knaplock* in that the plaintiff's claims were couched entirely within the terms of reference of the *Statute of Anne*,[43] it was dissimilar in that this action did not proceed to a full hearing. Rather, this was the first in a long line of cases in which the injunctions granted were interlocutory and nothing more.[44] Blackstone, as was the case with *Knaplock*, provided his own interesting, if erroneous, interpretation of the decision in the later case of *Tonson v Collins* (1762). He noted that, in this earlier case, *The Conscious Lovers* was "not stated to have been registered at Stationers Hall" and continued that this was a requisite of the 1709 Act, concluding that the injunction granted "must therefore

[37] At this point in the proceedings Foster J interjected that "[t]his was a legal right clearly within the Act of Parliament"; Blackstone replied: "I only mention it because here the injunction was perpetual". *Tonson v Collins* (1762) 1 Black W 329–30.

[38] Similarly the defendants arguments are largely couched within the terms of the Act.

[39] C 11 690/5; c 33 339/12.

[40] C 11 690/5; emphasis added.

[41] C 33 339/12. He also ordered that the plaintiffs were not "to prosecute the defendant on the penalty of the Act of Parliament", *ibid.*

[42] *Tonson v Clifton* (11 December 1722) c 11 690/21; c 33 340/30, 340/33, 340/114.

[43] In their bill the plaintiffs set out "that by vertue of the said assignment and an Act of Parliament... Your Orators became well intitled to the copy of the said Comedy and to the sole and separate right and liberty of printing and selling he same and all future editions for the term of 14 years", c 11 690/21.

[44] The injunction was granted "until the defendant shall fully answer the plaintiff's bill and this court make other order to the contrary", c 33 340/33.

have proceeded on the general common law right".[45] Again, Blackstone proves less than reliable, given that the plaintiffs, in their bill, made explicit reference to the fact that they *had* registered the work in accordance with the Act.[46]

Continuing in the vein of *Tonson* (1722), interlocutory injunctions were similarly secured in the last two cases begun in the 1720s. In *Gay v Read* (1729)[47] the author John Gay entered a bill of complaint, on 11 April, to prevent the printing of his work *Polly, An Opera* and by 12 May was granted an injunction until answer, by the court.[48] This case, however, unlike the previous one, was to run on for a further eight years resulting, after Gay's death, with the decision in *Baller v Watson* (1737).[49] The second was *Gilliver v Watson* (1729),[50] an action concerning Pope's *Dunciad*, in which the plaintiff's injunction was granted only 13 days after the filing of a bill and, as in the previous two cases, before any answer had been received by the court. This injunction, however, was later revoked for reasons connected with Pope's reluctance to be identified as the author of the work. To protect himself against retaliation by any of the "Dunces" satirised in his work, Pope, to disguise his authorship, assigned the poem to three friends, the Earl of Burlington, the Earl of Oxford, and Lord Bathurst. Gilliver then contracted with them for the right to print the work, and registered his interest in the poem on 12 April 1729. At this time however, the three Lords had yet to actually assign the work to him.[51] The defendants latched upon this fact, challenged the adequacy of the registration, invalidated Gilliver's claim and had the injunction dissolved.[52] Nevertheless, these cases had established the convention of seeking and securing injunctions, to protect those works, falling squarely within the terms of the 1709 Act, which had drawn the attention of the pirates. Moreover, this was a pattern which could be traced through a stream of subsequent cases: *Watson v Jeffries* (1738),[53] *Richardson's Case* (1740),[54]

[45] (1672) 1 Black W 330.
[46] C 11 690/21. Moreover, in the only answer entered to the court, on 24 January 1723, the defendants make no reference to the issue of registration at all; they simply choose to deny all the pertinent facts alleged in the plaintiff's bill. *Ibid.*
[47] *Gay v Read* (12 May 1729) c 33 351/305.
[48] *Ibid.*
[49] Below: The *Statute of Anne*, Polly, and the Perpetual Injunction.
[50] *Gilliver v Watson* (19 May 1729) c 33 351/284, 355/85.
[51] It would in fact be November of the same year before he could make an authoritative entry in the Company Register as the owner of the copy of the work.
[52] The defendants also argued that the plaintiff's bill was defective in that he had failed to identify the author of the work. King LC, reportedly accepting this argument, declared that it was not sufficient for Gilliver to state that he purchased or legally acquired the copy, without also indicating that he had purchased it from the author; (1722) 2 Eq Ca Abr 522. For a more in depth discussion of this litigation, see JR Sutherland, "The Dunciad of 1729" (1936) 31 *Modern Language Review* 347.
[53] *Watson v Jeffries* (January 1738) c 11 1541/37; c 33 370/148.
[54] *Richardson's Case* (6 May 1740) 2 Eq Ca Abr.

Rivington v Cooper (1740),[55] *Tonson v Mechell* (1740),[56] *Millar v Lynch* (1742),[57] *Pope v Gilliver* (1743),[58] *Pope v Illive* (1743),[59] *Pope v Bickham* (1744)[60] and *Tonson v Stevens* (1745).[61] In all of these cases the injunction awarded was simply until the defendant answer the plaintiff's bill and the court make order to the contrary. Time after time, booksellers were to turn to this equitable court seeking injunctions to secure their properties and muzzle the activities of the pirates.

There remains the question, however, as to why the Chancery injunction, initially at least, proved to be the preferred method of obtaining legal redress against the pirates. Why was it that, having so vigorously lobbied for the protections of the *Statute of Anne*, the booksellers then choose to ignore the remedies it provided them? Ransom provides one explanation. Discussing section 8 of the 1709 Act, which set out that should "a Verdict be given for the Defendant, or the Plaintiff become Non-suited, or

[55] *Rivington v Cooper* (8 June 1740) c 11 1566/42; c 33 374/295. In this case the plaintiffs were complaining that "the whole or great part" of the work (Miller's *Gardeners Kalender*) had been published in a book called *The Universal Pocket Book*, and that the defendant was threatening to print the rest of the work.

[56] *Tonson v Mechell* (23 October 1740) c 11 2462/49; c 33 374/2. Note that this case is erroneously reported in *Donaldson v Becket* (1774) 4 Burr 2408, as *Tonson v Mitchell* (6 November 1757).

[57] *Millar v Lynch* (October 1742) c 33 380/1. The injunction was requested here to protect Henry Fielding's novel *Joseph Andrews*. This appears to be the first case in which an injunction is requested and granted, before any pirate edition of the work was ever printed or published.

[58] *Pope v Gilliver, Lintot et al* (16 February 1743) c 11549/39; c 33 380/259. In this case there had been an agreement between Pope and Gilliver in 1728 for the "purchase of the copy or sole right of printing and publishing [*The Dunciad*] for a term of fourteen years pursuant to [the 1709]". Gilliver had sold one third of his interest to James Clark whereby it came to John Osbourne in August 1739, and then to Lintot early in 1740. Lintot then bought the further interest remaining with Gilliver, despite advice from Pope that the title to the work was to return to him in December 1742. In his bill Pope sets out that both Gilliver and Lintot were preparing to print a new edition, and claimed that they asserted that the assignment was not for 14 years "but that such assignment was indefinite and passed the perpetual right and interest and absolute property of the Author... and that he the said Lintot has by virtue thereof the sole absolute and entire property of the book without any restriction in point of time or otherwise". This appears to be the earliest claim to a perpetual right and interest outside the bounds of the 1709 Act. However Henry Lintot in his answer denies ever claiming a perpetual right. Rather he simply states that all he bought was what Gilliver contracted with Pope for, a contract which he had never seen.

[59] *Pope v Illive* (16 February 1743) c 33 837/14.

[60] *Pope v Bickham* (9 January 1744) c 11626/30; c 33 382/179. See also D Hunter, "Pope v Bickham: An Infringement of An Essay On Man Alleged" (1987) 9 *The Library* 268. This case has a peculiar point of interest. Bickham was an engraver and had produced a copy of Pope's *An Essay on Man*. In his bill Pope alleges that Bickham claims "a right to cast off as many copies of [the poem] and any other of Your Orator's works from plates engraved as he pleases" so long as they are not printed from type. Pope however asserts that "there is no difference whether the impression be made from plates Engraved or from Types, the injury [being] exactly the same". The niceties involved in resolving any potential conflict between the 1709 Act and the *Engraver's Act* however were avoided as Bickham failed to enter an answer.

[61] *Tonson v Stevens* (10 April 1745) c 11 2558/47.

Discontinue his Action, then the Defendant shall have and recover his full Costs", he comments that:

> [T]his section inevitably discouraged suits at common law by increasing the risks of the plaintiff. As a result, injured proprietors of copy resorted to threats or to actions in Chancery.[62]

Moreover, even if the booksellers had chosen to proceed under the *Statute of Anne*, it is clear that the common law penalties actually provided by the Act were considered to be difficult to follow for,[63] as well as "impracticable", and "inadequate".[64] Given that the Court of Chancery was prepared to grant an initial injunction upon mere submission of a bill (a lesson well learned from the patent cases), alongside the fact that these actions rarely proceeded beyond the pleadings stage, there can be no doubt that the route through Chancery was perceived to be considerably more expedient than following an infringer at common law. It was certainly effective, but was it appropriate? Edmund Curl in *Knaplock* (1722) once called into question the jurisdiction of the court to try the action, and grant an injunction. Having set out most of his defence, Curl charged that the court "will not any ways confirm any rights to the Complainants ... or injunctions", and continued:

> [I]f the said complainants think they have a better right to the said Book ... they may try their right with this defendant and justify their Right thereto at Common Law where this defendant is advised the same is properly Tryable.[65]

His appeal came to nothing. If there was some question mark hanging over the propriety of the court to decide upon such matters, it was to remain uncontested. The booksellers would continue to rely upon these Chancery injunctions, and any thought of pursuing a pirate through the common law courts would lie dormant for nearly three decades following the 1709 Act.

THE *STATUTE OF ANNE*, POLLY, AND THE PERPETUAL INJUNCTION

In *Gay v Read* (1729) John Gay entered his bill of complaint with the court, and on 12 May 1729 was granted an injunction until answer.[66] This case,

[62] H Ransom, *The First Copyright Statute* (Austin, University of Texas, 1956) 104.
[63] See *The Petition of the Booksellers of London against the Booksellers of Edinburgh and Glasgow*, 15 July 1746.
[64] See *The Petition of Daniel Midwinter*, 11 December 1747.
[65] C 11 690/5.
[66] C 33 351/305.

while similar to those others concerning works that fell squarely within the terms of the 1709 Act, merits special attention. Not only did it proceed to a final hearing, culminating in the decision of *Baller v Watson* (1737),[67] but at the hearing Lord Chancellor Talbot decreed that "the injunction formerly granted in this cause ... be perpetual".[68] In years to come the advocates of the common law copyright would make much of this declaration. For example, Alexander Wedderburn, in the case of *Tonson v Collins* (1761),[69] would later recount how the Lord Chancellor in *Baller* "made the injunction perpetual; which he could not have done merely under the Act".[70]

Unfortunately no copy of the bill originally filed by John Gay appears to have survived. The Court of Chancery's Book of Records from 1729 however, does provide some indication of the manner and tone of his application. Gay set out that he had written the work in question, *Polly, An Opera* and that he had published and registered it in accordance with the 1709 Act. He continued that the defendants had printed his work "contrary to the intent of the said Act of Parliament ... without the plaintiff's consent." Like those before him, he prayed for an injunction to prevent the defendants printing the work until they answered his bill and the court ordered to the contrary.[71] Whatever the significance of Lord Talbot's final decree, Gay certainly seems to have grounded his complaint within the context of the statute. Moreover, the various answers, twelve in all, submitted throughout the course of this litigation have little more to offer. The first joint answer of Thomas Read, James Watson and Robert Walker did suggest that, as was the case in *Gilliver* (1729), the plaintiff's registration was in some manner suspect; they had "heard and believe that some copies of the book were published before the complainants title to the same was registered".[72] This however was the first and last time that they proffered such a defence. The mainstay of this first answer lay in their demurrer to the author's call for discovery regarding the numbers of pirate copies printed, the profits made, and so on. Gay contested the sufficiency of the response and, on 3 March 1730, Lord Talbot declared it to be inadequate.[73] The remaining eleven answers, repetitive in nature and form, were given over to setting out the very details which Gay had sought in his initial call for discovery: how many editions had been printed; by whom; in what quantities; at what price; how many were sold; and for what profit. There is nothing in any of this to provide any insight

[67] *Gay v Read, Baller v Watson* (1729–37) c 11 1739/34, 1272/7, 2427/24, 1272/17, 1272/18, 1727/16, 2433/14, 2434/18, 1738/35; c 33 351/305, 353/5, 353/38, 353/153, 353/202, 353/292, 353/401, 355/20, 355/27, 357/132, 357/249, 357/271, 357/272, 357/273, 357/419, 357/547, 359/378, 361/14, 361/17, 367/5, 367/23, 367/37, 367/83, 367/188, 369/315.
[68] C 33 369/315.
[69] *Tonson v Collins* (1761) 1 Black W 301.
[70] *Ibid*, 305–6.
[71] C 33 351/305.
[72] C 11 1739/34.
[73] C 33 353/153.

as to the meaning behind the Lord Chancellor's decree. While it seems unlikely that Gay ever contemplated receiving any longer protection than that set out in the *Statute of Anne*, the precise significance of the Lord Chancellor's perpetual injunction raises something of a conundrum.

Today one might turn to any number of modern authorities to establish that the perpetual injunction is one "directed towards the final settlement and enforcement of the rights of the parties that are in dispute".[74] That is, the perpetual injunction is to be understood in simple contradistinction to the interlocutory; the latter is effective only until the day of the trial, while the former provides the final order that settles the dispute in question.[75] Moreover, it is also clear that such an injunction can be granted in respect of rights that are limited in duration.[76] However, what exactly did it mean to grant a perpetual injunction in 1737? Was Lord Talbot's injunction simply perpetual as to the process before him, or did he actually grant an injunction to *perpetually* protect what was otherwise a statutorily defined wasting asset? Early treatises on the law of equity in general, and on injunctions in particular, provide little assistance in this regard. Eden, in his work *A Treatise on the Law of Injunctions*, writes about injunctions "to restrain the Infringement of Copyright" noting that "[i]t rarely happens" that such suits are brought to a hearing. He continues: "The plaintiff is generally satisfied with having an injunction continued, and it becomes unimportant to seek for an account of profits". Of the perpetual injunction in particular, Eden simply observes that it "is final, and it is not necessary to revive upon the death of either of the parties, in order to keep it on the foot".[77] Neither Fowler,[78] Hinde,[79] Turner,[80] nor Lord

[74] ICF Spry, *The Principles of Equitable Remedies*, 4th edn (London, Sweet & Maxwell, 1990) 373. See also: JE Martin, *Hanbury & Modern, Modern Equity*, 16th edn (London, Sweet & Maxwell, 2001) 760; PV Baker and P St J Langan, *Snell's Principles of Equity*, 29th edn (London, Sweet & Maxwell, 1990) 646.

[75] See for example the distinction drawn in the first edition of *Kerr on Injunctions*:

> Injunctions are either interlocutory or perpetual … Perpetual injunctions are such as form part of the decree made at the hearing upon the merits, whereby the defendant is perpetually inhibited from the assertion of a right or perpetually restrained from the commission of an act which would be contrary to equity and good conscience. The perpetual injunction is in effect a decree, and concludes a right. The interlocutory injunction is merely provisional in its value, and does not conclude a right. The effect and object of the interlocutory injunction is merely to preserve the property in dispute in statu quo until the hearing or further order.

WW Kerr, *A Treatise on the Law and Practice of Injunctions in Equity* (London, Maxwell & Son, 1867) 11.

[76] Spry, *The Principles of Equitable Remedies*, n 74 above, 373.

[77] R Eden, *A Treatise on the Law of Injunctions* (London, 1821).

[78] DB Fowler, *The Practice of the Court of Exchequer upon Proceedings in Equity* (London, 1817).

[79] R Hinde, *The Modern Practice of the High Court of Chancery Methodized and Digested in a Manner Wholly New* (London, 1785).

[80] S Turner, *An Epitome of the Practice on the Equity Side of the Court of Exchequer* (London, Clarke & Sons, 1806).

Nottingham's *Manual of Chancery Practice* [81] contribute anything of any greater instruction. The basic ambiguity remains. When the injunction in *Baller* was decreed to be perpetual, was Lord Chancellor Talbot using the phrase "perpetual injunction" as a legal term of art to indicate the conclusion of the litigation, or did he intend to attribute to it its ordinary and literal meaning? Given the nature and the terms of the action brought by Gay in the first place, the former seems the more likely. And yet this can by no means be stated with great conviction. An argument could be made for either reading throughout the course of the eighteenth century. In *Millar v Taylor* (1765), when the plaintiff prayed for a perpetual injunction, it is reported that Lord Chancellor Nottingham considered such an injunction might be improper, as it seemed to imply a perpetual right. Rather, he observed that the "injunction ought to be continued, but it ought to be so framed as not to imply a right beyond the two terms of fourteen years."[82] Indeed, this judicial uncertainty as to the proper way to proceed in such cases was still evident nearly one hundred and fifty years later. In *Savory (Lim.) v Gyptian Oil Co. (Lim.)* (1904) the plaintiffs, who owned the copyright in four pictures copied by the defendants, sought an injunction from the court "perpetually restraining infringement". Farwell J, in response, commented that "a perpetual injunction ought not to be granted to protect a right having only a limited duration", and granted an injunction lasting the length of the plaintiff's copyright only.[83] Whatever Lord Talbot intended in 1737 remains unresolved. What is certain, however, is that the later proponents of the common law right would make much of his decree.

THE *STATUTE OF ANNE*, POLLY, AND THE PLEA FOR PROFITS

In John Gay's original bill to the court he had asked not just for relief by way of injunction, but also for discovery of a number of details concerning the extent of the piracy of his work: who had printed the books; how many editions had been printed; at what cost; at what price; and crucially, at what profit? At the hearing, in addition to granting a perpetual

[81] DEC Yale (ed), *Lord Nottingham's "Manual of Chancery Practice" and "Prolegomena of Chancery and Equity"* (Cambridge, CUP, 1965).
[82] *Hinton v Donaldson* (1773), see *Information for Alexander Donaldson*, 2 January 1773, B.M. 515. f. 15(2).
[83] (1904) 48 *Solicitor's Journal* 573. Indeed, this case led Paterson to observe in the sixth edition of Kerr on Injunctions that: "A perpetual injunction should not however be granted to protect a right having only a limited duration; in such a case the injunction should be limited to the period of the plaintiff's interest in the subject-matter of the action"; JM Paterson, *Kerr on Injunctions*, 6th edn (London, Sweet & Maxwell, 1927) 31.

injunction, Lord Chancellor Talbot also decreed that a Master of the Court:

> [T]ake an account against the several Defendants ... of the profits of the books mentioned in the Bill printed published or sold by the said Defendants [and that they] do respectively pay the same to the plaintiffs as the Master shall direct.[84]

This was a truly novel departure for the court. The Lord Chancellor had not ordered the Master to calculate what the penalties delineated in the *Statute of Anne* amounted to, but rather that he make an account of the profits which the defendants had actually made through the publishing of their pirate edition. The order for this account, mentioned nowhere in the legislation, enabled the London booksellers in the later case of *Midwinter v Hamilton* (1743-1748) to claim that, in the forty years since the passing of the *Statute of Anne*, "frequent Occasions have occured in England" wherein the "consequent Practice" of the Court of Equity has been to give relief by way of injunction as well as decrees "to account to the Proprietors for all the Profits" made by the sale of the pirate edition.[85] In fact, the only time such a decree had been made was in *Baller* (1737).

Prior to this action, it was generally the case that a plaintiff filing a bill would seek both writs of injunction and subpoena from the court, to prevent the defendant printing any more infringing books, and require him to answer to the plaintiff's charges. In a handful of cases, however, the plaintiffs included some form of further request in their bill. In *Knaplock v Curl* (1722) they sought "such further and other relief as Your Lordship shall seem meet and shall be agreeable to Right, Equity and Good Conscience".[86] In *Eyre v Walker* (1735) the plaintiffs requested "such further order and decree as to Your Lordship shall seem meet".[87] In *Motte v Faulkner* (1735) they followed for "such further or other relief in all and singular the premises as the nature of their case shall require".[88] Exactly what the plaintiffs had in mind was left unsaid. In any case, both *Eyre* and *Motte* failed to proceed to a full hearing, and although *Knaplock* did, the Lord Chancellor made no such order for any "other relief". Following Lord Chancellor Talbot's decree in *Baller*, however, barely an action went by without the plaintiffs making some reference to, or call for an account of,

[84] C 33/369.
[85] *The Petition of Daniel Midwinter, William Innes, Aaron Ward, and others, all of London Booksellers, and William Elliot Writer in Edinburgh their Attorney or Factor, Pursuers*, 9 December 1747. It is interesting to note that the plaintiffs were actually relying upon an opinion prepared for them by the then Solicitor-General, William Murray.
[86] C 11 690/5.
[87] C 11 1520/29. For more on this case, below: The *Statute of Anne* and Ancient Authors.
[88] C 11 2249/4. For more on this case, below: The *Statute of Anne* and Ancient Authors.

the profits which the defendants may have made from their piracies. The first application to the court, *Watson v Jeffries* (1738), coming less than two months after the decision in *Baller*, sought discovery of the amount of profits made with the request that "such further or other relief in the premises as the circumstances of this case requires".[89] With *Tonson v Mechell* (1740) a tradition emerged in which the complainants began to assert their claims somewhat more stridently. In this case, taking a more direct cue from *Baller*, the plaintiffs claimed that they:

> [O]ught in justice and equity to have a satisfaction and compensation made ... for the violation and injury... committed upon our said right and property ... [seeking that the defendants] each of them come to an account ... for the profits by them respectively made from or by the printing ... the book.[90]

This call for an "account of profits" was similarly taken up in the numerous actions which followed.[91]

While the Lord Chancellor's decree in *Baller* was responsible for this new profit-conscious rhetoric, a question remains as to whether or not the decision was, in and of itself, legitimate.[92] Upon what basis, authority or principle did Lord Talbot make such a decree? Seven years later, in *Jesus College v Bloom* (1745) the question facing the new Lord Chancellor, Lord Hardwicke, was whether a bill for account "ought to be entertained merely for satisfaction for timber cut down, after the estate of the tenant that cut it down is determined". As the tenant was no longer resident upon the land there had been no necessity to seek an injunction. Lord Hardwicke refused relief commenting that waste was a tort that was actionable at law. However, he did observe that, where the bill is for an injunction, and waste has already been committed, "the court to prevent a double suit, will decree an account, and satisfaction for what is past." He continued:

> [I]n all these cases, this court has gone further, merely upon the maxim of preventing multiplicity of suits, which is the reason that determines this court in many cases ... So in bills for injunctions, the court will make a complete

[89] C 11 1541/37. See also *Austen v Cave* (1739) c 11 1552/3, and *Rivington v Cooper* (1740) c 11 1566/42.

[90] C 11 2462/49.

[91] *Read v Hodges* (1740); *Pope v Curl* (1741); *Forrester v Walker* (1741); *Pope v Gilliver* (1743); *Pope v Illive* (1743); *Pope v Bickham* (1744); and *Tonson v Stevens* (1745). I have only been able to locate a c 33 reference, and not any c 11 documents, for *Tonson v Walker* (1739); *Hitch v Langley* (1739); *Gyles v Wilcox* (1741); *Millar v Lynch* (1742); and *Cogan v Cave* (1744). As such it cannot be stated with certainty that all the cases following *Baller* did in fact make some claim for an account of profits. However, this is likely to have been the case.

[92] For a discussion of the development of the remedy of account at common law and in equity see SJ Stoljar, "The Transformations of Account" (1964) 80 *LQR* 203, 220–21.

> decree, and give the party a satisfaction, and not oblige him to bring an action at law as well as a bill here.[93]

The decree for an account of profits in *Baller* may have been granted by the court along similar lines, that is, as ancillary to the injunction for reasons of expediency on the plaintiff's behalf.[94] The only problem with this explanation, however, is the fact that the availability of an order to account for profits must have been one that was, in any case, available at common law, and this had never yet been tested in the courts. Prior to this, only one action had been initiated before the common law courts, *Ponder v Bradyll* (1679), and that was never brought to a conclusion.[95] The Lord Chancellor may have granted the decree for an account of profits for

[93] *Jesus College v Bloom* (1745) 3 Atk 262–64.

[94] See further: W Ashburner, *Principles of Equity*, 2nd edn (London, Butterworth, 1933) 349–50; PV Baker and P St J Langan, *Snell's Principles of Equity*, 29th edn (London, Sweet & Maxwell, 1990), 637–38; H A Smith, *The Principles of Equity*, 5th edn, (London, Stevens and Sons, 1914) 558, 791.

[95] This involved a pirate edition of J Bunyan, *The Pilgrim's Progress*. Nathaniel Ponder had registered the work with the Stationers' Company, and just three months later, in the wake of the lapse of the Licensing Act 1679, began an action against his printer, Bradyll whom he accused of printing and selling more than Ponder had originally ordered. Harrison, writing about the action, provided an account of the case, taken from John Lilly's *Modern Entries*:

> Nathaniel Ponder complains concerning Thomas Braddill for the following reason: because when the aforesaid Nathaniel Ponder on the first day of May 30 Car: II [1678] in London namely in the parish of the Blessed Marie de Arcubus St Mary-le-bow in the Cheap Ward was and up till now the manifestly true proprietor of the same book entitled The Pilgrims Progress and which because he the aforesaid Nathaniel Ponder printed two thousand books of the same copy and the 20 day of January 30 Car: II [1679] in London had in his hands a hundred books and more of the impression on the same 20th January was printing four thousand books of the same copy although Thomas Braddill … afterwards (in fact on the same 20th January) … printed four thousand copies of the book itself of the aforesaid Nathaniel Ponder entitled The Pilgrims Progress … printed and at this time and in the same place exposed for sale.

Harrison himself commented:

> The so-called Licensing Act of 1662, which had actually lapsed in May 1679, and had not been renewed, made the case Ponder v Bradyll, of considerable interest to the legal profession, for it was evidently a moot point regarding Ponder's claim of copyright; and he had for his advocate John Lilly. The suit was really an "action on the case", in the Court of Common Pleas in Hilary Term, 30 Car. II [1679]; and the comment on it by the late Mr WA Copinger, shows that the case was evidently not proceeded with.. Ponder was a victim of circumstances, without the ghost of a chance of procuring redress.

FM Harrison, "Nathaniel Ponder: The Publisher of the Pilgrim's Progress" (1934–35) 15 *The Library* 257.

Harrison's reference to Copinger's comment on the case, was to the following passage: "In this case an action was brought for printing 4000 copies of the 'Pilgrim's Progress' of which the plaintiff was the true proprietor, whereby he lost the profit and benefit of the copy. There is no account of the case having been proceeded with." WA Copinger, *The Law of Copyright*, 3rd edn (London, Sweet & Maxwell, 1893) 23.

reasons of expediency, while at the same time implicitly acknowledging the existence of such a right at common law. Alternatively he may have made the order because John Gay had simply *asked* for such an account to be made. Again, what rationale lay behind Lord Talbot's actions remain with him alone. In any case, this was to be the one and only time such an order was ever made in the Court of Chancery, as the booksellers were soon to turn their attentions to the courts of common law.[96]

THE *STATUTE OF ANNE* AND THE UNPUBLISHED MANUSCRIPT

While the *Statute of Anne* had provided a fourteen-year protection for new works "to commence from the day of first publishing the same",[97] it left the issue of the unpublished manuscript unaddressed. In *Webb v Rose* (1732),[98] Sir Joseph Jekyll first considered the spectre of the manuscript work. Thirty years later Blackstone would find in Jekyll MR's decision evidence of an "original and natural right which every man has in his own composition".[99] In reality, the case concerned nothing of the sort. The plaintiff's father, Richard Webb, a lawyer, had prepared numerous manuscript copies of conveyances he had executed throughout his lifetime (*Precedents of Conveyancing*). Robert Southern, employed by Webb as a clerk and agent, also carried out business of his own and, upon Webb's death, left his chambers with a number of drafts belonging to both Webb and himself. Southern died in 1724, and all the manuscripts came into the possession of the defendants, Edward Rose and John Talbot. The plaintiff, William Webb, devisee of his father's estate, filed a bill against Rose and Talbot to prevent them from printing his father's manuscripts, and to reclaim the same. He was granted an interlocutory injunction against the printing[100] and the action proceeded to a full hearing. On 24 May 1732 Jekyll MR decreed that all the drafts in question be delivered up to Mr Elde, a Master of the Court, to determine which belonged to the plaintiff, and which to the defendant; he proceeded that "the injunction formerly granted in this cause ... is in the meantime continued".[101] When the plaintiff filed his bill it neither made reference to the 1709 Act, nor to the fact that he himself ever intended to print the papers in question. Webb was simply following the defendants for what he considered to be a

[96] See below, ch 5(1) Copyright at Common Law? A "Complicated" Action.
[97] S 1.
[98] *Webb v Rose* (24 May 1732) c 11 1881/156; c 33 354/11, 354/22, 354/33, 354/336, 356/336, 356/372, 356/376, 358/22, 358/78, 358/121, 358/308, 360/364, 360/381, 360/444.
[99] *Tonson v Collins* (1762) 1 Black W 329, 330–31. See also Wedderburn's comments in the same case, but a year earlier: *Tonson v Collins* (1761) 1 Black W 301, 302–3.
[100] C 33 354/22.
[101] C 33 358/308.

part of his father's personal estate. The issue at hand concerned the papers as physical property and not whether anyone, the plaintiff included, had an inherent right to print them. Despite the assertions of Blackstone and Wedderburn, this action had nothing to do with copyright whatsoever.

The next of these manuscript cases, *Forrester v Waller* (1741)[102] came before Lord Hardwicke, and concerned another set of legal texts, Forrester's *Reports*.[103] In his bill, Forrester set out that he had transcribed various cases and reports of the Court of Chancery "into a folio book now in his own custody" and had not sold or otherwise departed with "his property in the said manuscript". Neither, he asserted, had he given leave for anyone else to print the same. Nevertheless, the defendant had reproduced his manuscripts in a work entitled *Cases in Equity during the Time of the Late Chancellor Talbot*. Forrester continued that:

> [B]y means of his being the sole proprietor thereof and by virtue of an Act of Parliament [the 1709 Act] that no person whatsoever ought to print or publish [the] manuscript without licence or consent.[104]

Forrester's reliance on the 1709 Act obviously represents a departure from the line taken in *Webb*. The reason for this, lies in the fact that here, the defendant had "obtained the said cases or a copy of the same surreptitiously".[105] This case, unlike *Webb*, was not simply a question of securing the return of the actual physical manuscript itself; rather, Forrester had to convince Lord Hardwicke that he, and he alone, had the sole right to first publish his work. Despite that the Act remained silent as to what rights, if any, subsisted in an unpublished manuscript, Forrester sought to rely upon the *Statute of Anne*. Lord Hardwicke, as had been the case in all the previous cases coming before the court, granted the plaintiff an interlocutory injunction until an answer was submitted. The defendant acquiesced. Without an answer, the issue as to whether it was appropriate for Forrester to rely upon the 1709 Act remained unexplored.

The third in this triptych of cases, and arguably the most important, was *Pope v Curl* (1741),[106] again decided by Lord Hardwicke, and only four days after he had issued the injunction in *Forrester*. This case differed from *Forrester* in that Alexander Pope was not seeking to prevent Edmund Curl reproducing material that remained in the plaintiff's possession. It also differed from *Webb* in that neither was Pope trying to reclaim any

[102] *Forrester v Waller* (13 June 1741) c 11 867/54; c 33 375/439.
[103] *Cases and Reports of the High Court of Chancery*; c 11 867/54.
[104] C 11 867/54.
[105] It appears that Waller had tried to persuade Forrester that he had received the cases from another source, but when pressed as to whom it was, he replied that "the gentleman would not put his name to the said cases"; c 11 867/54.
[106] *Pope v Curl* (17 June 1741) 2 Atk 342; c 11 1569/29; c 33 376/350.

physical documents from Curl. Here, the plaintiff had written and sent a number of letters to and from the Rev Dr Swift; the letters Pope had written to Swift had subsequently come into Curl's possession. Pope was not contesting the ownership of the physical artefacts, these letters; that lay with Curl. Instead he was trying to regulate the reproduction of that correspondence within Curl's volume entitled *Dean Swift's Literary Correspondence for 24 Years from 1714–1738*. Pope entered his bill on 5 June 1741 and was granted an injunction until answer.[107] The bill itself, drafted by William Murray, later Lord Mansfield, provided little more than a factual account of the events leading up to the litigation, but followed *Forrester* in relying on the 1709 Act to protect the letters. It set out that Pope, being the "sole author of the said letters" and "never having disposed of the Copy right of such letters" to anyone "hath the sole and absolute right of printing, reprinting, vending and selling the same as he should think fit".[108] In relation to the correspondence Pope had received from Swift, the plaintiff also set out his hope that neither "those other letters which were sent and addressed to [him] would have been printed, published or sold without [his] consent".[109] Pope, somewhat inconsistently, was claiming authority over his own writings, regardless of the ownership of the physical letter, as well as the writings of others that had been addressed to him.

Curl moved to have the injunction dissolved with his answer filed on 17 June. He put it to the Lord Chancellor that the letters which Pope had sent were to be considered as gifts to the recipients, that they were no longer Pope's property, that he was no longer "the author and proprietor of all or any of the said letters".[110] In short, he claimed that Pope's dominion over the letters began and ended with the physical manuscript. Pope, on the other hand, argued that while he was no longer the proprietor of the letters in question, he was still their author, and as such retained the ability to decide whether or not they should be printed and published. It is in answer to this dilemma that we get one of the first truly remarkable judicial commentaries on the nature of the text as literary property. Lord Hardwicke, in the absence of any guidance from the *Statute of Anne*, sought to resolve this conflict between the author of the text and the owner of the letter. Rejecting Curl's thesis, he commented:

> I am of opinion that it is only a special property in the receiver, possibly the property of the paper may belong to him; but this does not give a licence to any person whatsoever to publish them to the world, for at most the receiver has only a joint property with the writer.[111]

[107] C 33 376/350.
[108] C 11 1569/29.
[109] *Ibid.*
[110] *Ibid.*
[111] *Ibid.*

Campbell, the author of *Lives of the Lord Chancellors*, working from manuscripts in his own possession written by a Mr Jodderell, a Chancery barrister, relates the Lord Chancellor's opinion on this issue in the following terms:

> [T]hat where a man writes a letter, it is in the nature of a gift to the receiver, I am of opinion that the receiver only acquires a qualified interest in it. The paper on which it is written may belong to him, but the composition does not become vested in him as property, and he cannot publish against the consent of the writer.[112]

Whether "special property" or "qualified interest", both reports of Hardwicke's analysis amount to the same thing: Curl was unable to print those letters that Pope had written.[113] As to the letters which he had received from others, while Atkyns records that the injunction was continued only as to those letters "written by him, and not as to those which are written to him",[114] Campbell recounts the Lord Chancellor's decision in the following way:

> [A]s for the letters in this volume written *to* Mr.Pope, I think that *he* cannot be heard to complain. They may possibly be published with the authority

[112] J Campbell, *Lives of the Lord Chancellors* (London, John Murray, 1857) vol VI, 202. About this report, Campbell writes: "It consists of four quarto volumes, beautifully written by Mr. Jodderell, an eminent Chancery barrister. He often does more justice to Lord Hardwicke than Atkyns or Vesey, sen.; and I am told that, upon a reference to the register's book, he is found to be more accurate"; 198.

[113] The use of both these phrases "special property" and "qualified interest" seem to have a precedent at the time, in the law and the language of bailments. Blackstone, writing in 1765, categorised personal property as either "property in possession" or "property in action". As to property in possession, he divided this category into "absolute property" and "qualified property". In relation to this second category, he wrote that "qualified, limited, or special property … is such as is not in its nature permanent, but may sometimes subsist and at other times may not subsist", noting that often "[t]hese kinds of qualification in property depend upon the peculiar circumstances of the subject matter, which is not capable of being under the absolute dominion of any proprietor". Blackstone continued that:

> Property may also be of a qualified or special nature, on account of the peculiar circumstances of the owner, when the thing itself is very capable of absolute ownership. As in the case of bailment, or delivery of goods to another person for a particular use; as to a carrier to convey to London, to an inn keeper to secure his inn, or the like. Here there is no absolute property in either the bailor or the bailee, the person delivering, or him to whom it is delivered: for the bailor hath only the right, and not the immediate possession; the bailee hath the possession, and only a temporary right. But it is a qualified property in them both; and each of them is entitled to an action, in case the goods be damaged or taken away: the bailee on account of his immediate possession; the bailor, because the possession of the bailee is, mediately, his possession also.

W Blackstone, *Commentaries on the Laws of England, Book the Second* (Oxford, Clarendon Press, 1766) 389–96.

[114] (1741) 2 Atk 343.

of the writers of them, and from copies taken from before they were sent to him.[115]

This whole issue was just one of a number of concepts that had been left untouched by the *Statute of Anne*: who had the right to first publish any written manuscript?, and, upon what foundation? The Act had specified protection for works upon first publication, but said nothing about the unpublished manuscript. This omission reflected the fact that the legislation had been lobbied for and secured on behalf of the book trade, albeit not in terms that entirely served their better interests. If the *Statute of Anne* only made reference to published works, this was because the booksellers were in the business of publishing works. If the Act said nothing as to an author's rights over his unpublished work, this was simply because it was a question that held no real interest for the bookseller.

It was in this vacuum that Lord Hardwicke had to negotiate the competing claims before him. While the *Statute of Anne* had set out for the first time that authors could own the property in their published work, it was as a result of what the Act had *not* said, that one such author was now addressing his court. In this absence, he began to formulate a policy-oriented approach to the rights of the author in relation to his text in light of the meaning and significance of the 1709 Act. To deny Pope any redress in the light of an Act that was passed for the encouragement of learning would have been wholly inappropriate, especially in light of the fact that epistolary exchanges of the time were often used to serve this very function. The letter in the eighteenth century was more than a simple carrier of personal news. As Ransom notes, it could be adapted to perform any number of disparate functions: carry news, entertain, chastise, persuade or inspire, as well as providing "a sound pedagogical device" for the instruction of others.[116] Indeed, the Lord Chancellor was certainly of the opinion that "no works have done more service to mankind than those which have appeared in this shape upon familiar subjects".[117] Moreover, in his view, it was very often *because* such letters were not intended for publication that they were so instructive; it was this very fact that often rendered them "so valuable".[118] If Pope had no control over his correspondence, he, and other authors, both current and future, may simply have abstained from writing such correspondence. Thus, while the *Statute of Anne* remained silent as to the unpublished work, the general principle

[115] Campbell, *Lives of the Lord Chancellors*, n 112 above, vol VI, 202.
[116] H Ransom, "The Personal Letter as Literary Property" (1951) 30 *Studies in English* 116, 118–19.
[117] Lord Hardwicke did, however, concede that it is often the case that "letters which are very elaborately written and originally intended for the press, are generally most insignificant, and very little worth any persons reading"; (1741) 2 Atk 342.
[118] *Ibid*.

underpinning the legislation suggested and enabled Lord Hardwicke to conclude that Pope's letters should be protected. More significant, however, was that in arriving at this decision, the Lord Chancellor provided one of the earliest elaborations upon the problematic nature of copyright, and the relationship between the author, the reader, the book and the text. Rose considers the decision of crucial significance, describing it as "a transitional moment in the conception of authorship and a pivotal moment in the production of the concept of intellectual property".[119] The observation is not overstated. In resolving the issue before him in the way that he did, in the way that best accorded with the underlying principle of the *Statute of Anne*, Lord Hardwicke divorced Pope's physical letter from its metaphysical content, splitting the book and the text asunder in a way that the legislators responsible for the Act had hardly contemplated.[120]

THE *STATUTE OF ANNE* AND ANCIENT AUTHORS

Despite that the *Statute of Anne* had provided the booksellers with a twenty-one year protection for those works already in print, eventually that statutory protection would expire. Inevitably, after 10 April 1731, a number of cases came to be litigated involving works falling outside the term dictated by the Act. The first of these was *Eyre v Walker* (1735),[121] a decision concerning a pirate edition of *The Whole Duty of Man*, first published in 1657. Like so many previous actions, Jekyll MR granted an interlocutory injunction, to

[119] M Rose, *Authors and Owners: The Invention of Copyright* (London, Harvard University Press, 1993) 60.

[120] The question of unpublished manuscripts would only be addressed in the courts a further two times throughout the rest of the period: *The Duke of Queensbury v Shebbeare* (1758) 2 Eden 329, and *Macklin v Richardson* (1771) Amb 694. *Queensbury* (1758) concerned a manuscript copy of Lord Clarendon's *History of the Reign of Charles II, from the Restoration to the Year 1667*, which he had given to his administrator thirty three years previously. Clarendon's administrator had subsequently passed it on to his son, Francis Gwynne, who had represented to the defendant Shebbeare that he was free to do with it what he wished. An injunction had been granted and the plaintiffs were seeking to show cause against its dissolution. The Lord Keeper continued the injunction until the hearing commenting that it was not to be presumed that Lord Clarendon, when he gave a copy of his manuscript to Mr Gwynne, intended that he should have the "profit of multiplying it in print" and that Mr Gwynne could make every other use of the manuscript bar that. In *Macklin* (1771) the plaintiff was the author of a two-act play called *Love a la Mode*, which he had staged at several theatres, but he had never allowed it to be printed or published. Before and after every performance, the author would bring the script to and from the particular theatre in question. The defendants, publishers of the *Gentleman* and *Lady's Magazine*, employed someone to go to a performance of the play and make a record of it "from the mouths of the actors". In April 1766 they printed the first act of the plaintiff's play in their magazine, advertising that they would print the second act in a future edition. The plaintiff sought an injunction to prevent them from doing so, and, in light of the decision of *Millar v Taylor* (1768) 4 Burr 2303, was granted a perpetual injunction.

[121] *Eyre v Walker* (9 June 1735) c 11 1520/29; c 33 363/419, 480, 525.

which Walker would subsequently acquiesce. The plaintiffs' bill was mostly concerned with setting out the history of the ownership, sale and resale of the work, passing through numerous hands, down to the present owners, a history "now near 4 score years without any other person or persons whatsoever invading or attempting to invade their right".[122] Throughout their petition, the plaintiffs variously alluded to the "benefit of the copy of the book", the "right, privilege and property of printing the work", their "right and property", the "copy of the book ... and the sole and exclusive right, privilege and property of printing and vending the same", the "copy of the book ... and all and every the profits thereby arising and also all the estate, right, title, interest, property, claim and demand whatsoever", and finally the "right, title, interest, part or parts, share or shares, property claim and demand of in or to certain copies or proprieties of copies or books",[123] without once making reference to the provisions of the 1709 Act.

To this, Robert Walker filed his answer on 10 October, seeking to demure to the injunction granted by the Court.[124] Querying the court's jurisdiction to provide the plaintiffs relief, Walker asked whether the bill had set out "any impediment which a Court of Equity ought to remove". He continued by challenging the plaintiffs' claim to the sole right to print the book in a number of ways. The defendant claimed to have "as good a right to print and publish ... as any other printer or publisher hath the works of any other ancient author", drew attention to the *Statute of Anne*, highlighting that the plaintiffs "do not suggest by their said Bill that they have complyed with or that they are within the statute", and pointed to the fact that the plaintiffs could make no claim to the printing of the work under any letters patent. Finally, Walker stressed that the plaintiffs did not know who the original author of the work was, nor could they prove that there was any original authority from the author to print the said work.[125] Despite these arguments, the case proceeded no further than the pleadings stage.

Towards the end of the same year Benjamin Motte and Charles Bathurst were granted an injunction by the court to prevent the printing of their *Miscellanies*, a three-volume work that included various pieces by Swift and Pope, some of which had originally been printed in 1701 and 1702. *Motte v Faulkner* (1735)[126] first began on 18 October 1733, when the plaintiffs presented their bill before Lord Talbot complaining that George

[122] C 11 1520/29.
[123] *Ibid*.
[124] Note those reports which record that the injunction granted was simply acquiesced in. Also note that the only reason that the defendants entered a demurrer at all was probably due to the fact that the Court had issued a warrant "to the Sherriffs of London" to "attach the defendant for not answering at the suit of the plaintiff", c 33 363/480.
[125] *Ibid*.
[126] *Motte v Faulkner* (28 November 1735) c 11 2249/4; c 33 366/18.

Faulkner, the Dublin bookseller, had printed their work in Ireland and was importing into England copies of the same for sale.[127] The plaintiffs were not seeking an injunction to prevent the works being printed in Ireland, as was suggested by William Murray, the Solicitor-General, in *Tonson v Walker* (1752). Indeed, they seemed to concede that Ireland was, in truth, a place "where Booksellers cannot pretend to any property in what they publish either by law or by custom".[128] Rather, Motte and Bathurst, noting that Faulkner had "brought over with him several editions" pretending to make "presents" of them, an act "which he insists to be legal", sought an injunction to prevent the pirate editions being printed or sold in England.[129] The approach of the plaintiffs in this action is immediately distinguishable from that adopted in *Eyre* in that they relied squarely upon the *Statute of Anne* for protection. By virtue of the "Act of

[127] The others named in the bill were Arthur Bettesworth, Charles Hitch, Charles Davis and John Hopkins.

[128] The Dublin bookseller George Faulkner made this declaration in 1733 in his newspaper *The Dublin Journal* (10 February), and it proved to be a reasonably accurate account of the legal position of Irish booksellers at the time. Pollard has extensively examined the nature of the book trade in Dublin throughout the seventeenth and eighteenth centuries. It was first formerly organised around the founding of the Guild of St Luke the Evangelist, by Charter, in 1670. This guild was established to facilitate the regulation of three disparate trades: cutlers, painter-stainers and stationers. Initially, only two stationers were named in the 1670 Charter, but by 1710, this number had risen to thirty three. In the early years of the Guild, the chief activity of this fledgling Irish book trade consisted of selling imported British books. With the passage of the *Statute of Anne* however, the face of the trade took on a new complexion. The fact that 1709 Act did not extend to Ireland had a dual impact. It meant that there was little if any incentive for Irish booksellers to pay copy money for the work of Irish (or British) authors, as a result of which most of the original work of these authors was lured away by London money. Secondly, in place of this vacuum, the Irish booksellers realised that it was possible to reprint original works first printed in Britain, for sale to Irish readers, with no fear of redress from the London booksellers. In this way, throughout the eighteenth century, until the passing of the *Copyright Act* 1801, the Irish book trade would thrive. As to the Irish booksellers' attitude towards the printing of each others' reprint works (and original works), Faulkner's declaration, while legally correct, did not necessarily resonate with the reality of trade relations existing at this time. His comments may have suggested a publishing free for all, yet this never actually seems to have been the case. While the Guild itself provided little direction for the regulation of the book trade, its stationer members had developed their own informal method of trade regulation. In essence, whichever Irish bookseller first publicly announced his intention to reprint a particular London imprint was free to do so without competition. Moreover, this agreement was understood to apply, not only to the bookseller's initial edition, but to future editions also. This ad hoc arrangement was described in 1742 by Thomas Bacon in the following terms: "There is a Rule among the Booksellers of Dublin, established by common Consent and Custom, that whoever shall first paste up Title-Pages, advertising their Resolutions of publishing any Book, the Property then becomes theirs". He concluded that "this appears to be necessary in a Country where no public Laws have been made in that Respect." While Pollard accepts that this system "operating solely by mutual consent with no ruling authority behind it, frequently broke down", he continues that, "considering the normal fierce rivalry of trade it is remarkable that it worked at all". In general, see M Pollard, *Dublin's Trade in Books, 1550–1800* (Oxford, Clarendon Press, 1989) 32–65, 165–226. See also, RC Cole, *Irish Booksellers and English Writers, 1740–1800* (Kent, Mansell/Humanities Press International, 1986) 1–21.

[129] C 11 2249/4.

Parliament", they claimed to be "[i]ntituled to the sole Right of printing the said Miscellanies for 14 years to commence from publishing the same", having first registered and published their work "in or about June 1727". Despite the fact that some of the individual pieces in the edited collection were originally printed at the turn of the century, the plaintiffs were claiming the protection of the Act for what they considered to be an entirely new work, first published in 1727. For Motte and Bathurst, their action had nothing to do with a work falling outside of the remit of the legislation. The plaintiffs tried to pre-empt an argument that the pirate editions "do contain other treatises besides those *Miscellanies* ... or do in some other manner differ from the same". They alleged that Faulkner made such a suggestion "merely to call or distinguish the books printed him by another name ... and thereby to prevent [us] from having remedy against him", and continued that, in actual fact, "all or the far greatest part of the said Miscellanies ... are transcribed and reprinted by him into his said books literally and with small or no variance".[130] Such emphasis on Faulkner's *literal* and essentially *entire* use of the *Miscellanies* only serves to reinforce that the protection the plaintiffs were claiming was for a new collection of older works, a publication falling within the fourteen year protection of the Act. On 12 November 1735, three of the named defendants entered an answer in which their essential tactic was to dispute all or most of the relevant facts set out by the plaintiffs.[131] Following this, on 28 November, an injunction was awarded "against the defendants Bettesworth, Hitch and Davis" until the hearing.[132] As with *Eyre*, the injunctions appeared sufficient to dispose of the action and the hearing was never pursued.

In *Walthoe v Walker* (1737),[133] the third in this curious quartet of cases, Jekyll MR once again granted the injunction, this time to prevent the printing of Nelson's *A Companion for the Festivals and Feasts of the Church of England*, a work originally published in 1703/4.[134] The only distinction of note, between this and the *Eyre* bill, is that in *Walthoe* the plaintiff restricted the nature of his claim to the "sole right of printing the book". Apart from this, the two bills are virtually indistinguishable in structure and form, which perhaps should not surprise given that they were both

[130] *Ibid.*

[131] Arthur Bettesworth, Charles Hitch and Charles Davies. In *Millar v Taylor* (1768) 4 Burr 2303, 2325 it is reported that Faulkner "was advised not to litigate further" but to submit to the injunction.

[132] C 33 366/18.

[133] *Walthoe v Walker* (27 January 1737) c 11 1534/62; c 33 368/127.

[134] Again this is only an injunction until answer; however, it is noteworthy is that the c 33 report makes reference to the fact that the plaintiffs were seeking an injunction to prevent the defendants printing the book "or any part thereof", which was the first time that such an injunction was either requested or granted.

prepared by the same counsel, William Hamilton. As with *Eyre*, there was no reference to the *Statute of Anne*, the main thrust of the plea relying upon the fact that the plaintiff had enjoyed untroubled proprietorial possession of the work to date. The initial injunction was granted upon Walthoe's assertion that he had:

> [Q]uietly had and enjoyed the sole and exclusive right of printing [the work] ever since the same was so first printed and published … without any other person or persons whatsoever invading or attempting to invade their right by printing or vending the same.

Walker submitted no answer to Walthoe's bill; nor did he enter one to the bill lodged on behalf of James and Robert Tonson. In *Tonson v Walker* (1739),[135] the last of this intriguing quartet of cases, the plaintiffs claimed title to John Milton's *Paradise Lost* under an assignment of the copy from the author in 1667.[136] William Murray, counsel for the plaintiffs, making no reference to the 1709 Act, asserted that his clients were "possessed of and intitled unto the copy" of the poem as well as a commentary by Elijah Fenton, *The Life of John Milton*, which had been written in 1727. He continued that the defendants, Robert Walker and James Abree, had printed their work, which "so far as the same goes is printed in the same words as the same poem and life printed by the said plaintiffs" and prayed for an injunction. Again, the injunction was granted.[137]

Taken in the round, these four cases represent a rather curious legal landmark. One of them, *Motte*, in the minds of the litigants, and probably the judge as well, simply concerned a work that did in fact fall within the terms of the 1709 Act. Of the other three, in each of them, Robert Walker, the defendant, had specifically chosen works falling outside the twenty-one year protection provided by the *Statute of Anne*, and on one occasion drew this to the attention of the court, albeit to no avail.[138] On all three occasions, the plaintiffs having secured an interlocutory injunction from the court, Walker failed to pursue the action. As such, they represent no more than another group of actions in which the court routinely granted injunctions to a complaining party. In this respect, they prove to be no different from *Watson* (1737), *Richardson's Case* (1740), or *Rivington* (1740). This was not, of course, how they came to be subsequently represented. William Murray, who had secured the injunction in *Tonson* (1739), later

[135] *Tonson v Walker* (5 May 1739) c 33 1753/208.

[136] The list of plaintiffs also included Aaron Ward, John Oswald, Samuel Birt, Edward Wickstead, Richard Chandler, James Hutton, Richard Wellington, Bethell Wellington, John Brindley and John Mew.

[137] C 33 1753/208.

[138] C 11 1520/29.

acting as the Solicitor-General in *Tonson v Walker* (1752), confidently described the decision in *Eyre* as that "which made a precedent".[139] Although *Motte* concerned a publication that, within the minds of the plaintiffs at least, fell clearly within the terms of the *Statute of Anne*, Aston J in *Millar v Taylor* (1768) recounted how Lord Talbot continued the injunction as to the entire book, despite the fact that many of the parts "were printed so long before as to entirely take it out of the Act".[140] Yates J, the dissenting voice in *Millar* (1768), tried to dismiss the relevancy of these decisions, commenting that one should: "let the injunctions be what they may, they were only till the hearing, without any final judgment".[141] Nevertheless, this did not prevent the same William Murray, now Lord Mansfield, from declaring, once again in *Millar*: "I look upon these injunctions as equal to any final Decree".[142]

THE *STATUTE OF ANNE* AND THE ALTERED TEXT

Although the *Statute of Anne* had provided a temporary protection for works already in print, and those works that would subsequently be published, this protection was expressed in terms of the "book", the whole book and nothing but the book.[143] As a result, Lord Hardwicke was presented with a novel point of law in two separate cases brought before him on the same day. In the first of these, *Austen v Cave* (1739),[144] the proprietors of Dr Joseph Trapp's book, *The Nature, Folly, Sin and Danger of Being Righteous Over Much*, complained that Edward Cave, under the pretence and title of printing an extract of the work, was in fact printing the whole of their work, by instalment, in his publication *The Gentleman's Magazine*. They were granted an injunction "to restrain the said Defendant ... from printing ... the said Book *or any part thereof*", until answer.[145] In *Hitch v Langley* (1739),[146] the complainants who had purchased "the Copy Right or sole privilege of printing" James Gibbs' two books on architecture, alleged that Langley had "printed coppyed published and sold great parts of the said books" without their consent. They too prayed that an

[139] *Tonson v Walker* (1752) 3 Swans 672. The report of Murray's argument runs as follows: "If the term is expired the Court does not refuse to interpose. Sir Joseph Jekyll who sat in Parliament when the act was passed, made a precedent, 9th June 1735."
[140] *Millar v Taylor* (1768) 4 Burr 2303, 2328.
[141] *Ibid*, 2379.
[142] *Ibid*, 2399.
[143] S 1.
[144] *Austen v Cave* (7 August 1739) c 11 1552/3; c 33 371/493, 535, 586, 373/41, 224, 415, 535. This case is often reported as having been decided on 17 May 1739.
[145] C 33 371/493.
[146] *Hitch v Langley* (7 August 1739) c 33 371/493, 541, 591.

injunction be awarded to prevent the defendant from printing either of the books "or any part or parts thereof" and were granted the same.[147]

No more information is available about the latter case, however, Cave entered a joint demurrer and answer in response to Austen's bill of complaint.[148] In this response Cave denied ever intending to print or reprint Trapp's work, explaining instead that "for several years last past" he had printed in his magazine, amongst other things, "short extracts, parts of books, pamphlets or other writings newly published on various subjects" without any "intent to prejudice the proprietors" of the same. Moreover, Cave asserted that his publishing such extracts "have many times if not mostly been agreeable to the proprietors of the books", adding that "the same hath never been complained of by them as being contrary to the said Act, or detrimental to them". As to the extent of his use of the plaintiff's work, he set out that of a work of around sixty-nine pages, he had only drawn upon thirty, and even then "several pages" were "wholly omitted" as well as "great parts of other pages" so that the material used occupied only three and a half pages of his magazine. Such use he considered was never intended to be prevented by the 1709 Act, as to hold otherwise would be "greatly prejudicial to the spread of knowledge and learning".[149] The Lord Chancellor considered the defendant's demurrer to be insufficient; Cave was given additional time to resubmit his pleadings. Predictably, they were never entered.[150] The only printed report of the case records that Lord Hardwicke rejected Cave's suggestion that the 1709 Act did not extend to the use of extracts from a work, commenting that "[i]t is not material what Title you give a book, nor whether you print all at once or not".[151] Presumably the Lord Chancellor remained unconvinced as to the evidence of Cave's motives and actions; the implication is that he considered that Cave, as the plaintiffs had alleged, was indeed intending to print the entire work, but in stages.[152]

Printing extracts of another's work, whether in isolation or by instalment, presented Lord Hardwicke with one kind of problem concerning the altered text. Printing an abridgement of a work raised an entirely

[147] C 33 371/493.

[148] C 11 1552/3. Cave demurred to so much of the bill as called for details of printing numbers and prices, arguing that so to do would expose him to the penalties in the Act.

[149] C 11 1552/3.

[150] C 33 373/41, 224, 415, 535.

[151] (1740) 2 Eq Ca Abr.

[152] Cave was involved in a similar action in *Cogan v Cave* (28 June 1743) c 33 379/485, 521, 547, 383/69. In this case the plaintiff prayed for an injunction to stay Cave publishing *parts* of Elizabeth Haywood's book, *The Unfortunate Young Nobleman*, in his magazine, which was duly granted until answer. There however the similarity ends as Cave, having entered his answer, petitioned that "the said Injunction may be dissolved" which was ordered "unless the said plaintiff ... shall [within a certain time] shew unto this court good cause to the contrary". Cogan failed to give cause and the injunction was dissolved.

different concern. Despite that Defoe, in 1704, had specifically identified the practice of printing abridged versions of an author's work, as a form of "press-piracy",[153] this issue would not come to the court's attention for nearly four decades. When it did it was, once again, Lord Hardwicke who would first consider the question. Exactly what was the nature of the relationship between an abridged text and the *Statute of Anne*? In *Read v Hodges* (1740)[154] the plaintiff had published a three-volume edition of John Motley's work *The History of the Life of Peter the First Emperor of Russia*. James Hodges, the defendant, then published the work in one volume under the title of *The Life and Reign of the Czar Peter the Great*. This, Read claimed was:

> [R]eally and truely the very same ... and almost wholly taken and copied therefrom and consists of the same paragraphs and almost of the same words and if the same doth in some particular places vary in some few words from Your Orator's said book such variations were only craftily made and contrived merely to deceive Your Orator but the same does not materially differ from Your Orator's said book except that some of the public memorials and copies of records are left out and omitted ... merely with Intent and Design to reduce the bulk of the said Book so that he might be able to sell the same at an under rate and cheaper than Your Orator could afford to sell his ... [155]

The court granted Read an injunction until answer, which was submitted on 29 April 1740. Hodges mounted three main rebuttals. First, he disputed that the plaintiffs had been to "very great expence, industry and pains" in preparing the book, given that a:

> [G]reat Part of the book is transcribed from and composed of several Publick tracts, memorials and translations of papers ... and particularly that no less than 108 pages [of Vol.3] are transcribed and with little or no variation of phrase from a book entitled *The Present State of Russia* (1722).

He then asserted that he himself had "compiled, printed and published an Abridgement" of their work, in which "there is not one whole page of the complainants said book transcribed into this defendants book without variation or abridging the same". His volume, he pointed out, was designed "for the entertainment of more ordinary and mean readers". Finally, Hodges argued that, in any case, his text was not the same work

[153] D Defoe, "An Essay on the Regulation of the Press", reprinted by the Luttrell Society (Oxford, Blackwell, 1958) 25–27.
[154] *Read v Hodges* (19 May 1740) c 11 538/36; c 33 374/153, 250, 255, 275, 299.
[155] C 11 538/36.

"but is of a different nature, and humbly insists that it is in the nature of an abridgment". He conceded that the two works must of course consist "of the same matter and substance" but continued that this "must be in the nature of things were an abridgment is fairly made."[156] Having concluded, the defendant asked that the injunction previously granted be dissolved.[157] The plaintiff questioned the adequacy of the defendant's answer, which matter was referred to Mr Sawyer, a Master of the Court, who, on 19 May, reported that the answer was sufficient, and the injunction was duly dissolved. On the same day, and following Sawyer's report, Lord Hardwicke heard submissions from both parties, and Read petitioned that the injunction may be revived. The Lord Chancellor granted his request "until the hearing of the case".[158]

When this action was cited to Lord Hardwicke in the later case of *Tonson v Walker* (1752) he is reported to have commented that he had considered Hodges' publication "an evasive abridgment", and so had allowed the reinstatement of the injunction until the hearing.[159] However, speaking in *Gyles v Wilcox* (1741),[160] less than a year after *Read* itself, he pointed out that the earlier decision had been "upon a motion only, and at the time I gave my thoughts without much consideration (and therefore shall not lay any great weight upon it)".[161] In *Gyles* itself, the plaintiffs complained about an abridgement of Sir Matthew Hale's *Pleas of the Crown*, in which they alleged the defendants, Wilcox and Barlow, had transcribed "the said Treatise or the greatest part thereof in the very words thereof" into a Book under the title of a *Treatise of Modern Crown Law*. Counsel for Wilcox denied that the second work had been transcribed from the former in the straightforward manner in which the plaintiffs suggested. Rather he set out that "severall intire chapters" of the original work had been deliberately omitted, while "several chapters of different Material not to be found" in the original had been included within the defendants' book. He continued that many "very valuable and learned" works which:

> [H]ave been published since the [1709 Act] have been abridged and translated by others without the consent of the authors or proprietors of the original

[156] *Ibid.*
[157] C 33 374/255.
[158] C 33 374/275, 299.
[159] (1752) 3 Swans 672, 679.
[160] *Gyles v Wilcox* (13 March 1741) c 33 375/274; 2 Atk 141; Barn C 368; 3 Atk 269.
[161] (1741) 2 Atk 142. In an alternative report of *Gyles* (Barn C 368) Lord Hardwicke is reported as commenting that, in *Read*, "the second Book that was published no otherwise varied from the first, than by leaving out certain parts of the former, and only by that Means shortening it, and the Court was of Opinion, that an Injunction ought to have been granted to restrain the printing of that second Book."

> works and he the defendant never understood that such abridgements or translations were within the words or meaning of the act or were adjudged or constrained so to be ... [162]

Two printed reports of this stage of the proceedings make interesting reading. Barnardiston records that the Lord Chancellor began by noting that the *Statute of Anne* was:

> [A]n Act made for the Encouragement of Learning, and is useful to that End. This shews that the Act is for the public Benefit and Advantage, and therefore the Act is not to be construed strictly, but according to the intention of the Legislature.

Considering the words of the statute, "any such Book or Books", he proffered that the relevant question has and should always be "[w]hether the second book has always been the same Book with the former". "Whether the second Book is the same as the former", Lord Hardwicke continued, "is a Matter of Fact, and a Fact of difficulty to be determined". Referring that task to a Master of the Court, assisted by "two Persons skilled in the Profession of Law",[163] he continued the injunction in the interim. Thereafter, it was decided that the second work was indeed a fair abridgement and so not within the statute; the injunction was dissolved. In the second of these reports, by Atkyns, the Lord Chancellor's reading of the 1709 Act is presented somewhat differently. He records that Lord Hardwicke considered:

> [T]hat it ought to receive a liberal construction ... as it is intended to secure the property of books in the authors themselves, or the purchasers of the copy, as some recompense for their pains and labour in such works as may be of use to the learned world.[164]

The Lord Chancellor's attitude to the decision in *Read* is recorded in more ambivalent terms. Atkyns relates that the judge perceived a problem in applying the decision in *Read* to all those cases involving abridgements; should he "extend the rule so far as to restrain all abridgements it would be of mischievous consequence". Again, the question for the Lord Chancellor was whether or not the two books were the same, for "where the second book has been an abridgement it has been understood not to be the same book, and therefore to be out of the Act". In this version of

[162] C 33 375/274.
[163] A Mr Cay and Mr Stephens.
[164] (1741) 3 Atk 269.

the case, Lord Hardwicke laid down several guidelines for dealing with situations of this kind:

> Where books are colourably shortened only, they are undoubtedly within the meaning of the Act of Parliament and a mere evasion of the statute, and cannot be called an abridgement.... But this must not be carried so far as to restrain persons from making a real and fair abridgement, for abridgements may with great propriety be called a new book, because, not only the paper and print, but the invention, learning and judgment of the author is shewn in them, and in many cases are extremely useful...[165]

Whichever reporter has provided us with the more accurate account, both reveal a Lord Chancellor who was well aware of the central focus of the *Statute of Anne*. As was the case in *Pope v Curl* (1741), Lord Hardwicke once again was confronted with an issue not contemplated by the drafters of the 1709 Act. If someone published merely part of an author's work, or published an abridged version of that work, was he acting in contravention of the legislation? The *Statute of Anne* proffered no guidance. Campbell, in his examination of Lord Hardwicke, portrays him as a judge "with a reputation which no one presiding in the Court of Chancery has ever enjoyed", the wisdom of whose decrees "was the theme of universal eulogy".[166] He continues that the Lord Chancellor "was anxious to bring every case within the scope of some general principle which he enunciated and defined".[167] Describing Lord Hardwicke's judicial approach while presiding over the Court of Chancery, Campbell writes that:

> [H]e reviewed all the authorities upon the subject, and, if none of them were expressly in point, he tried to educe from them by analogy a rule which harmonised with them in principle, and which might equally govern all cases similarly circumstanced.[168]

Such assessment certainly rings true when considering the judge's attempts to reconcile the problems raised by *Read* (1740) and *Gyles* (1741)

[165] (1741) 2 Atk 141, 143. Campbell's record of the Lord Chancellor's opinion accords most closely with Atkyns. He relates Lord Hardwicke's address in the following terms:

> When books are only colourably shortened, the statute is evaded, and the law will give redress. But this must not be carried so far as to restrain persons from making a real and fair abridgment. An abridgment may, with great propriety, be called a new book. Not only are the paper and printing the abridger's, but in his task he may show invention, learning, and judgment. In many cases, abridgments are extremely useful, though sometimes they are prejudicial, by curtailing and mistaking the sense of the author.

Campbell, *Lives of the Lord Chancellors*, n 112 above, vol VI, 202–3.
[166] *Ibid*, 197.
[167] *Ibid*, 196.
[168] *Ibid*.

with the central principle of the *Statute of Anne*. While that statute said nothing specifically about this issue, Lord Hardwicke contended that it was to be construed "liberally" and "according to the intention of the Legislature". The 1709 Act was predicated primarily upon a social bargain struck between the author, the bookseller and the reading public, in order to promote the continued production of useful books. It was this appreciation that informed the policy the Lord Chancellor adopted in relation to abridged texts. A balance had to be struck between protecting the author, who as a result of his own labour had produced something "of use to the learned world", and the genuine abridger, who through his own "invention, learning, and judgment" very often produced a work that was similarly "extremely useful". In striking this balance, informed by this central tenet of the *Statute of Anne*, the evasive abridger could be caught out, while the reading public would remain the principal beneficiaries.

The approach that Lord Hardwicke adopted in resolving various of the issues left in doubt by the legislation, proved both insightful and well-intentioned, guided as it was by the central principle underpinning the legislation itself. Unfortunately, Lord Hardwicke was given little opportunity to expand upon and develop his reasoning in this area for, although he held the office of Lord Chancellor until November 1756, apart from those cases which have already been touched upon earlier in this chapter, he would only be called upon to make one final determination involving the 1709 Act. This was not until *Tonson v Walker* (1752), which eventually took shape as a determination on an abridgement of the plaintiff's work.[169] Just as the Lord Chancellor was beginning to deliver judgments of such discerning quality, the attention of the London booksellers shifted from the metropolis and the Court of Chancery, to the activities of those booksellers operating north of border, to the Scottish Court of Session, and ultimately to the English common law courts. Moreover, the London booksellers began to apply themselves to a more fundamental issue, which ran to the very core of the *Statute of Anne*.

[169] See further, ch5(2) The Lawyers' Tales.

4

Be Careful what You Wish for

SAMUEL BUCKLEY

THE *STATUTE OF Anne* had provided that nothing contained therein was to prevent the importation of "any Books in Greek, Latin or any other foreign Language printed beyond the Seas".[1] Foreign language texts could not be reprinted in Great Britain, but they could be freely imported and sold without redress. One consequence of this provision was that, very often, authors and publishers would instead seek a royal privilege to protect their works and prevent others importing them.[2] An alternative strategy was that evidenced by Samuel Buckley. On 18 February 1734 Buckley petitioned, not the monarch, but the House of Commons to provide adequate protection for his edition of the Latin work *Thuanus' Histories*, seeking "such Privilege ... as is already granted to every British subject who is possessed of the Copy of any Book in English". In doing so he drew parallels between the protection granted foreign language works in France and Holland and the protection, or lack thereof, provided in England.[3] In Holland, it was commonplace for the Emperor to grant exclusive privileges to reprint works "published in the neighbouring Nations, in the learned Languages, or in French the common Language almost of Europe". Similarly, the French system of privileges allowed for importing any foreign impressions.[4] Having highlighted this divergence in national approach, Buckley continued with the appeal that the legislature:

> [T]reat a Native subject with the same Indulgence as all the neighbouring Governments do theirs, namely, by granting him an exclusive Privilege for Fourteen Years, for a Book that shall be compiled and published here in the

[1] 1709 Act, s 7.
[2] S Rogers, "The Use of Royal Licences for Printing in England, 1695–1760: A Bibliography" I (2000) *The Library* 133.
[3] S Buckley, "A Short State of the Publick Encouragement given to Printing and Bookselleing in France, Holland, Germany, and at London" in S Parks (ed), *English Publishing, the Struggle for Copyright, and the Freedom of the Press: Thirteen Tracts, 1666–1774* (New York, NY, Garland, 1975).
[4] For discussion of the French book trade in the eighteenth century see C Hesse, *Publishing and Cultural Politics in Revolutionary France* (Berkeley, CA, University of California Press,

> Greek, Latin, or any other foreign Language: That the Man may not, after an Expense of much Money and many Years Application and Study, be liable to lose the Profits he might justly promise to himself and Family from his Labours, and to have only the Honour at last of having made a very good Copy for a Dutch Bookseller to raise a Fortune by, Tax-free, quickly and surely, at no more Trouble than that of reprinting it.[5]

Buckley's plea did not fall upon deaf ears. Observing that he, "at a very great expence, by his own industry, and with the assistance of divers learned persons in the course of several years", had made "great additions and improvements" to the *Histories,* and noting that "the proviso [in the 1709 Act] was not intended for the advantage of foreigners in prejudice to the natives of this Kingdom", parliament granted him the sole right of printing his work for 14 years. This, the legislation explained, was to ensure:

> [T]hat he may not lose the fruit of his Expence and Labour by the Avarice of Foreign Printers, or suffer by an Act made for the Encouragement of Learning.[6]

Despite that this was an individual petition with an individual solution, Buckley had brought to parliament's attention the differential treatment that authors received in Britain as compared with their European counterparts, and the impact this had upon the English book trade. These issues were to provide a significant focus for legislative consideration throughout the next five years.

THE ENGRAVERS

A year later, in 1735, two further petitions were received in the Commons; the first on 7 February, the second on 3 March. The latter came from the booksellers. The former, *The Case of Designers, Engravers, Etchers &c. stated In a Letter to a member of Parliament,*[7] was submitted by a disparate group of seven artists: William Hogarth, George Vertue, George Lambert, Isaac Ware, John Pine, Gerrard Vandergucht and John Goupy.[8]

1991) and RL Dawson, *The French Booktrade and the "Permission Simple" of 1777: Copyright and Public Domain* (Oxford, The Voltaire Foundation, 1992).

[5] Buckley, "A Short State of the Publick Encouragement given to Printing and Bookselleing", n 3 above.
[6] *An Act for granting to Samuel Buckley, Citizen and Stationer of London, the sole Liberty of Printing and Reprinting the Histories of Thuanus, with Additions and Improvements, during the Time therein limited,* 7 Geo II, c 24.
[7] Lincoln's Inn Library, MP 102, Fol 125.
[8] CJ 22:364.

Hogarth, Lambert, Ware and Pine regularly met with other artists at Old Slaughter's Coffee House, in St Martin's Lane. Of these four, Hogarth and Lambert shared the closest relationship, having previously been involved in the founding of the gregarious *Sublime Society of Beefsteaks*. Vertue and Goupy generally moved in a different social set, the "Clubb of St Luke", based at the King's Arms, New Bond Street; Vertue described the St Luke Club as "the tip top Clubb of all, for men of the highest Character in Arts & Gentlemen Lovers of Art".[9] Of the seventh petitioner, Vandergucht, David Hunter notes that he was not known to have belonged to either group "though Vertue had worked for seven years with his father Michael".[10] Although Hunter suggests Vertue played a more significant role in the engravers' campaign than has traditionally been acknowledged,[11] Paulson nevertheless maintains that it was the Slaughter's group that acted as the "nucleus for the campaign", for which William Huggins, also a member of the *Beefsteaks*, provided the legal advice.[12]

Whether or not it was Hogarth and his group that provided the central driving force behind the engravers' petition,[13] the spur for their action did lie in Hogarth's experiences in marketing and selling his own work, rather than relying upon the existing trade structures of the London printsellers. Hogarth laid the groundwork for the passing of the *Engravers Act* when he himself published and distributed *A Harlot's Progress* in 1731–32. Working on a subscription basis, which subscriptions were taken only in his shop, he was able to guarantee a minimum return on this series of prints before he had even begun to engrave them. By April 1732, when the subscription came to an end, Hogarth had brought in over £1200 for this first independent series, and had done so in a way as to exclude the printseller from the entire business.[14] Not long after the series first appeared however, there were "no less than eight piratical imitations".[15] The printsellers had responded by making their own copies and undercutting Hogarth. As Paulson recounts, the next step for the engraver-entrepreneur, was to "secure my Property to myself".[16]

[9] Quoted in R Paulson, *Hogarth: His Life, Art, and Times* (New Haven, CT, Yale University Press, 1971) vol I, 347.

[10] D Hunter, "Copyright Protection for Engravings and Maps in Eighteenth-Century Britain" (1987) 9 *The Library* 128, 130.

[11] *Ibid.*

[12] Paulson, *Hogarth*, n 9 above, 359.

[13] There is a copy of the petition in the Victoria and Albert Museum which has a hand-written inscription claiming: "Hogarth got this drawn up"; R Paulson, *Hogarth's Graphic Works* (New Haven, Yale University Press, 1965) vol 1, 5. n 7.

[14] *Ibid*, 6–8.

[15] J Nichols, *Biographical Anecdotes of William Hogarth*, 2nd edn (London, 1782) 33, referred to in Hunter, "Copyright Protection for Engravings and Maps", n 10 above, 131.

[16] Paulson, *Hogarth's Graphic Works*, n 13 above, vol 1, 8.

Unlike the *Statute of Anne*, in which the booksellers had co-opted the authorial figure to secure and promote the economic interests of the book trade, now it was the artists themselves, these authors of engravings, who directly petitioned parliament for protection on their own terms. Moreover, unlike the situation in 1709, when the established booksellers sought to curb the excesses of those pirates who operated on the fringes of the trade, now it was the actions of the established print dealers that provided the engravers with the greatest cause for complaint. The artists set out in their petition that they were "opress'd by the tyranny of the Rich ... the Rich of that very trade which could not subsist without them": the printsellers. Not only did the printsellers "insist upon a most unreasonable share of the Profits for selling the Prints", but further, if a print proved successful, copies of it were made and sold in place of the engravers' originals. As well as impacting unfairly upon the individual artists, the tyranny of these existing trade practices had also operated to sink "the Arts themselves into the low Condition which they are at present in". To remedy this situation, the engravers' petition proposed that an Act "make it punishable ... for any one to copy the Designs of Another" which would secure "to every one the Fruits of his own Labour" and provide "the greatest and noblest Encouragement, that any Art can possibly receive". Securing such legislative protection would also enhance both the quality and quantity of these visual arts, as well as encouraging more "young Men of Taste and Genius ... to indulge their Love of Designing"; as a result, the purchaser would have "a greater variety of Prints to chuse out of". Further still, they contended, as designing was "the Foundation of Painting, Sculpture, Architecture" as well as "all the Train of inferior Arts", an improvement in the quality of designing and engraving would do nothing if not transform the nation's artistic and cultural canvas.[17]

Between identifying their problem and presenting this panacea, the petitioners proffered some justification as to why an engraver should be entitled to profit from his designs and prints at all. It was the work of the artist, they propounded, which gave a print "whatever Value it has above another common Piece of Paper". This value lay not in the physical page, but in the application of the artist's industry and skill in capturing a given subject upon that page. Thus, when someone simply took a direct copy of another's work, he did so "mechanically", with "absolutely no Skill in Designing requir'd." Moreover, they explained, when the copier did so:

> He does not indeed steal the very Paper, (which if he did, tho' it is not of near so great a Value, he knows he should suffer for it) but he steals from

[17] *The Case of Designers, Engravers, Etchers & c stated In a Letter to a Member of Parliament*, Lincoln's Inn Library, MP 102, Fol 125.

> him every Thing that made the Paper valuable, and reaps an advantage which he has no more right to, than He, who counterfeits a Note of Hand, has to the Money he receives by it.[18]

Central to their thesis, however, lay the significant concession that "[e]very one has undoubtedly an equal Right to every Subject". These artists were seeking to prevent the copying of their work, their prints, but not to prevent others making prints of their own, albeit of the same subject. Indeed, they submitted that anyone "who attempts a Subject already executed" without directly copying another's work, had "undoubtedly the same Rights to the Fruits of his Skill, that the first had".[19] Anticipating possible objections, they posed the following question: if every subject was free to be treated by every man, would this not give rise to numerous "frivolous and vexatious Law-suits", given that one engraver may claim that another has simply copied his work? To this they provided an answer that foreshadowed the emergence of the now commonplace dichotomy between the idea and the expression of an idea. The petitioners asserted that two different artists taking the same subject would produce two different works wherein the manner, shape and distances (that is, the form or the style in which each was rendered) would vary so greatly as to easily denote each work as original. It was self-evident to the engravers that one person's design would be just as unique and original as his handwriting, which likewise depended upon "the Manner, Distances and Shape of the Strokes which compose the Letters".[20]

Having laid the petition before the house it was ordered that it be referred to the consideration of a committee who were to provide their opinion upon the same.[21] On 14 February 1735 they reported that the petitioners had fully proved their allegations, and leave was given to bring in a *Bill for the Encouragement of the Arts of designing, engraving and etching, historical and other Prints, by vesting the Properties thereof in the Inventors and Engravers, during the Time therein to be mentioned*.[22] The Bill received its first reading on 4 March, was amended in committee, at the report stage, and upon its third reading, and then passed through the Lords unchanged.[23] The Act came into force on 25 June 1735, upon which day Hogarth issued his second major series: *A Rake's Progress*. By all accounts, the legislation proved remarkably effective. Of Hogarth's subsequent work, Paulson notes that "[a]side from a few Dublin piracies,

[18] *Ibid.*
[19] *Ibid.*
[20] *Ibid.*
[21] CJ 22:364.
[22] CJ 22:380–81.
[23] CJ 22:401, 414, 436, 442, 457; LJ 24:516, 517, 528, 530.

unauthorised copies ... virtually disappeared until the 1750s when the copyrights began to expire".[24]

Much of this *Engravers Act* derived from the *Statute of Anne*. While the artists' petition had made no explicit reference to the 1709 Act, the Journal of the Commons recounts that leave was sought to bring a Bill into the house to secure "the Properties of the Petitioners, as the Laws now in being have preserved the Properties of the Authors of Books".[25] The Act provided "every Person who shall invent and design, engrave, etch, or work in Mezzotinto or Chiaro Oscuro", with the "sole right and liberty of printing and reprinting" their work, "for the term of fourteen years to commence from the day of first publishing thereof". The first section replicated the terms of the earlier legislation, in that anyone who copied, printed, reprinted, sold or imported for sale, another's work would be subject to the various penalties detailed therein.[26] There were, however, two significant variations between both statutes in this regard. In the first place, the nature of the engravers' reproduction right was more extensive than its predecessor. The statutory prohibition was extended to prevent copying a work "in the whole or in part, by varying, adding to or diminishing from the main Design". This aspect of the Act was no doubt incorporated following the warning in the artists' petition that:

> It will be a very trifling evasion of the law to plead that one cannot be a copy of another, because there is a figure more or less in it, than in the original, when all the others can evidently be shown to be taken from it; and it is hoped, that by the wording of the Act, all such wicked attempts to render the design of it useless will be entirely prevented.[27]

Second, the new Act made clear, albeit implicitly, that it was only such work as was original to an engraver that would be protected. During the third reading of the Bill in the Commons, a proviso was inserted for the benefit of the engraver, John Pine. Pine had proposed to engrave a set of prints "copied from several Pieces of Tapestry in the House of Lords and His Majesty's Wardrobe" relating to the Spanish Invasion of 1588. The proviso ensured that Pine would be entitled to the benefit of the Act "in the same manner as if the said John Pine had been the Inventor and

[24] Paulson, *Hogarth's Graphic Works*, n 13 above, vol 1, 9.

[25] CJ 22:364.

[26] S 1. As there existed no artistic equivalent of the Stationers' Company there was no existing trade to support and regulate the registration of works. Instead, during the Bill's passage through the Commons, s 1 was amended to require that the name of the proprietor of every print be engraved upon every plate, and so reproduced upon every published print. This would ensure that no one would "through ignorance" fall foul of the penalties detailed within the statute.

[27] *The Case of Designers, Engravers, Etchers & c stated In a Letter to a Member of Parliament.*

Designer of the said Prints".[28] The need for providing explicit protection for Pine's suggested work, colours the way in which we must read the first section. It had set out that anyone who should "invent *and* design, engrave, etch [etc.]" work would receive the benefit of the legislation. Reading both sections together makes it clear that only those prints that were not copied from some other source were to be protected, Pine's work providing the only exception.[29]

The statute also contained a provision peculiar to the art of engraving. It was made explicit that anyone purchasing the engraved plates "from the original Proprietors thereof" was free to print and reprint from them without incurring the penalties detailed in the Act.[30] Just as the engravers themselves had drawn attention to the distinction between the physical page or print, and that which made it valuable, the image, here the legislature tried to account for, and give recognition to, the convergence of two types of property in the one form. To purchase the physical plates would have been of little value to a printseller were it not also clear that they were free to reproduce the engraved image itself. In a way that the *Statute of Anne* did not, here the legislators gave express statutory recognition to the difference between the physical and the non-physical, the tangible and the intangible. The purchaser of the engraved plates was buying two disparate but linked properties: the physical plates and the right to reprint and sell the image captured thereupon. While the influence of the previous legislation was apparent,[31] the engravers' petition and the Act that followed evidenced something new, a departure from what had gone before. The 1709 Act had secured the protection of printed books; it guaranteed the right to reproduce a given physical work. Now however, within this exchange between artist and legislature, there emerged a subtle shift away from the physical, the tangible. With this debate, and its resolution, it was accepted that the value of a print lies not in the print itself, not in the paper, but in the design. Moreover, while the subject matter of any number of prints may remain the same, it was the individual expression of that subject that set one artist's work apart from another's. It was in the expression of the given subject that the value of the work lay, an image that was entirely individual and readily

[28] S 5.

[29] Various provisions in the second *Engravers' Act* 1767, 7 Geo III, c 38, also indicate that this reading is the correct one to adopt. This later statute specifically provided that the benefit of the earlier *Engravers' Act* 1735 be extended to any person engraving a work "taken from any picture, drawing, model or sculpture, either ancient or modern", the implication being that engravers who worked as mere copyists, prior to 1767, were not extended any legislative protection for the works they produced For an examination of the cumulative effect of the two Acts see *Newton v Cowie* (1827) 4 Bing 234.

[30] S 2.

[31] *Engravers' Act* 1735, ss 1, 3, and 4.

identifiable, as unique as any person's handwriting. With the passing of the *Engravers Act* a silent revolution had taken place. In this legislation, copyright, as we understand and appreciate it today, first began to take embryonic form.

THE BOOKSELLERS

On 3 March 1735, the day before the *Engravers Act* received its first reading in the Commons, the house received a *Humble Petition of Several Proprietors of Copies of Books* praying for an Act to render more effectual the 1709 Act.[32] The main concern of the petitioners were the activities of the pirates not just at home, but also those "in foreign parts" who were reproducing the booksellers' works having paid "no consideration for the CopyRight in such Books". Also, paper could be purchased abroad "for half the expence that it can be furnished and provided in England", with the result that "the persons concerned in such foreign and surreptitious impressions" were making "an exhorbitant profit to themselves". This, they continued, tended "to the diminution of His Majesty's Revenue, the discouragement of the art of Printing and the Trade and Manufacture of this Kingdom".[33] In the sixteenth and seventeenth century the booksellers had aligned themselves with a monarchy desirous of regulating the printed word. In return for the sovereign's protection, they compacted to police the content of public literature. In the early part of the eighteenth century, the booksellers presented the author as public benefactor and private beneficiary to secure the *Statute of Anne*. Now, a third bargain was being offered to the government of the day. Buckley had generated a parliamentary awareness of issues concerning European trade and national revenues, and the booksellers, in the wake of the artist's petition, adopted his rhetoric. Now their tactic lay in emphasising economic reward for both their industry and the state. In return for renewed legislative protection, they promised an improved marketplace, increased manufacture, and additional revenues for the public purse.[34]

[32] CJ 22:400. What influence the engravers' petition had over the timing of the booksellers petition can only ever be speculative. However, for an exploration of some of the links that existed between the print trade and the book trade in general, see M Harris, "Scratching the Surface: Engravers, Printsellers and the London Book Trade in the Mid-18th Century" in A Hunt, G Mandelbrote and A Shell (eds), *The Book Trade and its Customers, 1450–1900* (Winchester, St Paul's Bibliographies, 1990) 95.

[33] BM 357 c 2 (80).

[34] Many of these arguments relating to national industry and trade were subsequently rehearsed in a number of the tracts produced by the booksellers during this period. See for example *Farther Reasons Humbly Offer'd to the Consideration of the Honourable House of Commons, for making more effectual an Act passed in the 8th Year of Q Anne*, BM 816 m 12 (51).

The petition was referred to the consideration of a committee that reported to the house on 12 March.[35] The booksellers' representations as to how the "good intentions" of the *Statute of Anne* had been "frustrated and evaded" took a number of forms. The first witness was Robert Aynsworth who had spent 20 years compiling a Latin and English dictionary; any profit that was to be made from the sale of such a worthy work would only come with the production of a second edition; this, he explained, would not happen for "some considerable time". John Knapton, Charles Rivington and John Basket next recounted how a number of the works they had published had subsequently been printed in Ireland and imported for sale in Great Britain.[36] Evidence was similarly provided concerning a number of works that had been imported from Holland.[37] It was highlighted that the duty payable on printed books imported from Holland was considerably less than for paper. Moreover, the price of paper in Ireland and Holland was considerably cheaper than in Great Britain. To conclude, they ended with a personal appeal, along the same lines as that of Samuel Buckley a year previously, from the Reverend Doctor Mangey. He explained that he was about to publish a work in Greek and Latin, *Philo Judeus*, which he had been to great expense in compiling. This, he feared, would soon afterwards "be reprinted in Holland, and imported and sold here, near One-third Part cheaper than what the original Impression can possibly be sold for". The committee was convinced, and it was ordered that leave be given to bring in a Bill.[38]

The *Bill for the better Encouragement of Learning, and for the more effectual securing the Copies of Printed Books to the Authors or Purchasers of such Copies, during the Times therein mentioned* was read for the first and second time on 26 and 31 March 1735 and then committed to the whole house. It was amended in committee, at the report stage, and again upon its third reading, before being sent up to the House of Lords on 6 May, where the second reading was delayed until parliament was prorogued.[39] This Bill, the first to refer to the "Copy:Right" in a book, proved to be something of a revised, updated and expanded version of the *Statute of Anne*.

[35] CJ 22:400, 411. For a handwritten copy of the original committee report see BM 357 c 2 (73).
[36] These works included: Dr S Clarke, *Sermons*; Miller, *The Gardener's Dictionary*; Delany, *Revelation Examined with Candour*; Lord Clarendon, *History of the Rebellion*; and Bishop Burnett, *History of His Own Time*.
[37] Various works by the Earl of Shaftesbury, the Duke of Buckingshamhire, the Duke of Normandy and Bishop Burnet.
[38] CJ 22:411.
[39] CJ 22:431, 438, 451, 460, 470, 475, 480, 482; LJ 24:543, 544, 548, 550. There exist two copies of this *Bill for the better Encouragement of Learning*. The first details the Bill as it was prior to its third reading in the Commons; Bodleian Library, MS Carte 114, 391. The second is a handwritten copy of the engrossed Bill as it was sent up to the Lords; see The Manuscripts of the House of Lords. In practice, there is very little difference between the two.

A number of booksellers' pamphlets had made clear that the 1709 Act was inadequate in many respects: the fourteen year protection needed to be increased; the three month time limit for prosecution was too short; the process for acting against infringers proved too hazardous and costly; the penalties provided were inadequate.[40] The new Bill would address all these defects. It began with a preamble that emphasised the "great Injury and Distress" suffered by the nation's authors, the securing of their property, the diminution of "his Majesty's Revenue" and the "Discouragement of the Trade and Manufacture of the Kingdom". This was lifted almost word for word from the booksellers' initial petition of 3 March. The protection granted to the authors and proprietors of books was revised. Any author who had not already transferred "to any other the whole Interest and Property in the Copy" of any printed work, was to have the right to print and reprint the same for a further period of seven years. The author of any work not yet printed, or even composed, would receive a twenty-one year protection for his work upon first publication.[41] Not only was it an offence to print and publish protected

[40] *The Case of Authors and Proprietors of Books*, BM 816 m 12 (54); *A Letter from an Author to a Member of Parliament occasioned by a Late Letter concerning the Bill now depending in the House of Commons*, Bodleian, MS Carte 207, 16. A number of other tracts were produced during this period: *A Letter to a Member of Parliament concerning the Bill now depending in the House of Commons*, Bodleian, MS Carte 207, 9; *A Second Letter from an Author to a Member of Parliament containing some Further Remarks on a Late Letter concerning the Bill now depending in the House of Commons*, Bodleian, MS Carte 207, 19; *Farther Reasons Humbly Offer'd to the Consideration of the Honourable House of Commons, for making more effectual an Act passed in the 8th Year of Q Anne*, BM 816. m. 12. (51); *Reasons for renewing the privilege of the term of 21 years in old copies; Reasons for granting authors a Privilege for 21 years rather than for 14; Some Reasons Humbly Offered to the Parliament of Great Britain for Making more effectual an Act made 8 Ann cap 49*, BM 18th century reel 3019/24, Bodleian library, M.S. Carte 207, 4.

[41] There is evidence that this was originally only a 15 year protection; below n 53. The arguments presented before the Commons by the booksellers, for altering the term of protection in this manner, were recorded at the time by Thomas Carte, who Feather describes as "a non-juring antiquary who had himself been a victim of the Irish pirates"; J Feather, *Publishing, Piracy and Politics: An Historical Study of Copyright in Britain* (London, Mansell, 1994) 74. Always careful to couch their rhetoric in the terms most beneficial to the author, the booksellers suggested that a simple twenty-one year term was more appropriate than the "precarious reversionary grant for a second term of fourteen years" as the author could command a higher price for his copy. Moreover they recounted that: the work of the author was more deserving than "the most Ordinary discoveries in any art or manufacture" as these may be discovered with "little or no experience"; the expense, labour and time invested in a "polite education" and then in "compiling an useful book" was, by contrast, a much greater endeavour, requiring a longer term of protection to ensure some reasonable profit; many works, such as Sir Walter Raleigh's *History of the World* and John Milton's *Poetical Works*, failed to achieve the recognition (and so recompense) which they deserved, until long after the expiration of the first fourteen years; a longer time to recover the costs of publishing allowed for greater print runs and so lower prices; and finally, the English nation's "great reputation for learning abroad" had in the last forty years gone into decline due to the work of the pirate booksellers, a trend which could only be reversed by ensuring this more secure property in books. See *Reasons for granting authors a Privilege for 21 years rather than for 14* Bodleian Library, M.S. Carte 207, 4.

books, but the pirate would now also be liable for publishing such works "in parcels at different times and by different publications". Where work was reprinted without authorisation the aggrieved party was to have twelve months to bring it to court. The recoverable penalties were also altered, removing the requirement that half of the money recovered be paid over to the crown, and providing that, should a plaintiff succeed, he would also be paid his costs as well as "all the Profits arising by and from the sale" of the infringing work.[42]

Alterations to the import provisions and the library deposit requirements saw parliament strive to strike a new balance between the promotion of trade and national commerce on the one hand and the encouragement of the dissemination of, and access to, learned works on the other. The issue of importing works was, unlike the 1709 Act, made the subject of a separate clause. Rather than forfeit the works and pay a penny for every infringing article, those who imported works contrary to the Bill would still forfeit the work, but now pay the much heftier penalty of twenty shillings for every work so imported. In contrast to the first clause of this Bill, wherein the litigant was to receive the benefit of the penalties provided by the Bill in full, now one half of the penalty for illegal importation was to go to the crown.[43] Parliament was clearly alive to the point that had been made about the loss of potential revenue as a result of the overseas book trade. In addition, the plea of Mangey was not ignored. The *Statute of Anne's* exemption for importing books "in Greek, Latin or any other foreign Language printed beyond the Seas"[44] was altered to cover only those books "originally composed, written and printed" abroad. Moreover, should "any new Edition of any Book in the said Learned or Foreign Languages" be first published in Great Britain, it too would receive the same protection as "any English Book or Books originally printed in this Kingdom".[45] No longer would men like

[42]Clauses 1, 10. There were a number of other minor amendments made to provisions from the 1709 Act: now when a book was registered the proprietor was required to state the exact nature of his share in the work, but was no longer required to register that "consent to print" had been granted (clause 3); the list of notaries able to enquire into the price of books was expanded to include the Speaker of the House of Commons, the Master of the Rolls, the Chancellors of the Universities, the Presidents of Sion College and of the College of Physicians, the Dean of the Arches and the Dean of the Faculty of Advocates; further, they were to be able to act upon their own initiative rather than waiting to receive a complaint to the same end (clause 5); the proviso for the Universities remained unchanged except for including the four Universities in Scotland (clause 15).

[43]Clause 2.

[44]S 7.

[45]Clause 2. Note that this clause speaks of the prohibiting various acts "during the *Continuance of the Property herein granted* to the original Author thereof ... under the same Penalties and Forfeitures to be had, sued for and recovered, in the same Manner ... as are herein before declared concerning the importing, vending and selling in this Kingdom, of any English Book or Books".

Buckley and Mangey be disadvantaged or "suffer by an Act made for the Encouragement of Learning".[46]

While this represented an encroachment upon the earlier settlement within the 1709 Act designed to improve the circulation of such foreign language and learned texts, a counterbalance was provided in the guise of a more robust system of library deposit. The Company of Stationers was now to take delivery of 14 copies of each new book printed, with the additional copies to go to the libraries of the Inner and the Middle Temple, Lincoln's Inn, Gray's Inn, and also to the Advocates in Doctor's-Commons. More significantly, these works were to be delivered whether the book was registered or not, failure of which no longer incurred a financial penalty, but resulted in the forfeiture of "all privilege and benefit given and intended to be secured ... by this or any other Act of Parliament".[47] The 1711 Act had set out certain conditions under which the protections of the *Statute of Anne* were to be enjoyed, or conversely removed: unless the relevant duties were paid upon pamphlets and newspapers, they were not to be regarded as copyright protected.[48] Now, without deposit, there was to be no property. It was almost as if the legislators had finally decided to act upon the suggestions of John Locke from forty years before.[49]

This willingness to circumscribe what protections and controls the legislature provided authors and booksellers was also evident in two of the three clauses within the Bill that bore no direct relationship with the 1709 Act.[50] The first of these took the unusual departure in letting anyone publish any work that had been allowed, by its proprietor, to become "scarce and out of print".[51] With the existence of the right to print the work free from invasion, there came a concomitant duty to ensure that the work would always publicly available. Should the owner of the work refuse to do so, a system of compulsory licensing was to operate to ensure that no work need ever fall out of print.[52] The second provision no doubt proved equally irksome to the booksellers. Focussing now upon the

[46] Buckley's Act 1734.

[47] Clause 7. Similarly clause 10 also set out that where nine copies "of all such books as have been printed since [the passing of the 1709 Act] or reprinted and published with additions" had not been delivered in accordance with the deposit requirement in the 1709 Act, then such deposits should be made, otherwise the proprietor of the work was to lose the protection of the new legislation.

[48] Ch 2, n 54 and accompanying text.

[49] Ch 1, n 35 and accompanying text.

[50] The third clause extended the protections of the Bill "any book or books of musick or any composition in musick whatsoever whether printed or engraved"; clause 12.

[51] This may well have been included as a result of the warning in *A Letter to a Member of Parliament* that various books "while they are a private Property, may long continue out of Print".

[52] Clause 6.

interests of the consumer, it sought to address the frequent practice among authors and publishers "that as soon as an impression has been sold to publish another edition thereof with some alterations, additions or notes". Should anyone do so within 21 years of the publication of the first work,[53] he was also required to provide a subsequent edition of these revisions for anyone who purchased the first edition at a proportionate cost. Like the deposit provisions, failure to adhere to these statutory requirements was to result in the author or publisher losing "all benefit and advantage" of the Act in relation to that subsequent edition, as well as having to pay the substantial penalty of "£50 to any person who shall sue for the same".[54] As was the case with the *Statute of Anne*, what protection the booksellers were to receive would come at a certain cost. With guaranteed rights, came social obligations. The tensions in marrying the competing interests of the public good and the private individual had resulted in the negotiated instrument that was the *Statute of Anne*; with the 1735 Bill that dynamic became even more exaggerated.

These tensions were similarly apparent in the lobbying that accompanied the progress of the Bill. Unlike the cohesion of the booksellers' print campaign of 1710, dissenting voices were now publicly apparent. With *A Letter to a Member of Parliament* there emerged a pamphleteer prepared to contest the utility of the proposed legislation; what objections the letter writer had, turned upon considerations of the public interest.[55] In relation to the suggestion that a new term of protection be extended to those works published prior to the *Statute of Anne*,[56] the booksellers argued that the 1709 Act had been so ineffective that they had older works remaining unsold, "to the value of Many thousands of Pounds". The legitimate trade had incurred substantial costs in printing these works and would require a further number of years to properly realise the returns upon their investment. In any case, they continued, such a step would do no more than replicate legal practice in Holland where licences were continually renewed as of course; this, it was suggested, had been found "by experience to be of great service for the Encouragement of Learning and the

[53] Note that this was changed from fifteen to twenty-one years after the third reading of the Bill in the Commons. It is most probable then that the first section also originally provided for a fifteen year protection which was changed at the committee stage.
[54] Clause 8.
[55] *A Letter to a Member of Parliament*, Bodleian, MS Carte 207, 9.
[56] In addition to the protections extended to authors, clause 1 provided that any bookseller who had previously purchased any book for publication was to have "the sole Right and Liberty of Printing and Reprinting such Book or Books for the Term of Seven Years, to commence from [24 June 1735], and no longer". This would necessarily have operated to reinstate a statutory protection for those works published prior to the *Statute of Anne*, despite that they had already received the 21 year protection afforded by that Act, which term had now expired.

Improvement of the Manufacture of Printing".[57] The author of *A Letter* responded with the warning that there was no good reason for granting a further term now, that could not similarly be invoked for granting it "again and again, as often as the Old ones Expire" resulting in "a perpetual Monopoly, a Thing deservedly odious in the Eye of the Law". He continued that rather than "having any real Tendency to the promoting of Learning", the Bill would instead "manifestly hinder its spreading in the World", "notoriously invade the natural Rights of Mankind, and subject the Publick to an exorbitant Tax". Drawing a parallel with the protection granted by the state to new inventions, the writer cast the relationship between the author and the public as one of a state sanctioned bargain, the legislature recognising the need to protect an author's work while at the same time judging it reasonable "that some Limitation should be set to that Term" so that the "Publick might have the common benefit of a Work, after they have for several years contributed to the Author's profit".[58]

The discourse generated between these two camps, those lobbying for and against the new legislation, also articulated a question which would occupy the highest courts of the land, both in England and Scotland, the legislature, lawyers, authors, academics and the wider populace, throughout the next 40 years: did there exist a common law property right of printing an author's work which pre-dated the *Statute of Anne*? The booksellers had become more strident in the claims they made as to the existence of a literary property at common law. Authors, they asserted, "have ever had a Property in their Works founded upon the same fundamental maxims by which Property was originally settled, and hath been since maintained."[59] This was the case prior to the invention of printing (which invention simply rendered the property of authors "more easy to be invaded"),[60] through the incorporation of the Company of Stationers, the parliamentary ordinances of 1641 and 1643,[61] the *Licensing Act* 1662 and the *Statute of Anne*, all of which was only ever

[57] *Reasons for renewing the privilege of the term of 21 years in old copies.* Bodleian, M.S. Carte 207, 4.
[58] *A Letter to a Member of Parliament occasioned by a Late Letter concerning the Bill now depending in the House of Commons*, Bodleian, MS Carte 207, 16.
[59] *The Case of Authors and Proprietors of Books*, BM 816 m 12 (54) See also *A Letter from an Author to a Member of Parliament occasioned by a Late Letter concerning the Bill now depending in the House of Commons*, Bodleian, MS Carte 207, 16, which boldly declared that "if there be such a Thing as Property upon Earth, an Author has it in his Work".
[60] *The Case of Authors and Proprietors of Books*, BM 816 m 12 (54).
[61] For more on these see H Ransom, *The First Copyright Statute* (Austin, Texas, University of Texas, 1956) 66–75. See also: LR Patterson, *Copyright in Historical Perspective* (Nashville, Vanderbilt University Press, 1968); M Rose, *Authors and Owners: The Invention of Copyright* (London, Harvard University Press, 1993); J Loewenstein, *The Author's Due: Printing and the Prehistory of Copyright* (London, University of Chicago Press, 2002).

intended as an "Affirmance of the Common Law".[62] Their arguments set out to create a story of property in books that bore a weighty measure of historical continuity. As against this, the one dissenting voice simply declared:

> Before the Act of the 8th of Queen Anne, there was no Law which vested in any one the sole Copy-Right of any Books which were published to the World; but when once a Treatise was made publick, every one was at liberty to make free with it. This to be sure, was a great Discouragement to Authors, who were by this means in great measure deprived of the Profit of their Works; and this was the Grievance which gave Occasion to the making of that Act.[63]

The final answer to the question of the existence of a common law right would have to wait. However, of significance is the fact that the terms and the language of the debate were at least attracting greater clarity than had been evident in 1710. A more subtle understanding as to the very nature of the property under discussion began to emerge. There was now less mention of the book and the copy, and more reference to an author's "Copy-Right", "the sole Copy-Right of any Books", and "such property or Copy-Right" as belonged to an author or bookseller. The precise meaning of such terms was perhaps not yet absolutely clear, yet it began to be realised, albeit imperfectly, that of concern was not the physical book but the author's work that lay therein, his writing, the text. "[T]he Privilege now desired by Authors", wrote one commentator, was "not to lay Restraint, with Regard to a Science in general, but only as to an individual Book, the Property not of a Community, but of a single Man." He continued:

> The Field of Knowledge is large enough for all the world to find ground in it to plant and improve. Let every Body do it; let them be encouraged and protected in so doing; let them write and print on the same Subject: But let them not lazily borrow that individual Work, which is the Produce of another's Labours, to make a Gain to themselves, to a deserving Author's Detriment or Ruin. There must be a fixed Property in this ...[64]

Such rhetoric recalls the earlier petition of the engravers: that even should two artists take the same subject, the work they produced would be as individual to each other as their own handwriting. This parallel,

[62] *A Second Letter from an Author to a Member of Parliament containing some Further Remarks on a Late Letter concerning the Bill now depending in the House of Commons*, Bodleian, MS Carte 207, 19.
[63] *A Letter to a Member of Parliament concerning the Bill now depending in the House of Commons*, Bodleian, MS Carte 207, 9.
[64] *A Letter from an Author to a Member of Parliament occasioned by a Late Letter concerning the Bill now depending in the House of Commons*, Bodleian, MS Carte 207, 16.

however, between the thesis proffered by the engravers and the emerging conception of the property in books was not exact. In the Bill's eighth clause, which imposed the obligation to provide editions of any revisions to a work for the original purchasers of that work, the author (or publisher) was exempt from the legislative requirement wherever the changes to the text arose from either "correcting the common errors of the press, or from a variation of expression only". The first leg of this exception seems eminently practical. The second, with its inference that changes in expression were permissible so long as the original content or the essence of the work remained, is more intriguing. With the *Engravers Act* an individual's stylistic rendering of a given subject was protected, while that subject itself remained free to all. Here however, a three-way interplay was being explored between subject, content, and expression. The book was the sum of the ideas that made up the work however they were expressed. It was the content of the work that was significant and so protected, not the manner in which it was expressed.

Whatever these parliamentarians understood copyright to mean, the Bill, in any case, foundered in the upper chamber, the Lords delaying its second reading until parliament was prorogued. As to why this was the case, there is much evidence to suggest that Alexander Pope was indirectly responsible.[65] While the Bill was being debated in parliament, Pope contrived to induce Edmund Curl into publishing a volume of his correspondence. His aim was to depict the behaviour of pirate booksellers such as Curl as overly invasive and morally repugnant, while at the same time developing public sympathy for the notion that an author should be free to control the dissemination of his own private correspondence. Ultimately what Pope wanted was to establish the right conditions for publishing an authorised edition of his letters himself.[66] On the same day that the booksellers' petition first came before the Commons, Pope wrote to the Earl of Oxford to ask him to send on a book of his letters that he had earlier entrusted to the Earl. He ensured that Curl published the correspondence, and arranged that he advertise the same. As McLaverty writes: "Pope wanted Curll to publish the edition of letters and to be caught doing it".[67] When Curl advertised his edition in the *Daily Post-Boy* he did so in the following terms:

> This Day are published, and most beautifully printed, Price five Shillings, Mr.Pope's *Literary Correspondence* for thirty Years; from 1704 to 1734. Being a

[65] J McLaverty, "The first printing and publication of Pope's Letters" (1980) 2 *The Library* 264.
[66] Rose writes that "[f]or a gentleman to publish his own letters would have seemed inexcusably vain, but a prior unauthorized publication by Curll would open the way for Pope to publish his own edition as a way of setting the record straight"; Rose, *Authors and Owners*, n 61 above, 60.
[67] McLaverty, "Pope's letters", n 65 above, 276.

> Collection of Letters, regularly digested, written by him to the Right Honourable the late Earl of Halifax, Earl of Burlington, Secretary Craggs, Sir William Trumbull, Honourable J. C. General ****, Honourable Robert Digby, Esq; Honourable Edward Blount, Esq; Mr.Addison, Mr.Congreve, Mr.Wycherly, Mr.Walsh, Mr.Steele, Mr.Gay, Mr.Jarvas, Dr.Arbuthnot, Dean Berkeley, Dean Parnelle, &c. Also Letters from Mr.Pope to Mrs.Arabella Fermor, and many other Ladies. With the respective Answers of each Correspondent. Printed for E.Curl in Rose-street, Covent-Garden, and sold by all Booksellers.[68]

Curl's advert made it sound like he was publishing correspondence of members of the Lords, which was, of course, in breach of privilege.[69] It appeared on 12 May, the same day as the second reading of the Bill was scheduled in the upper chamber.[70] Notice was taken of the advert in the Lords, whereupon it was ordered that the book be seized and that Curl, and a Mr J Whitford, should attend the house the next day.[71] Immediately after this, the second reading of the Bill was postponed. Curl duly appeared to give evidence and, after examination of the book, it was found that the he had not printed "any Letter of any Lord".[72] Despite this exoneration, the incident, regardless of Pope's original intention, resulted in the Lords developing a disingenuous attitude toward the passing of the Bill. Pope himself later wrote:

> Some of their Lordships having seen an advertisement of so strange a Nature, thought it very unfitting such a Bill should pass, without a Clause to prevent such an enormous License for the future ... BY THIS INCIDENT THE BOOKSELLERS BILL WAS THROWN OUT.[73]

THE HOUSE OF COMMONS

Concluding the *Narrative* which Pope produced detailing the events surrounding the publication of his correspondence, he wrote:

> [W]e have nothing to add but our hearty Wishes ... that the next *Sessions*, when the Booksellers Bill shall again be brought in, the Legislature will be

[68] Taken from "A Narrative of the Method by which the Private Letters of Mr Pope have been Procur'd and Publish'd by Edmund Curll, Bookseller" in G Sherburn (ed), *Correspondence of Alexander Pope* (Oxford, Clarendon Press, 1956) vol III, 458, 464.

[69] Ch 1, n 21, and accompanying text.

[70] The Bill was scheduled for its second reading on 9 May, but this was postponed until 12 May. McLaverty suggests that "Pope's allies in the Lords helped to fix this day for the debate"; McLaverty, "Pope's letters", n 65 above, 279.

[71] LJ 24:550.

[72] LJ 24:554, 556.

[73] Pope, "A Narrative" in Sherburn, *Correspondence of Alexander Pope*, n 68 above, vol III, 464.

> pleas'd not to extend the *Privileges*, without at the same time *restraining the Licence, of Booksellers*.

He had returned, once again, to the practice of certain booksellers in printing "a Gentleman's Private Letters".[74] Two years later, when, on 11 February 1737, leave was given in the House of Commons to prepare and bring in a *Bill for the Better Encouragement of Learning*, the legislature omitted to address Pope's request. In any case, the Bill, as with the previous one, would fail in the Lords,[75] and Pope would eventually turn to the courts, and Lord Hardwicke, for relief.[76] What the Bill did contain, however, was evidence of a more coherent legislative appreciation of what it meant to speak of property in books. By the time it had moved through the committee stage in the House of Commons, its title stated the purpose of the Bill as the promotion of the encouragement of learning "by the more effectual securing the *sole Right of printing Books* to the Authors thereof".[77] The preamble continued in the same vein. Stressing the ineffectiveness of the 1709 Act, that "Men of Learning are discouraged from pursuing Studies" through this violation of the author's property, and noting that "it may be just and reasonable to secure to Authors the property of their own Works" for a longer period than was detailed in the earlier Act, the Bill proposed to legislate with the purpose of "the more effectual vesting in Authors ... the *Property of their own Writings*".[78] The property in a book was one thing; the property in an author's text was another thing entirely. The language of this Bill was explicit, precise and confident when addressing the nature of the author's right.[79] Such clarity had been missing from the *Statute of Anne*, and was no more than fledgling in the 1735 Bill. The book was now no more than a vehicle; it was the text, and the act of printing that text, that was of consequence.

In terms of content, the Bill built upon much that had gone before, and much remained largely unchanged.[80] There was, however, sufficient to distinguish it from its antecedents. It separated the rights granted to the

[74] *Ibid*, 467.
[75] This Bill was brought in and passed through the lower house being amended both in committee and at the report stage. When carried to the Lords, the Bill was read twice, but the committee stage was continually postponed until parliament was prorogued; CJ 22:741, 756, 761, 764, 769, 800, 803, 832–33, 836, 838; LJ 25:73, 81, 91, 99, 106, 111, 142.
[76] *Pope v Curl* (1741) 2 Atk 342. See ch 3, n 106 and accompanying text.
[77] Emphasis added.
[78] Emphasis added.
[79] Note that rather than referring to the "author or proprietor", this Bill chose to proffer its protection to the "author, his executors, administrators or assigns". This construction however, was not always used consistently. In both clauses 4 and 6, the wording "author or proprietor" remained in the later draft of the Bill.
[80] A number of the provisions in this Bill had almost identical precedents in either the 1709 Act or the 1735 Bill. For example: the proviso relating to the free importation of foreign

author, and the penalties for infringement, into two distinct sections. As regards the rights provided, the distinction between old and newly published works was collapsed; all works, whether "already printed, or hereafter to be printed", were to receive the same protection. The author was granted the right of printing the work "during his natural Life" after which his "Executors, Administrators or Assigns" could print the same for a further eleven years. Moreover, if an author died leaving work unpublished, his executors were granted a twenty-one year term of protection from the date of first publication.[81] As to the nature of these rights, this Bill, like its predecessors also made clear that they were statutory in nature and subject to revocation. The clause from the 1735 Bill relating to subsequent editions with "alterations, additions or notes" was retained, but now only applying to works priced five shillings or more.[82] In addition, however, the 1737 Bill expanded the extent of the obligations of the booksellers by providing that, these subsequent editions were also subject to the library deposit requirement, again upon penalty of losing the benefit of the Act.[83] As if to emphasise the statutory nature of such property, the registration provisions were also revised.[84] The *Statute of Anne* and the 1735 Bill had set out that no one would be subject to the forfeitures therein contained unless the work had been registered. Instead, this Bill set out that the author by registration would not just ensure the benefit of the legislation, but "shall in and by such entry claim the Property of the said Book".[85]

The drafters of the 1737 Bill also brought a number of new ideas to the floor of the Commons. The first of these addressed the differential in the

language works originally printed overseas (clause 14); the mechanism for a public control over the price of books (clauses 18, 19); the protection of books of music (clause 23); the extension of the Act to Scotland (clause 24); the ability to plead the general issue (clause 25); the proviso saving the universities' printing privileges (clause 26); and a time limit for action, now extended to three years (clause 27).

[81] S 1. Should the author die within ten years of first publication, his executors were similarly entitled to print the work for twenty-one years after his death. The penalties for infringement followed those set out in the *Statute of Anne*, with the exception that the plaintiff would recover five shillings for each infringing copy, or sheet, instead of a penny, along with the costs of his suit; clause 2. The ability to sue for profits received by the pirate, which had been introduced in 1735, was made the subject of a separate clause, allowing the author to follow for the same in any of the Courts of Equity, upon waiver of the other penalties detailed in the Bill; clause 3.

[82] Clause 12. The Bill as originally drafted had envisioned that the author provide sufficient extra copies where he had made "material" alterations to his previous text. This qualification was subsequently dropped as the Bill proceeded through the Commons.

[83] Clause 13.

[84] Clauses 4, 6–11.

[85] Clause 4. It is curious to note that this Bill omitted to make any provision for the situation where the warehouse keeper of the Company of Stationers might refuse to register an author's work.

duty that was payable on imported paper as against imported books. That considerably less duty was payable upon printed material, than was the case for paper imported for use in the printing trade, had been brought to the attention of parliament by Buckley, and by the petitions and pamphlets of the booksellers in 1735. The loss of this potential revenue had obviously struck a chord. The Bill rendered it illegal to import, for sale, any book that had been printed first in Great Britain, and reprinted elsewhere.[86] The remaining provisions sought to nurture new conceptions about the relationships that existed between reader, author and bookseller. For one thing, authors could now publish anonymously while retaining protection for their work. Where the author wished to retain his or her anonymity, any other person was allowed to make the necessary entry in the stationers' register claiming the property in the work on behalf of the author for the term of twenty-one years.[87] A second clause considered, for the first time in a legislative context, the issue of abridgements and translations of works. It provided that should anyone within three years of first publication of a work "print, publish, import or sell any Abridgement of the same, or Translation thereof" without the author's consent, then they were to be subject to the same penalties as had been set out for reproducing the entire work. Interestingly this represented not just an expansion of the nature of the author's property right, but was also drafted with a form of authorial propriety in mind. It was considered that very often these "hasty and incorrect" re-workings, "not only lessen the Sale, but also frequently sink the Reputation of the original Composition".[88] Presumably three years was considered a long enough time for any work to either succeed or fail upon its own merit, establishing the repute of its author one way or the other, after which, anyone was free to re-present the text in modified form. The last of the new provisions was arguably the most radical. In trying to accommodate the fact that "the true worth" and "value" of books may "not be found out until a considerable time after the publication is known", it set out that:

> [N]o author shall have the power to sell, alienate, assign or transfer, except by his last will and testament, the right thereby vested in him to the original copy of any book ... for any longer time than 10 years, to commence from the date of such sale ... ; and all sales ... and all covenants for any sale ... for any longer time, or to commence from a future day, and all bargains and covenants for the renewal of the same ... shall be utterly void and of none effect.[89]

[86] Clause 21.
[87] Clause 5. Moreover, should the author reveal his identity, then he was to receive the ordinary protection granted by the Bill.
[88] Clause 22.
[89] Clause 15.

Not only did this ensure that a considerable element of financial control would remain with the author, but it also provided them with the opportunity "to alter and correct their compositions, upon maturer judgment and reflection".[90] Given that the author's work was to be protected for his lifetime plus eleven years, should the Bill pass, it would have resulted in a dramatic restructuring of the relationship between bookseller and author that would have been nothing short of revolutionary.

Pope, while not involved in the downfall of this legislative attempt, does provide some insight into why the Bill once again failed to secure the Lords' assent. Writing on 14 May 1737, he set out that:

> The Bill, about which some honest Men as well as I, took some pains, is thrown out, for this Sessions. I think I told you it was a Better Bill when it went into the H. of Commons, than when it came out. They had added some Clauses that were prejudicial (as I think) to the True Intention of Encouraging Learning; and I was not sorry the H. of Lords objected to them.[91]

The Commons had indeed introduced a number of changes during the Bill's passage through the House,[92] but it is difficult to cast any of them as

[90] About this clause, Pollard writes: "The 1730s in London saw further efforts by the booksellers to lengthen the periods of copyright protection and to clarify the prohibition on imported reprints by statute law. No less than three bills were prepared, one containing the revolutionary clause written by Swift that copyright would revert to the author after an initial ten years"; M Pollard, *Dublin's Trade in Books, 1550–1800* (Oxford, Clarendon Press, 1989) 70–71. Whether or not Swift actually penned this clause, it is clear that, while the 1735 Bill was still in committee in the House of Commons, William Pulteney sent Swift a copy of the Bill for comment. Pulteney wrote to Swift on 29 April 1735:

> I have sent you the Copy of a Bill now depending in our House, for the encouragement of learning, as the Title bears, but I think it is rather of advantage to Booksellers than Authors; whether it shall pass or not this sessions I cannot say, but if it should not, I should be glad of your thoughts upon it, against another. It seems to me to be extreamly imperfect at present. I hope you have many more Writings to oblige the world with, than those which have been so scandalously stolen from you, & when a Bill of this nature passes in England (as I hope it will next year) you may then secure the Property to any friend, or any Charitable use you think fit.

H Williams (ed), *The Correspondence of Jonathan Swift, 1732–1736* (Oxford, Clarendon Press, 1965) vol IV, 327. This provision was also responsible for the inclusion of the saving proviso that nothing in the Bill would "impeach, or make void, or make large, any contract" already subsisting; clause 17.

[91] Sherburn, *Correspondence of Alexander Pope*, n 68 above, vol IV, 68.

[92] For example they: made alterations to the title and the preamble of the Act; replaced the notion of a "proprietor" of a work with that of an author's "executors, administrators or assigns"; provided that those publishing subsequent editions lose all the benefit of the Act should they fail to comply with the requirements detailed therein; limited the property in an anonymous work to twenty-one years should the author prefer never to reveal his identity; ensured that music publishers were to benefit under the legislation; and last, included the provision addressing the abridgements and translations of an author's work.

inimical to the encouragement of learning. A more likely explanation for its failure lies in the fact that this statutory proposal was, from the point of view of the bookseller, the most contentious piece of parliamentary drafting to date. The *Statute of Anne* had engineered a balance that wavered primarily between the bookseller and the reading public. The author, although portrayed as central protagonist, had remained largely in the wings. The 1735 Bill, if anything, tipped the earlier balance in favour of the reader as consumer. However this 1737 Bill, for the first time, introduced the authorial figure as a significant third party. The prospect of having to renegotiate contracts with the author every ten years must have made most members of the London book trade baulk in disbelief. Add to this the fact that parliament seemed to be encouraging other booksellers to produce abridgements of anyone's work, albeit after three years, and the proposed legislation must have seemed more nightmare problem than dream solution. It was less likely to be those clauses prejudicial to the "true intention of encouraging learning", than those that prejudicial to the interests of the booksellers, that heralded an end to the support for this Bill.

STILL THE HOUSE OF COMMONS

Little under a year later a more modest attempt to legislate was undertaken in parliament, now specifically addressing the problem of cheap foreign imports and the resultant loss in trade and revenue that this represented. On 19 April 1738 leave was given to prepare and bring in a *Bill for Prohibiting the Importation of Books reprinted abroad that were Originally Printed in Great Britain*. Amended while in committee, both in the Commons and in the Lords, it was rejected upon its third reading in the upper house.[93] In its final version it prohibited importing for sale those works "first printed, composed or written and published" in Great Britain,[94] and revised the *Statute of Anne's* mechanism for controlling the price of books.[95] One year later, legislation was finally secured. Fully five years after Samuel Buckley first drew public attention to the inequities in competitive practices that existed between the British book trade and their continental counterparts, this sustained period of parliamentary activity eventually came to fruition in the guise of *An Act for the Prohibiting the Importation of Books reprinted abroad and first composed or written and*

[93] CJ 23:157, 158, 163, 169, 170, 171, 172, 185; LJ 25:242, 244, 251, 254, 255, 259.
[94] Clause 1.
[95] Clauses 2, 3. In effect this Bill represented no more than a restatement of clauses 18, 19 and 21 from the 1737 Bill.

printed in Great Britain and for limiting the Prices of Books.[96] On 6 April 1739 it was ordered that the Bill be prepared; on 14 June 1739 it received the Royal Assent.[97] The Bill that passed from the House of Commons to the Lords was, in essence, a restatement of the 1738 Bill with one main alteration.[98] An additional proviso had been inserted to the effect that nothing in the Act was to:

> [P]revent or hinder the Importation of any Book first composed or written, and printed in this Kingdom, which shall or may be reprinted abroad, and inserted among other books and tracts, and to be sold therewith, in any Collection, where the greatest part of such collection shall have been first composed and written, and printed abroad.

When the Bill came before the Lords however, they introduced a general exception to the offence outlined in the Act, by stating that it was not to extend to any work "that has not been printed or re-printed in this Kingdom within Twenty Years before the same shall be imported".[99] The intention, as was the case in the 1737 Bill, was to ensure that the reading public were not deprived of access to useful works by the action, or rather the inaction, of any bookseller. In the booksellers' favour, however, the Lords repealed that part of the *Statute of Anne* that enabled various public officials to investigate and cap what price the booksellers charged for their books. This legal mechanism, which had never yet been properly invoked, was simply removed.[100]

The Act, which had been limited in duration to seven years, was extended again and again, until its lapse in September 1795.[101] Predicated upon concerns of national industry, European trade, and His Majesty's revenue, concepts identified by Buckley and subsequently expanded upon by the bookselling lobby, the Act sought to encourage a more buoyant national trade. Moreover, by insulating the booksellers from the impact of the import book trade, and by providing them with a more effective means of redress against pirate operations, the government stood to gain through a more prosperous national industry and the

[96] *An Act for Prohibiting the Importation of Books reprinted abroad and first composed or written and printed in Great Britain and for limiting the Prices of Books* 1739, 12 Geo II, c 36.

[97] CJ 23:320, 325, 332, 337, 342, 355, 371; LJ 25:363, 368, 370, 374, 395.

[98] There was one other change in that the Dean of the Faculty of Advocates in Scotland was added to the list of people qualified to examine into and limit the price of books.

[99] S 1.

[100] S 3. The Lords also clarified that the Act was to extend to offences committed in Scotland, explicitly stating that the penalties outlined could be "recovered before the Court of Session there"; s 1.

[101] 20 Geo II c 47 (1747); 27 Geo II c 18 (1754); 33 Geo II c 16 (1760); 7 Geo III c 35 (1767); 14 Geo III c 86 (1774); 22 Geo III c 13 (1782); and 29 Geo III c 55 (1789). Note that from 1754 onwards, these Acts only renewed ss 1 and 2 of the 1739 Act.

amplified taxable revenue it would generate. To suggest however that the government alone provided the drive for the 1739 Act would be overly simplistic. The booksellers were equally interested in combating the import book trade. Moreover, they clearly had a hand in the shaping of the Act, as no one other than the booksellers had any interest in getting the price control on books revoked. The question remains then, as to why this powerful lobby should abandon its earlier efforts in extending the protections of the *Statute of Anne*, and limit their interest to the much narrower focus that was adopted in the 1738 Bill and the 1739 Act. The answer lies in an event that took place between the failure of the 1737 Bill, and the bringing of the 1738 Bill. The 1737 Bill remained in committee in the Lords until the end of the parliamentary session. Nearly a year later, in April 1738 the new Bill was introduced in the Commons. Between these two dates, the decision of *Baller* v. *Watson* (1737) was finally handed down by Lord Chancellor Talbot in the Court of Chancery,[102] a decision in which the executors of John Gay's estate had secured a "perpetual" injunction, as well as an order that the defendants account for the profits they had made from their pirate edition. The possibility of securing such a decree in Equity, when added to the existing protections of the *Statute of Anne*, meant that, for the booksellers, it became something of a redundant exercise to lobby for a replacement for the *Statute of Anne*. On the contrary, given the content of the 1735 and 1737 Bills and the measures that were likely to be foist upon the trade in return for additional protection, all the evidence pointed to the fact that should they continue, they would end up at a considerable disadvantage. If parliament was intent on redrawing the balance between the bookseller, the author and the reader, then the prudent course lay in retreat. It made more sense to begin to step away from a legislative body that might just give the booksellers what they wished for.

[102] Ch 3.

[...]
The Hidden Pivot

THE 1737 BILL, by contrast with the *Statute of Anne*, was actually a well-considered, comprehensible and mature piece of legislative drafting. From the booksellers' point of view however, it was unacceptable. Had the Bill carried, it would have seriously disrupted established market structures in giving the author a much more prominent role within trade negotiations, as well as imposing considerable obligations upon the publisher in the pursuit of what were considered to be socially desirable ends. In addition, an alternative threat to the position of the dominant London booksellers was beginning to manifest, but this time from the Scottish publishers, north of the border.[1] On the whole, these various factors signalled a new direction for the southern monopolists. Between the failure of the 1738 *Importation Bill* and the success of the *Importation Act* 1739, Andrew Millar, a Scottish bookseller in London, initiated an action against a number of booksellers in Glasgow and Edinburgh, for printing and selling numerous works by the Scottish poet James Thomson, in which he claimed the property under the *Statute of Anne*.[2] These various works included Thomson's *Seasons*, which series of poems was to provide the focus for the later action of *Millar v Taylor* (1768).[3]

Millar v The Booksellers of Edinburgh and Glasgow (1739) came before Lord Balmerino on 2 February 1739 with Anton Grant appearing for Millar, and James Balfour and Henry Home representing the Scottish booksellers. The plaintiffs, resting their case squarely on the protection

[1] For more on this see ch 5(1) Copyright at Common Law? A "Complicated" Action.
[2] The various defendants mentioned in Millar's bill are as follows: Andrew Stalker, John Barrie, James Brown, James Duncan, John Duncan, William Duncan, Alexander Millar and Alexander Hutchieson, all booksellers in Glasgow, and John Paton, Alexander Symner, Gavin Hamilton, Alexander Kincaid, James Davidson, John Freul, William Sands, Alexander Brymer, Gideon Crawford, Alexander Dunning, William Miller, Janet Brown, William Hamilton, Allan Ramsey, Andrew Menlin, John Aitken, Gavin Drummond, William Mombey, William Drummond and Samuel Clerk, all booksellers in Edinburgh.
[3] The other works of Thomson included: *Britannia, a Poem*, the *Poem, Sacred to the Memory of Sir Isaac Newton*, a *Hymn on the Succession of the Seasons*, an *Essay on Descriptive Poetry*, *A Tragedy entitled Sophonisba*, a poem called *Liberty*, A *Poem to the Memory of the Right Honourable Lord Talbot*, and a play entitled, *Agamemnon, a Tragedy*.

provided by the 1709 Act, sought an order for the forfeiture of the infringing books, for the payment of the penalties detailed in the legislation, but also "to hold Compt to the said Pursuer, for the Profits of all such Books as have been sold and disposed of them … and to make Payment to the Pursuer, each of them, of the Sum of One hundred Pound Sterling, in Name of Expences and Damages".[4] Balfour and Home raised a number of objections to the plaintiff's claim. They set out that the *Statute of Anne* was irrelevant as the defendants had "sold such books which is the natural privilege of every subject, except in so far as is prohibited by statute"; the Scottish booksellers had neither printed nor sold any of the books suggested by Millar. They also drew attention to the fact that the Act only provided for the forfeiture of infringing works, and the penalty of one penny for each sheet in the transgressors' custody, maintaining that no action for damages could be entertained. Moreover, they continued, that what redress was provided by the legislation had to be pursued for within three months, which time had already passed. Grant, in reply to these objections, conceded that the recovery of the penalties set out in the 1709 Act was limited to the period of three months, but drew a distinction between those penalties and the recovering of damages sustained on account of the defendants' actions. As the property in the copies of books was protected by the Act, he argued, this ensured that authors and proprietors had "thereby sufficient right and title to pursue for damages". Following this however, the action was dropped. James Graham, preparing a later brief, referred to this case, and explained that, after the northern booksellers "had been put to considerable Expence", the libel was "deserted and dropt".[5]

This action, generally overlooked by those who have written upon the development of copyright law throughout this period, provides a hidden pivot that encapsulates a crucial change in the position and attitude of the London booksellers at this time. Armed with the new decision of *Baller* (1737) and wary of the direction in which Parliament was developing the legislation which proposed to amend the *Statute of Anne*, the southern book trade chose to abandon their dependence upon the legislature. The London booksellers, rather than relying upon the corridors of power to safeguard their monopoly interests, turned instead to the hallowed halls of justice.

[4] CS 228/M3/4.
[5] *Additional Information for Mess Hamilton and Balfour*, 13 December 1744, 2.

Where great Courts are gathered of Kings or of great Lords, where is need of subtle counsel, there must Reynard find the subtle means. They may well speak and say their advice, but mine is best and what goeth before all.

W Caxton, *History of Reynard the Fox* (1481)

5(1)

Copyright at Common Law? A "Complicated" Action

AN UNSUCCESSFUL CLAIM FOR PROFITS IN EQUITY

THE ADVENT OF *Millar v The Booksellers of Edinburgh and Glasgow* (1739) heralded a decade in which booksellers, north and south, would engage in a more protracted legal battle, *Midwinter v Hamilton* (1743–1751).[1] Andrew Millar was, once again, one of the key protagonists.[2] It is clear, however, that members of the Scottish book trade had been engaged in printing and selling pirate works for a considerable time prior to either of these two actions.[3] What was it that motivated Millar and the other London booksellers to act in 1743? Most significant, perhaps, was that, in 1741, Robert Foulis established himself as a bookseller and publisher in Glasgow.[4] Foulis, later joined by his brother, Andrew, established a press which would come to be recognised as one of the finest in Britain, producing a quality of work that could rival, and even exceed, that of their London counterparts in every respect. Of the Foulis Press, John Ferguson comments:

> The works produced by it are quite entitled to rank with the Aldines, Elzevirs, the Bodonis, Baskervilles, which are all justly renowned for the varied excellances they possess, but no provincial, and certainly no

[1] This action will be referred to under two names, representing the two distinct stages of the process: *Midwinter v Hamilton* (1743–48) refers to the time spent before the Scottish Court of Session; *Millar v Kincaid* (1749–51) involves the appeal from the Scottish Court of Session to the House of Lords.

[2] The plaintiffs named in the initial action were as follows: Daniel Midwinter, William Innes, John Knapton, Paul Knapton and Andrew Millar. The defendants were Gavin Hamilton, John Balfour and Andrew Stalker.

[3] For details of a number of pirate editions that were produced and sold in Scotland throughout the 1720s and 1730s; see W McDougall, "Copyright Litigation in the Court of Session, 1738–1749, and the Rise of the Scottish Book Trade" (1988) 5 *Transactions* 2, 3.

[4] On the Foulis Press see generally: C Clair, *A History of Printing in Britain* (London, Cassell, 1965); FA Mumby, *Publishing and Bookselling: From the Earliest Times to 1870*, 5th edn (London, Cape, 1974); J Maclehose, *The Glasgow University Press 1638–1931* (Glasgow, Glasgow University Press, 1931).

> metropolitan press in the country has ever surpassed that of the two brothers.[5]

With the establishment of the Foulis Press, in addition to the fact that in general the Scottish trade had developed throughout the early 1740s to the point that, by 1743, the Glasgow printers were supplying a substantial part of the growing export trade to America,[6] it could be said that printing in Scotland was coming of age.[7] To the London booksellers it was becoming readily apparent that their northern counterparts were emerging as a powerful economic rival. Moreover, they were less susceptible to control than were pirate booksellers operating within England. As Feather notes:

> So long as would-be pirates (who had always existed) were in the capital, there were moral, commercial and legal pressures which could be brought to bear upon them ... Distant pirates, however, were a much greater danger, especially when they had easier access than the London booksellers to the rapidly developing provincial markets, and they could offer a cheaper product.[8]

In 1743, the same year in which Robert Foulis was appointed printer to Glasgow University, he published a work, on 28 February, containing Bishop Burnet's *A Treatise concerning the Truth of the Christian Religion*, and John Locke's *A Discourse on Miracles*. It was the publication of this edition, McDougall notes, which finally "galvanized Millar into action".[9]

On 6 April 1743 the plaintiffs complained of Scottish piracy of a number of works,[10] and sought the penalties delineated in the *Statute of Anne*, as well as damages and their costs. In June, when the case came

[5] J Ferguson, "The Brothers Foulis and early Glasgow Printing" (1889) 1 *The Library* 81.

[6] McDougall, "Copyright Litigation in the Court of Session", n 3 above. See also W McDougall, "Scottish books for America in the mid 18th Century" in R Myers and M Harris (eds), *Spreading the Word: The Distribution Networks of Print, 1550–1850* (Winchester, St Paul's Bibliographies, 1990) 21.

[7] This is not to overlook the dimensions and significance of the book trade within Scotland in the early modern period. Alastair Mann has recently established the case for concluding that the scale of the Scottish book trade throughout the sixteenth and seventeenth centuries was greater than most historiographers have traditionally been willing to infer. A Mann, *The Scottish Book Trade 1500–1720, Print Commerce and Print Control in Early Modern Scotland* (East Lothian, Tuckwell Press, 2000). For a commentary on copyright protection in Scotland during this period, see *ibid*, 95–124.

[8] J Feather, *A History of British Publishing* (London, Routledge, 1988) 77.

[9] McDougall, "Copyright Litigation in the Court of Session", n 3 above, 5.

[10] These were: *The History of the Reformation of the Church of England*, 2nd edn; and Bishop Burnett, *An Exposition of the Thirty-nine Articles of the Church of England*, 4th edn; J Armstrong, *The Oeconomy of Love*, 3rd edn; J Locke, *The Works*; H Fielding, *The History of the Adventures of Joseph Andrews*; J Foster , *Sermons on Several Important Subjects*; and E Chalmers, *Cyclopaedia, or, An Universal Dictionary of Arts and Sciences.*

before the Lord Ordinary, Lord Elchies, the plaintiffs' counsel restricted the libel to two books only, John Armstrong's *Oeconomy of Love*, and Ephraim Chambers' *Cyclopaedia*, afterwards adding Henry Fielding's *Joseph Andrews*, and declared that they would not insist for the penalties in the Act, but rather only pursue for the profits of sale and damages. Lord Elchies instructed both parties to hand in written memorials, and then submitted the matter to the Lords of Session for their consideration. In their second memorial,[11] the plaintiffs set out the substance of the 1709 Act and continued that the forfeitures and penalties therein contained "were found attended with such Difficulties, [and] that in no one instance ... have the same ever been prosecuted or recovered". Instead, they sought damages and their costs of action. Although the legislation made no provision for any other remedy, they claimed, relying upon the opinion of William Murray, later Lord Mansfield, that in England:

> Authors and Proprietors, waving the Penalties, always have recourse to a Court of Equity, which proceeds upon the foundation of the Property declared by the Act, and gives a specific remedy, by granting Injunction ... and decrees them to account to the Proprietors for all the Profits made by the Sale of any Copies of a Pirated Edition.

As proof that "the Practice of the High Court of Chancery, in many instances" had in fact conformed to Murray's claim, they pointed to the case of *Baller v Watson* (1737). As "the Court of Session in Scotland [was] a mixt Jurisdiction of Law and Equity",[12] they argued that it was open to the Court to grant them such relief as they might secure before the English Court of Chancery. This was neither a claim for the penalties of the 1709 Act, nor was it a claim for damages at common law; at this point, the London booksellers were seeking an account of profits in equity, of the kind that had been ordered in *Baller*. The basis of their claim, as had been the case in *Millar* (1739), remained the *Statute of Anne*. It had granted authors, and their assigns, a property in their work, and as with any other form of property, whenever it was subject to "the unjust Invasions of other People" a competent action for damages should be available.

Henry Home and James Graham submitted two responses on behalf of Hamilton, Balfour, Stalker and the other Scottish booksellers. Home, the future Lord Kames who, in *Hinton v Donaldson* (1773), would later declare that there existed in Scotland no copyright at common law, prepared the first.[13] In relation to the claim for damages, Home led with the general

[11] *Information for Daniel Midwinter*, 30 November 1744. Their first memorial does not appear to have survived.
[12] On the Court of Session as a court of common law and equity, see ARG M'Millan, *The Evolution of the Scottish Judiciary* (Edinburgh, W Green, 1941) 77–78.
[13] 3 December 1744.

point that "correctory laws are to be strictly interpreted", that the "letter of the law" need be observed, and that in relation to the claim for damages there was "not the least hint of such a process in the statute". The legitimacy of the plaintiffs' argument was dismissed as being:

> [E]ntirely founded upon a Mistake, in applying the Rights which are the consequences of Property strictly taken, to Matters which cannot be called Property but in a loose and vague sense.

The "sole liberty of printing" provided by the Act was not a property but "an exclusive privilege, or Monopoly, well calculated ... for the Benefit of Learning". For Home property lay in the physical book and nothing else; anyone who purchased a book, was just as able to dispose of a copy of the book, as he was the book itself. The only thing, in his opinion, that prevented anyone making and distributing copies of a book was "the exclusive privilege or monopoly granted by the Statute". As a consequence, the only remedies available were those detailed in the Act "[w]hich are all the checks the Legislature have thought proper to give the authors for the Security of their quasi-Property". As to the precedent of *Baller* he suggested that the plaintiffs could have followed for the penalties in the statute, but instead "chose to be moderate in their demands" by restricting their claim to the profits made by the defendants, which sum proved to be less than they might otherwise have enjoyed. It was not, as the plaintiffs would have it, an example of "an action for damages sustained, where an action for penalties was not competent".[14] In any case, he continued, a true action for damages would proceed upon the basis of "the real Loss sustained by the pursuer" and not simply the profit made by the transgressor.

The second of the defendants' responses was a different affair entirely. Graham expounded upon the recent development of the printing trade in Scotland, which trade he claimed, for "Beauty, Correctness, and Cheapness", rivalled printing anywhere else in Britain. Moreover, Glasgow lay "so conveniently situated for Trade to the American Plantations, that ... there is a very reasonable prospect, that a very large Branch of Trade will be opened in that Part of the Kingdom, heretofore unknown". It was for these reasons that the London booksellers had begun to raise processes against their northern counterparts: "to discourage the art of printing of Books in North-Britain"; to "secure the Monopoly thereof to themselves at London"; and, to ensure that Scottish Booksellers remained "mere Warehouse-keepers to the London

[14] Home suggested that the plaintiffs in *Baller* actually received about one tenth what they might have received under the 1709 Act.

Booksellers". This was not about the piracy of books, but about maintaining the status quo in a profession dominated by English monopolists. He conceded that the Glasgow booksellers had indeed printed works by Locke and Burnet but maintained they were at liberty to do so since any protections provided by the *Statute of Anne* had long since expired. Once these periods had elapsed "the Laws of the Land lay no Restraint upon any body". "[I]t is utterly impossible" he continued "that any Mortal can now have exclusive Title to the printing of those Books", before concluding with an appeal to the court to clarify the legal position as regards such works "so as they may be at a Certainty with respect to the free Privileges of Printing".

Whether as a result of Home's exposition of the law, or Graham's overtly politicised defence of the national trade, the Lords of Session reviewed the case, and on 4 July 1746 held that "no action of damages lay" upon the *Statute of Anne*.[15] This was not, however, a foregone conclusion. Lord Elchies' report of their decision is in the following terms:

> The Lords found that action of damages does not lie upon either of the acts 8vo Anne Cap.19, or 12th Geo.II. for printing, reprinting, importing & c. books contrary to these statutes. Haining and Strichen did not vote. Tinwald and I were very doubtful but voted for the interlocutor. President thought that the action did not lie for books imported contrary to 12th Geo.II. because the pursuers could not wave the penalties of that statute, but that it lay on all the offences against the 8vo Anne, because the penalties in that are not prescribed, and that it would have lain on the same act for importing books from abroad, had not the act 12th Geo.II. supervened.[16]

The decision was as close as it could have been: two to one, with two of the Lords abstaining. The Scottish court it seems was not entirely convinced that an action for such damages as the London booksellers were seeking would not lie.

A SUCCESSFUL APPEAL FOR PROFITS IN EQUITY

The pursuers appealed against the interlocutor. Less than two weeks after the decision of the Lords, they submitted the *Petition of the Booksellers of London against the Booksellers of Edinburgh and Glasgow*.[17] Their position, this time drawn up by Alexander Lockhart, remained

[15] Lord Elchies, *Decisions of the Court of Sessions from the Year 1733 to the Year 1754* (Edinburgh, WM Morison, 1813) vol 1, Appendix II, 2.
[16] *Ibid*, vol 2, 250. See also the report of the decision in Elchies, *ibid*, vol 1, Appendix II, 2.
[17] 15 July 1746, Bodleian Vet A4 e 2197. Note that there is also a copy of this in the Advocate's Library, Edinburgh, Elchies Papers, XV, A-B, 1741–49.

essentially the same. The *Statute of Anne* vested the property of books in authors, as a natural consequence of which there existed a claim for damages for the encroachment of that property. In support of this, Lockhart set out a distinction between those statutes that simply created an offence under certain penalties, and the 1709 Act. In the first situation "the Transgression of that Law cannot be otherways punished than by recovering the Penalties imposed by that Statute". The *Statute of Anne* however was of a different sort. In this case, where:

> [A] Right of Property is first granted to the Author of any Book, for the Encouragement of Learning; and in consequence thereof, an offence created ... Your petitioners must be forgiven to say, they can discover no good reason either in Law or in Equity, why a claim of Damages should not be competent, upon Waiver of the Penalties.

Having drawn the distinction between these two types of legislation, he drew a further distinction between the action for penalties and the claim to damages. The first, provided by the statute, was an *actio popularis*. That is, anybody was eligible to pursue an infringer for the statutory penalties. This statutory right was fundamentally different from the claim for damages. Again relying upon the authority of *Baller*, he continued that the latter remedy was only available as "the natural consequence of the Right of Property vested in the Author and claimable by no other person".

The Scottish booksellers provided two answers to this petition, the first dated 29 July, the second, 21 December 1746; both were now prepared by Home.[18] As regards the argument that the 1709 Act created a species of property that gave rise to a remedy for damages, he developed his earlier objections. This was not property *per se*, but an exclusive privilege, a monopoly. Home began to examine the nature of property itself. Elaborating upon the question of property in a book, he wrote:

> If a Man composes a Book, the Manuscript is his Property, and the whole edition is his Property after it is printed. But let us suppose that this whole

[18] *Answers for the Booksellers of Edinburgh and Glasgow to the petition of Andrew Millar and other Booksellers in London*, Bodleian, Vet A4 e 2197, see also the Advocate's Library, Edinburgh, Elchies Papers, XV, A-B, 1741–49 and *Answers for the Booksellers of Edinburgh and Glasgow to the Petition of Daniel Midwinter and other booksellers in London*, Bodleian Vet A4 e 2197, see also the Advovate's Library, Edinburgh, Elchies Papers, XV, A-B, 1741–49. There is in fact a third undated document which can be tied to this stage of the proceedings. The *Memorial for the Booksellers of Edinburgh and Glasgow, relating to the Process against them by some of the London Booksellers; which depended before the Court of Session, is now under Appeal*, can reasonably be linked to this stage of the litigation, as the unnamed author quotes directly from the pursuers immediately preceding petition (30 November 1744). Moreover, it is likely that this *Memorial*, like the two *Answers* for the Scottish booksellers, was prepared by Home; the reason for suggesting this, lies in the fact that when Home later comes to provide an account of the Lords decision of 7 June 1748, his account draws heavily upon this same *Memorial*.

> Edition is sold off, where then is his Property? Surely none of the books sold remain his Property. And as Property, by all Lawyers, antient and modern, is defined to be *jus in re*, there can be no Property without a subject.[19]

A book is property; the property is the book; there was nothing else. Whatever else the author may have was specifically granted by Parliament, it was "only a quasi Property", a property "*ad certum effectum* only".[20]

Picking up an earlier thread, Home elaborated upon the problematic aspect of actually establishing damages. The claim for damages and the right to profits were, he pointed out, two entirely different matters. The actual damage suffered might easily amount to more, or less, than the profits gained by the pirate. The endeavour of quantifying damages was, as a process, "plainly inexplicable". Moreover, he suggested that the legislature "forebore giving such a remedy, because they very well knew that it could have no other effect than leading People into inextricable processes". To support the point, he alluded to the fact that the legislature had not forgotten to provide the Universities with the ability to follow for the value of books not delivered to them under the library deposit requirements. *These* damages "were not overlook'd", but granted, as they could be easily ascertained. Home also drew upon the language of the statute itself in dismissing the legitimacy of this "new invented claim".[21] He suggested that the three-month time limit and the registration requirement were inconsistent with a claim, and highlighted the uneasy co-existence of a popular action for statutory penalties, with a private action for damages.[22]

In dealing with the supposed precedent offered in the guise of *Baller*, Home castigated Murray's reading of the case, and the practice of the Chancery court in general, as no more than a "private opinion", and one that was "an extreme bad comment upon the statute".[23] He accepted that there existed "a comitas betwixt Courts, Sovereign Courts especially, to make the decisions of one Court regarded in another". Nevertheless, where "the statute is so express and clear", where the pursuers could provide only one example of such practice and where that decision had not yet been affirmed in the House of Lords, he argued that "blind obedience is not expected" and the decision "ought to have no great weight with

[19] 21 December 1746.

[20] *Answers for the Booksellers of Edinburgh and Glasgow to the petition of Andrew Millar and other Booksellers in London*, Bodleian, Vet A4 e 2197.

[21] *Ibid.*

[22] He writes that: "[A]n absolute stranger, sueing for Penalties only, shall cut out the Proprietor, claiming only his Damages. This would be so disjointed a Thing, that there would be no apologising for it by any sort of Principles"; *ibid.*

[23] 29 July 1746.

any Court against Statute, and against Principles of Law". Whether in blind obedience or not, on Christmas Eve 1746, the slender majority of the earlier decision was reversed and the London booksellers were presented with a most welcome seasonal gift. Lord Elchies recorded their decision as follows: "In this case we . . . altered the former interlocutor as to books printed here, and found that the action does lie to the extent of the profits made".[24] Hamilton, Balfour and Stalker petitioned against the Court's determination.

A CLAIM UPON THE COMMON LAW, NOT THE *STATUTE OF ANNE*

The petition of the Scottish booksellers, now prepared by James Graham, re-presented much of what had gone before.[25] It rehearsed the desire of the London booksellers to maintain economic dominance of the printing trade within Great Britain, denied the pre-existence of any property in an author's work prior to the 1709 Act, recounted how any action for damages would in any event be "full of difficulties and inexplicabilities", and disputed the relevance of the singular Chancery decree relied upon by their counterparts. On this last point they also requested "a moderate time for looking into the Practice of the Law of England, and of other foreign Countries, with respect to this Point, and for laying such Authorities before you".[26] Concerned about the nature of the Lords' decree, they also appealed for clarification as to whether it extended to cover *any* works entered in the Stationers' Register or just those as fell within the time-limited protections of the legislation. "[I]f this Matter is not a little better fixed and settled" they complained, "no Man in Scotland will be able to know, what Books he can safely print and publish, and what not". In addition, they advanced a further argument drawing upon the theme that, while a man keeps "his

[24] Elchies, *Decisions of the Court of Sessions*, n 15 above, vol II, 250. See also Elchies, *ibid*, vol I, Appendix II, No 3. At this time, the Court also ordered that a hearing be held as to whether or not the penal action detailed in the *Importation Act* 1739, was limited by an earlier Elizabethan statute (31st Eliz) which provided a general limitation upon all penal statutes of three years. The hearing was held upon 13 January 1747, whereupon it was decided, by a bare majority, that the ability to claim under the 1737 Act was so limited. Lord Elchies provides an account of who the dissenting judges were: "[U]pon the hearing we (13 January 1747) found it was limited, five to five, and the Presidents casting vote. Against the interlocutor were Drummore, Strichen, Kilkerran, Shewalton and I (Elchies). The decision was contrary to what was found in 1737 in a question on the same act, that statute was not so limited". See also J Ferguson, *Decisions of the Court of Sessions from the Year 1738 to the Year 1752* (Edinburgh, 1775).

[25] *The Petition of Gavin Hamilton & John Balfour, and others, Booksellers in Edinburgh, Andrew Stalker and others, Booksellers in Glasgow, Defenders, Against Andrew Millar and others, Booksellers in London, Pursuers*, 15 January 1747.

[26] See later, the *Memorial for Gavin Hamilton*, 29 May 1747.

Lucibrations to himself ... he may be said to have a Property in his Noodle". However, they continued, "if he prints and publishes these Lucibrations, so soon as one buys a Copy of the Book ... the Person who buys has just the same Property that the Author had". The pertinent analogy lay with the inventor of a useful tool:

> Why should not an ingenious Carpenter or Joiner, who has made a new Plough, or a new Cart, be said to have a Property in such new Cart or Plough, and to have an Action of Damages competent to him, at least to the Extent of the Profits made, against all makers of such new Carts or Ploughs?

Rather, the only method of protecting one's invention, as was the case with books, was by an exclusive patent or statute. Moreover, as both book and invention were "a mere Creature of the Statute's" both "must be regulated by them alone, and cannot go one Inch beyond them".

Should the Lords maintain their decision that an action for damages was competent, the petitioners raised a number of issues specific to the detail of the interlocutor and the works in question. If an action was sustainable, they argued that it should extend only to those works entered in Stationers' Hall before publication of the book. If this were not the case, they suggested that altruistic authors would otherwise have no way to "bestow the Labours of their Brain freely upon all Mankind". If an author sought monetary return for his work, he could inform the rest of the world by registration before publication, which method had been set out in the *Statute of Anne*. In relation to Chamber's *Cyclopaedia*, they asserted that, as the book had been first published in 1727, and as Chambers had not survived fourteen years after this date, then the protection for the work provided by the 1709 Act had expired, upon termination of the first fourteen year term, in 1741. On 26 February 1747, they also presented evidence before the Court that both *Joseph Andrews* and the *Oeconomy of Love* were first published "for some time before the Pursuers had acquired the Right from the Authors, or entered the same in Stationers Hall".[27]

When William Grant submitted the London booksellers' answer to this petition, he adjusted the focus of their argument.[28] No longer relying upon the *Statute of Anne* as the source of the relevant property right, instead he began by suggesting that what rights an author had to reprint

[27] *The Petition of Gavin Hamilton and John Balfour Booksellers in Edinburgh, and Andrew Stalker, and others, Booksellers in Glasgow*, 26 February 1747.

[28] *Answers for Daniel Midwinter, William Innes, John Knapton, Andrew Millar and others, all of London, Booksellers, and their Attorney or Factor, Pursuers; to the Petition of Gavin Hamilton and John Balfour, and others, Booksellers in Edinburgh, Andrew Stalker and others, Booksellers in Glasgow, Defenders*, 27 February 1747.

his work pre-dated the legislation. The 1709 Act, he asserted, implicitly accepted a pre-existing property in books in the language used in the preamble with its reference to the "proprietors" of books, and the acknowledgement of the previous practice of registering works in Stationers' Hall. Both factors stood testament to the veracity of such a claim. In addition, he appealed to "the fair and unprejudiced Sense of Mankind", presenting the hypothetical author who, after spending a number of years composing his work, finds that upon publication a "pyrate" has acquired a copy and is issuing a cheaper edition, to the ruin of the author and his family. The logic then ran as follows:

> How can it be maintained that there was no Right or Property in the Author? For if there was no Right in him, there could be no injury done to the other; and if there was a Right, there must be a Remedy competent, in course of Law or Equity; and that Remedy which is founded in the Nature of the Case, is by no means taken away, by the super-added Penalties, introduced by a positive Statute.

From the injury, flows the right; from the right, flows the remedy. Grant further examined the nature of this right, in taking issue with Home's adherence to the understanding that property must be *jus in re*. It was indeed true that the purchaser of a book does become the proprietor of that book to the extent that "he may read it, or burn it, or give it away, or sell it again". However, what rights the purchaser had, existed only in relation to that volume, and that volume alone. Such rights as the purchaser had, did not affect that the author of the book "remains the *Proprietor of that Work or Composition*, and can only dispose of it, and print or reprint it at Pleasure". The author remained proprietor, not of the physical object, which by definition he would sell on to another, but of the work, the composition, the text. His property lay not in the tangible, but the intangible.

In responding to the more specific aspects of the Scottish booksellers' case, it was argued that the requirement for registration prior to publication affected only the ability to follow for the penalties in the statute, and in no way impeded the claim for damages. This addressed the argument that the petitioners had mounted in relation to *Joseph Andrews* and the *Oeconomy of Love*. As far as the objection in relation to Chamber's *Cyclopaedia* went, Grant insisted that the original work of 1727, had been so "greatly altered and improved, with large Additions in the after Editions of that Work" that it "had been rendered quite a different Book from that first published in the year 1727, altho' it still bore the same Name and Title". Thus the work still fell within the fourteen-year period of the 1709 Act. With these more specific points however, Grant unwittingly drew attention to an uneasy paradox lying at the heart of his argument. If indeed there existed, prior to the *Statute of Anne*, a common law property in books, why then was it necessary to establish that the three works in question all fell within the terms of that Act? This would not go unnoticed by Home.

On 29 May 1747 the Scottish booksellers submitted a further *Memorial*[29] followed one month later by a *Memorial and Condescendence*.[30] The first was presented by an unnamed Scottish bookseller, "one of the Defenders in this Cause";[31] the second was jointly prepared by Home and John Grant. Between these two submissions the defendants raised a number of additional arguments, further building upon the foundations they had already laid.[32] Having requested time to look into "the Practice of the Law of England, and of other foreign Countries",[33] they recounted a brief history of the printing trade in Europe. Relying upon other jurisdictions such as Venice, Florence, Spain and France, they illustrated that what protection was available had always proceeded upon the principle of granting temporary privileges, initially to the printer, then later to authors, which privileges were also very often conditional as to the price of the work, the quality of the materials used in its production, or indeed that several copies be donated for the benefit of certain libraries or universities. As to the English Act and its wording which seemed to support the thesis that it acknowledged the prior existence of a property in books, this was dismissed as simply reflecting the "By-Laws or Rules" the Company of Stationers had laid down for themselves, which "tis hop'd, the Pursuers will hardly prove they extend to Scotland". Moreover, a parallel was drawn between the position of the author and that of the engraver. Referring to the recently secured *Engravers Act* 1735, intended for "the Encouragement of the ingenious Mr.Hogarth", the question was asked: "[I]s not the Case of the Engraver and that of the Printer the same? and is not a Design in Engraving as much a Production of genius as a Book?" Until the passing of the 1735 Act, they observed, every engraver "was at

[29] *Memorial for Gavin Hamilton, and others, Booksellers in Edinburgh, Andrew Stalker, and others, Booksellers in Glasgow, Defenders; by way of Supplement to their Petition presently depending, and a Reply to the Pursuers Answers*, 29 May 1747.

[30] *Memorial and Condescendence for Messieurs Hamilton and Balfour and others Booksellers in Edinburgh, and Andrew Stalker and others Booksellers in Glasgow*, 29 June 1747.

[31] There is evidence to suggest that this was actually prepared by John Stevenson, then Professor of Logic at Edinburgh University. See McDougall, "Copyright Litigation and the Scottish Book Trade", n 3 above, 7.

[32] In relation to the three works in question, it was submitted that none of the three had even been printed in Scotland. *Joseph Andrews* had been pirated, but in *London* by "a well known Undertaker, Mr Hodge". Chamber's *Cyclopaedia*, if the fourth edition was indeed "quite a different Book from that first Published in the year 1727", fell foul of the Act in that the pursuers had failed to register it as a new work. And finally, the *Oeconomy of Love*, which had raised a "great Noise" in Scotland over a year before the pursuers began their process, was in any event "one of those Productions which the Law never meant to encourage".

[33] See the petition of 15 January 1747.

Liberty to copy precisely the Designings of another, without varying or improving them". The statute however had granted them a temporary monopoly, which was in no way different from that provided by the *Statute of Anne*. The pursuers, they claimed, could show nothing in their case "which can put it on a better Footing than that of Designers or Engravers."

In addition to these arguments drawn from historical and contemporary legal practice, the Scottish booksellers also examined the respective benefits of providing an author with a temporary or perpetual monopoly. The author, they claimed, would be no better off even with a perpetual protection, given the predominant situation of the bookseller, and the risk in publishing any unknown work. In contrast however, the author had everything to gain from a more limited term, as "all the Works of the Learned that have been before him lie open to his Lucubrations". They suggested that the author:

> [I]f he is a Critick, he may show their Beauties and Faults, explain their obsolete Language, rescue their true Readings from the Faults of careless Printers; if he is a Philosopher, supply the Defects of Reasoning, and, in a thousand various Ways, illustrate their Principles; nay, a Man of Reputation, by giving himself the trouble to wite (*sic*) a Preface, may give a forgotten Book a new run, and if he runs the Risque, what should hinder him to enjoy the Profits: 'Tis well known that Learned Men have gained sometimes more this Way than by their own Works, and served the Publick no less.

Not only would the author benefit from a wealth of available material, but the wider literary field, and indeed the nation also stood to gain. Denying the possibility of a perpetual monopoly held out the possibility of numerous benefits: improved trade and manufacture in Scotland; a fruitful increase in trade between England and Scotland; a more commanding position in the wider European market; a substantial growth in revenue generated on account of additional paper manufacture. All this was suggested, as well as the promise of improved political unity between the two nations. The unnamed bookseller asked:

> Will it hurt England to have their standard Authors so common among Persons of all Ranks, and even diffused into the remotest Corners of Scotland, so as gradually to diminish and annihilate the Seeds of Rebellion, and all Ideas of a separate Interest from that of the general Good of Great Britain.

Finally, and perhaps most importantly, the Scottish booksellers took issue with a number of inconsistencies that sprang out of the position that their southern counterparts were attempting to maintain. If indeed there existed at common law such a property as they claimed, then why limit their action to those works which seemingly fell within the *Statute of Anne*? Why not similarly pursue for damages for the works of Burnet and Locke? Why had no bookseller in Dublin ever been sued when the common law in Ireland remains the same as in England? Why not pursue against the London bookseller, Mr Osborne, who was printing the works of Shakespeare, which works Andrew Millar pretended an undoubted right to? Why not do any of these things? The answer, suggested Home and Grant, lay in the fact that they were afraid to do so. They were afraid that to do so would give occasion to "stating the true Question, and open many Eyes, which the Ignorance of the Rights of both *Scotland* and *England* blinds".

They bluntly stated the opposition's position as two maxims. The first, that an action of damages lay (at least to the extent of profits made), regardless of the requirements of the *Statute of Anne*, which was *perpetual* to the first author of a work, his heirs and assigns. Secondly, that the author's right to his work was "indefeasable and perpetual". Then, noting that "[i]n both the former Processes your Lordships could not, consistently with Form, explain the meaning of the Act of Queen Anne", they challenged the Lords to clarify their understanding and reading of the law. Nearly a year after their previous ruling the Lords of Council altered their position once again. Lord Elchies recorded that, on 2 December 1747, by unanimous decision, it was found that: no action lies for offences against the statute three months after the offence; no action on the statute lies for books not entered in Stationer's Hall; and, no action upon the statute lies for damages, but only for the penalties therein mentioned.[34] Of Lord Tinwald in particular, Lord Elchies recounted that, he:

> [W]ell observed, that the author of a book could have no better title at common law to the property or rather monopoly of his own labours and invention than the first inventor of printing or gunpowder had to the monopoly of that invention, and that this would be a *novus modus aquirendi dominii*.[35]

James Ferguson, Lord Kilkerran, recorded the opinion of the court in slightly different terms.[36] Having previously considered the author as having the right to pursue for profits, he continued that the Lords, "now on more mature consideration" were of the opinion:

> [T]hat as antecedant to the statute, an author had no property in a book composed and published by him, further than in the copies remaining in

[34] Elchies, *Decisions of the Court of Sessions*, n 15 above, vol 1, Appendix II, No 3.
[35] *Ibid*, vol 2, 251.
[36] Ferguson, *Decisions of the Court of Sessions*, n 24 above.

> his hand, as nothing remained with him after printing and publishing his book but the thought of his mind which does not admit the notion of property.

Never again would the Scottish judiciary entertain any notion of the existence of a common law copyright.

A CLAIM UPON THE *STATUTE OF ANNE* FOR COMMON LAW DAMAGES

Grant, in preparing the London booksellers' appeal against this latest decision of the Lords of Session, stepped back from the position he had advocated in the answer of 27 February 1747. His focus shifted once more from the position of the law prior to the *Statute of Anne*, to the "natural" consequences of the passing of that Act. "[H]owever the Law stood before the Act of the 8th of Queen Anne", he wrote, "it is by that Statute fixed and settled".[37] The pursuers took issue with the third leg of the Lords' previous declaration that "no action upon the statute lies for damages". These words they conceived to be ambiguous given that:

> [A]n Action upon the Statute, in the most obvious and proper Sense, signifies an Action that is directly and expressly given by the Statute itself, such as the Actions for the Penalties in the present Case.

Agreeing "that the Statute gives no such Action of Damages to the Proprietors of Books" they nevertheless continued that there existed in England "in Pursuance of the Property ascertained by this Statute of Queen Anne ... a double Remedy": the first was the popular action for the penalties in the 1709 Act; the second, "as a necessary Consequence of the Property given by the first Clause of the Statute", was the proprietor's ability to follow for damages. This represented an obvious retreat from their immediately previous stance in that the right to pursue for some measure of damages was implicitly recognised to extend only to those works protected by the *Statute of Anne*. The petitioners set out:

> That *in Consequence of the Property declared by the Statute to belong to the Authors of Books*, and their Assigns, there arises to such Proprietors ... an Action founded, not upon the Express words of the Statute giving such Action, but by the common Rules of Law, as a necessary Consequence of the

[37] *The Petition of Daniel Midwinter, William Innes, Aaron Ward, and others, all of London Booksellers, and William Elliot Writer in Edinburgh their Attorney or Factor, Pursuers*, 9 December 1747, Bodleian, 4 Jur X 136.

> Property itself established by the Statute, even as if the Law had gone no further than to declare such Property, without proceeding to superadd peculiar Remedies, by way of Penalty and Popular Action.[38]

This change in approach, however, did not involve a simple restatement of those arguments the London booksellers had put forward in their initial submissions of November 1744 and June 1746. At that time they were claiming, before the Court of Session, the same relief as they would have been provided by the Court of Chancery in England, that is, an equitable account of profits. While Grant no longer argued that the property in a book necessarily pre-dated the *Statute of Anne*, his language, the rhetoric of the claim, had shifted. Now, the ability to ensure "Redress of any Invasion of that Property" was expressed to lie "by an Action of the Case at Law, *or* a Bill in Equity, at the Suit of the Proprietors".[39] An aggrieved bookseller was free to pursue an account in Equity, or alternatively some other measure of damages at common law.

Six months after this petition was submitted for the Lords' consideration, on 7 June 1748 they issued their final ruling of this protracted litigation. The decision of the court was recorded by Home in his work, *Remarkable Decisions of the Court of Session, From the year 1730 to the year 1752.*[40] That this report is later furnished by Home, the senior counsel for the Scottish booksellers, and printed on behalf of Alexander Kincaid, one of the principal respondents in the litigation, is enough to raise suspicion as to the possibly partisan nature of the record. It is in fact a representation of the majority of a *Memorial* prepared for the Scottish booksellers at an earlier stage of the litigation, presumably by Home himself.[41] His record of the case then fails to furnish any of the rationale of the court then sitting. What can be said, however, is that nothing in the pursuers' petition persuaded the Lords of Session that they should alter their previous decision of 2 December 1747.[42]

[38] Emphasis added.

[39] Emphasis added. In support of their argument they once again relied upon the statement of William Murray (which they described as "not so much of an Opinion of the learned and honourable Person who gives it, upon a new Question or Point of Law, as a Report or Certificate of a notorious Matter of Fact"), the case of *Baller v Watson*, as well as an additional commentary "by another learned and eminent Practiser in the Court of Chancery" who remains unnamed.

[40] H Home, *Remarkable Decisions of the Court of Sessions, From the year 1730 to the year 1752* (Edinburgh, A Kincaid and J Bell, 1766).

[41] *Memorial for The Booksellers of Edinburgh and Glasgow, relating to the Process against them by some of the London Booksellers; which depended before the Court of Session, and is now under Appeal* (undated).

[42] Note that in *The Case of the Respondents*, 11 February 1751, the decision of the Lords of Session is reported in the following terms: "[T]heir Lordships found, That no Action of Damages does lie upon, or in Consequence of, the Statute, but only for the Penalties: And therefore adhered to their former Interlocutor". In *The Case of the Appellants*, 8 February 1751,

COMPLICATIONS WITH THE CLAIM AT COMMON LAW PROPER

The London booksellers appealed to the House of Lords.[43] On 8 January 1750 they entered their petition before the House, *The Case of the Appellants*.[44] The arguments presented on the booksellers behalf, by William Murray and Alexander Lockhart, evidenced a new direction. They began by reciting the 1709 and 1739 Acts and continued that "[u]nder the sanction of the Common Law, and of these two Acts of Parliament" the London booksellers had been encouraged to lay out great sums of money in purchasing various works and giving authors "such prices as were adequate to their Labour and Merit". Then, with echoes of the February 1747 petition prepared by William Grant, Murray and Lockhart freely advocated that the *Statute of Anne* "admits a property in copies of books to have existed in authors before the making of it". This property, they argued:

> [I]s grounded upon Principles of Common Right, and Publick good, and is not created to support the actions given by the statute; but, on the contrary, those actions are given to fence and preserve that property, as their object and foundation.

Stating that the "Rule of Equity" should be the same in England as in Scotland, they alluded to the Chancery cases that supported the reading of the 1709 Act as simply "declaratory of an author's property".[45] The Court of Chancery would, they maintained, "decree [the plaintiff] all the profits which have accrued to the defendant, and an injunction for the future with costs". Picking up on an argument Lockhart had made use of at an earlier stage of the proceedings,[46] they drew a distinction between the "common Informer" and the "Proprietor" of a work. The latter, they suggested, could pursue against an infringer, in Chancery as detailed above. The former, by contrast, was bound solely to the penalties and formalities of the statute. Why was the "Proprietor" not

the decision is recorded in the same terms, with the addition that the Lords "refused the Desire of the Bill". Of the decision, Falconer simply records that: "The Lords adhered", *Falconer's Decisions 1744–1751*, vol 1, No 256, 344–46. WM Morison, *The Decisions of the Court of Session from its Institution until the Separation of the Court into 2 Divisions in the Year 1808*, vol 39–40, Synopsis, vol 1–2 (1811), states: "Found, that no action lies upon the statute, except for such books as have been entered in Stationers' Hall in terms of the statute. And found, that no action of damages lies upon the statute." In an earlier volume, vol 19–20, Morison also provides exactly the same record of the case as that furnished by Home.

[43] LJ 22:488.
[44] BM, Eighteenth Century Reel, 4065/03.
[45] They omit to provide specific cases in support of this.
[46] 15 July 1746.

similarly restricted? Simply because "his *Property* is a sufficient title". The key then to understanding the passing of the *Statute of Anne* at all, was this distinction that they elaborated between the "common Informer" and the "Proprietor", and the fact that:

> The *penal* action given by the Act to the *Common Informer*, is totally distinct from the remedy and relief the *Proprietor* is intitled to; *That* depends upon the positive letter of the Statutes; *This* flows from the general Rules of Law and Justice, in consequence of property, and does not depend upon the Acts of Parliament.

Following this, just as the proprietor of a work was not confined to the penalties of the 1709 Act, as the common Informer was, neither was he "confined to the term of years mentioned in the Act". As a consequence, when a proprietor secured an injunction in Chancery under decree,[47] the decree would be "perpetual", that is, perpetual *in duration*. In support of this novel supposition, Murray and Lockhart referred to two works, *Paradise Lost* and *The Whole Duty of Man*, as examples of "old Books protected by Injunctions at this day".[48]

When the Scottish booksellers replied, their strategy, while successful, regretfully avoided addressing the novel claim that Murray and Lockhart were advocating.[49] They failed to respond to, or even acknowledge, that part of the plaintiffs' argument which made reference to the existence of a common law property in the "copies of books", instead relying upon objections of a technical nature to derail the Londoners' appeal. Essentially, they argued that the plaintiffs had embarked upon an action that was "complicated", maintaining that the action for damages, "if it is taken as an Action upon the Case, it cannot be joined with an Action for the Penalties". That is, it was inconsistent for the plaintiffs to bring a case for both common law damages and the statutory penalties in the same action. Moreover, they contended that the action was, in any event, improper since a single accusation was being brought against 24 separate booksellers "without charging them to be *joint* Offenders". The House of Lords agreed with the Scottish position, making the following declaration:

> That the Action brought by the Appellants in the Court of Session in Scotland was improperly and inconsistently brought, by demanding at the same Time a Discovery and Accompt of the Profits of the Books in Question,

[47] That is, upon a final hearing of the case.

[48] See *Tonson v Walker*, 1739, c.33 1753/208 and *Eyre v Walker*, 1735, c.11 1520/29.

[49] *The Case of the Respondents*, 11 February 1750, British Library, BM Eighteenth Century Reel, 4065/04.

> and also the Penalties of the Act of Parliament, which the Appellants have never absolutely waived in the Proceedings below; and also by joining several Pursuers claiming distinct and independent Rights in different Books in the same Action; and that therefore the Points determined by the said Interlocutors could not regularly come in Question in this Cause.[50]

As a result, "without Prejudice to the Determination of any of the said Points when the same shall properly be brought in Judgement", the issue was returned to the Court of Session to proceed with accordingly. The Scottish booksellers were not awarded their costs. The London booksellers were free to restart proceedings but chose to proceed no further.[51]

[50] LJ 27:489.

[51] Lord Dreghorn provides an account of Lord Hardwicke's opinion on the appeal: "The plaintiffs had mistaken the true course of proceedings, by mixing an action for the penalties with an action or suit for an account of profits". He continued however, that the 1709 Act "might be considered as a general standing patent to authors, for the term of years mentioned in that statute ... but he doubted whether the statute was declaratory of the common law, or introductive of a new law for the encouragement of learning and to give learned men a property which they had not before". Moreover, he continued that, "it was material to consider how the common law of Scotland was before the statute for that might be very material", and concluded that, "a great deal might be offered on this subject, when it came to be fully debated ... and would not be understood to give an opinion which might bind himself"; J MacLaurin, *Considerations on the Nature and Origins of Literary Property* (1768) 26–27, Bodleian, Johnson e. 386.

5(2)

The Lawyers' Tales

I KNOW YOU LAWYERS CAN, WITH EASE, TWIST WORDS AND MEANINGS AS YOU PLEASE;

THROUGHOUT THE ENTIRETY of the *Midwinter/Millar* (1743–1751) litigation, little else had been happening in the English courts.[1] The year after the declaration in the House of Lords however, Jacob Tonson once again clashed horns with Robert Walker over the printing of Milton's *Paradise Lost*.[2] Tonson's initial bill of complaint of 26 November 1751 set out the full history of the work as commodity, from the original assignment by Milton himself to Samuel Symonds, down to the present proprietors, including details of additional comments which had been annexed to the text by Elijah Fenton (in 1727), Richard Bently (in 1732), and most recently, the Rev Thomas Newton (in 1746). Omitting any reference to the *Statute of Anne*, the petitioners set out that they had hoped that:

> [W]hen their right and title to the said Book, Copy, Manuscript and Poem and to the several additional improvements had been established by such a length of uninterrupted possession, [they] should quietly have continued to enjoy the whole and sole right, benefit and advantage of printing [the same] And that no other person or persons would have invaded such Right by printing the same or any part thereof.[3]

In the earlier action, Walker had failed to enter an answer before the court; this time, along with J Marchant, he submitted a response on 12 December 1751. They disputed the claim that the plaintiffs had enjoyed quiet possession of the work in the past noting that "several eminent and learned authors have wrote upon the said Poem" including the "Rev. Paterson, Mr. Addison, the two Richardsons and several others". Their edition, whereby "persons unaquainted with the learned languages and

[1] The only cases that came before the Chancery Court throughout this period (April 1743–February 1750) were *Pope v Bickham* (1744) and *Cogan v Cave* (1744).
[2] Ch 3.
[3] *Tonson v Walker*, c 11 1106/18.

polite literature" were to be introduced to "the various Beauties and Excellancies of this Masterpiece of Heroic Poetry", drew upon all these authors, as well as those named in the plaintiff's edition, correcting their "many errors and imperfections". Their book they claimed was designed to introduce "to the publick in a plain and easy way the true sense and meaning" of the work. In support of this populist publication, they suggested that "every man has a right of writing and publishing his thoughts and remarks upon any book exhibited to the public". In relation to the claim by Tonson of an exclusive right to print the work of Milton itself, the defendants, implicitly referring to the 1709 Act, set out that:

> [T]hey do not dispute but that John Milton [had] a right and property in the fruits of [his] own genius, learning and application and had power to assign and convey such property to the said complainants, or those persons under whom they claim, *for such time as is allowed by the law* ...[4]

The case, for which there exists a report, came before Lord Hardwicke on 25 April 1752.[5] William Murray appeared for the plaintiffs, and Thomas Clarke for the defendants.[6]

Murray began to develop the position he had delineated before the Lords the previous year. Then, he had set out that the *Statute of Anne* was simply "declaratory of an Author's Property", and that this had been confirmed by the Court of Chancery. Now, consolidating this position, he presented before Lord Hardwicke three historical stories: the first preceding the 1709 Act; the second concerning the 1709 Act; the third following on from the 1709 Act. As to the first, he claimed that at common law "authors have a right to their productions ... upon principles of property, upon the constant opinion of all men". In support, he presented a pre-1709 historical sweep acknowledging the existence of common law copyright, through the *Licensing Act* 1662, the bye-laws of the Stationers' Company which were "confirmed by the Chancellor", and various seventeenth century cases concerning letters patent.[7] Throughout all of these, he insisted, there flowed the same notion: that there existed, prior to the *Statute of Anne*, a common law property in the

[4] *Ibid*, emphasis added.

[5] *Tonson v Walker* (1752) 3 Swans 672.

[6] That this was in fact Thomas Clarke is confirmed by a commentary of the case by Willes J in *Millar v Taylor*, reported by William Coke in 1771, where Willes is reported as saying that: "It was argued very diffusively by Lord Mansfield for the plaintiff, and by Sir Thomas Parker for the defendant". While Clarke's second name has been mis-reported in this report, every other report of *Tonson* (1752) refers to Clarke, appearing for the defendant.

[7] For an examination of the patent cases which preceded the *Statute of Anne*, see "Appendix II: A short note on the Patent Cases" in R Deazley, *On the Origin of the Right to Copy*, Doctoral Thesis, (Queen's University, Belfast, 2000). Interestingly, Murray chose to omit any reference to the wealth of letters patent cases post-dating the 1709 Act; ch 3.

reproduction of an author's work. As for the legislation itself, Murray posited that it had been secured at the request of a private petition, which petition asserted "as a thing uncontroverted, that they [the booksellers] had the right in the copies ... the provision by action on the case not being effectual". Moreover, he pointed out that the preamble established that the Act was "to encourage authors" and that "taking away copyright would not do it". Murray was correct in setting out that the booksellers had indeed argued the existence of a right "enjoined by Common Law above 150 years"; what was more, the 1709 Act as originally drafted seemed to confirm such claim. However, what he failed to acknowledge was that the Bill as initially drafted, and the Act as it now stood, were, in emphasis and design, two fundamentally different texts.[8] Third, and last, he presented a mass of Chancery caselaw, focusing almost entirely upon those cases which involved manuscript works (*Webb* (1732), *Forrester* (1741), and *Pope* (1741))[9] and those which involved works first printed well outside the twenty-one year term detailed in the legislation (*Eyre* (1735), *Motte* (1735), *Walthoe* (1737), and *Tonson* (1739)).[10] As manuscript works were not protected by the 1709 Act, he suggested, this was evidence of the fact that the court must have proceeded "on the original right". Similarly, despite the fact that a number of works seemed to fall outside the periods of protection provided by the legislation, injunctions were still granted by the court, which were subsequently acquiesced in. Moreover, on a number of these occasions, the acquiescee had in fact been Walker himself, the defendant.[11]

In a time when there were no official law reports, when cases and legal precedents were gathered in private manuscripts by judges and practising lawyers, manuscripts that were sometimes published, sometimes not, the factual accuracy of such reports was often difficult to ascertain or check. Veeder, examining the history and quality of English law reporting, writes that:

> [T]he long period from 1537 to 1785 is precariously covered by more than one hundred reporters of various degrees of merit. A few of them, such as Plowden, Coke, and Saunders, have long enjoyed an intrinsic authority; others are quite worthless; all are subject to limitations which should never be lost sight of in relying upon their authority as judicial precedents.[12]

[8] Ch 2.
[9] Ch 3. Lord Hardwicke had previously adjudicated over both *Forrester* and *Pope*.
[10] Ch 3. Lord Hardwicke had presided over *Tonson* in its earlier guise.
[11] Although the report does not record Murray as stating which cases he is referring to, it is clear that they are *Eyre* (1735), *Walthoe* (1737) and *Tonson* (1739).
[12] VV Veeder, "The English Reports, 1537–1865" in AALS (Wigmore ed), *Select Essays in Anglo-American Legal History* (Cambridge, CUP, 1908) vol II, 123.

Most commentators cite the advent of Burrow's reports (1757–1771) as marking "an epoch in law reporting".[13] Burrows, who was master of the Crown Office in Lord Mansfield's Court of King's Bench, is taken as heralding the appearance of professional law reporting and law reporters. As Baker comments, "[b]y the end of the [eighteenth] century periodical series were being commissioned for publication in respect of all four superior courts". This he continues, was a venture "which, once the profession accepted the high price of the volumes, ensured a steady succession of accurate and recent reports".[14] In the early 1750s then, when the availability of law reports was dictated by private enterprise, it was relatively easy for Murray to begin to re-present these cases, to re-tell them in the way that best suited his argument, and to effect a transformation in their meaning and relevance. In this action, he began a process in which the history of copyright came to be dictated, not so much by historical fact, accuracy or veracity, but by those stories that could deliver the greatest rhetorical impact. Moreover, it would become clear that for every story that could be spun out in favour of the perpetual right, for every thesis the booksellers could advance, there existed an equally plausible antithesis.

Having heard the plaintiffs' case, Lord Hardwicke commented that should the action proceed to a full hearing, he would "be inclined to send a case to the judges, that the point of law may be finally settled". However, the question as to whether or not to grant an injunction in the meantime remained. On this point, the Lord Chancellor observed that "Dr. Newton's notes come within the statute of Anne", which notes the defendants had admitted making use of in their edition. Reiterating that he was not intending "to determine the general issue" at this stage, Lord Hardwicke invited Walker's counsel to explain how the defendants' use of Newton's notes was "not within the statute". In response, Clarke advanced the premise that a "fair abridgement" did not violate the Act, relying in particular upon the decision of *Gyles v Wilcox* (1741), wherein Lord Hardwicke himself had adjudged that Wilcox had made a fair abridgement of Hale's *Pleas of the Crown*.[15] From this point onwards, the action became another in the series of Chancery cases addressing the issue of abridging a text that fell within the protections of the *Statute of Anne*.[16] Noting that the important question to ask was "whether the alterations make it a new work, or are intended evasively to colour a new edition",

[13] *Ibid*, 1, 43. See also JH Baker, *An Introduction to English Legal History*, 4th edn (London, Butterworths, 2002) 178–86 and AH Manchester, *A Modern Legal History of England and Wales 1750–1950* (London, Butterworths, 1980) 23–25.

[14] Baker, *An Introduction to English Legal History*, n 13 above, 184.

[15] Ch 3.

[16] *Ibid*.

the Lord Chancellor took some time to consider the various texts involved. Five days after the initial hearing, on 30 April 1752, despite reiterating that "a fair abridgement would be entitled to protection", he explained that he considered Merchant's work to be "a mere evasion". An injunction was granted "till Hearing", and Tonson was ordered "to speed his cause". Not surprisingly, he never did. As for the legal counsel in the case, it would be another decade before either Murray or Clarke would once again engage with the issue of property in books. However, when they did so, it was to be as members of the judiciary. By 1761, Thomas Clarke had become Sir Thomas Clarke, Master of the Rolls, sitting in the Court of Chancery. By 1761, William Murray had become Lord Mansfield, Chief Justice of the King's Bench.

THAT LANGUAGE, BY YOUR SKILL MADE PLIANT, WILL BEND TO FAVOUR EV'RY CLIENT;

In *Dodsley v Kinnersley* (1761)[17] the plaintiffs had published a work by Samuel Johnson, *Rasselas, The Prince of Abyssinia, A Tale* (in two volumes). The defendants reprinted part of the narrative in their *Grand Magazine of Magazines* but "left out all the reflections". Dodsley filed a bill for an injunction and an account of profits. For the first time, at this interlocutory stage before the Court of Chancery, Lord Keeper Henley refused to grant the plaintiff his injunction. Echoing Lord Chancellor Macclesfield in *Burnet v Chetwood* (1721),[18] Henley doubted whether *The Prince of Abyssinia* "was such a book as the statute of Queen Anne intended to protect". By the time the case came on for the hearing, before Sir Thomas Clarke, Dodsley sought only the injunction. The Master of the Rolls, unlike Henley, refused to become embroiled in questions of aesthetic judgment. Rather, he proposed to determine the case on the more straightforward point as to whether or not there had been any infringement of the property. Following on from this position, like *Tonson* (1752), this case became a simple enquiry as to an abridged text. Clarke MR began his consideration of this issue, with the observation that:

> [T]he subject matter of this suit has been so often before the Court upon other occasions that when a Case of this kind comes to be litigated, little more is necessary than to see whether it is adapted to the rules and principles before laid down.

[17] *Dodsley v Kinnersley* (1761) Amb 403.
[18] *Burnet v Chetwood* (1721) 2 Mer 441.

He continued however with the proviso that "no certain line can be drawn, to distinguish a fair abridgement but every case must depend on its own circumstances." It was determined that, by the date of the filing of the original bill, the defendants had lifted little more than one-tenth of the plaintiff's first volume, which was considered sufficient to adjudge the defendant's abridgement fair.

THAT 'TIS THE FEE DIRECTS THE SENSE TO MAKE OUT EITHER SIDE'S PRETENCE

While *Dodsley* (1761) was being decided in the Chancery court, another case was pending before the Court of King's Bench: *Tonson v Collins* (1761).[19] This case took up the position that had been earlier expounded by William Murray in *Millar* (1749–51) and *Tonson* (1752). It was not Murray, however, who would once again adopt the defence of the London booksellers. Now, he was presiding over the case in the guise of Lord Mansfield. Significantly, having previously advocated the existence of the common law right before Lord Chancellor Hardwicke, he was now presiding over the first case in which the booksellers argued the existence of a common law copyright before a court of common law. Rose, writing about the timing of *Tonson* (1761) suggests that it was this factor, Murray's recent elevation to the King's Bench, that prompted the booksellers to act. He continues:

> Also encouraging to them perhaps was the first decision in a literary-property matter handed down by Lord Mansfield's court, *Baskett v University of Cambridge* (1758), in which the court considered that the crown held a perpetual prerogative copyright on certain works that, like any other copyright, could be assigned.[20]

In *Basket* (1758) Thomas and Robert Basket, sons to John Basket, and executors of his estate, had complained about the University printing a work entitled *An Exact Abridgment of all the Acts of Parliament Relating to excise on Beer, Ale, Brandy, Vinegar or other Liquors, with some few Notes and References*. They claimed that they held the exclusive privilege of printing all Acts of Parliament, under the letters patent granted by Queen Anne in October 1713, which grant took effect on 10 January 1739. Joseph Bentham, the Cambridge University printer, argued on the other hand, that under a grant from Henry VIII to the University in July 1534, the

[19] *Tonson v Collins* (1761) 1 Black W 301.
[20] M Rose, *Authors and Owners: The Invention of Copyright* (London, Harvard University Press, 1993) 74.

University had the privilege of printing *omnes et omnimodos libros*, all manner of books, approved by the Chancellor. This included books of statute law.[21] The Court of King's Bench, treading a diplomatic line between the two parties, found that the plaintiffs were "intitled to the right of printing Acts of Parliament and abridgments of Acts of Parliament, exclusive of all other persons not authorised to print the same by prior grants". They continued, however, that by virtue of the 1534 grant, the University had been "intrusted with a *concurrent authority* to print Acts of Parliament... upon the terms in the said letters patent". While this vindicated the universities' right to print the works, it was implicit that they were to exercise such rights for the public benefit, for the advancement of education, but not explicitly for profit. Foster J, one of the members of Lord Mansfield's court, wrote to Oxford University following the conclusion of the case. Recounting the decision, he added that the court had considered "the powers given by the letters patent" as being ones entrusted "for public benefit, for the advancement of literature, and not to be transferred upon lucrative views to other hands". He continued by articulating his hope that "both the universities will always consider the Royal grants in that light".[22]

Tonson (1761), concerning a reprint of Addison and Steele's *The Spectator*, first published in 1711, developed the arguments used in *Millar* (1749–1751) and *Tonson* (1752).[23] Alexander Wedderburn,[24] arguing on behalf of the plaintiff, extended Murray's pre-history of copyright back through the bye-laws of the Company, the letters patent cases and the *Licensing Act* 1662; back through the various decrees of

[21] *Basket v University of Cambridge* (1758) 2 Keny 397; 1 Black W 105; 2 Burr 661.

[22] (1758) 1 Black W 105, 122.

[23] Feather writing about this case notes that "[i]n the lower courts, the jury had been unable to reach a verdict, and it was now for the King's Bench to resolve the issue"; J Feather, *Publishing, Piracy and Politics: An Historical Study of Copyright in Britain* (London, Mansell, 1994) 84. The actual report of the jury's "special verdict" runs as follows:

> That before the reign of Queen Anne, it was usual to purchase from authors the perpetual copy-right of their books, and to assign the same for valuable consideration, and to settle them in family settlements, for the provision of wives and children.... That the defendant, without licence of the plaintiffs, and knowing the said copy to have been purchased by said Jacob Tonson deceased, printed, published and sold several copies of the same in April and May 1759, whereby the plaintiffs were damnified; but whether the defendant is liable in law to answer damages, they are ignorant. But if the Court shall adjudge him liable, they find him guilty, damages 5l.; if otherwise, not guilty.

(1761) 1 Black W 301–2.

[24] Wedderburn, later, Lord Loughborough, Earl of Rosslyn, was appointed King's Counsel in 1763, the Solicitor-General in 1771, the Attorney-General in 1778, the Chief Justice of Common Pleas in 1780, and held the office of Lord Chancellor between the years of 1793–1801. See in general, AWB Simpson (ed), *Biographical Dictionary of the Common Law* (London, Butterworths, 1984).

the Star Chamber,[25] the incorporation of the Company of Stationers, and the origins of the prerogative copy-right; back to the very introduction of printing itself by Caxton in 1471. He also introduced ruminations upon the very nature of property, quoting from John Selden,[26] and relying upon Grotius for the maxim that "invention is one ground of property, occupancy another".[27] The right of the plaintiffs, he contested, was based upon invention. In support of this proposition he pointed to the "manuscript cases" which Murray had previously made use of in *Tonson* (1752), and asserted that "[w]hile a work is in manuscript, the author has entire dominion over it". Anticipating the objection that, even if such property was born of invention, it was incapable of possession, Wedderburn set out that the property in question was an incorporeal one; it was no more or less than the profits in a book:

> The right of authors is now to be determined; not of any particular bookseller. From the industry of the author, a profit must arise to somebody; I contend it belongs to the author; and when I speak of the right of property, I mean in the profits of his book, not in the sentiments, style, &c.

In addition, Wedderburn relied upon other of the earlier Chancery decisions, including the "ancient author" cases, as well as *Baller v Watson* (1737), important due to the fact that the Lord Chancellor had decreed a perpetual injunction, which, he argued, "he could not have done merely under the Act".

Edward Thurlow, acting for the defendant, set forth two main limbs to his counter-argument.[28] First, he insisted that the property argued for "does not exist naturally or flow from natural law". As to the existence such property in the "profits of a work", Thurlow posited that:

> Property in the profits of publication must presuppose property in the thing itself. And the subject of this property, if any, must be in the abstracted, ideal, incorporeal composition. Now, the idea of the composition, as it lies in the author's mind, before it is substantiated by reducing it into writing, has no one idea of property annexed to it.

He denied any distinction between the author and the inventor stating that "[i]f the labour of the head gives the right, the property is just

25 1566, 1586, and 1637. See ch 1, n 4.

26 John Selden (1584–1654), an English jurist, who wrote a number of works ranging over English law, history, the classics, Hebrew, Arabic, Turkish, Persian and oriental learning. See Simpson, *Biographical Dictionary*, n 24 above.

27 Hugo Grotius (de Groot), (1583–1645), the Dutch jurist, whose major work, *De iure belli ac pacis* (*On the law of war and peace*) (1625), sought to establish certain universal principles of law, which could be applied irrespective of time or place, deduced directly from man's nature, independent of theological considerations. *Ibid.*

28 Thurlow, later Lord Thurlow of Ashfield was appointed first Solicitor-General then Attorney-General in 1770, and later Lord Chancellor in 1778. *Ibid.*

the same". For Thurlow, there were two species of property: the physical book, protected by the ordinary rules of common law; and the composition, the incorporeal "labour of the head", which existed, as was the case for inventions, only so far as it was protected by the state. Once the statutory protection of this second form of property came to an end, every man was free to do what he pleased with his book, which included the freedom to reprint the work. Secondly, Thurlow endeavoured to undermine Wedderburn's pre-history by establishing that "where this kind of property has been spoken of by learned men, or even by Courts of Justice", they were merely referring to "the extraordinary Acts of the State". Since the introduction of the printed word, he observed, "privilegeing and printing went hand in hand". Such privileges, or patents, were "totally foreign to any notion of copy-right" having been created solely for "reasons of State".

Lord Mansfield decreed that the case stand over for further argument, suggesting that both counsel look further into two types of Chancery case. The first, he commented, were those in which "there had been no printing or publication at all", citing Lord Hardwicke's decision in the case of *Pope v Curl* (1741).[29] The second were those cases where "the term given by Act of Parliament has been clearly expired". Of these Lord Mansfield noted that he could "remember no case" when the merits had been fully argued, or the injunction made perpetual upon the hearing of the cause. Despite these limitations however, he thought fit to add: "[A]nd yet they have great authority". In directing counsel to those cases concerning unpublished manuscripts (*Webb* (1732), *Forrester* (1741), *Pope* (1741)) and those texts for which the protection of the *Statute of Anne* had expired (*Eyre* (1735), *Motte* (1735), *Walthoe* (1737)), Mansfield was, of course, directing them to those cases that he himself had presented before Lord Hardwicke in *Tonson* (1752).[30] Ten years earlier William Murray had sought to convince Lord Hardwicke that in these cases lay evidence of the earlier Chancery judiciary proceeding upon "the original right" of the author. Thurlow had simply dismissed the decisions arguing that none of them were contrary to the doctrine he advanced. Wedderburn had made reference to these cases, but his emphasis lay with the decree of perpetual injunction in *Baller*. Lord Mansfield, that "champion of the author's common law right",[31] with this direction, was encouraging a line of reasoning that would operate in the booksellers' favour. It was an argument that he himself had earlier written; the hint would not be ignored.

[29] *Pope v Curl* (1741) 2 Atk 342.
[30] *Tonson v Walker* (1752) 3 Swans 672.
[31] Rose, *Authors and Owners*, n 20 above, 74.

WHEN YOU PERUSE THE CLEAREST CASE, YOU SEE IT WITH A DOUBLE FACE;

The case was reheard in 1762, this time with William Blackstone as plaintiff's counsel, and Joseph Yates representing the defendants.[32] Blackstone, who would later be one of the eleven judges to give an opinion in the seminal decision of *Donaldson v Becket* (1774),[33] took up what Wedderburn had previously begun. Commenting that "it is more satisfactory, first to convince by reason, than merely to silence by authority", he embarked upon an extensive discourse on the existence of common law copyright "[a]s founded in reason". The aim was "to sift right to the bottom, and to argue on principles". Blackstone's philosophical rock proved to be the writings of John Locke.[34] Asserting that the natural foundation of property was "invention and labour" he explained that an original composition exhibited both these qualities: its *originality* implied invention; the *composition* implied industry and labour. Of labour in particular, he argued that the "exertion of animal faculties" and "the exertion of the rational powers" should have "as fair a title to confer property" as each other. "Property" he declared "may with equal reason be acquired by mental, as by bodily labour". Blackstone was clearly influenced by Locke's *Second Treatise on Government*, but had obviously failed to acquaint himself with Locke's personal views as to what property subsisted in books.[35] He continued with two logically spurious arguments. The first, born out of common utility, operated as follows:

> Without some advantage proposed, few would read, study, compose or publish. This advantage can only arise from the profits of publication: and those profits can only be secured, by vesting in the author an exclusive right of publication. Universal law has established a permanent perpetual property in bodily acquisitions: and reason requires, that the property in mental acquisitions should be equally permanent.

The second turned upon the fundamental premise that "[t]he one essential requisite of every subject of property is, that it must be a thing of value". From this he continued that value consists in an object's capacity to be exchanged for other valuable things. Therefore, if something can be so exchanged, it must have value and "[w]hatever therefore has a value is the subject of property". That is, property equals value equals

[32] *Tonson v Collins* (1762) 1 Black W 321.
[33] *Donaldson v Becket* (1774) 4 Burr 2408; 2 Bro PC 129.
[34] Blackstone made reference to Locke's *Second Treatise of Government*, "Chapter V: Of Property", reprinted in J Locke, JW Gough (ed), *The Second Treatise of Government* (Oxford, Blackwell, 1966); in particular see ss 27–28.
[35] Ch 1, n 12 and accompanying text.

opportunity to exchange; therefore, an ability to exchange equals value equals property.

In contradistinction to Thurlow, Blackstone maintained that "a literary composition, as it lies in the authors mind" had, before being reduced to writing, "the essential requisites to make it the subject of property", and proceeded by examining the nature of the property in question. Also rejecting Wedderburn's claim that the property lay not in the "sentiment" or "style" of a book, but simply in the profits to be made from the sale of the book, Blackstone substituted a tripartite understanding of the work. He suggested that there exists *the physical book*, the *ideas* conveyed in that book, and *the composition*, "those words in which an author has clothed his ideas". "Characters are but the signs of words, and words are but the vehicles of sentiments". For Blackstone it was the composition, or the sentiment, that proved the thing of value from which the profit should arise. It followed from this exposition, that the purchaser of a book, while he acquires certain rights over the book as property,[36] did not however acquire "a right to the sentiment, so as to multiply copies". Noting that printing was no more than an "art of speedily transcribing", Blackstone continued:

> If an author has an exclusive property in his own composition, while it lies in his mind, when clothed in words, when reduced to writing; he still retains the sole right of multiplying the copies, when it is committed to the press.

Having exhausted the position from principle, Blackstone then turned to the law. After re-presenting Wedderburn's pre-history of copyright, he embarked upon a more in depth exposition of those cases that had come "out of Chancery": *Webb* (1732), *Eyre* (1735), *Motte* (1735), *Walthoe* (1737), *Tonson* (1739), and *Pope* (1741). Admitting that they were "not quite decisive", as few had proceeded to a final decree, he nevertheless continued that they showed "the uniform opinion of that Court, that a copy-right may, and does subsist, independent of the Statute of Queen Anne". The argument resonated with Mansfield's own stance in *Tonson* (1752) when he had argued that "at the common law, authors have a right to their productions, exclusive and independent" of the *Statute of Anne*, and that "subsequent determinations and expositions show that it has been so understood".[37] Having finished his examination of the Chancery

[36] Blackstone commented: "The purchaser of a single book may make any use he pleases of it; but no man, without leave from the author, has the right of making new books, by multiplying copies of the old. If a man has an opera ticket, he may lend it to as many friends as he pleases; but he may not counterfeit the impression, and forge others".
[37] *Tonson* (1752) 3 Swans 672, 674.

authorities, Blackstone concluded his opening dialogue by stating that the property argued for was "founded on the principles of reason, universal justice, public convenience and private property".

Yates, who would later deliver the only dissenting opinion in the case of *Millar v Taylor* (1768),[38] began by conceding the point that the faculties of the mind could give a property just as well as those of the body. He continued however, that such property as exists in an author's "sentiments", may "be rendered common by the act of the proprietor". The crucial event was that of *publication*. Until that time the author maintained dominion over his text. Upon publication however, the author's property was "thrown into a state of universal communion". While Blackstone stressed the concepts of invention, labour and value, Yates focussed upon the importance of two fundamentals of property: *possession*, and *indicia*. As to the first, he relied upon Pufendorf and Bynkershoek, as authorities for the proposition that property "must be something susceptible of possession". Upon publication of one's ideas, however, the author could no longer claim to retain anything capable of "separate and exclusive enjoyment". For Yates, property was, above all, a physical rather than a metaphysical entity; it was something "that may be seen, felt, given, delivered, lost or stolen", something that one could lay one's hand upon. In the case of indicia, he asked what marks of appropriation existed to ascertain which "property" belonged to whom. Referring to Lord Kames who, in his work, *History of Property*, laid down "visible possession ... as an essential condition of property", Yates asked, "[w]hat are the marks?", and "[h]ow is an author to be distinguished"? He continued, in a familiar vein, that "the act of publication has thrown down all distinction, and made the work common to everybody; like land thrown into the highway it is become a gift to the public".

Moving on to consider "the local law of the kingdom", Yates elaborated upon Thurlow's earlier synopsis of the pre-history to the *Statute of Anne*. The stationers' bye-laws were characterised as "private regulations", the letters patent were "merely privileges", the King's prerogative had nothing to do with the present case, and the decrees of the Star Chamber were dismissed as being merely political in scope and intent. He re-examined the wording of the 1709 Act itself, as well dismissing the significance of the Chancery cases arguing that "whatever that Court prohibits" was not necessarily "actionable at law". The Lord Chief Justice, at this point, interjected with the observation that "[i]f the injunction be well founded, the same determination would be at law". Having stated Blackstone's position, in stronger terms than Blackstone himself had, Mansfield LCJ continued by reminding Yates of his opposing counsel's argument that

[38] *Millar v Taylor* (1768) 4 Burr 2303.

works outside the terms of the Act, as well as unpublished manuscripts, seemed to go "upon the original right". Yates replied that for those cases where the term was expired, the injunctions were only until answer, and as to unpublished manuscripts, that the author had dominion over the text, but only until the point of publication. Again, at the point of publication, he commented, the author "emancipates" his work "and makes it common". In Yates' consideration there could exist no natural common law right to literary property. Only the state, through legislative intervention could provide succour for the author. Agreeing with Thurlow, that there was no difference between the work of an author and that of an inventor, Yates observed:

> Both are the productions of genius, both require labour and study, and both by publication become equally common to the world. The Legislature seems to have judged so.

Lord Mansfield did not restrict himself to the one comment, during the course of the defendant's argument. When Yates had described property as something that had to be "seen, felt, given, delivered, lost or stolen", the Lord Chief Justice interrupted once more, essentially dismissing the counsel's position, with the question: "How would you steal an option, or the next turn of an advowson?" Yates' reliance upon the physical, failed to take account of those incorporeal forms of property that had been acknowledged by the common law, and Blackstone was quick to capitalise upon both Yates' omission, and Mansfield's interjection. Given the opportunity to reply, Blackstone commenced by pointing out that Yates' analysis had "omitted the distinction between corporeal and incorporeal rights". Both, he suggested, were considered a good basis for property. Capitalising upon Mansfield LCJ's interjection, Blackstone made reference to numerous examples of incorporeal hereditaments, including options, advowsons, commons and ways, drawing parallels between grazing cattle on common land, between exercising a right of way over another's land, and the publishing of a book. Denying that the act of publication was fatal to the existence of a common law right and rejecting the opinion that "a book when published, is a gift to the public, like land thrown into a highway", Blackstone drew what he considered to be a more apposite analogy:

> [I]t is more like making a way through a man's own private grounds, which he may stop at pleasure; he may give out a number of keys, by publishing a number of copies; but no man who receives a key, has thereby a right to forge others, and sell them to other people.

The story of copyright in books had travelled a long way in little over fifteen years. Throughout *Midwinter v Hamilton* (1743–1748), the London booksellers' strongest position came with an understanding which advocated that:

> [I]n Consequence of the Property declared by the Statute to belong to the Authors of Books, and their Assigns, there arises ... an Action founded, not upon the Express words of the Statute giving such Action, but by the Rules of common Law, as a necessary Consequence of the Property itself established by the Statute.[39]

In short, the *Statute of Anne* had *created* a property right, which, by definition carried certain common law penalties for invasion. By now, however, something new, something altogether different had begun to surface.

Lord Mansfield, commenting that the issue in question had never yet been finally determined, decided that it should be debated before all the twelve judges of the courts of common law, and so ordered that the case be adjourned, to stand over for further argument.[40] As before however, he gave some indication of how he himself might decide the issue, in remarking that:

> [A] fair argument will arise from Sir Joseph Jekyll's, Lords Macclesfield's, Talbot's and Hardwicke's proceedings, that they thought there was a property in the author at common law: else they would not have granted the injunctions that have been cited.

Having been referred for the consideration of all twelve common law judges sitting *en banc*, it emerged that the action had been a collusive one, directed by Tonson, designed to obtain a judgment favouring the existence of the common law right. The judges refused to proceed with their determination, considering the precedent of a collusive action, a dangerous one to set. Willes J, in *Donaldson v Becket* (1774), who favoured the existence of a common law copyright, later recounted the incident in the following manner:

> After these two arguments, the case was adjourned into the Exchequer Chamber. I have been informed from the best authority [Lord Mansfield], that so far as the Court had formed an opinion, they all inclined to the plaintiff. But as they suspected that the action was brought by collusion;

[39] *The Petition of Daniel Midwinter*, 9 December 1747.

[40] Rose commenting upon Lord Mansfield's decision to refer the case to the twelve common law judges, writes: "[the] unusual decision to have the case heard by all twelve common-law judges — the judges of King's bench, Common Pleas, and Exchequer assembled *en banc* — was evidently intended to give the decision the widest possible authority so that, even if no appeal were filed, the court's determination would stand"; Rose, *Authors and Owners*, n 20 above, 75.

and a nominal defendant set up, in order to obtain a judgment, which might be a precedent against third persons; and that therefore a judgment in favour of the plaintiff would certainly have been acquiesced in; upon this suspicion, and because the Court inclined to the plaintiff, it was ordered to be heard before all the Judges. Afterwards upon certain information received by the Judges, "that the whole was a collusion, and that the defendant was nominal only and the whole expence paid by the plaintiff," they refused to proceed in the cause though it had been argued bona fide, and very ably, by the counsel, who appeared for the defendant. They thought this contrivance to get a collusive judgment was an attempt of a dangerous example, and therefore to be discouraged.

FOR SCEPTICISM'S YOUR PROFESSION; YOU HOLD THERE'S DOUBT IN ALL EXPRESSION.[41]

[41] J Gay, "The Dog and the Fox" in *Fables By the late Mr Gay. Volume the Second* (1738), reprinted in J Gay, *Fables, Two Volumes in One* (Menston, The Scholar Press Limited, 1969).

6

Property and the Pamphleteers

> I also give and bequeath to the said Mr. Warburton the property of all such of my Works already printed, as he hath written, or shall write Commentaries or Notes upon, and which I have not otherwise disposed of, or alienated; and all the profits which shall arise after my death from such editions as he shall publish without future alterations.[1]

SO RAN THAT part of Alexander Pope's will which, in 1744, appointed William Warburton as guardian, editor, and beneficiary, of his literary estate. In June 1751 John Knapton published *The Works of Alexander Pope Esq., In Nine Volumes Complete. With his last Corrections, Additions and Improvements; As they were delivered to the Editor a little before his Death: Together with the Commentaries and Notes of Mr. Warburton*.[2] The editor's profits from the first five editions of the work ran in excess of £2,500.[3] Four years earlier Warbuton had edited *The Works of Shakespear in eight volumes* for Jacob Tonson, the same publisher who had twice previously tussled with Robert Walker over the printing of Milton's *Paradise Lost*. That same year, 1747, Warbuton wrote *A Letter from an author, to a Member of Parliament, concerning literary property*.[4] In doing so, he proved to be one of the first of a number of writers to contribute to the developing debate over literary property outside the confines of the courtroom. A beneficiary of Pope's literary estate as well as an author and editor in his own right, Warburton was, not surprisingly, robust in his defence of the author's right to control the publication of his work in perpetuity. It would be fifteen years, however, before another writer took up the pen to publicly address this issue of property in books. In 1762, while *Tonson v Collins* was under debate, two epistles appeared. The first, *An Enquiry into*

[1] Quoted in DW Nichol, *Pope's Literary Legacy: The Book-Trade Correspondence of William Warburton and John Knapton with other letters and documents, 1744–1780* (Oxford, The Oxford Bibliographical Society, 1992) xxxii.

[2] The other booksellers involved in the production of this edition were: Henry Lintot, Jacob and Richard Tonson, Somerset Draper, Paul Knapton and Charles Bathurst.

[3] Nichol notes that the exact figure was £2,626 0*s* 9*d*. Nichol, *Pope's Literary Legacy*, n 1 above, xxxiii.

[4] *A letter from an author, to a Member of Parliament, concerning literary property* (London, Knapton, 1747) reprinted in *The Works of William Warburton* (London, Cadell & Davies, 1811) vol 12.

the Nature and Origin of Literary Property, was very much a belated reaction to Warburton's earlier treatise;[5] *A Vindication of the Exclusive Right of Authors, to their own works*, responded, in kind, to *An Enquiry*. Two further pamphlets were to be published on the subject before the consideration of the case *Millar v Taylor* (1768) by Lord Mansfield's court.[6] *Some Thoughts on the State of Literary Property* was printed in 1764 by the Scottish bookseller Alexander Donaldson,[7] accompanying the opening of his "shop for cheap books two doors east from Norfolk-street, in the Strand" in London. The second, four years later, was *Considerations on the Nature and Origin of Literary Property*. Not written, but published by Donaldson, like the Scottish bookseller's tract, it supported the view that literary property was vested in the author by the *Statute of Anne* and so was limited to the finite time for protection laid down in that Act.[8] The author of this last pamphlet was John MacLaurin, later Lord Dreghorn, who would subsequently lead the defence for Alexander Donaldson, before the Scottish Court of Session, in the case of *Hinton v Donaldson* (1773).[9] To these various publications can be added William Blackstone's *Commentaries on the Laws of England*, which appeared in four volumes between 1765 and 1769. The second volume of this work, published in 1766, was given over to the consideration "Of the Rights of Things" in which Blackstone specifically considered "the right which an author may be supposed to have in his own original literary compositions".[10] Not surprisingly, his commentary on this species of property did not stray overmuch from the position he had advocated in *Tonson v Collins* (1762), nor from the one he would adhere to, as a judge, in *Donaldson v Becket* (1774).

These various publications contributed to the numerous rhetorical strands that had emerged through *Midwinter* (1743–1748), *Millar* (1749–1751), *Tonson* (1752) and *Tonson* (1761, 1762). These writers created a

[5] *An Enquiry into the Nature and Origin of Literary Property* (1762) reprinted in S Parks (ed), *Horace Walpole's Political Tracts 1747–1748 with Two by William Warburton on Literary Property, 1747 and 1762* (New York, NY, Garland, 1974). This has often been misattributed to Warburton himself. That he should adopt such a contrary position is unlikely, given that in 1759, fifteen years after Pope's death, he supervised the sale of John Knapton's share in Pope's works to Andrew Millar and Somerset Draper, and in the same year, wrote to Mercy Doddridge sharing his thoughts on copyright with her in the following terms: "If the work was written within fourteen years, the property is secured by Act of Parliament; when that time is elapsed, it is then claimed by Common Law"; see Nichol, *Pope's Literary Legacy*, n 1 above, lix, 129.

[6] Ch 7.

[7] *Some Thoughts on the State of Literary Property*, reprinted in S Parks (ed), *The Literary Property Debate: Six Tracts 1764–1774* (New York, NY, Garland, 1975).

[8] *Considerations on the Nature and Origin of Literary Property*, Bodleian, Johnson e 386. See also his later essay: *On the Origin and Progress of Literary Property* (1798) reprinted in RA Macfie, *Copyright and Patents for Inventions* (Edinburgh, T&T Clark, 1879).

[9] Ch 7.

[10] W Blackstone, *Commentaries on the Laws of England* (Oxford, OUP, 1766) vol II.

dialogue that both rehearsed and extended an existing debate. These two traditions, those for and against the common law right, embraced the earlier proponents of their cause, and engaged each other in argument and counterargument, thesis and antithesis. Between them they generated a debate that was legally, intellectually and historically unique, a chain-story that would fashion the very nature of literary property.[11] Much was made of the law, both written and unwritten, that had gone before: the pre-history of the *Statute of Anne* was addressed; comparisons were drawn with other continental systems of protection; the wording of the Act itself received multifarious interpretations; the Chancery caselaw was subject to contrasting readings; common law precedents were sought. This placed the debate in a legal-historical framework. Alongside this, deliberations of a more ontological character were generated. The very nature of property itself was considered, as well as the way in which literary property sat within that broader analysis. This more conceptual methodology inevitably invited comparisons, and distinctions, with similar and dissimilar property rights. In addition to the legal and the theoretical, a third framework emerged: what consequences would follow should the existence of a common law copyright be vindicated? The impact that the decision would have upon both the reading public in general, and the book trade in particular, were considered at some length, in addition to which, constitutional arguments were raised about the role of the judiciary, their relationship with the legislature (in the guise of the *Statute of Anne*), and their place in resolving the issue at hand. Three conversational streams: law, theory, consequence.

LAW

William Murray had incorporated a seventeenth century tale of common law copyright into his argument in *Tonson* (1752), which was later extended by Alexander Wedderburn in *Tonson* (1761) back through the seventeenth and sixteenth, back to the introduction of printing into England by Caxton. Edward Thurlow seeking to undermine Wedderburn's thesis, established his own pre-history, characterising the earlier precedents as "extraordinary Acts of the State". While Blackstone in *Tonson* (1762) made reference to the "antient usage" of the stationers, the

[11] Of this period, Sherman and Bently write: "[O]ne of the reasons why the battle of the booksellers is so interesting and why it has received so much attention in intellectual property scholarship is that it was not only the first but perhaps the only time in which so many issues were discussed at such length and in such detail"; B Sherman and L Bently, *The Making of Modern Intellectual Property Law, The British Experience, 1760–1911* (Cambridge, CUP, 1999) 15.

Licensing Act, and the prerogative grant cases, Joseph Yates expanded upon Thurlow's historical meditation, dismissing bye-laws, patents, the Crown's prerogative, and Star Chamber decrees respectively, as private regulations and mere privileges, purely political in design, and so, essentially irrelevant. The author of *An Enquiry* took "the history of literary property" back even further than Yates, back to the times when "[t]he first Bards strolled from House to House ... little dreaming of Property in those unpremeditated Strains which flowed from the Warmth of their Fancy". Examining the literary tradition of the ancient poets he declared "neither the Authors nor their Assigns, in the Republics of Greece and Rome, ever claimed an exclusive Right in their Copies after their Publication." As printing was introduced into England, he explained, "it became a Part of the Prerogative". When the prerogative was limited "and the Liberty of the Press established, this Right must of Necessity vanish". As with Yates before him, a distinction was drawn between the remaining prerogative printing rights, and those rights that the author was entitled to under the 1709 Act. The former he pointed out were:

> [P]urely founded on Maxims of Policy, because these books are of public importance. Matters of public concern, and things that relate to the government, were never left to any man's liberty to print that would. This cannot be made a precedent in favour of the right claimed in other copies, which stand on a different foundation.

The response in *A Vindication*, took the form of a treatment of the history of literature and its place in English society. In the time of Henry VII, when the press was in its infancy, the king "was not distinguished by his love of literature". In the succeeding reign of Henry VIII, when the "king himself was an author", "learning made a rapid progress" even if it was mostly concerned with "ecclesiasticks". Under Elizabeth's guidance "literature reaped a bounteous harvest", however, he continued, it was the reign of "the unfortunate Charles" which contributed "more than all those preceding, to enlighten the bulk of the people". After this, he maintained, "Real learning ... shone forth in its full lustre in the days of queen Anne". His purpose in charting this alternate pre-history to the *Statute of Anne*, was to establish the reason as to why the author's right was never before made manifest. In times past, when authors were supported by "the especial patronage of the great", there was simply no need for them to assert their natural rights over their work. Now however, "since authors and readers are multiplied", now that the public had become "the patrons of learning", now "the case is extremely different". Whereas before, authors could rely upon "liberal gratuities from the bounty of their patrons", now, by necessity, they had to be concerned with the "circulation of their copies" and the profits raised thereby.

The discussion in *An Enquiry* was not however limited to the British experience. He conjectured that some weight might be added to what had already been said "if it be shown that the sense of other Nations on this point, corresponds with the policy of our common law". The comparison with these other continental jurisdictions provided useful material for those arguing against the perpetual right. On 15 January 1747, James Graham, arguing for the Scottish booksellers in *Midwinter* (1743–1748), had requested of the Court of Session "a moderate time for looking into the Practice of the Law of England, and of other foreign Countries". On 29 May, they recounted, for the court, a brief history of printing in Europe, noting that these other jurisdictions, such as Venice, Florence, Spain and France, had always rewarded the labours of authors and printers, through the principle of granting temporary privileges. This reading was echoed by MacLaurin in *Considerations* who observed that the art of printing was early claimed as part of the prerogative. Upon this footing:

> [S]tood these Privileges all over Europe, it never having been once dreamed, that they were granted *ex justicia* in Virtue of a *perfect* Right, but indulged from favour, and a View to public Expediency.

The author of *An Enquiry* recounted the example of the case that Galilæo brought against Simon Marius, before the Lords Reformers of the University of Padua, in Venice, in 1607. Marius had printed a Latin translation of Galilæo's work of the year before, in the name of one of his disciples, Capra. The Lords, finding that "Galilæo had been abused", ordered that all the remaining copies of the pirate work be brought before them "to be suppressed in such Manner as they shall think fit". Despite the fact that this affair "was not cognizable by the Common Law of Venice", the Lords Reformers nevertheless had "a peculiar Jurisdiction in literary Disputes"; they decreed that Marius had contravened the "Laws of Printing".

In addition to these competing pre-histories, there emerged a considerable difference of opinion as to the meaning and significance of the *Statute of Anne*. That the wording of this Act, could, at the same time, positively support as well as refute any notion of a pre-existing property in books, stood testament to the peculiar skill of those who had drafted this "perfidious measure". In February 1747, William Grant, acting on behalf of the London booksellers in *Midwinter* (1743–1748), had tentatively suggested that the Act's preamble implicitly accepted the existence of the author's natural right. In the same year, Warburton, asserted that:

> [I]gnorance and knavery have concurred to represent [the 1709 Act] as a *restrictive*, and not *accumulative* law; and consequently, to suppose it the *sole foundation*, instead of an *additional support*, of literary property.

He too relied upon the preamble of the Act, describing it as "plainly declarative" of the existence of a previous property. In addition, he suggested that the proviso for the universities, setting out that nothing in the Act would extend either to "prejudice or confirm" any existing right, was evidence that the legislators had two things in mind, namely, "the *natural right*, and that which is founded on patents". As to the fourteen year limitation? This was an entirely pragmatic calculation by the legislature, designed to support the author when the temptation to invade his property was greatest, "which is, generally, on the first publication of a book, and some few years afterwards". In *A Vindication* the writer cited, with approval, Warburton's assessment of the 1709 Act as a cumulative and not a restrictive law. Moreover, he suggested that the very first section of the Act, referring as it did to "the author of any book, who *hath not transferred* the copy to any other", made manifest the proposition that "the Act does not *create* a right in the author or bookseller, but presumes a right already subsisting". If this were not so, "[c]ould an author *transfer* that in which he had not an exclusive property?"

Thurlow in *Tonson* (1761) was the first to proffer some form of contrary analysis of the text of the statute. He observed that what reference there was to "property" in the Act, was derived "from the wording of the Orders of the Company of Stationers in 1691" who clearly had a vested interest in asserting such a right. He continued that the second fourteen year term, returning control of the work from the publisher to the author, was contrary to any ability to assign the work for any longer period. Moreover had the legislature considered that a right existed in the author in perpetuity, it would never have repealed that part of the Act that provided an external control over the price of books, for were it otherwise, "it would be extremely inconvenient". Yates, in 1762, stressed that the legislation "*vested* the copies in authors", which implied that "[i]t was not therefore vested before", as well as the fact the statute contained "negative words" in that, the right granted was to last for fourteen years "and no longer". "This alone", he claimed, "might determine the merits of this case". John MacLaurin, in *Considerations*, provided the first truly in depth examination, not only of the Act itself, but also of the parliamentary stages through which it had passed. Drawing upon the original petition of the booksellers which, he suggested, only set forth "that there had been a constant usage of selling Books to be held *as* a Property", MacLaurin highlighted that the title of the Act was changed from one "securing the property of copies of books", to one simply "vesting the copies" of such books. Moreover, he emphasised that what had been vested in the author, was the "sole right and liberty of printing" and nothing more. Addressing

Warburton's reading of the preamble, he argued that the inclusion of the term "proprietors" was:

> [P]alpably an inaccuracy owing to the inaccurate expression in the petition from the booksellers ... which procured the Act and is partly transcribed into its Preamble.

Similarly, rejecting the inference that Warburton drew from the universities proviso, he noted that should it be interpreted "to mean any more than a salvo upon patents [it] must operate a repeal on all the preceding clauses". Ultimately however, "what renders the question entirely insignificant", was the inclusion of the negative stipulation that the protection granted last for a limited term "*and no longer*".

MacLaurin's analysis also incorporated a commentary upon some of the existing case-law, reproducing Lord Kames' report of *Midwinter* (1743–1748) in full. He continued by recounting the English booksellers' appeal to the House of Lords, concluding with an extensive account of Lord Chancellor Hardwicke's opinion on the action. Relating that Hardwicke LC suggested that the *Statute of Anne* "might be considered as a general standing Patent to Authors, for the Term of Years mentioned in that Statute", he continued that the Lord Chancellor "doubted whether the statute was declaratory of the common law". Moreover, MacLaurin reported that Hardwicke LC "observed on the Precedents cited ... in support of the contrary opinion, that they were made on motion and hearing of one side only, therefore of little weight". Throughout *Midwinter* itself, counsel for the London booksellers had relied upon William Murray's analysis of *Baller v Watson* (1737) as evidence of judicial acceptance of a property in books, given the order that damages be paid to the plaintiff. The potential import of those judicial decisions that seemed to support the author's right was not lost to Warburton. MacLaurin had omitted to examine the Chancery case-law; Warburton, like Murray, Wedderburn and Blackstone to come, embraced it. In 1747 he suggested that:

> [I]n cases where the sense of the Legislature is uncertain or obscure, There the interpretation of the supreme Magistrates of Justice hath been always deemed to have the force of a legal decision. And this decision hath been made in favour of property, on the Act in question. For, in the High Court of Chancery, actions for damages have been sustained, where the action for forfeiture and penalties on this statute was not competent in any other court.

He argued, in much the same way as Murray and Lockhart in *Millar* (1749–1751), that these unnamed Chancery decisions were illustrative of the fact that the *Statute of Anne* was an accumulative, not a restrictive, measure. The Chancery court, he suggested, evidently agreed that there existed a right previous to the statute, for, were it otherwise, they would not have extended beyond the letter of the law.

The proponents of the perpetual right claimed the Chancery precedents were predicated upon, and illustrative of, the common law. It was not however until 1762, with publication of *An Enquiry*, that the question was raised as to what exactly had been determined previously at common law. The writer alluded to the fact that, should such a right exist, "[t]here must have been many violations of Literary Property in the course of several centuries, since the Introduction of printing". Despite this, he continued, the advocates of the perpetual right "have not produced a single determination at Common Law". MacLaurin, in *Considerations*, raised a similar point. Focussing, not on the lack of common law precedent from the distant past, but directing his attention to the events of the previous few decades, he considered it:

> [R]emarkable that [the booksellers] have never once attempted to call the booksellers of ireland to account, though they have suffered most by them; which seems to indicate that they themselves have no faith in this new Doctrine of a Right at Common Law, which must have supported them equally in Ireland as in Britain, though the [1709 Act] could not reach that country.

The author of *A Vindication* responded in kind to the more general issue raised by the *Enquirer*. His earlier examination of the historical development of literature within English society provided him with the solution to this lack of common law precedent. The shift from the earlier system of patronage, to one in which reading and writing had become a widespread and public phenomenon, in which the public were "now become the patrons of learning", had led to the necessity that authors pursue their natural right to their works. Such a right, he argued, was always inherent, but given that "learning was in its infant state, confined within a very narrow sphere", authors simply did not need to pursue such claims.

THEORY

Warburton, in the same year that William Grant had tentatively suggested to the Court of Session that the *Statute of Anne* implicitly accepted a pre-existing literary property, began the first real exposition as to the nature and classification of property and its relevance to, and relationship with, an author's work. This examination, he claimed, would prove "that an author has an undoubted right of property in his works". Beginning his classification of property with the observations that property, as traditionally understood, exhibited two essential criteria "that they be *useful* to mankind, and that they be capable of having their possession *ascertained*", he proceeded:

> Of these, some are *moveable*, as goods; some *immoveable*, as lands: and they become property either by first *occupancy*, or by *improvement*. Of *moveables*, some are things *natural*; others, things *artificial*. Property in the first is gained by occupancy, in the latter, by improvement.

Moveable property was of two kinds: "the product of the *hand*, and of the *mind*; as an *utensil* made; a *book* composed"; moreover, "the product of the *mind* is as well capable of becoming property as that of the *hand*". This, for Warburton, was self-evident in that a product of the mind had in it "those two essential conditions ... namely common *utility*, and a capacity of having its possession *ascertained*." His classification, and argument, thus travelled full circle. Later in his exposition, however, Warburton considered it necessary to concede the purposive omission of a third kind of artificial moveable: a third category "of a complicated nature", that of "*mechanic engines*". In these, the division of mental and manual labour broke down. They partook of "the nature of manual works" and yet, at the same time, "the operation of the mind [was] intimately concerned" in their construction. For Warburton, the "mathematical machine, holding of the nature of both, but more essentially of the former" meant that there was no way to satisfy the owner thereof without recourse "to a licence of monopoly, for a term of years, as on a claim of right". The invention, as a species of property, an imperfect right, stood apart.

In contrast to Warburton's efforts to differentiate between the work of the inventor and author, those opposing the common law right considered it an effective strategy to argue, by analogy, that no intelligible distinction could be drawn between the two. Thurlow, in *Tonson* (1761), asked why books and inventions should receive different protections, as both were products of "the labour of the head". Yates continued in this vein in denying any fundamental difference between the inventor of some art or a mechanical engine, and a literary composition. "Both are the productions of genius, both require labour and study, and both by publication, become equally common to the world". "The Legislature", he concluded, "seems to have judged it so". The author of *An Enquiry* considered "every Distinction ... between an Utensil and a Book" to be "idle and frivolous". If it was admitted that an inventor, at common law, had no exclusive right over his invention, "it must necessarily follow that the Author had none in his Copy". This tactic of argument by analogy was perhaps the strongest line that the opponents of the perpetual right were able to develop throughout the ontological debate. Certainly, in *A Vindication*, the writer felt that to break this link would "demolish the strongest hold, wherein the opponents of literary property have entrenched themselves".

Blackstone, in *Tonson* (1762), dismissed this idea that no distinction could be drawn between the case of an invention and a literary composition.

> Style and sentiment are the essentials of a literary composition. These alone constitute its identity. The paper and print are merely accidents, which serve as vehicles to convey that style and sentiment to a distance. Every duplicate therefore of a work ... if it conveys the same style and sentiment, is the same identical work, which was produced by the authors labour and invention. But a duplicate of a mechanic engine is, at best, but a resemblance of the other, and a resemblance can never be the same identical thing.

Following this, he concluded with the untenable if scare-mongering appeal against treating literary and mechanical compositions as similar in nature. Accepting such a premise, he suggested, would not in fact lead one to the conclusion that property in books should be similarly limited, but rather could only lead to a conclusion that the perpetual property subsisting in books "should also be allowed in machines", a prospect which in Blackstone's opinion ran contrary to the "natural liberty" of the world at large.

It was Blackstone who also provided the most detailed and elaborate analysis and classification of the law in this area. This he expounded not only in *Tonson* (1762), but at some length in his *Commentaries on the Laws of England*. The second volume of this work, published in 1766, was given over to the consideration of the "Rights of Things". Embarking on a historical sweep of the law in this area, Blackstone asserted that it was the concept of occupancy that gave "the original right to the permanent property in the substance of the earth itself". Property was classified into real property (land) and personal property (moveables), and both, he argued, were "originally acquired by the first taker". While occupancy was the original source of all property, Blackstone continued by acknowledging that, as time passed, as a result of "the introduction and extension of trade and commerce", the law had "learned to conceive different ideas" of personal property. In all, he suggested, personal property might be acquired in twelve different ways: by occupancy, prerogative, forfeiture, custom, succession, marriage, judgment, gift, contract, bankruptcy, testament, or, finally, by administration. Within the first of his twelve categories, Blackstone detailed a number of examples such as the goods of an enemy, moveables found upon the surface of the earth, and emblements, and continued that there was yet another species of property which "being grounded on labour and invention, is more properly reducible to the head of occupancy than any other". Drawing upon Locke, that the right of occupancy was founded "on the personal labour of the occupant", he asserted that:

> When a man by the exertion of his rational powers has produced an original work as he pleases ... any attempt to take it from him, or vary the disposition he has made of it, is an invasion of his right of property.

Property, in this case, was predicated upon occupancy, occupancy was defined by the expenditure of labour, and, as an author expended personal labour in writing his text, he therefore had a property in the text produced. Earlier, in *Tonson* (1762) Blackstone had asserted that a literary composition had all "the essential requisites to make it the subject of property". In the *Commentaries*, Blackstone had set out his classification of the property in things, into which he sought to place literary property. Literary property was considered *similar* to those recognised forms of property popularly cast as being founded upon the combined principles of occupancy and labour.

The opponents to the perpetual right denied that an author's work was "susceptible of property" at all. When Yates, in *Tonson* (1762) had raised the argument that property had to be something that could be "seen, felt, delivered, lost or stolen", he had been criticised by both Mansfield LCJ and Blackstone for ignoring the distinction that could be drawn between corporeal and incorporeal rights. By contrast with Yates, the writer of *An Enquiry* began with the explicit recognition that "[p]roperty is either corporeal or incorporeal". He continued however that those incorporeal properties acknowledged in law, were of two kinds:

> [E]ither *original* as Bonds, Contracts and Obligations, (for these arise from Compact and Agreement of the Parties) or *derivative*, as Estovers, Advowsons, and Rights of Common, which imply a prior Property from whence they issue.

The property claimed, he asserted had to fall within this second category, and yet all these derivative incorporeal rights were predicated upon the prior existence of a corporeal body. Before there could exist a right of common, there had to be created a Manor. Before estovers could be granted, a property had to subsist in the wood or forest. The goodwill of an Inn could not precede the building of the Inn itself. Without a theatre there could be no right of "setting in a Theatre". In this respect, he continued, the perpetual right "totally differs from every other incorporeal Right which the Law acknowledges" and if it existed at all "must necessarily partake of the Nature and Qualities of a corporeal Property". This he concluded would truly be a "strange Phenomenon!"

For Warburton, the product of the mind, the book composed, was not confined to the physical manuscript or book. Rather what was protected was "the doctrine contained in it"; that was, "the true and peculiar property in a book". A book as "a composition of paper and ink drawn out in artificial characters" was a work of the hand; however, "the complete idea of the book" incorporated the work of the mind, the composition, "a doctrine contained". It was this very notion of an original incorporeal right that the author of *An Enquiry* rejected. That an idea could be the subject of property, he argued, was inconsistent with the ability to draw clear and definable boundaries around that property. Delineating the boundaries of this "airy Phantom" would simply prove to be too problematic. As Yates had pointed out in *Tonson* (1762), a man had to be able to both possess his property, and exclude others from its enjoyment. Literary property however defied both of these qualities. It was not Warbuton, but Blackstone who met these criticisms in detailing a more essential distinction between the book, the ideas conveyed in that book, and "those words in which an author has clothed his ideas". "Style and sentiment are the essentials of a literary composition"; "[t]hese alone constitute its identity". Blackstone's conceit was developed by the author of *A Vindication* who drew out the differences between the book, the doctrine contained therein, and the expression of that doctrine. A book, he suggested, could be conceived of as both a doctrinal composition, and a mechanical composition. The doctrinal composition could be further divided into the ideas it contained, and the language of the author in conveying those ideas. The book as "visible permanent characters on paper", and the ideas it contained, were free for the reader to do with what he would:

> [F]or he who obtaineth my copy may appropriate my stock of ideas, and by opposing my sentiments, may give birth to a new doctrine; or he may coincide with my notions, and by employing different illustrations, may place my doctrine in another point of view: and in either case he aquireth an exclusive title to his copy, without invading my property: for though he may be said to build on my foundation, yet he rears a different superstructure.

Ideas common to the public could be confined within the private language of the individual author. What remained with the author after publication was his individual expression, the particular sentiments he employed in conveying his doctrine to the reader. This distinction between mechanical and doctrinal composition also helped to meet the analogy that had been drawn between the invention and the book. The completion of a machine, the mechanism itself, he suggested was "the end to which the ideas of the inventor are directed". The book however was different. Where the machine embodied a single set of ideas, the book embodied two, "both tending to different ends". The first set of these ideas, like that of the machine, was "directed towards the executing of the mechanical composition, which" he observed "is the end the printer has in view". However, the second set of ideas, present in the book, was applied "to the framing of the doctrinal composition, which is the end the author proposes". It was with the printer, and not the author, that the inventor most identified. With the machine, it was the object that was the end in and of itself. With the book, however, "the *mechanical* part, that is, the writing or printing, is, with respect to the author, only the *mean* for promulgating the doctrinal part, which is the *end*".

That there emerged no lucid or coherent response to this strain of philosophical conjecture was largely due to the nature of the counter-position that the opponents of the common law right had adopted. They advocated that property subsisted in the tangible unitary event of the book and nothing more. Denying that the general tenets of property law admitted any such thing as literary property, necessarily ruled out any examination of the nature of literary property itself. It also required an adherence to the concept that what protection authors should receive could only be provided by a paternalist legislature, by an extraordinary act of the state. This necessarily bound them to the language of the *Statute of Anne*, which was itself grounded in the tangible, in "the copies of printed books", in "the sole liberty of printing and reprinting such book or books". The proponents of the general right however, freed of the strictures of the 1709 Act, were able to explore and advance a more intellectually beguiling theory as to the "true" nature of the relationship between the author, the book and the text.

CONSEQUENCE

Warburton's reliance upon the concept of utility as one of the fundamental attributes denoting the existence of property came under attack in *An Enquiry*. In particular, it was suggested that Warburton had omitted from his analysis of the utility of literature, considerations of the reading public and the advancement of learning. The author argued that, to demonstrate the utility in any species of property, it had to be established "that a restrained Use and separate Enjoyment of it is more beneficial to Mankind, than a common and free Participation". The advancement of learning he contended, was not supported by an exclusive and perpetual right. William Murray, in *Tonson* (1751), had advocated the reverse. He suggested to Lord Hardwicke that "[i]f the property is not secured, there can be no fine editions of new books", that "books are the production and property of a man's ingenuity", and that "the property in them, is the only encouragement of letters". Both Wedderburn and Blackstone, in *Tonson* (1761, 1762) echoed these sentiments. Wedderburn asserted that "learning would be prejudiced, if authors may be stripped of this independant provision for themselves", while Blackstone declared that "the end of establishing and protecting property" lay in its "public utility to mankind". "Without some advantage proposed", he continued, "few would read study compose or publish". In short, in the absence of the perpetual right, a literary wasteland beckoned. Developing this, the author of *A Vindication*, argued that "no public injury can ensue from an author's perpetual exclusive right over his own works". Such a right, he argued, had no tendency to "confine the powers of genius".

Rather, drawing upon the tri-partite analysis of the book, the ideas contained therein, and the composition, he suggested that a perpetual property in an author's individual expression of his ideas did not deprive others from drawing upon those ideas as expressed. While the author's text was protected, his "stock of ideas" remained free for public consumption and conjecture.

Donaldson, in *Some Thoughts*, shifted the focus from the general public to the book trade in particular. He maintained that what was really under discussion was, not the rights of the author, but the threat to the dominance of the London booksellers over the entire trade. It was they, he asserted, who would benefit most from the granting of such a monopoly, in being able to fix "a most extravagant price" upon their books, which prices were "sometimes double or triple their real value". MacLaurin added more, with the contention that "every consideration of public Utility strongly opposes the Perpetuity claimed by the booksellers of London". He suggested that recognising the perpetual right would "depress and discourage all other Booksellers and Printers in the Kingdom", impacting negatively upon the health of the book trade in general. In addition to this, he predicted a threat to the quality in the production of books in that a less vital market place would "occasion Slovenliness, Inelegance and Incorrectness in Printing". Finally, he argued that denying the common law right would "greatly increase the Revenue arising from the Consumption of Paper", which could only be of considerable benefit to the national economy.

Maintaining a healthy, free exchange in books and knowledge were not however the only considerations highlighted by the opponents to the perpetual right. They also reflected upon an argument of considerable constitutional importance. That the judiciary were playing a crucial role in determining the nature and extent of this property right was becoming increasingly self-evident. It was apparent that this debate was not simply a dispute between the London and the provincial booksellers, between two commercially self-interested bodies. This entire process was also developing into a conflict between the sanctity of the legislature and the ability of the judiciary to supercede parliamentary authority through their development of the common law. The author of *A Vindication*, towards the end of his article, summarised his position. Having "endeavoured to shew that a literary copy is a subject susceptible of property", and that its recognition "will produce no inconvenience, either with regard to the author or to the public", he proceeded: "[I]t remains to hope that *this right may be judicially established*, and preserved inviolably to the latest posterity". MacLaurin, not surprisingly, did not think it was for the courts to make such a declaration. In his *Considerations*, he accepted as "indisputable" that "the author of a book, or of a machine or art useful in life" should have "the exclusive right of selling his work for such a length of time, as ought to reimburse him of his expense, and recompense him for his trouble". He continued however:

> [I]t by no means follows that this right ought to be informed by the ordinary Courts of Justice. Courts of Justice can only interpose their authority to make perfect rights effectual, not imperfect ones ... The proper remedy is an application to the Supreme Magistrate, or Legislature of the country, for a privilege.

After the decision of Lord Mansfield's court in the case *Millar v Taylor* (1768), Donaldson, on 8 May 1769, published *A Letter from a Gentleman in Edinburgh, to his Friend in London*. Referring to the protection provided to authors by the *Statute of Anne*, he asked:

> I should be glad to know, if any judge or court of law, have a power to dispense with the laws of the country, or to lay aside an act of parliament: If they have such power, I will venture to say, that none of His Majesty's subjects can be safe in their lives or properties; for whether they obey or disobey the laws, they are alike liable to be punished. The legislature can repeal or amend acts, but such appeals or amendments can have no retrospect; whereas if a judge can lay aside a statute, or punish a person who has observed it, surely he has more power than the King, Lords and Commons: If such a maxim should ever be established, then there is an end of the constitution.

***

Throughout the sixteenth and seventeenth centuries a mutually beneficial courtship had existed between the Stationers' Company and the monarchy. In return for guaranteed protections securing their trade, the stationers offered to monitor and regulate a potentially subversive press. This relationship ended with the lapse of the *Licensing Act* 1662 in 1695. In the twenty years that followed, during which there were no less than ten general elections, and when political activity became clearly delineated along discernible party lines, there were numerous attempts to re-establish this censorial legislation in one form or another. Alongside these attempts however, with the existence of an increasingly influential electorate, the potential of an effective and efficient propaganda machine began to be realised. As a popular and political press emerged, parliament became more and more intolerant of each passing legislative attempt to censure the book trade. What attempts were made to legislate became increasingly reactive in nature, spawned in the main by individually contentious publications. Moreover, it was becoming obvious that controlling the content of such books could be carried on without enlisting the help of the members of the book trade themselves. In the absence of the *Licensing Act*, parliament developed its own mechanisms to control the dissemination of licentious, criminal and seditious materials. Earlier intertwined notions of the content and the physical context of the book became increasingly disentangled, and the booksellers' regulatory links with the censorial state came to an end.

A number of figures had been prominent throughout this early period of politics and propaganda: Locke, Clarke, Freke, Harley, and Defoe. Defoe's interest in the situation of the book trade continued up until the passing of the *Statute of Anne*. He provided the booksellers with an alternative approach with which to court the sympathies of the legislature. It was Defoe who drew the explicit link between the benefit to society as a whole that comes with the general encouragement of learning, and the provision of some form of statutory protection for the printing of books. The earlier bargain with the stationers had been struck in the interests of controlling a sometimes dangerous and volatile press. This was superceded by an altogether different compact, in which the author and the contribution he could make to contemporary social development were given centre-stage. The first draft of the *Statute of Anne* set out that the copy of a book was a form of property equal in stature to any other tangible. This, of course, had been heavily influenced by the nature of the booksellers' petition to the Commons. While they had adopted the rhetoric of Defoe's argument, the booksellers did so to vigorously promote their own best interests. However, throughout its passage through parliament, the emphasis of the legislation underwent significant transformation. What began as a Bill to secure the property of authors, emerged as an Act primarily concerned with the continued production of "useful books", and the encouragement of learning. Moreover, the Commons was concerned to ensure that these useful books were available to the public at reasonable prices. The central focus of the statute was, and remains, a *quid pro quo*. Parliament was not concerned with the recognition of any pre-existing authorial right, nor was it primarily concerned with the regulation of the book trade. Rather it sought to encourage "learned Men to compose and write useful Books", through the striking of the economic, social and cultural bargain first articulated by Defoe. What the Act made up for in its general intent, however, it lacked in its details. It was and remains a poorly drafted piece of legislation. Although a clear rationale for the Act is readily identifiable, there is nothing to suggest that the drafters, and parliament in general, had any real understanding of the various ideas with which they were dealing. Their failure to define any of the concepts central to the statute illustrates that, while they may have fully appreciated the rationale of their actions, this did not necessarily mean that anyone fully understood what was meant by a statutory property in books.

When the booksellers turned to parliament again, following the expiration of the protections provided by the *Statute of Anne*, they did so in the light of a new focus that had been raised for the consideration of the Commons. Samuel Buckley, in 1734, had brought to parliament's attention the differential treatment that authors received in Britain compared with their European counterparts. Considerations of the health and state of a national trade were now of some import. The booksellers sought new legislation upon the strength of a third social bargain. With the *Licensing Act* 1662, they had promised effective regulation of work that was inimical to the health of the political nation. With the *Statute of Anne* parliament had granted the booksellers a measure of support on the supposition that the ultimate benefactor would be the state of learning and education within Great Britain. Now the booksellers stressed that the different treatment of the bookselling trade, abroad and at home, was contributing to "the diminution of His Majesty's Revenue, the discouragement of the art of Printing, and the Trade and Manufacture of this Kingdom". It was the state of the commercial nation that was to be addressed, and, upon this new platform the booksellers hoped to get the 1709 Act redrawn in their favour. The *Statute of Anne* had attempted to strike a balance between the interests of the book trade and the book buying public. The Bill that was drafted in 1735, if anything, tipped this balance away from the booksellers, towards the reader as consumer. The author, although presented as central protagonist in both these dramas, had, as yet, remained largely in the wings. The House of Commons, however, with the 1737 Bill, introduced the author as a significant third character, with a piece of legislative drafting that was even more hostile to the interests of the booksellers than either the *Statute of Anne* or the 1735 Bill had been. Six months after the 1737 Bill foundered in the Lords, *Baller v Watson* (1737), after eight years of litigation, was finally concluded. Lord Chancellor Talbot, in the Court of Chancery, granted to the executors of John Gay's estate a perpetual injunction protecting Gay's work, as well as an order for an account of profits. The possibility of securing such a decree in Equity, in contrast to the tone of an increasingly antagonistic legislature, meant that, for the booksellers, there was little to be gained in pursuing their lobby to redraft the *Statute of Anne*. On the contrary, all the indications pointed to the fact that should they continue, they would end up in a considerably worse position than they had secured in 1709. Instead, the attentions of parliament were directed solely to the issue with which the booksellers had begun this more recent campaign, the problem of cheap foreign imports and the resultant loss in trade and revenue which this represented to the booksellers in particular, and the country at large. As a result, in 1739 the *Importation of Books Act* was secured.

The London booksellers were not only reacting to the mood of the Commons and the unsympathetic tone of the 1737 Bill, but also to a new commercial threat manifesting north of the border. Between the failure of the 1738 *Importation Bill* and the securing of the 1739 Act, Andrew Millar initiated the first action taken against a number of Scottish booksellers before the Court of Session. This action, subsequently abandoned, neatly encapsulated the changing attitude and concerns of the southern monopolists. Relying upon the decision in *Baller*, they turned away from the legislature and instead sought relief from the judiciary. Taking up their campaign against the emerging Scottish trade in *Midwinter v Hamilton* (1743–48), it was argued that, as a result of the protection granted by the *Statute of Anne*, the booksellers were not only able to follow for the penalties detailed within the legislation, but also to follow for what damages they sustained by its impugnment. These damages, they claimed, were the same as those ordered in *Baller*, the equitable remedy of an account of profits. The Scottish booksellers, on the contrary, asserted that their pursuers were entitled to nothing more than the penalties outlined in the legislation. The resolution of this contest turned on whether the 1709 Act was concerned with property *per se*, or an exclusive privilege similar to the prerogative patent grants. The debate over the meaning of the *Statute of Anne* and the nature of literary property had, in part, begun. When *Midwinter* was appealed to the House of Lords, as *Millar v Kincaid* (1749–51), the plaintiffs' counsel, William Murray and Alexander Lockhart explicitly argued that the statute admitted "a property in copies of books to have existed in authors before the making of it". The London booksellers had made such claims before, albeit tentatively; now, however, they began to embark upon a sustained defence of this point of view. Most of the subsequent actions taken up to the time of the decision in *Donaldson v Becket* (1774) would be concerned with pressing or refuting this basic position that there existed a common law copyright in authors and their assigns. With the limits of the discussion framed in such terms, the time had come for developing and voicing those arguments that would support these diametric claims.

Perhaps most remarkable about the legal and ontological debate that emerged between *Millar v Kincaid* (1748–51) and *Millar v Taylor* (1768), is that it had little to do with the ultimate resolution of this question of literary property. The conceptual merit or historical veracity of either side of the discussion would not prove decisive in the end. This is not to say however that the generated debate was of no significance. On the contrary, despite the fact that the anti-monopolists would eventually emerge as victorious in this battle of the booksellers, it was the position that had been developed by the London booksellers that was to have a lasting influence over our understanding of the nature of literary property, over the very essence of copyright. While the debate itself was essentially irrelevant in terms of resolving the issue that was to come before Lord Mansfield's court, the Scottish Court of Session, and the House of Lords, the real legacy of these years of argument and counter-argument, thesis and antithesis, lies in the fact that, through the process of contesting the meaning of the copyright legislation, the concept of copyright itself came to be defined.

It would be tedious and tautologous, to repeat the arguments of the Counsel at the Bar, or the Cases and Authorities cited by them; as they were all of them, so fully and amply taken up again from the Bench, and so elaborately expatiated upon, canvassed, and discussed by the Judges, in delivering their Opinions, and the Reasons whereupon they formed them.

Let is suffice to say in general, that the Counsel for the Plaintiff insisted, 'That there is a *real Property* remaining in Authors, *after Publication* of their Works; and that they only, or Those who *claim under them*, have a Right to *multiply* the copies of such their literary Property, at their Pleasure, for Sale.' And they likewise insisted, 'That this Right is a *Common Law* Right, which *always has existed*, and does still exist, *independent of and not taken away by* the Statute of 8 Anne c19.'

On the Other side, the Counsel for the Defendant absolutely *denied* that any such Property remained in the Author, *after the Publication* of his Work: And they treated the Presentation of a *Common Law* Right to it, as mere *Fancy* and *Imagination*, void of any Ground or Foundation. They said that formerly the *Printer*, not the Author, was the person who was supposed to have the Right, (whatever it might be) And accordingly the Grants were all made to *Printers*. No Right remains in the Author, at *Common Law*.

J Burrow, *The Question Concerning Literary Property* (1773)

7

Millar v Taylor; *The Temporary Perpetual Triumph*

WILLIAM BLACKSTONE PRESSED the existence of a common law copyright, when representing the plaintiff in *Tonson v Collins* (1762). Joseph Yates, counsel for the defendants, comprehensively argued the contrary position. The twelve common law judges, sitting *en banc*, declined to proceed in their determination of the case, having discovered the action to be a collusive one, engineered by Tonson in the hope of extracting a favourable judgment. Following this, there was little in the way of encouragement for the London booksellers, as a number of subsequent Chancery decisions seemed to militate against the acknowledgment of a perpetual right. The first decisions, reported by Eden, came before Lord Chancellor Northington, two on the same day, 1 July 1765: *Osbourne v Donaldson* and *Millar v Donaldson*.[1] Both involved the same defendant, Alexander Donaldson, who had first begun to print and publish books in Edinburgh in 1750. His decision, to embark on a career as a bookseller, had been taken in the wake of *Midwinter* (1743–1748). Donaldson, in 1774, explained how, having "consulted some of the ablest advocates both in England and Scotland", they had confirmed his belief that "literary property depended entirely upon, and was wholly regulated by, the statute of Queen Anne". As a result, he "entered very largely into the bookselling business" publishing new works as well as "a great number of old and valuable books".[2] This was neither the first nor the last time that Donaldson appeared before the courts. In 1761, the Scottish printers, Gavin Hamilton and John Balfour, initiated an action before the Court of Session for money owed in respect of work they had carried out

[1] (1765) 2 Eden 329.

[2] "To the Honourable the Commons of Great Britain, in Parliament assembled, The Humble Petition of Alexander Donaldson, Bookseller in St. Paul's Church-yard, London, in Petitions and Papers relating to the Bill of the Booksellers, now before the House of Commons", reprinted in S Parks (ed), *The Literary Property Debate: Eight Tracts 1774–1775*, (New York, NY, Garland, 1974).

for Donaldson. On 13 July 1764 it was ordered that he pay, to the plaintiffs, 56*l*.16*s*.2*d*.[3] This was fairly typical of the type of claims brought before the court by the Scottish book trade. If they resorted to the courts at all, it was generally to enforce an outstanding debt, as in *Young v Lundie* (1764),[4] *Marshall v Lang* (1765),[5] *Groat v Barry* (1772),[6] and *Ruddiman's Trustees v Urie and Miller* (1772).[7] Donaldson himself commenced at least two actions, the first against his former partner, John Reid, for a large quantity of books he suspected Reid of embezzling from their business,[8] and the second for non-payment of a bill for books he had exported to Patrick and Andrew Thomson, merchants in New York.[9]

The London booksellers, since losing in *Millar v Kincaid* (1751), had chosen not to engage their northern counterparts in court. The only instance of such recourse is documented in the manuscript Minute Books for the Court of Session, when, in February 1762, a "decreet" was ordered in favour of Jacob Tonson, Andrew Millar and Thomas Wright, against John Orr and John Gilmour, booksellers in Glasgow, and John Wood, a bookseller in Edinburgh.[10] That is not to say they ignored the activities of the Scottish reprint industry. Instead, the southern book trade tried to adopt a more pragmatic approach. Rather than proceed in law, they turned "to the English provincial booksellers who were the main channels of sale for the Scots reprints south of the border".[11] In April 1759, John Whitson wrote two letters to John Merrill a bookseller in Cambridge, that were intended for circulation throughout all of the provincial booksellers in England. In them, Whitson described how the London booksellers had entered into a scheme "for totally preventing the sale of Scotch and Irish books, which were first printed in England". They were to replace all the provincial sellers' copies of Scottish and Irish reprint works, with English editions of the same books, to the same value. Once this had been done, it was promised that any bookseller found selling any offending reprints would "be proceeded against in Chancery, with the utmost severity". For the purpose of facilitating such prosecutions, a fund had been established, which was to be administered by a committee

[3] CS 238 H 3/4, CS 231 D 1/35/D, and CS 231 Misc 1/20.
[4] CS 21, 15 December 1764.
[5] CS 25 No 2, 5 February 1766.
[6] CS 21, 4 March 1772.
[7] CS 229 R 2/11.
[8] *Donaldson v Reid*, CS 231 D 1/36, CS 238 D 2/15.
[9] CS 29, 5 March 1767.
[10] CS 16 1/111, 16 February 1762.
[11] J Feather, *Publishing, Piracy and Politics: An Historical Study of Copyright in Britain* (London, Mansell, 1994) 83. For information on distribution networks in England at this time, see CY Ferdinand, "Local Distribution Networks in 18th-Century England" in R Myers and M Harris (eds), *Spreading the Word: The Distribution Networks of Print, 1550–1850* (Winchester, St Paul's Bibliographies, 1990) 131–49.

comprising of Jacob Tonson, Andrew Millar, Charles Hitch, John and James Rivington, John Ward and William Johnston, to which fund each had made a substantial contribution. Moreover, all of the metropolitan booksellers were expected to endorse the scheme, and contribute towards the established fund, under the penalty of being denied entrance to any future trade sales of "quire books, or copies".[12] The devised scheme, however, proved more bark than bite. Although over £3,000 was gathered in, this was never going to be sufficient to replace all the existing Scottish reprints, to keep in regular employ a team of riders "to inspect all the booksellers shops in England, [to] give intelligence of what they can find out", as well as taking legal redress against all those found offending. The plan would ultimately prove too impractical. As Feather comments, "[t]he truth was that the Londoners had no way of policing the provincial trade, and were unable to prevent the penetration of their markets by the reprinters".[13]

Whatever the reasons for Tonson, Millar and Wright coming before the Scottish court in 1762, the actions taken by Millar and Osbourne, before the English Court of Chancery, were precipitated by the opening of Alexander Donaldson's shop in London, near Norfolk Street, in the Strand. At the end of his tract, *Some Thoughts on the State of Literary Property*, he included the following advertisement:

> This is to give notice, that Alex. Donaldson, from Edinburgh has now opened a shop for cheap books, two doors east from Norfolk-street, in the Strand, where they are sold from thirty to fifty per cent. under the usual London prices. — The London booksellers ... have prevented their brethren from dealing with him, have forced him, in self-defence, to establish this shop. — Good allowance is made to merchants who buy for exportation, and to country booksellers.

Donaldson's audacity, in bringing his reprint business into the very heart of the capital, could not go unchecked. Millar and Osbourne, upon submission of their bills of complaint, were granted an injunction until answer, to prevent Donaldson printing various works: *The Seasons* by the poet James Thomson; *Homer's Iliad* by Pope; and *Miscellanies*, a collection

[12] Copies of these letters are reproduced in Donaldson, *Some Thoughts on the State of Literary Property* (1764), reprinted in S Parks (ed), *The Literary Property Debate: Six Tracts 1764–1774* (New York & London, Garland, 1975).

[13] Feather, *Publishing, Piracy and Politics*, n 11 above, 83. Elsewhere Feather writes that "[t]he sheer cost of the operation seems to have been the rock on which the scheme foundered, for it was not until November that a printed letter was generally circulated to the country trade explaining the intentions and motives of the Londoners". And again, he comments that "[t]he 1759 exercise may have been a salutary warning; but it was far too expensive to become a permanent system of policing"; J Feather, *The Provincial Book Trade in Eighteenth-Century England* (Cambridge, CUP, 1985) 8, 10.

of Swift's writing, which included a *Life of Swift* by Hawkesworth. When Donaldson entered his answer he made it a question whether:

> [A]s the two terms of fourteen years each, under the statute 8 Anne, was expired, the plaintiff was entitled to the sole printing and vending the books on the foot of the common law right.[14]

In response, the plaintiffs moved that the injunctions formerly granted by the court be continued until the hearing of the cause. When this motion came to be argued before Lord Chancellor Northington, only the plaintiff's counsel, Mr Yorke, was given time to make any representations on the issue. Yorke made reference to a number of cases, however Lord Northington considered that only *Tonson* (1752) had any relevance to the action at hand, and continued that even that case may have turned on the fact that the works of Milton printed with additional notes could be considered a new work. Without hearing any more, the Lord Chancellor dissolved the injunctions initially granted against Donaldson.[15] He explained that the issue was a point of so much difficulty and consequence that he desired not to decide it at the hearing but was instead inclined to send it to law for the opinion of the judges. Emphasising that he wished to be understood as giving no opinion on the subject, he nevertheless observed that "it might be dangerous to determine that the author has a perpetual property in his books". The reason? "[S]uch a property would give him not only a right to publish, but to suppress too" and this "would be a fatal consequence to the public".[16]

Failing to gain satisfaction against Donaldson, Millar turned to the courts again, but now choosing the less formidable figure of Robert Taylor, a printer from Berwick, as well as a work that fell within the protection of the *Statute of Anne*. In *Millar v Taylor* (1765), Millar and James Dodsley complained that the defendant Taylor had printed "several thousand copies" of Edward Young's book of poems *Night Thoughts* and sought an account of profits and an injunction from the court.[17] In 1743 and 1744 Young had sold his rights in the first volume of the work to Robert Dodsley, which had, in 1759, been subsequently transferred to James Dodsley.[18] In his defence Taylor relied squarely upon section 11 of the 1709 Act. Admitting that he had exchanged one hundred and fifty

[14] (1765) 2 Eden 329.
[15] A report of the Lord Chancellor's comments is also provided in Donaldson's "Information" for the later case of *Hinton v Donaldson* (1773).
[16] *Ibid*.
[17] C 33 426/60.
[18] The first five parts of the poem were sold in 1743; the sixth part of the first volume was sold in 1744.

copies of Young's work for other books with Alexander Donaldson, he challenged the plaintiffs' ability to follow for the small gain he had made. He argued that:

> [T]he Author of Books of Genius and Composition of the Brain or their Assignees have not vested in them by Law a perpetual indefinite Right or property to the copies of such Books.

Rather, "the sole liberty given to the authors" was restrained to the first term of fourteen years provided by the statute after which, he continued, "the sole property of printing and disposing of the copies" returned to the author, Young, who was still very much alive. Conceding that he had printed the works in question, Taylor argued that while Edward Young may have been able to bring a case against him, Millar and Dodsley could not.[19] Sewell MR ordered that the injunction "be continued for the remainder of the two terms of fourteen years and fourteen years" during which Young, as the author, and the plaintiffs "as standing in his place" held the printing right. This decision, he continued, was "without prejudice" to any right the plaintiffs may have had "beyond the said two terms".[20]

Less than a week after this decree, a further order was made by the court in relation to a second action Millar had taken against Taylor. This action, like the one he had previously taken against Donaldson, concerned an edition of Thomson's *Seasons*.[21] On 26 November 1765, counsel for Millar and Taylor appeared before the court. Millar did not allege that Taylor had printed his work, but rather based his case upon the fact that he had *vended and sold* it. Where Millar had failed with Donaldson, he sought to succeed against Taylor. The defendant, once again relying explicitly upon the *Statute of Anne*, denied the right of a purchaser of a given work to print it for longer than the first fourteen year period delineated in the legislation. Moreover, he pointed out that, unlike Young's work, *The Seasons* "was first printed and published about 30 years ago, and the author has been dead about 15 years". "[B]y the event of the Author dying after the expiration of 14 years", Taylor submitted:

> [Thomson's] works were become the property of the publick uncontrolled and unaffected by any Acts either of the Author or proprietors thereof which extended beyond the term of 14 years.[22]

[19] C 33 426/60.
[20] *Ibid*. It was also ordered that one of the Masters of the Court "take an account of the defendant of the profits of the Books mentioned in the plaintiffs Bill" and that "the said defendant do pay the same as the master shall direct".
[21] It was in fact the very edition Donaldson had printed.
[22] C 33 426/68.

It had become clear that the Court of Chancery was not the forum for deciding upon the existence of a perpetual common law right. Lord Northington had considered it "a capital question of law, subtile in its nature and extensive in its consequences" and, as such, had left the parties to proceed at law should they wish. The Master of the Rolls had been careful with Young's *Night Thoughts* to restrict the extent of the injunction to the times specified in the Act. Now, faced with a work falling outside the protection of the *Statute of Anne*, he ordered that "a case be made for the opinion of the judges of the Court of King's Bench" reserving the right to issue judgment "till after the judges shall have made their certificate". The injunction, formerly granted, was continued in the meantime.[23] His direction gave rise to *Millar v Taylor* (1768).[24]

Millar explained that on 20 January 1763 he had printed two thousand copies of Thomson's *Seasons*, following which, on 20 May 1763 Taylor had published, exposed to sale, and sold one thousand copies of the same work. These pirate editions were declared to have been "injuriously printed by some person or persons" without Millar's licence or consent. In fact these were the very editions printed by Donaldson of which Millar was all too aware. Omitting any reference to Donaldson, Millar claimed to have suffered damage to the amount of £200, which represented the profit that would have been realised from the thousand copies of his own edition that remained unsold. In response, Taylor pleaded the general issue, "Not Guilty", and the case proceeded to trial before a jury. The jury found that, before the *Statute of Anne*:

> [I]t was usual *to purchase from Authors* the Perpetual *Copy-Right* of their *Books*; and to *assign* the same from Hand to Hand, for valuable Considerations; and to make the same the Subject of *Family Settlements*, for the provision of *Wives and Children*.

[23] *Ibid.*

[24] There are two main reports of the decision in *Millar v Taylor* (1768). The first is a transcript of the decision printed by the Leith bookseller William Coke in 1771: *Speeches or Arguments of the Judges of the Court of King's Bench in April 1769; In the Cause of Andrew Millar against Taylor for printing Thomson's Seasons, to which are added Explanatory Notes, And an appendix, containing a short state of Literary Property, by the Editor.* The second is a note of the case by Sir James Burrow, printed in 1773: *The Question Concerning Literary Property, determined by the Court of the King's Bench, on 20th April 1769, in the cause between Andrew Millar and Robert Taylor, with the separate Opinions of the four Judges and the Reasons given by each in support of his opinion* (London, Strahan and Woodfall, 1773). Note also that there is essentially an exact transcript of this 1773 report in (1768) 4 Burr 2303–8. Given that the editor of Coke's edition apologises that the speeches "are not so complete as he could have wished", and that Burrows concedes that "[i]t is impossible to take down every Thing that is said, with Accurate precision", it should not surprise that there are variations between the two texts. For the most part, what differences exist are relatively minor in nature, the largest divergence between the two texts coming at the very end of Lord Mansfield's speech: Compare Coke, 104–6, to Burrows, 124–27.

They confirmed the facts of the action as asserted by Millar, but sought the advice of the court as to whether or not Taylor was "liable in law *to answer the Damages* sustained by the said Andrew Millar". If the court found that Taylor was so liable, then the jury would find Taylor guilty of the charge levelled against him, and set damages at *one shilling*.[25] If the court considered Taylor not so liable, then he would be found not guilty, and the action dismissed.

The first arguments were delivered to the court, on 30 June 1767, by John Dunning for the plaintiff and Edward Thurlow for the defendant. Thurlow, had previously appeared against the common law right in *Tonson* (1761). Following these, the court ordered the cause to stand over to the following term for second argument. On 7 June 1768 Blackstone set out the arguments on behalf of the plaintiffs; Arthur Murphy responded. After the delivery of this second set of arguments, it was ordered that the cause once again stand over until the next term for the opinion of the court. On 8 June 1768, however, Andrew Millar died. Millar's state of health must have been made apparent to the court, for at the time that the order was made that the issue stand over for judgment, it was also ordered, with the consent of the counsel for both parties, that "the judgment which shall be then given shall be entered up as a judgment of this term, in the same manner as if the judgment had been given on this day". Although the decision of the court was not handed down until 20 April 1769, it stands as having been delivered on 7 June 1768.

The four judges of the King's Bench presiding over the case were Willes, Aston, Yates JJ and Lord Mansfield, the Lord Chief Justice. Yates J, of course, had earlier represented the defendant in *Tonson* (1762), arguing at length against the existence of a common law right. Lord Mansfield, William Murray, had been one of the key protagonists in *Millar v Kincaid* (1749–1751), appearing as counsel on behalf of the London interest, as well as arguing in favour of the perpetual right in *Tonson v Walker* (1752). Beginning his judgment, Mansfield LCJ acknowledged that this was "the first instance of a final difference of opinion in this court ever since I sat here", a small matter of some thirteen years.[26] Despite each of the four having communicated their thoughts on the matter to each other, having "*talked* the Matter over, several times", and having "all equally endeavoured to persuade one another",[27] Yates J nevertheless felt compelled to dissent from the opinion of the other three judges. Unanimity of thought upon this issue was not to be achieved. Given the question was "so important to the Literary World" Yates J expressed his regret that

[25] In addition to this Millar was to be awarded 39 shillings costs and charges.
[26] Mansfield was appointed Lord Chief Justice in November 1756.
[27] Burrows, n 24 above, 112.

"there should be any Disagreement upon this Bench".[28] For Lord Mansfield, the lack of accord was not so problematic; indeed he implied the reverse, suggesting that the dissent actually strengthened the force and conviction of the majority decision.

> I do not know whether it may not be very advantageous, that there has been a difference of opinion, for it has been the occasion of going into the whole of the question, and the whole of the arguments much more at large; and it is a general question that concerns a vast number of people, now and for the time to come, it concerns the whole kingdom: And therefore I think it is of publick advantage that we have had different perceptions of this question, that has occasioned its being so minutely and so thoroughly gone into.[29]

For Willes J, delivering the first judgment, there were two relevant questions for consideration: "Whether the copy of a book, or literary composition, belongs to the author, by the common law", and, "[w]hether the common law-right of authors to the copies of their own works is taken away by 8 Ann. c.19.".[30] Aston J framed the problem slightly differently:

> 1st, Whether an author's property in his own literary composition is such as will entitle him, at common law, to the sole right of multiplying copies of it, or 2ndly, supposing he has a property in the original composition, whether the copy-right by his own publication of the work, is necessarily given away ... or, 3rdly, taken away from him, or restrained, by the Statute of Queen Ann.[31]

All three of the majority judges made reference to the patent cases of the late seventeenth century and the more recent decision of *Baskett* (1758),[32] as well as the various Chancery cases following the 1709 Act, both of which strands, they found, supported the existence of a common law right pre-dating the *Statute of Anne*. Similarly, all three investigated the wording of the 1709 Act, finding nothing therein that was contrary to the author's right at common law. While Willes J examined the pre-history of the 1709 Act at some length, Aston J preferred instead to enquire into the nature of property itself. It was appropriate "to consider certain great truths and propositions, which we, as rational beings, that is, to whom reason, as the great law of nature, has laid down the obligation of being governed by". Relying then upon truths "respecting mankind in general, antecedent to all human laws", Aston J expounded a "great theory

[28] *Ibid*, p 63.
[29] Coke, n 24 above, p 106. Note that this passage is omitted from the Burrows' report.
[30] Burrows, n 24 above, 11.
[31] *Ibid*, p 41.
[32] *Basket v University of Cambridge* (1758) 2 Keny 397.

of property", drawing upon Pufendorf, Locke and Grotius, ending with the declaration that:

> [A] Man may have Property in his *Body, Life, Fame, Labours*, and the like; and, in short, in anything that can be called *His*: That it is incompatible with the *Peace* and *Happiness of Mankind*, to violate or disturb, by *Force* or *Fraud*, his Possession, Use or Disposal of those Rights; as well as against the Principles of *Reason, Justice*, and *Truth*.[33]

Where Aston J drew upon "great truths and propositions" as to the nature of property, Lord Mansfield turned to fundamental principle as the cornerstone of the common law. Having set out that "what is agreeable to natural principles is common-law; what is repugnant to natural principles is contrary to common-law", he continued: "[I]t is agreeable to natural principles that an author should have a copy of his own works before publication". Why?

> [B]ecause it is *just*, that an Author should reap the pecuniary Profits of his own Ingenuity and Labour. It is *just*, that Another should not use his Name, without his consent. It is *fit*, that He should judge when to publish, or whether he will ever publish. It is *fit* he should not only choose the Time, but the Manner of Publication; how Many; what Volume; what Print. It is *fit*, that he should choose to Whose care he will Trust the Accuracy and Correctness of the Impression; in whose Honesty he will confide it, not to foist in Additions ... I allow them sufficient to shew "it is agreeable to the Principles of Right and Wrong, the Fitness of Things, Convenience, and Policy, and therefore to the Common Law to protect before Publication .... The 8th of Queen *Ann* is no Answer. We are considering the *Common Law*, upon Principles *before* and *independent* of that Act.[34]

This focus upon principle, upon reason and justice, and upon the rights of the author as central protagonist, for Yates J, obscured the wider social implications of the majority position. That is, the "rest of mankind" were being overlooked. He found it impossible to accept that a right could or should accrue to an author in perpetuity, and it was this element of *perpetuity*, and its consequences, which the majority judges had omitted from their reasoning:

> Shall an *Author's* Claim continue, *without Bounds of Limitation*; and *for ever restrain all the Rest* of Mankind from their natural rights, by an *endless Monopoly*? Yet *such* is the claim that is now made; a Claim to an *exclusive* Right of Publication, *for ever*: For, Nothing less is demanded as a Reward and Fruit of the Author's Labour, than an *absolute Perpetuity*.[35]

[33] Burrows, n 24 above, p 42–44.
[34] *Ibid*, p 115–16.
[35] *Ibid*, 70.

It was essential to explore "the consequences the publick will feel, if this claim should be established". The exclusive property sought by the booksellers would hand them the opportunity either to suppress works or sell them at whatever exorbitant price they considered appropriate. Could this really be considered "an encouragement of the propagation of learning?" He stressed the prospect of perpetual litigation over a property that bore no "proprietory marks in itself, and by common law is not bound to any formal stipulation", as well as disputes arising between authors "whether the work of one ... were or were not the same as those of another". Such questions would be liable to "great uncertainties and doubts". Such a property right would "imbroil the peace of society with frequent contentions, most highly disfiguring the face of literature, and highly disgusting to a liberal mind". Yates J concluded:

> [I]t is equally my duty, not only as a judge, but *as a member of society*, and even as a friend to the cause of learning, to support the limitations of the statute.[36]

Despite his protestations, Yates J remained in the minority, and following the decision, Millar's executors returned to Chancery. It had now been established that when Millar had originally filed his bill against Taylor he *did have* a property in the writings of James Thomson, he *had had* a property in *The Seasons*. In July 1770 the new Lord Chancellor, Lord Apsley, ordered Taylor to account for all the copies he had sold and the plaintiffs were granted a perpetual injunction preventing him printing the work again. Moreover, unlike the injunction granted by Lord Talbot in *Baller* (1737), there was to be no ambiguity about the duration of this decree. This one was clearly anticipated to last in perpetuity. For the first time, the London booksellers had secured an authoritative affirmation of the author's common law right to print and publish his work in perpetuity, and, by extension, had secured their monopoly over the trade's most profitable titles. The debate that had begun following *Midwinter* (1743–1748) had finally been brought to an explicit determination, and while the result did not have the authority of all twelve common law judges sitting *en banc*, as had been sought by Mansfield in *Tonson* (1762), it did bear the weight of the most senior common law court in the land. The decision, handed down by Lord Mansfield's court, represents no less than a triumph of creative historical revisionism and legal advocacy. Notwithstanding the reality of the *Statute of Anne*, and its immediate legal progeny, the history of the first four decades of lawful book publishing in Britain had been carefully re-crafted. The London monopolists had picked

[36] *Ibid*, 108–11; emphasis added.

a number of disparate legal-historical threads, bound them together within a compelling ontological framework, and created a new, altogether different, coherent form. The perpetual common law right had literally been written, talked and argued into existence.

***

On 24 October 1770, only three months after Millar's executors had been granted their perpetual injunction, a summons was issued in Scotland by John Hinton and Alexander McKonochie against Donaldson, John Wood and James Meuros, for printing, publishing and selling the Rev Thomas Stackhouse's *History of the Holy Bible*. In the summons, Hinton set out how Stackhouse, having first published his *History* in 1738, sold "the Copy Right and Sole Privilege of printing reprinting and selling" the work to Stephen Austin, in January 1740. He then traced the ownership of the work through Austin's death in December 1750, to his wife Elizabeth, who had subsequently married Hinton in August 1752. John MacLaurin, acting for Donaldson, raised two initial objections upon which Lord Coalston, on 11 July 1771, ordained that both parties give in memorials for his consideration. The first set out that Austin's will had made reference only to his "wife" and that nothing had been produced to prove that at the time of the making of the will he was married to Elizabeth. Second, he argued that what property Elizabeth might have had, which took the form of a chose in action, did not automatically become Hinton's property upon marriage.[37] In response, Hinton stated that there was a difference between a personal chattel *in action*, and one *in possession*, and observed that:

> The copy Right belonging to authors in their own work, is understood in the law of England to be a right of property, transferable to assignees, and passing to executors; and where an author or his executor or assignee, is in possession of that right, and in the use of exercising it, what occasion has he for an action to recover it.[38]

He continued that he and his wife:

> [W]ere in the actual possession of the manuscript, they were in the daily use of printing editions of the work, of publishing it and receiving the produce, and ... they do not see what further they could do, unless they were to bring

[37] On the method of acquiring property in goods and chattels upon marriage at this time, see W Blackstone, *Commentaries on the Laws of England*, vol 2 (Oxford, Clarendon Press, 1766) 433–35.

[38] CS 231 42/4.

> a declaratory action [against] the whole world to have it found and declared that they had right to a thing that the law already gave them a right to, that they were in full possession of.[39]

Lord Coalston considered that MacLaurin's objections involved specific issues of English law and directed the parties to take the advice of the English Bar. On 9 August 1771 Messrs Dalrymple and MacDonald provided their opinion upon both of the issues raised. On the first point, Elizabeth was found to be the wife in whose favour Austin had made his bequest. As to the second matter, they observed:

> Property in Copy rights stands now determined by the late judgment in the court in the case of Millar v Taylor to be perpetually vested in the author, his heirs and assigns, And it was admitted by the learned judge who differed in opinion from the court that this property could be no other than a personal chattel. Personal chattels are distinguished into, choses in action and choses in possession. The former arise from some contract express or implied; and require the interposition of legal judgment and execution to reduce them into possession; The latter, not requiring such interposition, but so called when the right and occupation are found to concur. Property in copyright can therefore not be called a chose in action, because it is a vested exclusive power of printing and publishing such copy; requiring no remedy of law to ascertain.[40]

As a result, on 16 November 1771, Lord Coalston ordained Donaldson to be ready to plead his defences *in causa*, against the next calling. Both parties submitted memorials upon the merits of the cause and on 5 August 1772, after which the matter was referred to the Lords of Session. Hinton and Donaldson were required to hand in printed *Informations* to the Lords' boxes;[41] on 12 January 1773, they were "inrolled" in the Innerhouse Rolls.

Between the time of both Hinton and Donaldson submitting their memorials for the consideration of Lord Coalston, and the final decision of the Lords of Session in July 1773, a number of other actions were brought before the Scottish court. In July 1772 Edward and Charles Dilly, proprietors of Thomas Nugent's *A New Pocket Dictionary of the French and English Languages in two parts* (corrected and improved by John Astrue),

[39] *Ibid.*

[40] *Ibid.*

[41] *Information for Mess John Hinton of London, Bookseller, and Alexander Mackonochie, Writer in Edinburgh, his Attorney, Pursuers; against Mess Alexander Donaldson and John Wood, Booksellers in Edinburgh, and James Meurose, Bookseller in Kilmarnock, Defenders,* (2 January 1773) reprinted in S Parks (ed), *The Literary Property Debate: Six Tracts, 1764–1774* (New York, NY, Garland, 1975); *Information for Alexander Donaldson and John Wood, booksellers in Edinburgh, and James Meurose, Bookseller in Kilmarnock, defenders; against John Hinton, Bookseller in London, and Alexander McConochie, Writer in Edinburgh, his Attorney, Pursuers* (January 2 1773) reprinted, *ibid.*

alleged that William Anderson and William Gordon had been importing Irish reprints of the work for sale in Scotland. As a consequence the London booksellers sought payment of the penalties detailed in the *Importation Act* 1739.[42] In December of the same year, William Johnston complained that John Reid and others[43] had printed an edition of Brooke's *The Fool of Quality, or the History of the Earl of Moreland*. Having purchased the work from Brooke, Johnston asserted that it was "secured" to him by "the common law of Great Britain" and "sundry Acts of Parliament made anent Literary Property and particularly by an Act made in the 8th year of Queen Anne".[44] Although making reference to the common law, it was clear that Johnston rested his claim firmly upon the *Statute of Anne*. After setting out in full those sections of the 1709 Act which he considered relevant, he gave an assurance that he had also registered his work in Stationers' Hall, in accordance with the requirements of the statute. The defenders, he continued, had printed and sold the work "in open defiance of the Laws and Acts of Parliament concerning Literary Property", as a result of which he sought delivery of the books remaining in their possession for the purpose of being damasked and made waste, the penalties provided in the 1709 Act, as well as "sufficient reparation" for the damages he had sustained "in his property".[45] In the same month as Johnston's action, William Griffin proceeded against Gilbert and Alexander McPherson, printers in Edinburgh, and John McLeish, Robert Clark and William Darling, booksellers in Edinburgh. Griffin did not even make reference to "the common law of Great Britain" but simply set out that "by sundry Acts of Parliament made anent Literary Property, and particularly by an Act made in the eight year of Queen Anne" he had "the sole right of printing and vending" a number of books, (*The West Indian, a Comedy, The Brothers, a Comedy, The Fashionable Lover, a Comedy*, and *The Grecian Daughter, a Trajedy*), all of which had been "regularly entered in Stationers-Hall as the Law directs". Several persons had printed these works, as a result of which Griffin sought delivery of the defenders remaining books that they may be damasked, payment of the penalties contained in the Act, as well as £500 "in the name of Damages" and a further £100 for the expense of taking the process.[46]

[42] CS 16 1/150, CS 237 D3/12, 15.

[43] John Robertson, William Darling, Robert Clark, Alexander McCaslan, John Wood, James McLeish and William Anderson.

[44] CS 16 1/152, CS 229 J/55.

[45] *Ibid.* Two months later, in February 1773, Johnston, in conjunction with Benjamin Collins (the same Collins of *Tonson v Collins* (1761, 1762)) complained, in essentially the same terms as his earlier libel, that Robert Mundell, William Darling, Robert Clark and John Wood, Alexander McCaslan, James McLeish, William Anderson, Charles Elliot and James Dickson, had printed and sold an edition of Tobias Smollett's *The Expedition of Humphry Clinker*; CS 16 1/154, CS 229 J/56.

[46] CS 16 1/154, CS 237 G2/31.

The language of these actions is instructive. Despite the decree in *Millar* (1768) in favour of the perpetual common law right, all of these claims were positioned squarely within the terms of the existing legislation, both the *Statute of Anne* and the *Importation Act* 1739. That this should have been the case is in one sense not surprising, given that all the contested works fell within the time limits delineated in those statutes. However, an additional explanation for the London booksellers' legal temerity perhaps lies with the developments that were occurring in *Hinton v Donaldson*. It was clear that the Scottish booksellers in general, and Donaldson in particular, were challenging the author's right as had been previously recognised in the English King's Bench. Even if the issue of perpetual copyright had been decided in England, it was still contestable in Scotland given that the *Act of Union* 1707 had specifically preserved the independence of the Scottish judiciary to decide upon questions of private law.[47] While the 1707 Act may have established a politically unitary state, it had also allowed for the existence of a unique system of legal pluralism.[48]

Returning to *Hinton v Donaldson* (1773), the arguments assembled for the benefit of the Lords of Session were, not surprisingly, remarkably similar to those that had already been amassed and developed over the past three decades, and finally expounded before Lord Mansfield's court. Hinton maintained he had a property "at common law, and in the general principles of reason and justice"; Donaldson denied the claim. In addition, however, both did explicitly address the position of literary property within the law of Scotland. Hinton sought to refute any implication to be drawn from the fact that, prior to the *Act of Union* and the *Statute of Anne*, what protection works of literature had historically received in Scotland, was all by way of prerogative grant. Instead, he suggested, the common law right was not "affected by any municipal law or custom of Scotland" and, "without entering deeper into the nature and rise of patents for the printing of books", continued that "there is nothing in that practice repugnant to an author's having an inherent natural right in his own work". If there was nothing *inconsistent* with the laws of Scotland, then it remained the case that the

[47] Art 18 of the *Act of Union* stated "that the Laws which concern publick Right, Policy and Civil Government, may be made the same throughout the whole United Kingdom; but that no Alteration be made in Laws which concern private Right, except for evident Utility of the Subjects within Scotland"; *An Act for an Union of the two Kingdoms of England and Scotland*, 5&6 Anne, c 8.

[48] On the legal union of the two nations: BP Levack, *The Formation of the British State: England, Scotland, and the Union 1603–1707* (Oxford, Clarendon Press, 1987) 68–101; AL Murray, "Administration and the Law" in TI Rae (ed), *The Union of 1707: Its Impact in Scotland* (Edinburgh, Blackie & Son, 1974) 30; AJ MacLean, "The 1707 Union: Scots Law and the House of Lords" (1983) 4 *Journal of Legal History* 50.

common law right was "agreeable to, and warranted by it". Why must this be so? Because:

> [E]very right which is either deducable from natural principles, or from the laws of nations, and rules of found policy, must be considered as aided and supported by every system of laws and administration of justice, that have the good and happiness of mankind for their object.[49]

Donaldson, on the other hand, having examined "the civil law", "our own ancient customs", "acts of legislature", the "authorities of our lawyers", and the "judicial determinations of our Courts", discovered "not the least glimpse ... of literary exclusion, independent of special grant". On the contrary, there were "ample materials to show, that it is adverse to every notion of the common law of this country". Unlike the English common law system, the Scottish legal system had been strongly affected and influenced by the Romano-Germanic civilian tradition. Where the English legal system had remained largely isolated from the reception of Roman law, throughout the sixteenth century, the Scottish system had aligned itself, as did most of Europe, with the legal inheritance of Justinian's *Corpus Iuris Civilis*.[50] Donaldson was quick to point out that "[t]he only literary property acknowledged in the civil law, was that which was in the owner of the paper, or parchment". In short, Roman law did not admit of incorporeal properties.[51] Moreover, as to the practice of granting patents in literary works, these he maintained were "indulged from favour" and were understood to be part of the prerogative, upon which footing "stood the exclusive privileges of printing all over Europe". Asserting that they were "creative" and "not corroborative of the author's right", Donaldson listed a number of patents granted to some of the foremost eminent lawyers in Scottish history. Works by Sir Thomas Craig, by Lord Durie, Sir John Nisbet, Lord President Gilmour, Lord President Falconer, Sir George Mackenzie, Sir James Dalrymple of Stair and Sir James Stuart had all been protected by patent grant. This very fact, he argued, illustrated:

> [M]ore clearly what was understood to be the law of Scotland, than the most direct authorities from their books could have done. Their works are silent upon the subject, but the reason is plain, because the notion of literary property was not then conceived in Scotland. All that any of our authors ever

[49] *Information for Mess John Hinton of London, Bookseller, and Alexander Mackonochie, Writer in Edinburgh, his Attorney, Pursuers; against Mess Alexander Donaldson and John Wood, Booksellers in Edinburgh, and James Meurose, Bookseller in Kilmarnock, Defenders,* (2 January 1773) reprinted in S Parks (ed), 19–24.

[50] MC Meston, WDH Sellar and The Rt Hon Lord Cooper, *The Scottish Legal Tradition, New Enlarged Edition* (Edinburgh, The Saltire Society & The Stair Society, 1991) 29–64.

[51] *Information for Alexander Donaldson*, n 41 above, 25–38.

> looked for, was an exclusive right by patent, or by act of parliament, for a certain number of years.[52]

The hearing before the Court of Session began on 20 July 1773. David Rae, Alexander Murray and Allan Maconnochie spoke on behalf of Hinton; John MacLaurin, Ilay Campbell and James Boswell represented Donaldson. After one week the Lords issued the following interlocutor:

> On report of Lord Coalston, and having advised the Informations *hinc inde*, and heard parties procurators in the cause, the Lords sustain the defences, and assoilize and decern.[53]

They decision was contrary to Lord Mansfield's earlier decree and against the perpetual right. It was also by majority, with one dissenting voice, Lord Monboddo, providing a neat reversal of the earlier decision in *Millar* (1768).

Of the thirteen judges present, eleven voted for Donaldson, eight of whom provided an opinion on the issue.[54] The Scottish judges were quick to draw a marked distinction between the law of England and the law of Scotland. Lord Hailes commented that "English law, as to us, is foreign law"; Lord Kennet pronounced "it ought to have no influence in determining upon the law of Scotland".[55] The Lord Justice Clerk set out that:

> The law and judicatures of Scotland will give their aid to an Englishman, and to every foreigner, for rendering effectual every property, and every right established in him by the right of his own country, not averse to the property and rights of the subjects of this country, established in them by the common law of Scotland.[56]

52 *Ibid*. For a recent commentary on the manner in which literary works were granted legal protection in early modern Scotland, see A Mann, *The Scottish Book Trade 1500–1720, Print Commerce and Print Control in Early Modern Scotland* (East Lothian, Tuckwell Press, 2000) 95–124.

53 *The Decision of the Court of Session, upon the Question of Literary Property; in the cause Hinton against Donaldson, & c, Published by James Boswell, Esq, Advocate, one of the Counsel in the cause; Printed by James Donaldson, for Alexander Donaldson* (1774) in Parks, *The Literary Property Debate: Six Tracts*, n 41 above.

54 Two of the Lords of Session, Lord Strichen and Lord Alemore, were absent. Of the thirteen that were present, that only twelve in total voted, is explained by the fact that the Lord President traditionally did not cast his vote, unless the rest of the Lords were equally divided upon the issue before them, in which case he exercised his casting vote. That the Lord President did not vote however, did not prevent him from delivering an opinion upon the case before him. He did so in *Hinton*, and it is clear that he agreed in principle with the majority of the Lords.

55 See also Lord Coalston who dismissed the relevance of *Millar* (1768) commenting that "the decision in the present case ... must be determined, not according to the law of England, but by the law of Scotland", in *The Decision of the Court of Session*, 30.

56 *Ibid*, 16.

Only Monboddo, the dissenting voice, expressed the opinion that "the common law of Scotland and England, must, I think, be the same in this case" given that the common law of any nation "is founded upon common sense and the principles of natural justice". These principles required "that a man should enjoy the fruits of his labours".[57] For the majority however, this was solely a Scottish action, and as such, the decision in *Millar* (1768) had little relevance. Instead, three central tenets emerged, woven throughout the majority of the judicial opinions. A common law copyright was deemed to have no foundation either in the *law of nature*, or the *law of nations*, nor was any vestige of such a right to be found in the *law of Scotland*.

As to the first of these, property, as a concept, was fundamentally concerned with the tangible and corporeal. Lord Gardenston noted that "[t]he ordinary subjects of property are well known, and easily conceived... lands and tenements, houses and gardens, fishings, and moveables of great variety". "But", he continued, "property, when applied to ideas, or literary and intellectual compositions, is perfectly new and surprising".[58] For Lord Kames, the meaning of property involved a right to "some corporeal subject, that can be possessed, that can be transferred from hand to hand, that goes to heirs, that may be stolen or robbed, and that may be demanded by a real action".[59] Property, in Lord Coalston's opinion had to be "descendible to heirs, affectable by creditors, and forfeitable for crimes", none of which characteristics were applicable to "abstract ideals".[60] While a man had an interest in "the productions of his own brain", if he should commit his thoughts to "paper, parchment, or any other material, he then has a *res corporalis*, which is a proper object for *dominium*, or property". If however he should sell or otherwise alienate his manuscript, Lord Alva continued, "he therewith conveys his whole interest".[61] In regard to the law of other nations, Lord Gardenston observed that "[t]he principles of reason and justice, as approved by all civilised nations, do support the author's claim to a temporary protection or privilege, [but] not to a property or perpetual right".[62] Lord Coalston considered it significant that:

> [T]hough supposed to be a common-law right, [it] has not been acknowledged in any country except England; and even then it appears to be a modern invention, always disputed, and never settled, till a late decision in the Court of King's Bench, which was not unanimous.[63]

[57] *Ibid*, 11.
[58] *Ibid*, 25.
[59] *Ibid*, 18.
[60] *Ibid*, 28.
[61] *Ibid*, 32.
[62] *Ibid*, 22.
[63] *Ibid*, 27.

Agreeing that "[n]o trace of it can be discovered in modern nations... England only excepted", the Lord Justice Clerk noted that it was on account of "the love of knowledge, and the admiration of the works of learning and genius" that "mankind are prone to give to authors, not only the merit, but the reward that is due to them for their works". Moreover, it was upon this basis that "every civilised state in modern times has introduced exclusive privileges to authors".[64] With respect to the law of Scotland in particular, Lord Hailes pointed out that:

> From Lord Stair down to Forbes all our authors are silent concerning it: from Lord Stair down to Forbes all our authors have acted as if there had been no such right.

Again the Lord Justice Clerk concurred. Having examined "our statutes, the Roman law, the ancient customs of the kingdom, the doctrines of our lawyers, and the decisions of this court" he could find no trace "of this idea of a *copy-right* or property in an author".[65]

On the one hand, it is tempting to dismiss the stark contrast between the judicial reasoning displayed in *Millar* (1768) and that in *Hinton* (1773) as reflecting two divergent legal traditions, common and civil law. However, the Lords of Session framed their opinions in such a way as to make it clear that, not only did Scottish law prevent recognition of the perpetual right, but that, in any case, they intrinsically disagreed with the position adopted by the English court. Ignoring obvious jurisprudential differences, the Scottish judiciary would have arrived at a decision that was contrary to the Court of King's Bench anyway. More than one judge considered the wording of the *Statute of Anne* "to be against the common law right",[66] in addition to which the Lord President considered the very passing of the *Importation Act* 1739 as "inconsistent with a common-law right".[67] Moreover, the Lord Justice Clerk, Lord Gardenston, Lord Kames and Lord Coalston all expressed difficulty in drawing any meaningful distinction between the author of a book, the inventor of a machine, or the engraver of a work of art. All were "equally the works of genius and industry, and in their publication may be useful to mankind".[68]

The Scottish judges, like Yates J, were also fundamentally concerned with the social implications of holding in favour of a perpetual right. Lord Coalston indicated that, while this was not a question that would

[64] *Ibid*, 14–15.
[65] *Ibid*, 16.
[66] Lord Kennet, *ibid*, 1.
[67] *Ibid*, 34.
[68] Lord Justice Clerk, *ibid*, 15.

actually affect the position of the author very much, nevertheless it represented a question:

> [I]n which the booksellers of London, on the one side, and the whole subjects of the country in general, and more particularly all the other booksellers in Britain, on the other side, are deeply concerned.[69]

Lord Alva indicated his satisfaction in arriving at such a decision as "justice, and the encouragement of learning and industry, require", and concluded with the caustic observation that he did "not envy any other state or country, where either common or statute law may have carried it farther".[70] However, it was Henry Home, Lord Kames, who proved the most forthright. "So far from being founded on common law", he considered the right contended for as "contradictory to the first principles of society". Should such a right exist, "it would be a sad day for learning, and for the interest of learning in general" as a perpetual monopoly would "unavoidably raise the price of good books beyond the reach of ordinary readers" and leave "the commerce of books ... in a worse state than before printing was invented". "[A] perpetual monopoly of books", he considered, "would prove more destructive to learning, and even to authors, than a second irruption of Goths and Vandals". For Kames, God had planted "the branch of the common law" in the hearts of men for the good of society, and that common law was "too wisely contrived to be in any case productive of mischief".[71] Just as easily as Lord Mansfield could perpetually protect an author's work according to the "principle of right and wrong, the fitness of things, convenience [and] policy", Lord Kames was able to dismiss the claim for the perpetual right as "contrary to law, as ruinous to the public interest, and as prohibited by the statute". The common law in England might sanction such a state of affairs, but the common law of Scotland could never do so. "[I]t belongs to judges", he commented, "to look forward; and it deserves to be duly pondered whether the interest of literature in general ought to be sacrificed to the pecuniary interests of a few individuals."[72]

***

In the England of 1709, when the London booksellers petitioned the House of Commons for a legal protection of its property, there existed little in the way of provincial printing. What printing did subsist outside of

69 *Ibid*, 27.
70 *Ibid*, 32.
71 *Ibid*, 18–21.
72 *Ibid*.

London was directed primarily towards the production of local newspapers, handbills, tickets and catalogues, rather than the book market.[73] At the beginning of the eighteenth century, and indeed throughout this century, printing and publishing in England remained firmly metrocentric. As Feather remarks, "[t]he English book trade was unshakeably metropolitan in its organisation".[74] One consequence of this was that, when the booksellers lobbied Parliament for legislative protection they did so, at that time, with a united voice, representing all those legitimately involved in the book trade. By the middle of the eighteenth century however, the Scottish book trade began to provide an unwelcome challenge to the Londoners' stranglehold over book publishing.[75] The Scottish trade were well able to supply many of the provincial booksellers in England with cheap imprints of London editions. Moreover, with ports in Glasgow, Greenock and Leith, Scotland was eminently well placed to capitalise upon the growing export trade in books to America, as well as establishing links with Norway, Russia, the Netherlands, Germany, France, Portugal and Spain.[76] As time moved by, it became apparent that the southern booksellers no longer spoke on behalf of what was now a truly British industry. Put simply, in McDougall's words, "[t]he Scots saw the copyright question differently".[77]

The period following *Millar* (1768) should perhaps have been a time in which the perpetual common law copyright dominated the publishing landscape within England. And yet, the reality of the decision's immediate impact upon the book trade was not so dynamic as one might expect. There were, initially, only two actions before the Court of Chancery in which perpetual injunctions were granted against piratical editions. The first of these was *Millar* (1770) itself,[78] and the second was *Macklin v Richardson* (1770).[79] That there were only two such injunctions does indicate that illegitimate printing in the capital was not the London book trade's main concern. Rather, it was the Scottish reprint industry. However, when a case was brought in Scotland, involving a work that fell outside the terms of the *Statute of Anne*, the argument in favour of the perpetual common law right was comprehensively rejected by the Scottish Lords of Session. This was a decision that did not sit easily with the earlier adjudication of Lord Mansfield and the Court of King's Bench, and in effect insulated the main threat to the predominance of the London book trade from legal challenge.

[73] Feather, *The Provincial Book Trade*, n 13 above, 98–121.
[74] *Ibid*, 120.
[75] In general, see McDougall, "Copyright Litigation and the Scottish Book Trade" 9–14.
[76] *Ibid*, 4, 14–22.
[77] *Ibid*, 3.
[78] *Information for Alexander Donaldson* (January 2 1773) 71.
[79] (1770) Amb 694; ch 3, n 120.

The legal plurality of a politically united British state allowed for the legitimisation of two fundamentally opposed concepts of copyright, one in the north and one in the south. This tension was, in reality, almost inevitable. It seems unlikely that Lord Mansfield's court, given the centrality of his earlier participation in the development of the booksellers' position, would ever have decided other than in favour of the London booksellers. By the same token, it is equally unlikely that the Lords of Session would ever have adjudicated other than against the perpetual right and the southern monopolists, in support of an indigenous industry that promised economic, social and cultural benefits for Scotland as a whole. What was needed was a final and authoritative resolution to the question of literary property, the opportunity for which came sooner rather than later.

Just three months after Hinton had issued his summons in Scotland, on 24 January 1771, John Rivington and a number of other booksellers entered a bill of complaint in the Court of Chancery against Donaldson and his brother John, for printing a one-volume edition of Henry Fielding's *The History of the Adventures of Joseph Andrews*.[80] In Donaldson's answer to the charge, dated 25 June 1771, he pointed out that the right to print the work had been first assigned to Andrew Millar in 1742, and, given that Henry Fielding had died in 1754; this meant that Millar could not have become entitled to print the work beyond the first fourteen year term after publication. What right Millar had over the work had come to an end in April 1756. For the Donaldson brothers this meant that, when Rivington and his associates had purchased Fielding's work at the trade sale of Millar's literary estate, they, in effect, had not purchased anything at all. Barely a week and a half after Rivington had entered his bill of complaint, a second was entered against the Donaldson brothers, this time by Thomas Becket and others, objecting to an edition of Fielding's *The History of Tom Jones*.[81] Donaldson responded to them both continuing to assert the supremacy of the *Statute of Anne* and challenging the London booksellers' victory in *Millar* (1768). He admitted publishing the works, but on the terms of the "literal and true meaning" of the *Statute of Anne* wherein each had become "common property" and "a lawful subject of commerce to all printers and booksellers in the

[80] John Rivington, Thomas Cadell, Thomas Beckett, Thomas Davies, Thomas Caslon, Thomas Longman, Stanley Crowder, Thomas Loundes, William Johnston, William Strahon, Robert Horsefield, George Robinson, and John Roberts c 12/1323/15.

[81] The other booksellers mentioned in the bill are Thomas Caslon, Thomas Cadell, Edward Dilly and Charles Dilly, Thomas Longan, John Rivington, Thomas Davies, Lacey Hawes, William Clark and Robert Collins, William Richardson and John Richardson, William Strahan, William Johnston, Thomas Lowndes, George Robinson, John Roberts, Stanley Crowder and Elizabeth Baldwin. c 12/1321/9.

kingdom of Great Britain".[82] It was in relation to a third bill entered against Donaldson, once again by Becket and his associates, that the opportunity arose to re-examine *Millar* (1768), and resolve the difference that existed between the English and Scottish courts, one way or the other. The stage was set for a compelling and comprehensive finale.

[82] C 12/1323/15.

8

Donaldson v Becket; *A Game of Numbers*

I must tell you a tale that happened Friday last. One Monsieur Pleinouf, a foreign minister was brought into the House of Lords whilst a cause was a trying, to satisfy his curiosity. Lord Sunderland made up to him and asked how he liked the place? "Pray", says Pleinouf, "what are these gentlemen with gowns and bands at the Bar?" "Why," says my Lord, "they are lawyers." "And what are they a doing?" My Lord answered, they were arguing a cause. "Pray, my Lord, where are the judges?" "Why," says my Lord, we, the peers, are the judges!' "Hola! mon Dieu," cries the Frenchman, "You, the judges! And is [there] not one in the House [that] minds the least morsel of the cause? You are all a talking to one another or to me!" "It's no matter for that," answers the peer, "there are three or four Lords in the House who understand the laws very well and give attention; and the House always gives in to their opinion." "Very well," says Pleinouf, "then you, the rest of the lords, take it upon your conscience and honour, not that the cause is just or unjust, but that the lords who listen are good lawyers and just judges. But pray, my Lord, do these lords never differ in opinion? How does the House govern itself in a law of that kind?"[1]

THE APPEAL TO THE LORDS

THOMAS BECKET, ON 21 January 1771, filed a bill in Chancery against Alexander Donaldson, and his brother John, praying for an injunction to prevent them from printing James Thomson's *The Seasons* as well as an account of the profits they had made from the publication of their pirate edition. As was the usual practice, upon submission of the bill, an interlocutory injunction was granted. Donaldson filed his answer in July, arguing that any right that existed in Thomson's work was limited to the times set out in the *Statute of Anne*. On 16 November 1772 the case was heard before Lord Chancellor Apsley. Taking note of

[1] This story, about an incident that occurred in the House of Lords on 25 March 1720, was related by Duncan Forbes to Lord Grange (Mar and Keille MSS, SRO, GD 124/15/1197/33), and is quoted at length in AJ Rees, *The Practice and Procedure of the House of Lords 1714–1784*, Doctoral Thesis, (University of Wales, Aberystwyth, 1987) 157.

Millar (1768), he decreed that the injunction formerly granted be made perpetual and referred the case to a Master of the Court to take account of what profit had been made by Donaldson for the purpose of paying the same to Becket.[2] Less than a month had passed when, on 10 December 1772, the petition and appeal of Alexander and John Donaldson against the decision was read to the House of Lords; Becket, along with the other booksellers interested in the cause, was ordered to put in an answer to the Donaldson's claim. He submitted it one week later, after which, on 24 December, it was ordered that the House would hear the cause "by Counsel at the Bar, on the First vacant Day for causes after those already appointed".[3] This however would not be for another thirteen months.

To properly understand *Donaldson v Becket* it is crucial to appreciate the method by which appeals could be brought before the House, as well as the way in which such legal issues were resolved by the lords.[4] In the eighteenth century the judicial capacity of the House could be invoked in one of two ways, either by writ of error,[5] or by a petition of appeal which provided a method for contesting decisions of the Lord Chancellor sitting at first instance in Chancery. On such occasions, the case was heard once again before the Lord Chancellor, but now sitting in his capacity as the Speaker of the House, and now to be heard *de novo*. Bringing these appeals, however, was not entirely straightforward. Petitions had to be presented by a peer, and the petitioner was required to provide a security of £100 before the case could proceed, ensuring that the respondent's costs would be met should the appeal fail. Moreover, all of the clerks and officers of the House were entitled to charge whatever fees they considered appropriate for the services they provided throughout the various stages of the proceedings.[6] To Donaldson, who had made a considerable fortune with his reprint business, these costs proved neither prohibitive nor discouraging. He declared that it was his "fixed purpose that the law should be finally settled in the Supreme Court of the kingdom".[7]

[2] (1774) 2 Bro PC 129.
[3] LJ 33:476, 483, 492.
[4] R Stevens, *Law and Politics: The House of Lords as a Judicial Body, 1800–1976* (London, Weidenfeld and Nicholson, 1979); AS Turberville, *The House of Lords in the Reign of William III* (Oxford, Clarendon Press, 1913); AS Turberville, *The House of Lords in the Eighteenth Century* (Oxford, Clarendon Press, 1927); AS Turberville, *The House of Lords in the Age of Reform, 1784–1837* (London, Faber, 1958); T Bevan, "The Appellate Jurisdiction of the House of Lords" 17 *LQR* 357, 1901; Rees, *The Practice and Procedure of the House of Lords*, n 1 above.
[5] Rees, *ibid*, 187.
[6] *Ibid*, 153.
[7] *The Humble Petition of Alexander Donaldson, Bookseller in St. Paul's Church-yard, London, in Petitions and Papers relating to The Bill of the Booksellers, now before the House of Commons*, (1774) in S Parks (ed), *The Literary Property Debate: Eight Tracts 1774–1775* (New York, NY, Garland, 1974).

The jurisdiction of the Lords to hear such appeals had only been authoritatively established with the decision in *Shirley v Fagg* (1675).[8] What *Shirley* did not resolve, however, was the role the lay peers played in the determination of such cases.[9] Their function, in such appeals, was simply to affirm or reverse the previous decision of the lower court, and it was understood that this was the work of the entire House.[10] In practice, however, the lay peers rarely became embroiled in such matters. Stevens notes that as a result of the increasing number of appeals coming before the House in the eighteenth century "the majority of peers took part actively in only the most important of cases".[11] When they did become involved, the lords had a right to give an opinion and vote on such proceedings as and when it suited them to do so. Generally however, the House would simply acquiesce to the opinions of the law lords, those peers present who had previously held judicial office. In addition to the law lords, the twelve judges of the common law courts also had a role to play as attendants and officials of the House.[12] The lords, when faced with a particularly complex or difficult legal issue, could call upon the common law judges to proffer expert advice for the consideration of the House. The judges, if summoned, took up their position upon the woolsack, a position that was not considered to lie within the limits of the House.[13] As a consequence, technically they "had no voice in the House" and could not give an opinion "unless formally asked for".[14] When they were asked for an opinion, if unanimous in their thinking, the senior judge present would deliver a collegiate address. If, however, there existed disagreement then the judges would be asked to answer the lords' questions, each in turn, in order of increasing seniority.[15] Having heard the opinions of the judges, the peers would then give their vote accordingly. Turberville comments that:

> Even if several other peers took part in the proceedings, they were bound, if they had any common sense, to be guided by the knowledge of the experts;

[8] *Shirley v Fagg* (1675) 6 St Tr 1121.
[9] Stevens writes that "[c]larification of the appellate juridical work of the Lords by no means ensured the clarification of the function of the lay peers in the operation of that process"; Stevens, *Law and Politics*, n 4 above, 11.
[10] Turberville, *The House of Lords in the Eighteenth Century*, n 4 above, 8–9.
[11] Stevens, *Law and Politics*, n 4 above, 13. See also Turberville, *The House of Lords in the Age of Reform*, n 4 above, 200.
[12] Stevens, *Law and Politics*, n 4 above, 11; Bevan, "The Appellate Jurisdiction of the House of Lords", n 4 above, 365; Rees, *The Practice and Procedure of the House of Lords*, n 1 above, 151–52.
[13] J MacQueen, *The Appellate Jurisdiction of the House of Lords and Privy Council* (London, 1824) 24.
[14] Rees, *The Practice and Procedure of the House of Lords*, n 1 above, 27.
[15] *Ibid*, 152.

> and in effect the judgments given by the House were in the vast majority of cases the judgments of the most illustrious judges of the country. [16]

The point must be made however that the lords were not actually bound to follow the opinions of the judges and did sometimes arrive at a contrary decision. It was at these times that the overtly political nature of such decisions came to the fore with greatest clarity. Peers were not averse to lobbying on behalf of a decision that they favoured, regardless of the opinion of the judiciary.[17] Bevan details three such instances, *Bertie v Falkland* (1696),[18] *Bishop of London v Ffytche* (1783),[19] and *Seymour v Lord Euston* (1805–1806),[20] in which the judgment of the House was given in defiance of the judges.[21] To this list of comparatively scarce examples should be added the decision of *Donaldson v Becket*. There is ample evidence to suggest that the vote of the House was contrary to the opinion expressed by the majority of the common law judges present.

IN THE HOUSE OF LORDS

Despite the fact that the lords were ordered to hear Donaldson's cause in December 1772, his petition was not read to the House until January 1774.[22] Originally scheduled to begin on 28 January, Donaldson petitioned the House that the hearing be adjourned for a month, as it would have been "impossible for the Petitioners to be ready for the hearing by the Day appointed". The hearing was duly put off until 4 February. The reason for delaying the hearing of the case had more to do with the readiness of Boswell's account of the Scottish decision of *Hinton* (1773) than it had to do with the readiness of Donaldson's counsel. On 1 February 1774, three days before the commencement of the case in the Lords, Donaldson advertised in the *Morning Chronicle* that his edition of Boswell's *Decision of the Court of Session upon the Question of Literary Property* was available

[16] Turberville, *The House of Lords in the Age of Reform*, n 4 above, 200.

[17] Hale commented that "it is grown a fashion in the lords' house for lords to patronise petitions: a course, that, if it were used by the judges of Westminster Hall, would be looked upon, even by parliament itself, as undecent, and carrying a probable imputation or temptation at least to partiality"; quoted in Stevens, *Law and Politics*, n 4 above, 11. See also Rees, *The Practice and Procedure of the House of Lords*, n 1 above, 158.

[18] *Bertie v Falkland* (1696) 1 Salkeld 231.

[19] *Bishop of London v Ffytche* (1783) 2 Bro PC 211.

[20] *Seymour v Lord Euston* (1805–1806) W Cobbett, *Parliamentary Debates*, vol 7, London, Hansard, 1813, 577, 669.

[21] Bevan, "The Appellate Jurisdiction of the House of Lords", n 4 above, 366–70.

[22] The reason this took so long was because Donaldson's case had been laid before a Mr Chambers (Robert Chambers, Vinerian Professor of English law at the University of Oxford), Lord's counsel, for "perusal and approbation". Chambers however had since been "appointed one of the judges to go to the East Indies" as a result of which he had not settled Donaldson's case until 7 January 1774. LJ 34:13.

for purchase.[23] On 4 February the twelve common law judges were ordered to attend the House where Edward Thurlow, the Attorney-General, opened on Donaldson's behalf.[24] Thurlow had long been involved in the literary property debate, having argued against the common law right both in *Tonson v Collins* (1761) and *Millar v Taylor* (1768). Alexander Wedderburn, the Solicitor-General, and John Dunning were heard on behalf of Becket.[25] Both Wedderburn and Dunning had earlier appeared against Thurlow, in *Tonson* and *Millar* respectively, arguing for the existence of the common law right.

After these arguments had been delivered, Lord Chancellor Apsley, who had earlier granted the injunction in Becket's favour, put three questions to the judges:

1. Whether at Common Law, an author of any book or Literary Composition, had the Sole Right of first printing and publishing the same for sale, and might bring an action against any person who printed, published, and sold the same without his consent?
2. If the Author had such Right originally, did the Law take it away upon his printing and publishing such Book or Literary Composition, and might any Person afterward reprint and sell, for his own Benefit, such Book or Literary Composition, against the Will of the Author?
3. If such Action would have lain at Common Law, is it taken away by the Statute of 8th Anne; and is an Author, by the said Statute, precluded from every Remedy except on the Foundation of the said Statute, and on the Terms and Conditions prescribed thereby?

These were in essence the same three questions that Aston J had asked himself when considering his decision in *Millar* (1768). Lord Camden, however, tabled a further two questions for the consideration of the judiciary and the House:

4. Whether the Author of any Literary Composition, and his Assigns, had the Sole Right of printing and publishing the same, in Perpetuity, by the Common Law?
5. Whether this Right is any way impeached, restrained, or taken away, by the Statute 8th Anne?

[23] M Rose, *Authors and Owners: The Invention of Copyright* (London, Harvard University Press, 1993) 95–96.

[24] LJ 34:19. There were two other counsel representing Donaldson: Sir John Dalrymple and Arthur Murphy.

[25] Becket's third counsel was Francis Hargave.

While both sets of questions amounted, in the end, to the same thing, there does exist a fundamental difference between them, identified by Patterson who comments that "analytically, the first three questions were directed to the rights of the author, the latter two to the rights of the booksellers".[26] Lord Apsley's questions focussed solely upon the position of the author, omitting any reference to the fact that the common law right claimed was one that lasted in perpetuity. Given that this cause was in effect an appeal against the decision in *Millar*, that Lord Apsley should take his cue from the questions examined in that case is not altogether surprising. Lord Camden however was clearly wary of the ease with which the perpetual right might be confirmed under the simple rubric of an author's right. Carefully stressing the place of an author's "assigns" and the perpetual nature of the right under discussion, his two questions covered the same ground as the Lord Chancellor's, but in a way that sought to direct the attention of the House from the author to the bookseller. Lord Camden's questions were then, and remain now, direct, to the point, and quite unambiguous. Did there exist a perpetual common law copyright?, and if such right did exist, was it removed by the *Statute of Anne*? Lord Apsley's questions, however, were not so straightforward.

The judges requested that they be allowed some time for consideration. On Tuesday 15 February, the Lord Chancellor informed the House "[t]hat the judges differed in their Opinions upon the said Questions", whereupon the judges were ordered to deliver each of their answers to the five questions. On this first day, Eyre B, Nares, Ashurst and Blackstone JJ gave their answers, and the matter was adjourned until Thursday 17 February. Then came Willes, Aston JJ, Perrott B, Gould J and Adams B, whereupon the issue was again adjourned until Monday 21 February. On this third day Smythe LCB and De Grey LCJ delivered the remaining opinions. One judge refrained from giving an opinion upon the five questions at all: Lord Chief Justice Mansfield. Six different sources record the various opinions delivered by the judiciary. First, there exists a record contained within the Journal of the House of Lords itself which is also replicated at the end of Burrow's report of *Millar v Taylor*.[27] The third is provided in Cobbett's *Parliamentary History of England*.[28] A fourth was printed in 1774 for Wilkin, entitled *The Pleadings of the Counsel before the House of Lords in the great Cause concerning Literary Property*;[29] the fifth was

[26] LR Patterson, *Copyright in Historical Perspective* (Nashville, Vanderbilt University Press, 1968) 176.
[27] LJ 34:12–32; *Donaldson v Becket* (1774) 4 Burr 2408.
[28] Cobbett, *Parliamentary Debates*, vol 17, 953–1003.
[29] S Parks (ed), *The Literary Property Debate: Six Tracts, 1764–1774* (New York, NY, Garland, 1975). This shall be referred to as the *Pleadings* account.

also printed in 1774, to which was added *Notes and Observations and References by a Gentleman of the Inner Temple*.[30] Finally, there is an account of the case, which includes only the judges' decision upon the third question, by Brown.[31] Of these various reports only Burrow provides any kind of explanation as to why Lord Mansfield might have remained silent. Noting that "[i]t was notorious, that Lord Mansfield adhered to his opinion [*Millar*]" he continues that "it being very unusual, (from reasons of delicacy,) for a peer to support his own judgment, upon an appeal to the house of Lords, he did not speak".[32]

A traditional reading of the votes of the eleven judges who did speak follows that detailed by Birrell.[33] He recounts the voting upon the five questions as follows: that there existed a right to first print and publish an author's work (10 to 1);[34] that this was not taken away upon publication of the work (7 to 4); that this right was taken away by the 1709 Act (6 to 5); that an author had a perpetual common law right to print his work (7 to 4); but that this right was taken away by the 1709 Act (6 to 5). This account details that a large majority of the judges considered that there did exist a perpetual common law copyright, while a smaller majority believed it had been impeached through the passing of the *Statute of Anne*. The reality however was somewhat different. In relation to his first question in particular, that ten votes were cast in favour of the right to first print does not mean that ten judges were in agreement as to the existence of a common law copyright, or even in agreement as to what the question actually meant. While Lord Apsley himself no doubt well understood the implications of the debate before the House, there is nevertheless an ambiguity at the heart of his first question that has created confusion in the subsequent reporting and understanding of the judicial responses to it. Abrams suggests that, in essence, Lord Apsley's first question amounted to asking: "At common law, did the author have a copyright in an unpublished manuscript?"[35] In recasting the enquiry in this light, however, he fails to articulate the

[30] *Ibid.* This shall be referred to as the *Gentleman's* report.

[31] *Donaldson v Becket* (1774) 2 Bro PC 129.

[32] *Donaldson v Becket* (1774) 4 Burr 2417. Birrell echoes this observation, writing that Lord Mansfield "did not think fit to attend, considering himself too deeply committed"; A Birrell, *Copyright in Books* (London, Cassel and Co., 1899) 124. For more on the reasons as to Lord Mansfield's silence, see Rose, *Authors and Owners*, n 23 above, 99–101.

[33] Birrell, *Copyright in Books*, n 32 above, 124–27.

[34] This is sometimes represented as an 8 to 3 vote. See for example J Whicher, "The Ghost of Donaldson v Beckett: An Inquiry into the Constitutional Distribution of Powers over the Law of Literary Property in the United States – Part 1" (1961–62) 9 *Journal of Copyright Society of the USA* 102, 128.

[35] H Abrams, "The Historic Foundation of American Copyright Law: Exploding the Myth of Common Law Copyright" (1983) 29 *Wayne Law Review* 1119, Appendix A, 1188.

question's inherent ambiguity that touches upon both the tangible and the intangible. With his first question the Lord Chancellor had asked whether an author had the "right of *first* printing and publishing"[36] his work and there are two distinct ways in which this question can be understood. Of these two competing readings the first, addressing the intangible, implies the existence of a common law copyright in a manuscript. This marries with Abrams' rendition of Lord Apsley's question — did copyright exist at common law? The second reading, however, has nothing to do with copyright in a manuscript whether published or not. This alternative reading of the Lord Chancellor's first question simply relates to the existence of certain rights at common law that flow from ownership of a given tangible object, which happens to be, in this case, a manuscript. In other words, the question simply addressed the rights of the owner of the physical manuscript to decide whether or not to publish it to the rest of the world. As shall be seen, when different judges were answering this first question, they were in fact answering different questions.

The day after the judges had delivered their opinions, Tuesday 22 February, it was proposed that the House reverse the former decree of the Court of Chancery. This was objected to, and after a debate, in which Lords Camden, Apsley, Lyttleton and Howard, as well as the Bishop of Carlisle, all expressed their own opinions on the matter, the question was put to the House once again. Of these five speakers only one, Lord Lyttleton, spoke in favour of the common law right. The proposal was resolved in the affirmative, and the decree of 16 November 1772 was accordingly reversed.[37] Given the history of the case in the Lords it was perhaps inevitable that *Donaldson* would generate much confusion and that the traditional reading of the case is not entirely accurate. Here were two sets of the same, yet different, questions, the individual meaning of which was a matter of some conjecture. Add to this the fact that the peers and legal reporters were left to ascertain each of the judge's answers in the light of a more general, and often lengthy, response (many of the judges not providing an explicit answer to any or all of the five questions) and it should not surprise that the traditional reading delivered by Birrell is not entirely accurate. *Donaldson v Becket*, and the question of literary property, had become something of a lottery. Two sides, six counsel, four speakers, five questions, twelve judges, delivering eleven opinions, over the course of seven days; one proposal, five further comments, a four to one split, one vote, and, eventually, six separate and inconsistent reports.

[36] Emphasis added.
[37] LJ 34:29, 30, 32.

THE VOTES OF THE JUDGES

Of all the judges who gave opinions in favour of Donaldson, Eyre J proves the least problematic (Figure 1). Put simply, he rejected any notion of the existence of a common law copyright and in any case considered that, should one exist, the *Statute of Anne* would have taken precedence.

EYRE	1	2	3	4	5
Lords' Journal	N	Y	Y	N	Y
Cobbett	N	Y	Y	N	Y
Burrows	N	Y	Y	N	Y
Pleadings	N	Y	Y	N	Y
Gentleman's	N	Y	Y	N	Y
Brown	-	-	Y	-	-

Figure 1

NARES	1	2	3	4	5
Lords' Journal	Y	N	Y	Y	Y
Cobbett	Y	N	Y	Y	Y
Burrows	Y	N	Y	Y	Y
Pleadings	Y	N	N	Y	N
Gentleman's	Y	N	N	Y	N
Brown	-	-	Y	-	-

Figure 2

Nares J, by contrast, concluded that there did exist a common law copyright (Figure 2). There is, however, a discrepancy in the records of his opinion upon the third and fifth questions. The majority of reports give it that Nares J decided that the common law right, after publication, was removed by the *Statute of Anne*. However, as Abrams and Rose have pointed out,[38] and as is apparent from the various reports themselves,[39] there is sufficient evidence to indicate that he was clearly of the opinion that the common law right was *not* impeached by the 1709 Act.[40]

[38] Rose, *Authors and Owners*, n 23 above, 154–58; Abrams, "The Historic Foundation of American Copyright Law", n 35 above, 1166–69.

[39] Cobbett, *Parliamentary Debates*, 975; *Pleadings*, 17–18; *Gentleman's*, 35.

[40] Cobbett's report notes that "[Nares] stated to the House why he thought a common law right in literary property did exist, and why the statute of Anne did not take it away" and yet records a vote of "yes" for the third question; *Parliamentary Debates*, vol 17, 975. The *Pleadings* report sets out the same position and continues that "[a]fter having spoken near an hour [he] concluded with answering the questions in a manner directly opposite to that of Mr Eyre"; 17–18. The *Gentleman's* report cites Nares J as commenting that "as it is admitted on all Hands that an author has a beneficial Interest in his own manuscript before Publication, it is a most extraordinary circumstance, that he shall lose that beneficial interest, the very moment he attempts to exercise it. The Statute my Lords, does not take away the common law remedy, although it gives an additional one"; 35. In addition to the speeches of the judges themselves, Rose also provides evidence of contemporary newspaper reports which indicate that Nares in fact voted "no" to the crucial third question; *Authors and Owners*, n 23 above, 154–58.

Moreover, this was an opinion shared by Ashurst, Blackstone and Willes JJ who followed (Figure 3).

ASHURST, BLACKSTONE, WILLES	1	2	3	4	5
Lords' Journal	Y	N	N	Y	N
Cobbett	Y	N	N	Y	N
Burrows	Y	N	N	Y	N
Pleadings	Y	N	N	Y	N
Gentleman's	Y	N	N	Y	N
Brown	-	-	N	-	-

Figure 3

Given the nature of Aston J's answers to the third and fifth questions, one might have anticipated that his votes would have followed the same pattern as the judges immediately preceding him (Figure 4). However, something is clearly amiss with the record of his answers to Lord Apsley's second question. How to account for the "yes" vote recorded in Cobbett, the *Pleadings*, and the *Gentleman's* report? Cobbett sets out that Aston J noted:

> If this right originally existed, what but an act of his own could take it away? By publication, he only exercised his power over it in one sense; when one book was sold, it never could be thought that the purchaser had possessed himself of that property which the author held before he published the work. A real abandonment on the part of the first owner must have taken place, before his original right became common. In all abandonments, Judge Yates hath defined my Lords, that two circumstances are necessary; an actual relinquishing the possession, and an intention to relinquish it; in the present case neither can be proved.[41]

Despite the obvious inference to be drawn from these comments, Cobbett continues: "judge Aston gave his opinion in favour of the first, second and fourth questions".[42] In this light, the conflicting record of his response to the second question is best explained as being simply erroneous. Aston J's vote, as noted in the Lords' Journal, followed the same pattern as the four previous judges, as well as that of Lord Smythe CB who spoke last but one.[43]

[41] Cobbett, *Parliamentary Debates*, vol 17, 980–81.
[42] Both the *Pleadings* and the *Gentleman's* report are the same.
[43] The record of Smythe CB's answers follows the same pattern as that for Aston J (Figure 4).

ASTON	1	2	3	4	5
Lords' Journal	Y	N	N	Y	N
Cobbett	Y	Y	N	Y	N
Burrows	Y	N	N	Y	N
Pleadings	Y	Y	N	Y	N
Gentleman's	Y	Y	N	Y	N
Brown	-	-	N	-	-

Figure 4

PERROTT	1	2	3	4	5
Lords' Journal	Y	Y	Y	N	Y
Cobbett	N	N	Y	N	Y
Burrows	Y	Y	Y	N	Y
Pleadings	N	N	Y	N	Y
Gentleman's	N	N	Y	N	Y
Brown	-	-	Y	-	-

Figure 5

Perrott B, Gould J and Adams B followed. There are conflicting accounts of both Perrott and Adams BB's response as to the existence of the common law right. The Lords' Journal records that Perrott B agreed that an author had the sole right of first printing "but could not bring an action against any person who printed, published and sold the same unless such person obtained the copy by fraud or violence", an answer that is often interpreted as a "conditional yes" vote (Figure 5).[44] By contrast Cobbett suggests that Perrott B "answered the first, second, and fourth questions in the negative, being fixed in the opinion that there never existed a common-law right, and that an author had no claim to his manuscript after publication".[45] That there is conflict in these reports at all lies in the inherent ambiguity of the first question referred to earlier.

It was not the case that Perrott B thought there existed a common law copyright that was removed by the law upon publication. Rather, he was suggesting that an author had certain rights over his manuscript by virtue of the fact that it was an item of tangible property. Cobbett records that "[r]especting the statute of queen Anne, [Perrott B] was perfectly convinced that it was the only security that authors or booksellers had". Beginning with the observation that "the argument for the existence of a common law right, and the definition of literary property, as chattel property, was in his idea exceedingly ill founded and absurd", the report continues:

> An author certainly had a right to his manuscript; he might line his trunk with it, or he might print it. After publication, any man might do the

[44] Note that while the Burrow's account is identical to that of the Lords' Journal, Abrams incorrectly suggests that Burrow in fact recorded a "no" vote from Perrott on this point. See Abrams, "The Historic Foundation of American Copyright Law", n 35 above, 1189.
[45] Cobbett, *Parliamentary Debates*, vol 17, 983.

> same ... if a manuscript was surreptitiously obtained, an action at common law would certainly lie for the corporeal part of it, the paper. So if a friend to whom it is lent, or a person who found it, multiplied copies, having surrendered the original manuscript, he had surrendered all that the author had any common law right to claim.[46]

Perrott B's attitude to the first question is grounded in an author's rights in relation to the physical manuscript as a tangible piece of property: "he might line his trunk with it, or he might print it". For Perrott B there was no common law copyright, only such rights as follow from the ownership of the physical text.[47]

ADAMS	1	2	3	4	5
Lords' Journal	Y	Y	Y	N	Y
Cobbett	N	N	N	N	N
Burrows	Y	Y	Y	N	Y
Pleadings	N	N	N	N	N
Gentleman's	N	N	N	N	N
Brown	-	-	Y	-	-

Figure 6

GOULD	1	2	3	4	5
Lords' Journal	Y	N	Y	Y	Y
Cobbett	Y	N	Y	Y	Y
Burrows	Y	N	Y	Y	Y
Pleadings	Y	-	Y	-	Y
Gentleman's	Y	-	Y	-	Y
Brown	-	-	Y	-	-

Figure 7

[46] *Ibid*, 981–83.

[47] In relation to Perrott B, the way in which the various accounts record his answer to the first question affects how his answer to the second question is documented. Abrams suggests that the second and fourth questions "[o]stensibly ... both ask the same question: is there a perpetual common law copyright after an authorised publication of a manuscript", and continues that, as a result, "the logically consistent answers to the second and fourth questions would be opposites"; "The Historic Foundation of American Copyright Law", n 35 above, 1158. The pattern of votes from the judgments prior to Perrott B would appear to confirm his observation. Again, however, Abrams is guilty of a dangerous oversimplification. While it is possible to read both questions in the way he suggests, this is to forget that the second question is specifically linked to the first, while the fourth question stands alone. In recording a "yes" vote to the first question, the Lords' Journal catalogued Perrott B's conviction that an author did have rights at common law; such rights however were inextricably linked to the physical manuscript. In relation to the second question, any rights that were contingent upon ownership of the manuscript must, by definition, be lost upon publication of the work. Moreover, to record a vote of "yes" to the first two questions, understood in this light, is not inconsistent with Perrott B's "no" vote in relation to the fourth question. Similarly, considering the account in Cobbett's, the *Pleadings* and the *Gentleman's* report, to suggest that Perrott B voted "no" to the first two questions makes sense when one reads the first question as addressing the existence of a common law copyright. Perrott B clearly considered one did not exist, and if one did not exist in the first place, then there was nothing to lose upon publication. Read in this manner, the six different reports are actually entirely consistent.

As was the case with Perrott B, so is the case with Adams B (Figure 6). The Lords' Journal records the same series of answers for Adams B, as it did for Perrott B. Namely, that there was a right of first printing the work, but that one could not bring an action against another "unless such person obtained a copy by fraud or violence".[48] Abrams, discussing Adams B's judgment at some length, draws on the observation of Adams B in Cobbett's report, that "authors never dreamt of any claim in their favour, after they had parted with their manuscript", and suggests that the implication is that "they had some rights in unpublished manuscripts".[49] That they have "some rights" in their manuscripts is without doubt. However, Abrams erroneously infers that Adams B supported the existence of a common law copyright, based on his comments concerning an author's rights in the tangible unpublished manuscript. Rather, it is clear that Adams B, like Perrott B, recognised certain rights in the author flowing from ownership of the manuscript as property, while rejecting any idea of a common law copyright.[50]

Gould J's position is different again (Figure 7). Both the *Pleadings*, and the *Gentleman's* report begin that he "agreed, that an author had a right at Common Law to his manuscript, previous to publication". One might assume that he was agreeing with both Perrott and Adams BB, between whom he spoke, however, Cobbett's report indicates that Gould J's overall approach was markedly different. He records that Gould J agreed "that an author had a right at common law to his manuscript previous to publication, [but] he thought that right should continue to him under certain restrictions after publication". He continues that Gould J "thought that if a book was kept out of print for an unreasonable time, it was a kind of abandonment of property in the original possessor, and the subject of it ought, for public convenience, to become common".

"Under this idea", Cobbett notes, "he answered the first, second, and fourth questions".[51] This, unlike the conventional wisdom about Perrott and Adams BB, does in fact represent a form of qualified common law

[48] Again, as was the case with Perrott B, Abrams records a "no" vote, rather than this "conditional yes" vote. Abrams, while commenting that Adams B's "position on rights in unpublished manuscripts is ambiguous" records a "yes" vote in Cobbett's account and continues that the *Pleadings* and the *Gentleman's* reports "do not touch the question". This is difficult to square with the fact that all three reports recount that Adams B answered all five questions in the negative.

[49] Abrams, "The Historic Foundation of American Copyright Law", n 35 above, 1190.

[50] Cobbett records his opinion that "till of late years no idea was entertained that a common-law right existed respecting what was now termed literary property ... He was clearly of the opinion that, previous to the statute of queen Anne, authors and printers had no security but by patents ... [and that] [t]he Act most evidently created a property which did not exist before"; *ibid*, 985.

[51] *Ibid*, 984–85. Both the *Pleadings* and the *Gentleman's* reports fail to record Gould J's answer to either the second or the fourth question.

copyright protection. Of all the judicial responses, Gould J is the one that stands apart. The brief reports of his opinion suggest that he did consider that a qualified form of copyright existed at common law, that in certain circumstances this could be circumscribed for "public convenience", but that in any case, it had certainly been removed through the passing of the *Statute of Anne*.

After Lord Smythe CB (Figure 8),[52] the last to speak was Lord Chief Justice De Grey (Figure 9). While all of the records agree that he voted "yes" upon the first of the five questions, a close examination of these various texts reveal that his understanding of the issue actually accorded with that of Perrott and Adams BB.[53] He began that "[w]ith respect to the first question, there can be no doubt that an author has the sole right to dispose of his manuscript as he thinks proper; it is his property, and, till he parts with it, he can maintain an action of trover, trespass, or upon the case, against any man who shall convert that property to his own use".

SMYTHE	1	2	3	4	5
Lords' Journal	Y	N	N	Y	N
Cobbett	Y	Y	N	Y	N
Burrows	Y	N	N	Y	N
Pleadings	Y	Y	N	Y	N
Gentleman's	Y	Y	N	Y	N
Brown	-	-	N	-	-

Figure 8

DE GREY	1	2	3	4	5
Lords' Journal	Y	Y	Y	N	Y
Cobbett	Y	N	Y	N	Y
Burrows	Y	Y	Y	N	Y
Pleadings	Y	N	Y	N	Y
Gentleman's	Y	N	Y	N	Y
Brown	-	-	Y	-	-

Figure 9

However, he continued:

> [B]ut the right now claimed at the bar, is not a title to the manuscript, but to something after the owner has parted with, or published his manuscript; to some interest in right of authorship, to more than the materials or manuscript, on which his thoughts are displayed, which is termed literary property ... which right is the subject of the second question proposed to us. [54]

[52] See n 43 above and accompanying text.
[53] Cobbett, the *Pleadings* and the *Gentleman's* report are all essentially the same.
[54] Cobbett, *Parliamentary Debates*, vol 17, 988.

Clearly De Grey CJ, in addressing the first question, was not answering the question of whether or not there exists a common law copyright. He simply asserted that everyone has certain rights flowing from the fact of ownership of a given tangible property. This was not a common law copyright, but simply a case of common law rights over your copy. It was not until he turned to the second question that he considered himself to be addressing the issue of the existence of a common law copyright. Upon this matter he commented that "this new doctrine", this "idea of a common-law right in perpetuity ... cannot be supported upon any rules or principles of the common law of this kingdom".[55] In short, Lord De Grey, like Eyre, Perrott and Adams BB, comprehensively rejected any notion of copyright at common law.

Overall, examining the substance of the opinions of each of the eleven judges, three definable approaches to the question of literary property emerge. On the one hand there were six judges in support of the common law copyright, who did not believe that such a right was lost either upon publication of the work, or as a result of the enactment of the *Statute of Anne* (Nares, Ashurst, Blackstone, Willes, Aston JJ and Smythe CB).[56] On the other hand, there were four judges who, rejecting any notion of a perpetual right, did recognise the existence of a right to first print, which had nothing to do with a common law copyright, but was rather a consequence of owning the physical manuscript (Eyre J, Perrott, Adams BB and De Grey CJ). For these four judges, what rights an author had over his work after publication, were entirely defined by the *Statute of Anne*. Third, standing somewhere between both of these camps, was Gould J, who delineated the existence of a common law copyright (albeit a qualified one), but considered the right lost upon the passing of the 1709 Act. For Gould J the legislature had definitively settled the issue. Over the course of a week, the House of Lords had heard a majority of the speaking judges (seven) concede the existence of a common law copyright, as well as a majority of those judges (six) consider this common law right pre-eminent over the *Statute of Anne*. That was what the peers had heard; whether they had listened was an entirely different affair.

ONE DEBATE; FIVE SPEAKERS; A FOUR TO ONE SPLIT

On the day after De Grey CJ had delivered the last of the judicial commentaries, five further opinions were added to what had already been said. The first to speak was Lord Camden, one of the upper chamber's

[55] *Ibid*, 992.
[56] To these six judges can of course be added the opinion of Lord Mansfield.

law lords,[57] who had introduced the fourth and fifth questions for the consideration of the judges. He began by castigating the "pretended precedents and authorities" that had been relied upon in support of the common law right, portraying them as a "Heterogeneous heap of rubbish … calculated to confound your Lordships, and mislead the Argument". The patent cases, the Star Chamber decrees, the stationers' bye-laws, all were dismissed. Of the Chancery injunctions, he asked "[w]here then is the Chancellor who has declared ex Cathedra that he had decided upon the Common Law Right?" Only once he had "cleared the way of those spurious, pretended authorities", did Camden consider the real question could begin "to assume its natural shape".[58] He decried that authors should write for anything other than glory,[59] and yet it was not the author that remained Camden's main concern. Rather, it was the bookseller. With his additional two questions he sought to move the focus of the House away from the rights of the author, to the consequences of such rights existing in a bookseller, the author's assign, in perpetuity. Remember, he warned, that "the common law right now claimed at your bar is the right of a private man to print his works for ever, independent of the crown, the [stationers'] company, and all mankind".[60] Should the lords vote in favour of the perpetual right "[a]ll our Learning would be locked up in the hands of the Tonsons and the Lintots of the age". Such booksellers, such "engrossers", could set upon books whatever price "their avarice chose to demand, till the Public became as much their slaves, as their own Hackney Compilers are". This pretended common law right was to Camden "as odious and selfish as any other; it deserves as much reprobation, and is become as intolerable". It was the free market of ideas and not the market place of the bookseller that remained of paramount importance.

> If there be any thing in the world, my Lords, common to all Mankind, Science and Learning are in their nature *publici juris*, and they ought to be as free and general as air or water. They forget their creator, as well as their fellow-creatures, who wish to monopolize his noblest gifts and greatest benefits. Why did we enter into Society at all, but to enlighten one another's minds, and improve our faculties for the common welfare of the species?

"Knowledge and science", he maintained, "are not things to be bound in such cobweb chains".[61]

[57] Having been called to the bar in 1738, he had been appointed Attorney-General in 1757, Chief Justice of the Court of Common Pleas in 1761, and held the position of Lord Chancellor from 1766 to 1770; AWB Simpson, *Biographical Dictionary of the Common Law* (London, Butterworths 1984) 434–35.
[58] Cobbett, *Parliamentary Debates*, vol 17, 993–96.
[59] Camden observed that "[i]t was not for gain that Bacon, Milton, Newton, Locke, instructed and delighted the world"; *ibid*, 1000.
[60] *Ibid*, 994.
[61] *Ibid*, 999–1000.

Lord Chancellor Apsley, who had granted the original injunction now under discussion, spoke next. Unfortunately, none of the reports of the case provide an in depth account of what exactly was said. In general we are told that Lord Apsley:

> [E]ntered into a very minute discussion of the several citations and precedents that had been relied upon at the bar, shewed where they failed in application to the present case; and one by one described their complexion, their origin and their tendency; in each of which he proved that they were foreign to any constructions which could support the respondents in their argument; he was no less precise and full in exposing the absurdity of the authorities derived from the Stationers' Company ... He then very fully stated the several cases of injunctions in the court of Chancery, produced several original letters from Swift to Faulkner and others, relative to the statute of queen Anne, and gave an historical detail of all the proceedings in both Houses upon the several stages of that Act, and the alterations it had undergone in the preamble and enacting clauses, all tending to shew the sense of the legislature, at the time of passing it, to be against the right.[62]

He explained that in granting the original injunction, he was acting "entirely as of course", regarding it as "merely a step in the gradation to a final and determinate issue in the House of Peers". The Lord Chancellor, the Keeper of the Great Seal, the Speaker of the House of Lords, informed his peers that had he been free to do so, he would never have granted the injunction in the first place. Instead he declared that he "was clearly of opinion with the Appellants".[63] What force this had upon the House can only ever be guessed at, but, following as it did Lord Camden's high impact rhetoric, it can only be supposed that Apsley's role in determining the final outcome of *Donaldson* was of much greater significance than has traditionally been recognised.

Of the three remaining speakers, Lord Lyttleton, the Bishop of Carlisle and Lord Howard, only Lyttleton favoured the perpetual right. Regarding it as of "infinite importance to every country, that the arts and sciences should be cultivated and protected", Lyttleton rejected Camden's assertion that authors write "for fame only". "This is", he commented, "a proper and noble observation, but it will not hold generally". In his view:

> Genius is particular to no clime, it belongs to no country, it is more frequently found in the cottage than the palace; it rather crawls on the face of the earth than soars aloft.

62 *Ibid*, 1001–2.
63 *Ibid*, 1002.

"[W]hen it does mount", he continued, "its flight should not be impeded". For Lyttleton, the perpetual right offered "a lasting encouragement", while making such works free to all was "like extending the course of a river so greatly, as finally to dry up its sources".[64] By contrast, Lord Howard, echoing sentiments that Lord Northington had expressed nearly ten years earlier,[65] considered the prospect of perpetual control dangerous "to the constitutional rights of the people", as politicians and ministers might buy up the rights to print critical pamphlets "thereby choaking the channel of public information".[66] His fear was one of unchecked political suppression.

The Bishop of Carlisle took up a different constitutional point. He began by commenting upon the "many foreign topics" that had been introduced into the arguments at hand. Questions such as:

> Whether it is a property properly so called, or only a right to some property? Whether such property be a corporeal one, or incorporeal? What is the subject to which it adheres? Whether it lies in the Letters of a Book, or the ideas, or in both? Whether it be a perfect, an imperfect, or only a quasi right? Whether it is real, or personal, original or derivative? Whence it might derive its origin, and what is its extent and duration? How far it is deducible from ancient practice, or grounded in the authority of precedents? How it has stood in different countries, or in our own at different periods, before or after the art of printing? [67]

Such speculations, the very lifeblood of the debate born out of *Midwinter v Hamilton*, which debate had now spanned over three decades, while "always entertaining", he considered "in a great measure foreign to the main point". Instead he directed the peers simply to consider the *Statute of Anne*. Such legislation he argued, however flawed, stood "directly opposite to the notion of any abstract independent perpetual copy-right". Even if such right did previously exist, he suggested, "it is now plainly circumscribed and subjected to certain restrictions".[68] The real issue for the Bishop remained one concerned with the sovereignty of parliament, and the relationship between the legislature and the judiciary.

> If it once comes to the established maxim, that Acts of Parliament can have no effect on claims subsisting at common law; in vain surely does the Legislature employ itself in framing any concerning them.

[64] *Gentleman's*, 55–56.
[65] Ch 7.
[66] *Gentleman's*, 59.
[67] *Ibid*, 56.
[68] *Ibid*, 56–59.

So long as the *Statute of Anne* remained in force, "it must exclude all that right paramount and inextinguishable, which is exhibited along with it".[69] Camden had earlier expounded upon the same theme. He had clashed with Mansfield CJ on numerous issues in the past,[70] and on matters of constitutional jurisprudence they were certainly not of the same mind. Where Mansfield CJ would freely base his judicial reasoning upon fundamental principle, often at the expense of recognised precedents, Camden held up the example of "[t]hat excellant Judge, Lord Chief Justice Lee" who would always ask counsel: "Have you any case?". For Camden, judges should "always copy [Lee CJ's] example, and never pretend to decide upon a claim of property, without attending to the old black letter of our Law". Lord Mansfield advocated the development of the law through concerted, principled judicial activism, whereas Camden championed the supremacy of the legislature and judicial conservatism. He reminded the judiciary that "[t]heir business is to tell the suitor how the law stands, not how it ought to be". "[O]therwise", he continued, "each judge would have a distinct tribunal in his own breast", and "[c]aprice, self-interest, [and] vanity would by turns hold the scale of justice, and the law of property be indeed most vague and arbitrary".[71] In short, for Camden, the judge should interpret and explain the law, not make it.

THE VOTE OF THE PEERS

Lord Camden began his speech to the House with a reference to De Grey CJ's opinion, expressing the hope that "what was yesterday so learnedly told your lordships, will remain deeply impressed on your minds". Whether or not De Grey CJ's speech had remained fresh in the minds of the peers is impossible to gauge. By the time Lord Howard had finished speaking, the lords had been presented with sixteen different opinions over the course of a week. Eight had endorsed the existence of a common law right, and eight had rejected such a notion, though those positions were not necessarily clear to the House. Nor was it immediately apparent what the judges' position had been upon the relationship between an existing copyright and the *Statute of Anne*. If the clerk of the House of Lords, and Cobbett, could mistake Nares J's position on the third and fifth questions, there is no reason to believe that some, all, or any of the peers present, could not have made a similar mistake. Moreover, while the

[69] *Ibid.*
[70] Rose, *Authors and Owners*, n 23 above, 99.
[71] Cobbett, *Parliamentary Debates*, vol 17, 998–99. See D Lieberman, *The Province of Legislation Determined, Legal Theory in eighteenth-century Britain* (Cambridge, CUP, 1989) 95–98.

judges were tied to the questions asked by the House, the lords who spoke were not so bound. While they all addressed the existence or not of the common law right, only two, Camden and the Bishop of Carlisle, made any comment upon the relationship between a common law right, should one exist, and the statute, both determining that the Act "plainly circumscribed" the common law.[72] In any event, the Lords decided, by a majority vote, that "[t]he decree of the Court of Chancery was accordingly reversed".[73]

The nature of the mechanism for deciding the appeal to the House renders it difficult to settle upon a definitive reading of *Donaldson*. There are a number of possible explanations for the vote of the peers. Perhaps they mistakenly voted against the existence of the perpetual right, believing that they were in fact voting with the majority of the judges. Perhaps the peers knew that the majority of judges were in favour of the perpetual right and, moved by the rousing sentiments of Camden and the denunciation by the Lord Chancellor of his own earlier decision, voted in defiance thereof. Perhaps the truth lies somewhere between these two poles. On balance, it seems most likely that the peers did appreciate that they were voting in defiance of the opinion of the majority of the judges. As such the decision in *Donaldson* should take its place alongside those of *Bertie*, *Ffytche* and *Seymour*. The judges in the majority had expressed sentiments that broadly concurred with those of the silent Mansfield LCJ. By contrast, the majority of those lords who spoke denied outright the existence of the common law right and it was this position that the House embraced. Lord Camden had identified and expounded upon two central themes that rang true in the heart of the upper chamber. The first concerned the nature of the relationship between the Houses of Parliament and the un-elected judiciary, and the supremacy of the legislative body. The second concerned the relationship between the author, his work, and the public good. When the *Statute of Anne* had been passed, it had been for the purpose of benefiting society through the encouragement of learning and the continued production of useful books. In seventy years it would seem that little had changed about this basic impulse. There was still a want and need for useful books and there remained the desire that they be produced and made available at an affordable cost.

[72] *Gentleman's*, 53–58.

[73] Only Cobbett provides any indication of the numbers involved in the vote itself; *Parliamentary Debates*, vol 17, 1003.

There is nothing which so generally strikes the imagination, and engages the affectations of mankind, as the right of property; or that sole and despotic dominion which one man claims and exercises over the external things of the world, in total exclusion of the right of every other individual in the universe. And yet there are very few, that will give themselves the trouble to consider the original and foundation of this right. Pleased as we are with the possession, we seem afraid to look back to the means by which it was acquired, as if fearful of some defect in our title; or at best we rest satisfied with the decision of the laws in our favour, without examining the reason or authority upon which those laws have been built.

W Blackstone, *Commentaries Vol II* (1766)

9

An Ending and a Beginning

ON 28 FEBRUARY 1774, six days after the House of Lords handed down their decision in *Donaldson v Becket*, a petition was received in the House of Commons, from the "booksellers of London and Westminster". In this petition, the booksellers complained that they "had constantly apprehended, that the [*Statute of Anne*] did not interfere with any copy-right that might be invested in [them] by the common law". "[B]y a late solemn decision of the House of Peers" however:

> [S]uch common law right of authors and their assigns hath been declared to have no existence, whereby your petitioners will be very great sufferers thro' their involuntary misapprehension of the law.

It was ordered that the petition be referred to the consideration of a committee of the House for examination.[1] One month later, the committee made its report. William Johnston had given evidence on behalf of the London booksellers that it was always presumed that they had a "perpetual right in the copies they had purchased", that had this right not existed the booksellers would not have invested so heavily in the works they had bought, that without any relief being granted the trade would suffer greatly, on top of which there was a danger that "elegant editions" of "valuable books" would soon run out of print. As a result of this testimony, it was decided, by a vote of fifty-four to sixteen, that a *Bill for the Relief of the Booksellers* [2] should be brought before the house. Amongst those charged with preparing the Bill were Alexander Wedderburn and John Dunning. Amongst those voting against the motion was Edward Thurlow.

Following this decision the booksellers and printers of Edinburgh petitioned the Commons claiming that the "the special indulgance prayed for by the London booksellers" would be highly injurious to everyone concerned in "Bookselling, the Paper manufacture, the Art of printing, and

[1] CJ 34:513.
[2] *A Bill for the Relief of Booksellers, and others, by vesting the Copies of printed Books in the Purchasers of such Copies from Authors or their Assigns, for a Time therein to be limited.*

other Branches therewith connected". Acknowledging that the Scottish book trade was primarily concerned with "re-printing English books", when the terms of the 1709 Act permitted it, they declared that extending the monopoly asked for by the London booksellers would "be the ruin of many families in Scotland", as well as being "prejudicial to the community at large".[3] Similarly, "sundry booksellers in London and Westminster", the "printers and booksellers of the City and University of Glasgow", and the "booksellers, printers and bookbinders of York", all spoke out against the deleterious consequences of passing the Bill.[4] Not surprisingly, Alexander Donaldson did not remain silent. He delivered his own petition, referring to the decision he had secured before the Lords, and expressing his mortification at seeing "the victory, which he obtained with great risk and labour, ready to be snatched out of his hands by the very people who have been hitherto guilty of oppression". Should the Bill pass into law:

> A very dangerous monopoly will be thrown into the hands of a few wealthy booksellers, who have already enjoyed the fruits of usurpation, and will, no doubt, make the best use of the further time now expected, by continuing such prices as will best answer their thirst of gain, to the great detriment of the publick, to the injury of letters, and the utter ruin of the inferior booksellers both in town and country.

Rejecting the "pretence of hardship" adopted by the London booksellers, he prayed to the house that the *Statute of Anne* "expressly made for the encouragement of learning" should not now be altered "for the encouragement of the London booksellers only".[5]

The Bill was first presented to the house on 22 April. During its passage through the Commons arguments were heard against it on behalf of the petitioners from Edinburgh, Glasgow, London and Westminster.[6] To these were added further petitions, from a number of provincial booksellers,[7] all advocating the retention of the 1709 Act. These had no more impact than the previous pleas; on 27 May 1774, the *Booksellers Bill* was read for a third time and passed.[8] Drawing no distinction between those works in which copyright had already expired and those which were still protected under the *Statute of Anne*, this Bill simply provided that any author, or, crucially, his assign, who had already printed and published his

[3] CJ 34:665–66.
[4] *Ibid*, 668, 698.
[5] *Ibid*, 679. See the report of this petition in *Petitions and Papers relating to the Bill of the Booksellers*.
[6] CJ 34:669, 736, 752.
[7] These petitions came from New Malton, Nottingham, Bawtry, Leeds and Knaresborough; *ibid*, 757.
[8] *Ibid*, 788.

work, should, from 4 June 1774 "have the sole and exclusive liberty of printing such book ... for the term of fourteen years ... and no longer".[9] Four days later, on 31 May, the Bill was received in the House of Lords, whereupon it was ordered that it be read for the first time on 2 June.[10] On this day the Bill was read and it was suggested that it be read a second time two months hence. The proposal was initially objected to, but after debate was affirmed and the order was made.[11] In effect, this signalled its demise as later that month the parliamentary session came to an end. Once again, the House of Lords had been the undoing of the London booksellers.

***

The London monopolists were not however the only interested parties alarmed by the decision in *Donaldson* (1774). Carter writes that:

> As soon as the House of Lords decided in 1774 that no subject had a perpetual copyright in a published work and had thrown out a Bill (which the Commons had passed) aimed at reversing its decision, the Universities took steps to secure exceptional treatment.[12]

In April 1775 leave was given in the Commons for Lord North, the Chancellor of Oxford University at the time, to prepare and bring in a *Bill for enabling the Two Universities to hold in Perpetuity the Copy Right in books, for the advancement of useful Learning, and other purposes of Education, within the said Universities*.[13] North, although a peer, presented the Bill, steered it through the Commons, and brought it before the Lords in less than three weeks.[14] The *Universities Bill* was presented to the Lords on 15 May, read for the second time the next day, and then committed. Two days later, Lord Scarsdale reported that the house had gone through the Bill without any amendment, and on 19 May it was read for a third time and passed. Three days after that, on 22 May 1775, after only eight days in the upper chamber, *An Act for enabling the Two Universities in England, the Four Universities in Scotland, and the several colleges of Eton, Westminster, and Winchester to hold in Perpetuity their Copy Right in Books given to or bequeathed to the said Universities and Colleges, for the Advancement of useful Learning, and other Purposes of Education*, received the Royal Assent.[15]

[9] *An Act for Relief of Booksellers and others, by vesting the Copies of Printed Books in the Purchasers of such Copies from Authors, or their Assigns, for a limited Time.*
[10] LJ 34:222.
[11] *Ibid*, 232.
[12] H Carter, *A History of the Oxford University Press, vol 1 to the year 1780* (Oxford, OUP 1975), 367.
[13] CJ 35:299.
[14] *Ibid*, 340, 351, 370, 373.
[15] 15 Geo III, c 53. LJ 34:451, 454–55, 458, 462–63, 470.

Modelled on the *Statute of Anne*, this Act dictated that the various universities and colleges should "have, for ever, the sole Liberty of printing and reprinting all such books as shall at any time heretofore have been" bequeathed to them by any author. This was granted in order that the selling of such works could contribute to funds "for the Advancement of Learning, and other beneficial Purposes of Education within the said Universities and Colleges".[16] In a matter of weeks, the universities managed to secure what the London booksellers had unsuccessfully pursued for over thirty years.

That parliament should sanction the granting of a perpetual copyright in certain books was not in itself considered problematic. What mattered, to the House of Lords at least, was who had control over these perpetual monopolies and why. When those in control were some of the country's most prestigious seats of learning, and when the perpetual monopoly they commanded was to be directed towards the betterment of those educational establishments, then both parliamentary chambers could agree that a perpetual copyright, framed in such terms, was not such a controversial prospect. Moreover, the educational parameters of this new legislation were made more than explicit. Should any university sell any of their perpetual copyrights on to another, the statute provided that the "the Privileges hereby granted are to become void and of no effect, in the same manner as if this Act had not been made".[17]

***

With the passing of the *Universities Act* 1775 we have come full circle. The *Statute of Anne* and the *Universities Act* stand as twin pillars. Both concerned the copyright in printed books, and both were secured on the strength of the social impact that each Act would have. Both were fundamentally concerned with the advancement of education and learning within Great Britain, and both supported the continued production of useful books. With the *Statute of Anne* a necessary, if finite, bargain had been struck with the author and the bookseller; with the *Universities Act* a useful, non-finite, source of revenue was provided for the support of various venerable seats of learning. Two contrasting measures directed toward the same end. Mirror images. Moreover, the success of the university lobby in 1775, in contrast with the failure of the London booksellers to secure further legislation in 1774, serves to reinforce that the decision in *Donaldson*, regardless of the wealth of argument and counterargument on the nature of literary property, turned primarily upon the same basic impulse that underscored both of these legislative bookends: a desire to

[16] Preamble, s 1.
[17] S 3.

encourage and promote the advancement of learning, to nurture a buoyant marketplace of ideas. In all of this, the interests of wider society were paramount.

***

In *Donaldson* the Lords were asked whether or not the decree for the perpetual injunction granted by Lord Chancellor Apsley to Thomas Becket in 1772 should be reversed. They voted that it should. Despite the fact that five questions had been put to the judges, only one question had been put for the consideration of the peers. In light of the various opinions expounded within the upper chamber, this single question approximated most closely to a choice between the perpetual common law right and the time-limited *Statute of Anne*, with the protection offered by the legislation being preferred. However, this still left open the issue of whether the Act had simply created a new property right in printing books, or whether it had abrogated a pre-existing common law copyright. The decision to reverse the Lord Chancellor's decree said nothing of this. However, while the actual vote of the peers ignored this issue, Lord Apsley *had* addressed it, and as Abrams correctly observes, while "the judicial statements were only advisory", "the Lords' statements were the law of the case".[18] This was the Lord Chancellor who "entered into a minute discussion of the several citations and precedents that had been relied upon at the Bar", who "proved that they were foreign to any constructions which could support the Respondents", who exposed "the absurdity of the authorities derived from the Stationers Company", who "very fully stated the several cases of injunctions in the Court of Chancery", and who "gave an historical detail of all the proceedings in both Houses upon the several stages" of the *Statute of Anne* "all tending to shew the sense of the legislature, at the time of passing it, to be against the right".[19] Lord Apsley, speaking in the House of Lords, explicitly denied the existence of the common law right.

That this represents the position adopted by the Lords is further reinforced in the petition for, and the drafting of, the *Booksellers Bill*. Drawing upon the language of the booksellers' petition to the commons in February 1774, as well as the preamble to the Bill itself, it is clear that the decision of the peers was initially understood to have dismissed any notion of the common law right. The booksellers complained that *Donaldson* declared the common law right "to have no existence"; had

[18] H Abrams, "The Historic Foundation of American Copyright Law: Exploding the Myth of Common Law Copyright" (1983) 29 *Wayne Law Review* 1119, 1169.

[19] *The Pleadings of the Counsel before the House of Lords in the cause concerning Literary Property*, 35, reprinted in S Parks (ed), *The Literary Property Debate: Six Tracts, 1764–1774* (New York, NY, Garland, 1975).

the Bill passed into law, its preamble would have recounted that it had "lately been adjudged in the House of Lords that *no such copy right in authors or their assigns doth exist at common law*". In the opinion of the booksellers themselves the House of Lords had denied that any common law copyright pre-dated the *Statute of Anne*; the legislation had in fact created a new, temporally limited, property right in literary works.

That the House of Lords in *Donaldson* rejected the existence of any common law copyright is not of course how their decision is popularly portrayed or understood. In the most recent edition of *Copinger and Skone James on Copyright*, Garnett, Rayner James and Davies write that, in *Millar* "[t]he Court held that there was a common law right of an author to his copy stemming from the act of creation and that that right was not taken away by the Statute of Anne".[20] They continue:

> The decision was finally overturned, however, by the House of Lords in *Donaldson v Beckett* in 1774, a case which decided that copyright was the deliberate creation of the Statute of Anne and thereafter treated as statutory property. Thus, the effect of the Statute of Anne was to extinguish the common law copyright in published works, while leaving the common law copyright in unpublished works unaffected. [21]

Laddie, Prescott and Vitoria open their "historical review" of copyright with the observation that:

> There are contained in the various law reports thousands of cases on copyright law going back some 280 years. However, few were decided under the current Act; and while a great many are still relevant today, some are not, can positively mislead, and have mislead judges in the past.[22]

Such commentary seems entirely apposite when re-reading *Donaldson*. Because of the nature of the single vote in the appeals process to the House of Lords, the lack of attention that the speeches of the Lords themselves have attracted, the emphasis that has been placed upon the eleven judicial opinions delivered to the house, and the misreporting of key aspects of those opinions, this singular determination in *Donaldson* has provided a conclusion to the debate over copyright that that has mislead judges,

[20] K Garnett, J Rayner James and G Davies (eds), *Copinger and Skone James on Copyright*, 14th edn (London, Sweet & Maxwell, 1999) vol 1, para 2–16.
[21] *Ibid.* Similarly see: H Laddie, *et al*, *The Modern Law of Copyright and Designs*, 3rd edn (London, Butterworths, 2000) vol 1, 55, 321; P Torremans, Holyoak & Torremans, *Intellectual Property Law*, 3rd edn (London, Butterworths, 2001) 10; D Brennan and A Christie, "Spoken Words and Copyright Subsistence in Anglo-American Law" (2000) 4 *IPQ* 309; D Burkitt, "Copyrighting Culture – The History and Cultural Specificity of the Western Model of Copyright" (2001) 2 *IPQ* 146.
[22] Laddie, *et al*, *The Modern Law of Copyright and Designs*, n 21 above, 51.

practitioners and academics for over two hundred years. When the peers voted in favour of reversing the earlier decree, they were voting against the perpetual right, but, regardless of their actual intention, their vote has been taken to correspond with the (mis)reported opinion of the majority of the speaking judges.

One of the first English copyright cases to reconsider the decision of *Donaldson* was that of *Beckford v Hood* (1798).[23] In this case the plaintiff was the author of *Thoughts Upon Hunting*, a work that fell within the twenty-eight year protection provided by the *Statute of Anne*. The plaintiff had not registered the work in accordance with the legislation but was seeking damages by an action upon the case, rather than the penalties of the statute. The question for the King's Bench was whether or not such an action could be sustained. Lord Kenyon, the Chief Justice, based his decision upon the 1709 Act, observing that "it vests the right of property in the authors of literary works, for the times therein limited" as a consequence of which "the common law remedy attaches, if no other be specifically given by the Act".[24] It was, however, Grose J who specifically addressed the decision in *Donaldson*, and its relationship with the issue before the court.

> I was struck at first with the consideration, that six to five of the Judges who delivered their opinions in the House of Lords ... were of opinion that the common law right of action was taken away by the Statute of Anne; but upon further view, it appears that the amount of their opinions went only to establish that the common law right of action, could not be exercised beyond the time limited by that statute.[25]

Such adoption of the eleven judges' opinions as the law in *Donaldson* has not been limited to this jurisdiction. In one of the seminal copyright decisions of the United States Supreme Court, *Wheaton v Peters* (1834),[26] a case that ultimately turned upon what measure of the English common law relating to literary property had been adopted by Pennsylvania upon its formation, both *Millar* (1768) and *Donaldson* were discussed at some length. In a majority decision, the Supreme Court concluded that the common law copyright did not transfer to Pennsylvania, which decision, as Abrams notes, "essentially concedes that common law copyright did exist in England".[27] Justice McLean delivered the majority opinion of the court

[23] *Beckford v Hood* (1798) 7 TR *620*.
[24] *Ibid*, 628.
[25] *Ibid*, 629.
[26] *Wheaton v Peters* (1834) 33 US 591. Abrams has described the case of *Wheaton* (1834) as defining "the underlying philosophy of copyright in the United States"; Abrams, "The Historic Foundation of American Copyright Law", n 18 above, 1185.
[27] *Ibid*, 1183.

relying upon Burrow's account of *Donaldson* in the process. Following an examination of the five questions, he continued:

> It would appear from the points decided, that a majority of the judges were in favour of the common law right of authors, but that the same had been taken away by the statute. [28]

It quickly becomes clear why the opinions of the judges in *Donaldson* bear so much importance. It is not because they were decisive of the issue, but because they were later believed to represent an accurate summary of the collective opinion of the house itself. Ultimately, what was taken away from *Donaldson* was that there *did* exist a perpetual common law copyright, that this right was *not* lost upon publication of an author's work, but that it *was*, upon publication, prescribed by the *Statute of Anne*. With the reversal of the Lord Chancellor's decree, the existence of a common law copyright in an author's *unpublished* manuscript was given life, and a perpetual common law copyright in the unpublished manuscript was *created* which would exist until the passing of the *Copyright Act* 1911.[29] Moreover, this popular reading of *Donaldson*, with its acknowledgement of a common law copyright, also required that a suitable theory of literary property exist to underpin this common law phenomenon. In theory, if the author had perpetual control over his work, then an appropriate explanation was needed as to how he might publish his work to the world and yet still retain absolute control. The relationship between the author his work and the reading public demanded proper definition. It was in this way that the ratiocinations of Blackstone and Wedderburn came to embody and inform popular conceptions of what copyright, as a property right, actually entailed. What was protected was not the book itself, nor the ideas contained in that work, but the words in which the author clothed those ideas. What was protected was not the book, the tangible, but the text, the writings of the author, the intangible. The London booksellers, in arguing for the existence of the perpetual right had developed, over time, a convincing, accessible and necessary theory of literary property. This remains their real legacy. The London monopolists, while they may have not won the battle of the booksellers, won the war of words.

[28] (1834) 33 US 656. Justice Thompson, one of the two dissenting judges in *Wheaton*, after examining the first two questions in *Donaldson* (1774), commented that: "The vote upon these two questions settled the point, that, by the common law, the author of any literary composition, and his assigns, had the sole right of printing and publishing the same in perpetuity", 679. More recently, in *Eldred v Ashcroft* 537 US 186 (2003), the US Supreme Court, in a majority decision, declined to resolve the issue as to whether or not any common law copyright protections pre-dated the US 1790 Copyright Act. For a brief commentary on the case, see R Deazley, "Re-reading Donaldson (1774) in the Twenty-First century and Why it Matters" (2003) 25 *EIPR* 270, 275–79.

[29] *An Act to amend and consolidate the Law relating to Copyright*, 1911, 1&2 Geo 5 c 46.

Conclusion
The Myth of Copyright; Moving While Standing Still

> Copyright today is entirely the creature of statute. It is no longer an emanation of the common law. It extends to both published and unpublished works. The old controversies are now dead. But, although the debate has died, much that was said lives on, to guide us in reading the statutes.[1]

FOR THOSE CONCERNED with the history and development of copyright the *Statute of Anne*, and the legislative and judicial debates that were to follow, inevitably stand out as warranting particular and special attention. For Ransom, the Act operates to mark "a middle ground, where early regulation was summarized and where a new law concerning literature began",[2] thus functioning as a unique and pivotal moment in legal, cultural and social influence. On the one hand it signals the end of an earlier time, when the censorship and ownership of the published press moved, seemingly conspiratorially, hand in hand. By and by, the censorial state falls away, and the publishers, aligned along new trade structures, lobby for and secure a new form of protection for themselves. From the ashes of the common hangman's dwindling fires, springs forth a strong, independent and powerful metropolitan industry. Following this, the pivot begins to tip and the statute, Janus-like, turns its gaze forwards. The focus shifts away from the bookseller and over the course of the next seventy years the *Statute of Anne*, and copyright law, comes to signal and embrace the emergence of the modern proprietary author. As Rose suggests, this second story is one of progression from trade regulation and marketplace economics to the liberal culture of possessive individualism.[3] Contributing to this seesaw tale of two halves are numerous voices: Birrell, Ransom, Patterson, Feather, Rose and Loewenstein to name but a few.[4]

[1] *Pacific Film Laboratories Pty Ltd v The Commissioner of Taxation of the Commonwealth of Australia* (1970) 121 CLR 154, 166 (Windeyer J).

[2] H Ransom, *The First Copyright Statute* (Austin, Texas, University of Texas, 1956) 6.

[3] M Rose, *Authors and Owners: The Invention of Copyright* (London, Harvard University Press, 1993) 142.

[4] A Birrell, *Copyright in Books* (London, Cassell & Co, 1899); Ransom, *The First Copyright Statute*, n 2 above; LR Patterson, *Copyright in Historical Perspective* (Nashville, Vanderbilt

This orthodoxy, concerning copyright's singular transformation in Britain throughout the eighteenth century, is however open to challenge. Saunders for one rejects the idea that the natural authorial right stands "as the necessary goal or destiny of law on literary and artistic rights".[5] The material presented within this book, and the explication of the movement of the law during this period, has thrown up a narrative that is by its nature complex, which often confounds, is sometimes banal, but is, hopefully, always authentic. What transpires is a movement, from the *Statute of Anne* to *Donaldson v Becket* (1774), from the bookseller's to author's right, which cannot be traced along any single, unfolding axis. The orthodox tale buckles under the weight of numerous identifiable but disparate threads of influence. This movement is instead one of twists and turns, of stops and starts, of repetitions and tangents. Its direction has been influenced by individual moments of political sensitivity, by unconnected matters of constitutional import, a dominant personality, the forging of a fruitful relationship; by the publication of a volume of personal correspondence, one erroneous decision, an unsympathetic legislature; by personal belief and bias, an absence of verifiable fact, and considerations of national industry; through misreporting, misunderstanding, and by careful and deliberate re-branding. These individual movements, moments, threads, provide an engaging reality that exposes the fiction of the larger, unified and coherent form. In these details, these smaller vignettes, the true movement of the law is unearthed.

Not only are these transient influences overlooked, but in tracing an overarching progression of the law from the *Statute of Anne* to *Donaldson*, other moments of considerable significance can also go unobserved. Throughout the years of legal and literary point and counterpoint, in the three decades following *Midwinter* (1743),[6] through the process of contesting the meaning and significance of the copyright legislation, the concept of copyright itself came to be defined. The ontology developed at that time, in support of the common law right, has since come to inform our understanding of copyright, as *Donaldson* was mistakenly taken to validate the existence of that common law right. The relationship between the author, his work and the reading public came to be understood in terms of the book, the ideas contained therein, and the way in which those ideas

University Press, 1968); J Feather, *A History of British Publishing* (London, Routledge, 1988); J Feather, *Publishing, Piracy and Politics: An Historical Study of Copyright in Britain* (London, Mansell, 1994); Rose, *Authors and Owners*, n 3 above; J Loewenstein, *The Author's Due: Printing and the Prehistory of Copyright* (London, University of Chicago Press, 2002).

[5] D Saunders, "Approaches to the Historical Relations of the Legal and the Aesthetic" (1992) 23 *New Literary History* 505, 512.
[6] See ch 5(1) Copyright at Common Law? A "Complicated" Action.

were expressed. The book was the province of the purchaser. The ideas contained therein were the province of anyone who might read that book. But, what remained with the author, even after publication, was the way in which he chose to express those ideas. No-one put this concept more eloquently than Francis Hargrave, third counsel for the London booksellers in *Donaldson*. Hargrave, not given the opportunity to voice his arguments before the House of Lords, published them instead as *An Argument in Defence of Literary Property* (1774). Examining the "subject of the property" under discussion, he commented that "[e]very man has a mode of combining and expressing his ideas peculiar to himself" so that "[t]he same doctrines, the same opinions, never come from two persons, or even from the same person at different times, clothed wholly in the same language". Hargrave continued that:

> [T]here is such an infinite variety in the modes of thinking and writing, as well as in the extent and connection of ideas, as in the use and arrangement of words, that a literary work really original, like the human face, will always have some singularities, some lines, some features, to characterize it, and to fix and establish its identity.[7]

That this concept, which still informs contemporary copyright thought, was formulated throughout the course of the battle of the booksellers, operates to compound the way in which *Donaldson* has become synonymous with the validation of a common law copyright and the emergence of the modern proprietary author. And yet, this theory, this tri-partite division, so beguiling, so attractive, so comprehensible, did not uniquely develop at this time. It had already seen legal and cultural articulation.

When Hogarth and his contemporaries drew up their petition, for the consideration of the House of Commons, in 1735, they explained that it was the artist's work that gave a print "whatever Value it has above another common Piece of Paper". This value lay not in the physical page, but in the application of the artist's industry and skill in capturing a given subject upon that page. They expounded that "[e]very one has undoubtedly an equal Right to every Subject", and asserted that anyone "who attempts a Subject already executed, without directly copying the Design of another, [has] undoubtedly the same Rights to the Fruits of his Skill, that the first had". Here exists the same tri-partite division in the guise of the artistic subject, the individual's design of that subject, and the print itself. Moreover, the engravers continued that two different artists taking the same subject would necessarily produce two entirely different

[7] F Hargrave, *An Argument in Defence of Literary Property* (London, W Otridge, 1774) reprinted in S Parks (ed), *Four Tracts on Freedom of the Press, 1790–1821* (New York, NY, Garland, 1974).

works. Why necessarily so? Because each of the two works would exhibit the individual "manner", "shape" and "distances" of the artists. They asserted that one person's design would be just as unique as his handwriting, which similarly depends upon "the Manner, Distances and Shape of the Strokes which compose the Letters".[8] Each person's work was as recognisable as his handwriting, or, to draw a different analogy, as recognisable as the individual features of his face. In lobbying parliament these artists and engravers were not seeking recognition of any natural common law rights they might have in their creations. They spoke not of their inherent proprietary rights but of being defrauded of the "Profits of the Sale of their Prints", and sought that it be made "punishable by Act of Parliament for any one to copy the Designs of Another". As a consequence, they were granted a fourteen-year protection for their work, in an Act that was modelled upon the *Statute of Anne*, but judicially aligned, initially at least, with the fourteen-year patents safeguarded by the *Statute of Monopolies* 1624. The engravers' manifesto, and the statutory protection granted, prefigured the factual conclusion of *Donaldson v Becket*, and its resolution to the conundrum of literary property, by nearly forty years.

And yet, although the conclusion to the contest over literary property emerges as no more than an echo of events past, *Donaldson* has come to mean something different. When Grose J delivered his opinion in *Beckford v Hood* (1798), that the House of Lords had earlier decided that "the common law right of action could not be exercised beyond the time limited by that statute", he signalled the nascent development of the *Donaldson* myth. Four years after the *Beckford* decision, Joshua Montefiore published a short treatise, only 59 pages in length, exclusively devoted to the law of copyright, commenting that "in the opinions of no less than eight of the twelve judges" in *Donaldson*, the common law right "was allowed and perpetuated by the common law of England; but six held it abridged by the statute of Anne".[9] Just over twenty years later Isaac Espinasse set out that an author had:

> [T]he sole right of printing and publishing his own work ... by common law ... but the exercise of that right was by the operation of [the 1709 Act] limited and restrained to fourteen years, with an extension of a further fourteen years if the author was living at the expiration of the first.

The result of the enactment of the *Statute of Anne*, he continued, was to give the author "an additional remedy by penalty, which he had not before" while leaving him "his common law right, limited to the term of

[8] *The Case of Designers, Engravers, Etchers & c. stated In a Letter to a member of Parliament*, 1735, Lincoln's Inn Library, MP 102, Fol 125.
[9] J Montefiore, *The Law of Copyright* (London, 1802) 2.

twenty-eight years at the utmost".[10] Robert Maugham's text of 1828, which incorporated a 62-page "Historical View of the Law", sought to "review the subject of literary property as it anciently stood, according to the common law" and asserted that by that common law "an author was entitled to the exclusive enjoyment of his copyright in perpetuity".[11] Next came John Lowndes who, in 1840, published the first text to exclusively address the historical development of copyright, in which he sought to establish in the mind of the reader that copyright "did formerly exist at common law".[12] When Lord Philips, in *Ashdown v Telegraph Group* (2002), described the nature of copyright stating plainly that it had "its origins in the common law, but is now derived from the provisions of the Copyright Act",[13] he might have been quoting from Montefiore, Espinasse, Maugham or Lowndes.

William Murray, in *Millar* (1749–1751) and *Tonson* (1752), had proved adept at recasting existing cases, transforming them in meaning and significance, to develop a rhetorical fiction that was otherwise unwarranted by the historical fact.[14] *Donaldson* has provided the point of focus for a similar reconstitution. Of greater importance is not the reality of the events surrounding *Donaldson* but instead the story of those events. In a sense, both parties to the action have been vindicated. Consequential fears have merged with the ontological arguments drawn out in support of the perpetual right. Elements from both camps have been fused in a way that has precipitated a re-writing of the legal and historical framework surrounding the decision. That is, a myth has developed concerning the nature of copyright law and its origins, which has since taken on a life and vitality that has proved ultimately more influential than the reality. Without close investigation it would be impossible to identify and locate the presence of this phenomenon, and it is only in recognising the influence this myth has borne over the later development of copyright, that we begin to fully appreciate the essential role played by those persons who actively engage in *writing the law*. The way in which this myth has come to dominate the story of copyright in the eighteenth century has also functioned to obscure one of the most fundamental and constant features of this narrative. In rushing to understand the *Statute of Anne* as the culmination of the previous one hundred and fifty years, as a result of a developing system of trade regulation, a central theme of

[10] I Espinasse, *A Treatise on the Law of Actions on Statutes ... and on the Statutes Respecting Copyright* (London, 1824) 89.
[11] R Maugham, *A Treatise on the Laws of Literary Property* (London, 1828) 6–7.
[12] JJ Lowndes, *An Historical Sketch of the Law of Copyright* (London, Saunders and Benning, 1840) Preface.
[13] *Ashdown v Telegraph Group Ltd* [2002] RPC 235, 243.
[14] See ch 5(2) The Lawyers' Tales.

the legislation has been overlooked. That parliament chose to proffer protection to the stationers and booksellers in return for a verifiable benefit for wider society, in the guise of a continued production of useful books, has too often and by too many commentators been overlooked. Equally so, this element has been omitted from discussion of and argument about the battle of the booksellers and the decisions of *Millar v Taylor* (1768) and *Donaldson*. The reality of the *Donaldson* decision is lost, and the import and significance of the *Booksellers Bill* 1775 and the *Universities Act* 1775 are disregarded. The centrality of the public interest, identifiably there, is once again concealed.

Copyright, in eighteenth century Britain, was never simply concerned with the bookseller or the author. What emerges from a close study of the movement of the law during this period is that copyright, with both the passing of the *Statute of Anne* and the factual decision of *Donaldson*, was primarily defined and justified in the interests of society and not the individual. A statutory phenomenon, copyright was fundamentally concerned with the reading public, with the encouragement and spread of education, and with the continued production of useful books. In allocating the right to exclusively publish a given literary work, the eighteenth century parliamentarians were not concerned primarily with the rights of the individual, but acted in the furtherance of these much broader social goals. The pre-eminence of the common good as the organising principle upon which to found a system of copyright regulation is revealed. This element of the public interest, overlooked or perhaps ignored in other historical tales of the origin of copyright, once moved to its very core.

Alice never could quite make out, in thinking it over afterwards, how it was that they began: all she remembers is that they were running hand in hand, and the Queen went so fast that it was all she could do to keep up with her: and still the Queen kept crying 'Faster! Faster! but Alice felt she could not go faster, though she has no breath left to say so.

The most curious part of the thing was that the trees and the other things round them never changed their places at all: however fast they went they never seemed to pass anything. ' wonder if all the things move along with us?' thought poor puzzled Alice. And the Queen seemed to guess her thoughts, for she cried 'Faster! Don't try to talk!'

L Carroll, Through the Looking-Glass, and What Alice Found There (1871)

Postscript
Thomas Becket's Claim for Penalties

ON 4 AUGUST 1775, three months after the passing of the *Universities Act* 1775, and a year and a half after *Donaldson* (1774), Thomas Becket returned to the courts of law. A summons was executed on his behalf, acting in conjunction with Thomas Cadell, William Straton and Alexander MacConnochie, against a number of Scottish booksellers, before the Court of Sessions.[1] In it they set out how they had purchased, from Laurence Sterne, a number of books including *The Life and Opinions of Tristram Shandy* and *A Sentimental Journey through France and Italy by Mr. Yorick*, while complaining that the Scottish booksellers had imported and sold foreign editions of these said works, in contravention of the *Importation Act* 1739, as well as printing and selling their own editions in direct violation of the *Statute of Anne*. To remedy the offence they requested that the Court order the defenders to "desist and decease from all further printing, publishing, importing and selling" the books in question, to deliver up any copies in their possession for damasking, that they make "payment of the penalties" outlined in the two Acts, in addition to their legal costs and £1,000 in damages.

John Bell and a number of the other booksellers mentioned in Becket's summons entered a representation early in 1776 recounting Becket's allegation that they had imported copies of the work from Ireland. They flatly denied the claim and, while the Lord Ordinary's decree that both parties be ready to debate the issue, this aspect of the action nevertheless stalled. Instead, Becket's focus turned to one bookseller in particular, David Willison. It was he who had printed the Scottish editions of the two works, and after a series of representations and answers by Willison and Becket, the process came on to be heard before the Lord Ordinary on 25 June 1778. Speaking on behalf of the pursuers, Alexander MacConnochie alleged that, sometime between March and July 1775, Willison had printed 1015 copies of an edition of Laurence Sterne's works, which included their copy of *A Sentimental Journey*. The edition printed by

[1] The Scottish booksellers listed in the action were Robert Mundell, David Willison, Charles Elliot, William Gordon, John Bell, William Gray, James Brown, James McCleish, William Darling, James Dickson, John Wood and Lachlan Forsyth (CS 229/B/3/20).

Willison consisted of 80 sheets, of which the pursuers work occupied 24. Moreover, Willison had printed 500 additional copies of *A Sentimental Journey*, occupying a further six (and one-sixth) sheets. MacConnochie continued that the statutory penalty for the whole of the aforesaid sheets, set out in the 1709 Act, amounted to "one hundred and twelve pounds nineteen shillings and seven pence halfpenny sterling", which Becket and the other claimants sought to recover, along with their expenses in bringing the process. Neither Willison nor his counsel attended the hearing, and the Lord Ordinary ordered that the same be paid to the pursuers. Nearly seventy years after the passing of the *Statute of Anne*, the statutory penalties that parliament had considered sufficient for the securing of an author's copyright began to be awarded against those booksellers guilty of literary piracy.

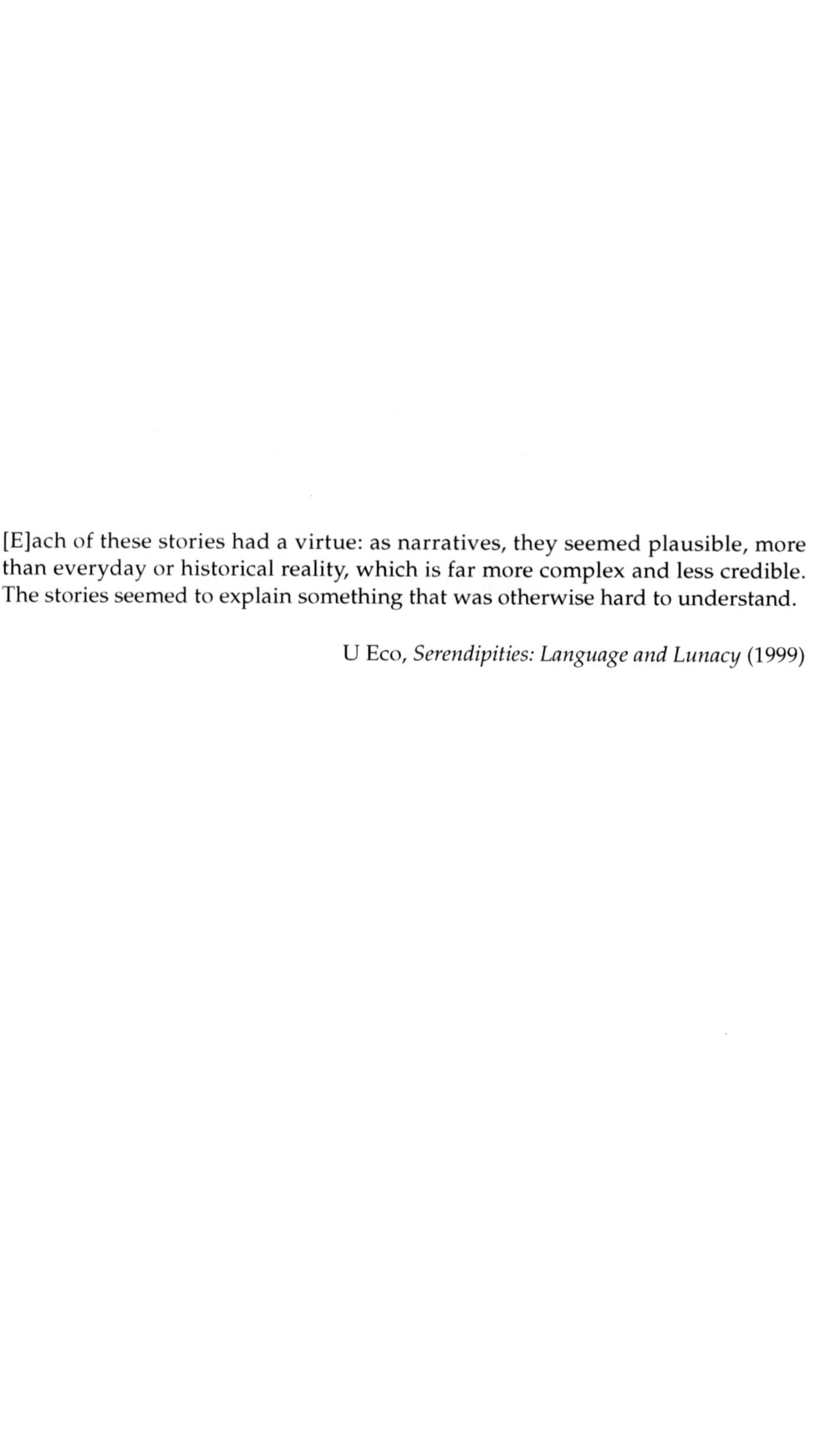

[E]ach of these stories had a virtue: as narratives, they seemed plausible, more than everyday or historical reality, which is far more complex and less credible. The stories seemed to explain something that was otherwise hard to understand.

U Eco, *Serendipities: Language and Lunacy* (1999)

Appendix I: The Statute of Anne 1709

AN ACT FOR THE ENCOURAGEMENT OF LEARNING, BY VESTING THE COPIES OF PRINTED BOOKS IN THE AUTHORS OR PURCHASERS OF SUCH COPIES, DURING THE TIMES THEREIN MENTIONED

Whereas printers, booksellers and other persons have of late frequently taken the liberty of printing, reprinting and publishing, or causing to be printed, reprinted and published, books and other writings, without the consent of the authors or the proprietors of such books and writings, to their very great detriment, and too often to the ruin of their families: For preventing therefore such practices for the future, and for the encouragement of learned men to compose and write useful books; may it please Your Majesty that it may be enacted, and be it enacted by the Queen's most Excellent Majesty, by and with the advice and consent of the Lords Spiritual and Temporal, and Commons, in this present Parliament assembled, and by the authority of the same,

s.1 That from and after the [10 April 1710], the author of any book or books already printed, who hath not transferred to any other the copy or copies of such book or books, share or shares thereof, or the bookseller or booksellers, printer or printers, or other person or persons who hath or have purchased or acquired the copy or copies of any book or books, in order to print or reprint the same, shall have the sole right and liberty of printing such book and books for the term of [21] years, to commence from the [10 April] and no longer; and that the author of any book or books already composed, and not printed and published, or that shall hereafter be composed, and his assign or assigns shall have the sole liberty of printing and reprinting such book or books for the term of [14] years, to commence from the day of the first publishing the same, and no longer; and that if any other bookseller, printer or other person whatsoever, from and after the [10 April 1710], within the times granted and limited by this Act as aforesaid, shall print, reprint or import, or cause to be printed, reprinted or imported, any such book or books without the consent of the proprietor or proprietors thereof first had and obtained in writing, signed in the presence of two or more credible witnesses; or knowing the same to be so printed or reprinted without the consent of the proprietors, shall sell, publish or expose to sale, or cause to be sold, published or exposed to sale, any such book or books, without such consent first had and obtained as aforesaid; then such offender or offenders shall forfeit such book or books, and all and every sheet or sheets, being part of such book or books, to the proprietor or proprietors of the copy thereof, who shall forthwith damask and make waste paper of them; and further, that every such offender or offenders shall forfeit one penny for every sheet which shall be found in his, her or their custody, either printed or printing, published or exposed to sale, contrary to the true intent and meaning of this Act; the one moiety thereof to the Queen's most Excellent Majesty, Her Heirs and Successors, and the other moiety thereof to any person or persons that shall sue for the same, to be recovered in any of Her Majesty's Courts of Record at Westminster, by action of debt, bill, plaint or information, in which no wager of law, essoign, privilege or protection, or more than one imparlance shall be allowed.

s.2 And whereas many persons may through ignorance offend against this Act, unless some provision be made whereby the property in every such book, as is intended by this Act to be secured to the proprietor or proprietors thereof may be ascertained, as likewise the consent of such proprietor or proprietors for the printing or reprinting of such book or books may from time to time be known; Be it therefore further enacted by the authority aforesaid, That nothing in this Act contained shall be construed to extend to subject any bookseller, printer or other person whatsoever, to the forfeitures or penalties therein mentioned, for or by reason of the printing or reprinting of any book or books without such consent as aforesaid, unless the title to the copy of such book or books hereafter published shall, before such publication, be entered in the Register Book of the Company of Stationers, in such manner as hath been usual, which Register Book shall at all times be kept at the Hall of the said Company; and unless such consent of the proprietor or proprietors be in like manner entered as aforesaid, for every of which several entries sixpence shall be paid, and no more; which said Register Book may, at all reasonable and convenient times be resorted to, and inspected by any bookseller, printer or other person, for the purposes before mentioned, without any fee or reward; and the Clerk of the said Company of Stationers shall, when and as often as thereunto required, give a certificate under his hand of such entry or entries, and for every such certificate may take a fee not exceeding sixpence.

s.3 Provided nevertheless, that if the Clerk of the said Company of Stationers for the time being, shall refuse or neglect to register, or make such entry or entries, or to give such certificate, being thereunto required by the author or proprietor of such copy or copies, in the presence of two or more credible witnesses, that then such person and persons so refusing, notice being first duly given of such refusal, by an advertisement in the *Gazette*, shall have the like benefit as if such entry or entries, certificate or certificates had been duly made and given; and that the clerks so refusing shall, for any such offence, forfeit to the proprietor of such copy or copies the sum of twenty pounds, to be recovered in any of Her Majesty's Courts of Record at Westminster, by action of debt, bill, plaint or information, in which no wager of law, essoign, privilege or protection, or more than one imparlance shall be allowed.

s.4 Provided nevertheless, and it is hereby further enacted by the authority aforesaid, that if any bookseller or booksellers, printer or printers, shall after the said [25 March 1710], set a price upon, or sell, or expose to sale any book or books at such a price or rate as shall be conceived by any person or persons to be too high and unreasonable; it shall and may be lawful for any person or persons to make complaint thereof to the Lord Archbishop of Canterbury for the time being, the Lord Chancellor or Lord Keeper of the Great Seal of Great Britain, for the time being, the Lord Bishop of London for the time being, the Lord Chief Justice of the Court of Queen's Bench, the Lord Chief Justice of the Court of Common Pleas, the Lord Chief Baron of the Court of Exchequer for the time being, the Vice-Chancellors of the two Universities for the time being, in that part of Great Britain called England; the Lord President of the Sessions for the time being, the Lord Justice General for the time being, the Lord Chief Baron of the Exchequer for the time being, the Rector of the College of Edinburgh for the time being, in that part of Great Britain called Scotland; who, or any one of them, shall and have hereby full power and authority, from time to time, to send for, summon or call before him or them such bookseller or booksellers, printer or printers, and to examine and enquire of the reason of the dearness and inhancement of the price or value of such book or books by him or them so sold or exposed to sale; and if upon such enquiry and examination it shall be found that the price of such book or books is inhanced, or any wise too high or unreasonable, then and in such case the said Archbishop of Canterbury, Lord Chancellor or Lord Keeper, Bishop of London, two Chief Justices, Chief Baron, Vice-Chancellors of the Universities, in that part of Great Britain called England, and the said Lord President of the Sessions, Lord Justice General, Lord Chief Baron, and Rector of the College of Edinburgh, in that part of Great Britain called Scotland, or any one or more of them, so enquiring and examining, have hereby full power and authority to reform and redress the same, and to limit and settle the price of every such printed book and books, from time to time, according to the best of their judgments, and as to them shall seem just and reasonable; and in case of alteration from the rate or price from what was set or demanded by such bookseller or booksellers, printer or printers, to award and order such bookseller or booksellers, printer or printers, to pay all the costs and charges that the person or persons so complaining shall be put unto, by reason of such complaint, and of the causing such rate or price to be so limited and settled; all which shall be done by the said Archbishop of Canterbury, Lord Chancellor or Lord Keeper, Bishop of London, two Chief Justices, Chief Baron, Vice-Chancellors of the Universities, in that part of Great Britain called England, and the said Lord President of the Sessions, Lord Justice General, Lord Chief Baron, and Rector of the College of Edinburgh, in that part of Great Britain called Scotland, or any one of them, by writing under their hands and seals, and thereof publick notice shall be forthwith given by the said bookseller or booksellers, printer or printers, by an advertisement in the *Gazette*; and if any bookseller or booksellers, printer or printers, shall after such settlement made of the said rate and price sell or expose to sale any book or books at a higher or greater price than what shall have been so limited and settled as aforesaid, then and in every such case such bookseller or booksellers, printer or printers, shall forfeit the sum of five pounds for every such book so by him, her or them sold or exposed to sale; one moiety thereof to the Queen's most Excellent Majesty, Her Heirs and Successors, and the other moiety to any person or persons that shall sue for the same, to be recovered with costs of suit, in any of Her Majesty's Courts of Record at Westminster, by action of debt, bill, plaint or information, in which no wager of law, essoign, privilege or protection, or more than one imparlance shall be allowed.

s.5 Provided always, and it is hereby enacted, that nine copies of each book or books, upon the best paper, that from and after the [10 April 1710] shall be printed and published as aforesaid, or reprinted and published with additions, shall, by the printer and printers thereof, be delivered to the Warehouse-Keeper of the said Company of Stationers, for the time being, at the Hall of the said Company, before such publication made, for the use of the Royal Library, the libraries of the Universities of Oxford and Cambridge, the libraries of the four Universities in Scotland, the library of Sion College in London, and the library commonly called the library belonging to the Faculty of Advocate's at Edinburgh respectively; which said Warehouse-Keeper is hereby required, within ten days after demand by the Keepers of the respective libraries, or any person or persons by them or any of them authorised to demand the said copy, to deliver the same for the use of the aforesaid libraries; and if any proprietor, bookseller or printer, or the Warehouse-Keeper of the said Company of Stationers, shall not observe the direction of this Act therein, that then he and they so making default in not delivering the said printed copies as aforesaid, shall forfeit, besides the value of the said printed copies, the sum of five pounds for every copy not so delivered, as also the value of the said printed copy not so delivered; the same to be recovered by the Queen's Majesty, Her Heirs and Successors, and by the Chancellor, Masters and Scholars of any of the said Universities, and by the President and Fellows of Sion College, and the said Faculty of Advocates at Edinburgh, with their full costs respectively.

s.6 Provided always, and be it further enacted, that if any person or persons incur the penalties contained in this Act, in that part of Great Britain called Scotland, they shall be recoverable by any action before the Court of Session there.

s.7 Provided, that nothing in this Act contained do extend, or shall be construed to extend to prohibit the importation, vending or selling of any books in Greek, Latin, or any other foreign language printed beyond the seas; any thing in this Act contained to the contrary notwithstanding.

s.8 And be it further enacted by the authority aforesaid, that if any action or suit shall be commenced or brought against any person or persons whatsoever, for doing or causing to be done anything in pursuance of this Act, the defendants in such action may plead the General Issue, and give the special matter in evidence; and if upon such action a verdict be given for the defendant, or the plaintiff become nonsuited or discontinue his action, than the defendant shall have and recover his full costs, for which he shall have the same remedy as a defendant in any case by law hath.

s.9 Provided, that nothing in this Act contained shall extend or be construed to extend, either to prejudice or confirm any right that the said Universities or any of them, or any person or persons have or claim to have, to the printing or reprinting any book or copy already printed, or hereafter to be printed.

s.10 Provided nevertheless, that all actions, suits, bills, indictments or informations for any offence that shall be committed against this Act, shall be brought, sued and commenced within three months next after such offence committed, or else the same shall be void and of none effect.

s.11 Provided always, that after the expiration of the said term of fourteen years, the sole right of printing or disposing of copies shall return to the authors thereof, if they are then living, for another term of fourteen years.

Bibliography

PRIMARY SOURCES

1695–1704. Before the *Statute of Anne*

Bill for the Better Regulating of Printing and Printing Presses, March 1695
Reprinted in DeBeer, *The Correspondence of John Locke*, vol V, 791–95

Bill for the Regulating of Printing and Printing Presses, November 1695
Cambridge University Library, Oo.6.6.93; Lambeth Palace Library, Todd MS, 640/17

An Abstract of the said Bill, 1695
Lambeth Palace Library, Todd MS, 640/18

Oxf: obj: ag: scheme of Printing Act, December 2 1695
Lambeth Palace Library, 939/10

Reasons humbly offer'd to the Consideration of the Honourable House of Commons, shewing the great necessity of having a Bill for the Regulating of Printing and Printing-Presses, dated "1698?", 1697
Lincoln's Inn Library, MP102, Fol.311; British Library, 1887.b.58.(7)

A Letter to a Member of Parliament, showing that a restraint on the Press is inconsistant with the Protestant religion, and dangerous to the liberties of the nation, 1697
Reprinted in Holmes and Speck, *The Divided Society*, 69–70

Bill for the Better Regulating of Printing and Printing Presses, January 1699
The Manuscripts of the House of Lords, Vol III, New Series, 1679–99

A Letter to the Archbishop of Canterbury from Mr. Harley concerning the Draught of a new Bill containing very good methods to have a printer or author answerable for every thing which is published, January 8 1702
Lambeth Palace Library, Todd MS, 930/25

An Act for the better regulating of Printers and Printing Presses, January 1702
Lambeth Palace Library, Todd MS 640/19

Some Observations on the said bill, 1702
Lambeth Palace Library, Todd MS, 640/201

The Case of the Booksellers and Printers, Relating to the Patentees for the sole Printing all Books of the Common Law, 1704
Lincoln's Inn Library, MP102, Fol.308

1705–1710. The *Statute of Anne*

Reasons Humbly Offer'd for a Bill for the Encouragement of Learning, and Improvement of Printing, cir.1706
Lincoln's Inn Library, MP102, Fol.312

How J, *Some Thoughts on the Present State of Printing and Bookselling* (London, How, 1709)
British Library, BM 11901.A.2(3)

Reasons Humbly offered to the Consideration of the honourable House of Commons Relating to the Bill, For Securing Property in Books &c., 1709?, 1707
Lincoln's Inn Library, MP102, Fol.102

A Bill for Encouragement of Learning, and for Securing the Property of Copies of Books to the Rightful Owners thereof, 1709
Lincoln's Inn Library, MP102, Fol.98; Bodleian Library, MS Rawl, 922, 380–386

An Abstract of the Bill for Encouragement of Learning, and for Securing the Property of Books to the Rightful Owners, 1710
British Library, L.23.c.6.(88)

The Booksellers humble address to the Honorable House of Commons In behalf of a Bill for the Encouragement of Learning, 1710
Bodleian Library, Fol.w, 666(227)

A Letter from Holland, concerning the Right which Booksellers have in the Copies, or Sole Power of Printing their respective Books, in that Nation, 1710
Lincoln's Inn Library, MP102, Fol.104

Reasons Humbly Offer'd for the Bill for the Encouragement of Learning and for Securing the Property of Copies of Books to the Rightful Owners thereof, 1709
Lincoln's Inn Library, MP102, Fol.100

More Reasons Humbly Offer'd for the Bill for Encouraging Learning and Securing the Property of Copies of Books, 1709
Lincoln's Inn Library, MP102, Fol.101

The Case of the Booksellers Right to their Copies, or sole Power of Printing their respective Books, represented to the Parliament, 1709
Lincoln's Inn Library, MP102, Fol.103; British Library, 1887.b.58(3)

1734–1740. A Flurry of Legislative Activity

A short State of the publick Encouragement given to Printing and Bookselling in France, Holland, Germany and at London. With Reasons humbly offered to the Lords Spiritual and Temporal in Parliament assembled, for granting to S. Buckley such Privilege for Thuanus in Latin, as is already granted to every British subject who is possessed of the Copy of any Book in English, Samuel Buckley, 1734
Reprinted in Parks (ed.), *English Publishing ... Thirteen Tracts*

The Case of Designers, Engravers, Etchers, &c. stated in a Letter to a member of Parliament, 1735
Lincoln's Inn Library, MP102, Fol.125

A Bill for the Encouragement of the Arts of designing, engraving and etching, historical and other Prints, by vesting the Properties thereof in the Inventors and Engravers, during the Time therein to be mentioned, 1735
Bodleian Library, MS Carte 207, 5

The Humble petition of several Proprietors of Copies of Books whose names are hereunto Subscribed on Behalf as well as of the Authors and Compilers of such Books as of themselves and a great Number of others concerned in the Manufacture of Printing, 1735
British Library, BM 357.c.2.(80)

Report of the Committee upon the Stationers Bill, 1735
British Library, BM 357.c.2.(73)

A Bill for the better Encouragement of Learning and the more effectual securing of the Copies of Printed Books to the Authors or Purchasers of such Copies, during the Times therein mentioned, 1735
Bodleian Library, MS Carte 114, 391–6

A Bill for making more effectual an Act passed in the Eighth Year of the Reign of her late Majesty Queen Anne, 1735
Bodleian Library, MS Carte, 207, 10, 11, 12, 13, 15

A Bill for the better Encouragement of Learning and the more effectual securing of the Copies of Printed Books to the Authors or Purchasers of such Copies, 1735
House of Lords Parchment Collection, Manuscript List, 1714–1814

An Act for the better Encouragement of Learning and the more effectual securing of the Copies of Printed Books to the Authors or Purchasers of such Copies, 1735
Bodleian Library, MS Carte, 207, 14

The Case of Authors and Proprietors of Books, 1735
British Library, BM 816.m.12.(52), (54); Bodleian Library, MS Carte 207, 20

A Letter to a Member of Parliament concerning the Bill now depending in the House of Commons, for making more effectual an Act in the 8th year of the Reign of Queen Anne, entitled, An Act for the Encouragement of Learning, by Vesting the Copies of Printed Books in the Authors or Purchasers of such Copies, during the Times therein mentioned, 1735
Bodleian Library, MS Carte 207, 9

A Letter from an Author to a Member of Parliament occasioned by a Late Letter concerning the Bill now depending in the House of Commons, 1735
Bodleian Library, MS Carte 207, 16

A Second Letter from an Author to a Member of Parliament containing some Further Remarks on a Late Letter concerning the Bill now depending in the House of Commons, 1735
Bodleian Library, MS Carte 207, 19

Farther Reasons Humbly Offer'd to the Consideration of the Honourable House of Commons, for making more effectual an Act passed in the 8th Year of Q.Anne, 1735
British Library, BM 816.m.12.(51); Bodleian Library, MS Carte 207, 7

Reasons for granting authors a Privilege for 21 years rather than for 14, 1735
Bodleian Library, MS Carte 207, 4

Reasons for renewing the privilege of the term of 21 years in old copies, 1735
Bodleian Library, MS Carte 207, 4

Some Reasons Humbly Offered to the Parliament of Great Britain for Making more effectual an Act made 8 Ann. cap.49, 1735
British Library, BM 18th century reel, 3019/24

A Bill for the Better Encouragement of Learning by the more Effectual Securing the Copies of Printed Books to the Authors or Purchasers of such Copies, 1737
British Library, BS 68/16.(1); Bodleian Library, MS Carte, 207, 14

An Act for the Encouragement of Learning by the more Effectual Securing the sole Right of printing Books to the Authors thereof, their Executors, Administrators or Assigns, during the Times therein mentioned, 1737
British Library, BM 357.c.7.(41.)

An Act for the Encouragement of Learning by the more Effectual Securing the sole Right of printing Books to the Authors thereof, their Executors, Administrators or Assigns, during the Times therein mentioned, 1737
House of Lords Parchment Collection, Manuscript List, 1714–1814

A Bill for Prohibiting the Importation of Books reprinted abroad that were Originally Printed in Great Britain, 1738
House of Lords Parchment Collection, Manuscript List, 1714–1814

A Bill, intituled, An Act for prohibiting the Importation of Books re-printed Abroad, and first composed or written, and printed in Great Britain; and for limiting the Prices of Books, 1739
Reprinted in Torrington (ed.), *Lords Papers 1739 to 1743–44*

1743–1751. *Midwinter v Hamilton, Millar v Kincaid*

Information for Daniel Midwinter, William Innes, John Knapton, Paul Knapton, Andrew Millar, and others, all of London Booksellers, and their Attorney or factor, Pursuers, against, Gavin Hamilton, Andrew Stalker and others, Booksellers in Edinburgh and Glasgow, Defenders, November 30 1744
Advocate's Library, Edinburgh

Information for Messr. Hamilton and Balfour, Booksellers in Edinburgh, Andrew Stalker, Booksellers in Glasgow, and other Booksellers in these cities, Defenders against Andrew Millar and others, Booksellers in London, Pursuers, December 3 1744.
Bodleian Library, Johnson d.247

Additional Information for Mess. Hamilton and Balfour, Andrew Stalker, and others, Booksellers in Edinburgh and Glasgow, Defenders; against Andrew Millar, and others, Booksellers in London, Pursuers, December 13 1744
Advocate's Library, Edinburgh

Petition of the Booksellers of London against the Booksellers of Edinburgh and Glasgow, 15 July 1746
Bodleian Library, Vet.A.4.e.2197; Advocate's Library, Edinburgh

Answers for the Booksellers of Edinburgh and Glasgow to the petition of Andrew Millar and other Booksellers in London, July 29 1746
Bodleian Library, Vet.A4.e.2197; Advovate's Library, Edinburgh

Answers for the Booksellers of Edinburgh and Glasgow to the Petition of Daniel Midwinter and other booksellers in London, December 21 1746
Bodleian Library, Vet.A4.e.2197; Advovate's Library, Edinburgh

The Petition of Gavin Hamilton & John Balfour, and others, Booksellers in Edinburgh, Andrew Stalker and others, Booksellers in Glasgow, Defenders, Against Andrew Millar and others, Booksellers in London, Pursuers, January 15 1747
Advocate's Library, Edinburgh

The Petition of Gavin Hamilton and John Balfour Booksellers in Edinburgh, and Andrew Stalker, and others, Booksellers in Glasgow, February 26 1747
Advocate's Library, Edinburgh

Answers for Daniel Midwinter, William Innes, John Knapton, Andrew Millar and others, all of London, Booksellers, and their Attorney or Factor, Pursuers; to the Petition of Gavin Hamilton and John Balfour, and others, Booksellers in Edinburgh, Andrew Stalker and others, Booksellers in Glasgow, Defenders, February 27 1747
Advocate's Library, Edinburgh

Memorial for Gavin Hamilton, and others, Booksellers in Edinburgh, Andrew Stalker, and others, Booksellers in Glasgow, Defenders; by way of Supplement to their Petition presently depending, and a Reply to the Pursuers Answers, May 29 1747
Advocate's Library, Edinburgh

Memorial and Condescendence for Messieurs Hamilton and Balfour and others Booksellers in Edinburgh, and Andrew Stalker and others Booksellers in Glasgow, June 29 1747
Advocate's Library, Edinburgh

Memorial for The Booksellers of Edinburgh and Glasgow, relating to the Process against them by some of the London Booksellers; which depended before the Court of Session, and is now under Appeal (undated)
Reprinted in Parks (ed.), *The Literary Property Debate: Seven Tracts*

The Petition of Daniel Midwinter, William Innes, Aaron Ward, and others, all of London Booksellers, and William Elliot Writer in Edinburgh their Attorney or Factor, Pursuers, December 9 1747
Bodleian Library, 4 Jur.X.136

The Case of the Appellants, February 8 1751
British Library, BM 18th century reel, 4065/03

The Case of the Respondents, February 11 1751
British Library, BM 18th century reel, 4065/04

1747–1770. A Public Discussion

A letter from an author, to a Member of Parliament, concerning literary property (London, John and Paul Knapton, 1747)
Reprinted in *The Works of William Warburton*, Vol.12, (London, Cadell & Davies, 1811)

An Enquiry into the Nature and Origin of Literary Property, 1762
Reprinted in Parks (ed.), *Horace Walpole's Political Tracts*

A Vindication of the Exclusive Right of Authors, to their own works: A subject now under consideration before the 12 judges of England (London, Griffiths, 1762)
British Library, BM 1130.d.4b

Some Thoughts on the State of Literary Property, 1764
Reprinted in Parks (ed.), *The Literary Property Debate: Six Tracts*

A Letter from A Gentleman in Edinburgh, to his Friend in London, 1769
Reprinted in Parks (ed.), *Freedom of the Press and the Literary Property Debate*

1769. *Millar v Taylor*

Speeches or Arguments of the Judges of the Court of King's Bench in April 1769; In the Cause of Andrew Millar against Taylor for printing Thomson's Seasons, to which are added Explanatory Notes, And an appendix, containing a short state of Literary Property, by the Editor, Printed for William Coke, Bookseller in Leith, 1771
Reprinted in Parks (ed.), *The Literary Property Debate: Seven Tracts*

The Question Concerning Literary Property, determined by the Court of the King's Bench, on 20th April 1769, in the cause between Andrew Millar and Robert Taylor, with the separate Opinions of the four Judges and the Reasons given by each in support of his opinion, James Burrow, Printed by W. Strahan and M. Woodfall, Law Printers to the King's Most Excellant Majesty, for B. Toley in Bell Yard, near Lincoln's Inn, 1773.
British Library, BM 515.f.16.(1)

See also the Table of Cases.

1773. *Hinton v Donaldson*

Information for Alexander Donaldson and John Wood, booksellers in Edinburgh, and James Meurose, Bookseller in Kilmarnock, defenders; against John Hinton, Bookseller in

London, and Alexander McConochie, Writer in Edinburgh, his Attorney, Pursuers, January 2 1773
British Library, BM 515.f.15.(2)

Information for Mess. John Hinton of London, Bookseller, and Alexander Mackonochie, Writer in Edinburgh, his Attorney, Pursuers; against Mess. Alexander Donaldson and John Wood, Booksellers in Edinburgh, and James Meurose, Bookseller in Kilmarnock, Defenders, January 2 1773
British Library, BM 515.f.15.(2)

The Decision of the Court of Session, upon the Question of Literary Property; in the cause Hinton against Donaldson, &c., Published by James Boswell, Esq., Advocate, one of the Counsel in the cause; Printed by James Donaldson, for Alexander Donaldson, 1774
British Library, BM 6573.g.11

See also the Table of Cases.

1774. *Donaldson v Becket*

The Cases of the Appellants and Respondents in the Cause of Literary Property, before the House of Lords wherein the Decree of Lord Chancellor Apsley was Reversed, 26 Feb. 1774, with, The Genuine Arguments of the Council, the Opinions of the Judges, and the Speeches of the Lords, who distinguished themselves on that Occasion, With Notes and Observations and References by a Gentleman of the Inner Temple, London, 1774
British Library, BM 515.f.16.(2)

The Pleadings of the Counsel before the House of Lords in the cause concerning Literary Property; together with the Opinions of the Learned Judges on the common law copyright of authors and booksellers, To which are added, the Speeches of the Noble Lords, who spoke for and against reversing the Decree of the Court of Chancery, London, 1774
British Library, BM 515.f.16.(3)

See also the Table of Cases.

1774–1775. After *Donaldson*

Bill for the Relief of Booksellers, and others, by vesting the Copies of printed Books in the Purchasers of such Copies from Authors or their Assigns, for a Time therein to be limited, 1774
House of Lords Parchment Collection, Manuscript List, 1714–1814

An Act for the Relief of Booksellers and others, by vesting the Copies of Printed Books in the Purchasers of such Copies from Authors, or their Assigns, for a limited Time, 1774
British Library, BM 21.b.18.(3)

Petitions and Papers relating to the Bill of the Booksellers, now before the House of Commons, 1774
Reprinted in Parks (ed.), *The Literary Property Debate: Eight Tracts*

To the Honourable the Commons of Great Britain, in Parliament assembled, The Humble Petition of Alexander Donaldson, Bookseller in St. Paul's Church-yard, London, in Petitions and Papers relating to the Bill of the Booksellers, now before the House of Commons, 1774
Reprinted in Parks (ed.), *The Literary Property Debate: Eight Tracts*

Remarks on the Petitions of Mr. A. Donaldson and others, against the Petition now depending in Parliament for affording Relief to the Booksellers of London and Westminster, 1774
British Library, BM 2581.c.5.(9)

Further Remarks and Papers on the Booksellers Bill, 1774
Bodleian Library, 4 Jur., 136, 8

Observations on the Case of the Booksellers of London and Westminster, 1774
British Library, BM 215.i.4.(99)

Considerations In Behalf of the Booksellers of London and Westminster, petitioning the Legislature for Relief, 1774
Reprinted in Parks (ed.), *English Publishing ... Thirteen Tracts*

Bill for enabling the Two Universities to hold in Perpetuity the Copy Right in books, for the advancement of useful Learning, and other purposes of Education, within the said Universities, 1775
House of Lords Parchment Collection, Manuscript List, 1714–1814

SECONDARY SOURCES

ABRAMS H, "The Historic Foundation of American Copyright Law: Exploding the Myth of Common Law Copyright", 29 *Wayne Law Review* 1983, 1119
ASHBURNER W, *Principles of Equity*, 2nd ed. (London, Butterworths, 1933)
ASTBURY R, "The renewal of the Licensing act in 1693 and its Lapse in 1695", 33 *The Library* 1978, 296
AUSTER P, *The New York Trilogy* (London, Faber and Faber, 1988)
BAINBRIDGE D, *Intellectual Property*, 4th ed. (London, Financial Times, Pitman Publishing, 1999)
BAKER J H, *An Introduction to English Legal History*, 4th ed. (London, Butterworths, 2002)
BAKER P V/P ST J LANGAN, *Snell's Principles of Equity*, 29th ed. (London, Sweet & Maxwell, 1990)
BEVAN T, "The Appellate Jurisdiction of the House of Lords", 17 *LQR* 1901, 357
BIRRELL A, *Copyright in Books* (London, Cassell & Co, 1899)
BLACK J, *The English Press in the Eighteenth Century* (London & Sydney, Croom Helm, 1987)
BLACKSTONE W, *Commentaries on the Laws of England, Book the Second* (Oxford, Clarendon Press, 1766)
—— *Commentaries on the Laws of England, Book the Third* (Oxford, Clarendon Press, 1768)

BLAGDEN C, *The Stationers' Company, A History, 1403–1959* (London, George Allen & Unwin, 1960)

BOWREY K, "Who's Writing Copyright History?", 6 *EIPR* 1996, 322

—— "Who's Painting Copyright's History?", in McClean D/Schubert K (eds.), *Dear Images: Art, Copyright and Culture* (London, Institute of Contemporary Arts, 2002)

BRENNAN D/A CHRISTIE, "Spoken Words and Copyright Subsistence in Anglo-American Law" 4 *IPQ* 2000, 309

BREWER J, *The Sinews of Power: War, Money and the English State, 1688–1783* (London, Unwin Hyman, 1989)

BROWN A, *Snell's Equity*, 9th ed. (London, Sweet & Maxwell, 1899)

BURKITT D, "Copyrighting Culture — The History and Cultural Specificity of the Western Model of Copyright" 2 *IPQ* 2001, 146

CAMPBELL J LORD, *Lives of the Lord Chancellors and Keepers of the Great Seal of England*, vol.VI (London, John Murray, 1857)

CARPENTER K E (ed.), *Books and Society in History* (New York and London, Bowker Company, 1983)

CARROLL L, *Through the Looking-Glass, and what Alice found there*, in *The Complete Works of Lewis Carroll* (London, Penguin Books, 1988)

CARTER H, *A History of the University Press, Volume I, to the Year 1780* (Oxford, Clarendon Press, 1975)

CAXTON W, *The History of Reynard the Fox*, (London, George Routledge & Sons Ltd)

CHALMERS A, *The Tatler. A Corrected Edition, with Prefaces historical and biographical, in Four Volumes* (London, Nicholson & Son, Fleet Street, 1806)

CLAIR C, *A History of Printing in Britain* (London, Cassell, 1965)

COBBETT W, *Parliamentary History from the Norman Conquest, in 1066, to the year 1803*, 44 Volumes, Vol. 17, (London, T Hansard, 1813)

COLE R C, *Irish Booksellers and English Writers, 1740–1800* (Kent, Mansell Publishing Ltd., Humanities Press International, Inc., 1986)

COLLINS A S, *Authorship in the Days of Johnson* (New York, Dutton, 1929)

COOMBE R J, "Challenging Paternity: Histories of Copyright", 6 *Yale Journal of Law and the Humanities* 1994, 397

CORNISH W R, *Intellectual Property: Patents, Copyright, Trade Marks and Allied Rights*, 3rd ed. (London, Sweet & Maxwell, 1996)

COPINGER W A, *The Law of Copyright*, 3rd ed. (London, Sweet & Maxwell, 1893)

CRANFIELD G A, *The Press and Society: From Caxton to Northcliffe* (London and New York, Longman, 1978)

—— *The Development of the Provincial Newspaper, 1700–1760* (Oxford, Clarendon Press, 1962)

CRANSTON M, *JOHN LOCKE, a biography* (London, Longmans, Green & Co., 1957)

CRIST T, "Government Control of the Press After the Expiration of the Printing Act in 1679", 5 *Publishing History* 1979, 49

CRUICKSHANKS E/S HANDLEY/D W HAYTON (eds.), *The House of Commons 1690–1715*, vol.III (Cambridge, Cambridge University Press, 2002)

DAWSON R L, *The French Booktrade and the "permission simple" of 1777: copyright and public domain* (Oxford, The Voltaire Foundation, 1992)

DE BEER E S (ed.), *The Correspondence of John Locke, in Eight Volumes* (Oxford, Clarendon Press, 1978)

DEAZLEY R, "The Myth of Copyright at Common Law", 62 *CLJ* 2003, 106

—— "Re-reading Donaldson (1774) in the Twenty-First century and Why it Matters", 25 *EIPR* 2003, 270

DEFOE D, *An Essay on the Regulation of the Press* (Oxford, Basil Blackwell, Published for the Luttrell Society, 1948)

—— *A Review of the Affairs of France, and A Review of the State of the British Nation*, reprinted in *Defoe's Review in 22 Fascimile Books*, Published for the Facsimile Text Society, (New York, Columbia University Press, 1938)

DOWNIE J A, *ROBERT HARLEY and the press: Propaganda and Public Opinion in the Age of Swift and Defoe* (Cambridge, Cambridge University Press, 1979)

DUGAS D-J, "The Book Trade in London in 1709 (Part One)", 95 *Papers of the Bibliographical Society of America* 2001, 31

—— "The London Book Trade in 1709 (Part Two)", 95 *Papers of the Bibliographical Society of America* 2001, 157

ECO U, *Serendipities, Language and Lunacy* (London, Phoenix, 2000)

EISENSTEIN E, *The Printing Press as an Agent of Change* (Cambridge, CUP, 1980)

ELCHIES LORD, *Decisions of the Court of Sessions from the Year 1733 to the Year 1754*, vols 1, 2 (Edinburgh, W M Morison, 1813)

ESPINASSE I, *A Treatise on the Law of Actions on Statutes…and on the Statutes Respecting Copyright* (London, 1824)

FEATHER J, *The Provincial Book Trade in Eighteenth-Century England* (Cambridge, Cambridge University Press, 1985)

—— *A History of British Publishing* (London & New York, Routledge, 1988)

—— *Publishing, Piracy and Politics: An Historical Study of Copyright in Britain* (London, Mansell, 1994)

—— "The Book Trade in Politics: The Making of the Copyright Act of 1710", 8 *Publishing History* 1980, 19

—— "The English Book Trade and the Law 1695–1799", 12 *Publishing History* 1982, 51

—— "From Censorship to Copyright: Aspects of the Government's Role in the English Book Trade 1695–1775", in Carpenter K E (ed), *Books and Society in History* (New York and London, Bowker Company, 1983)

FERGUSON J, *Decisions of the Court of Sessions from the Year 1738 to the Year 1752* (Edinburgh, 1775)

FERGUSON J, "The Brothers Foulis and Early Glasgow Printing", 1 *The Library* 1889, 81

FIFOOT C H S, *LORD MANSFIELD* (Oxford, Clarendon, 1936)

FINKELSTEIN D/A MCCLEERY (eds), *The Book History Reader* (London and New York, Routledge, 2002)

GAINES J M, *Contested Culture: The Image, the Voice, and the Law* (London, BFI Publishing, 1992)

GARNETT K, JAMES J R, DAVIES G, *Copinger and Skone James on Copyright*, 14th edn, vol.1 (London, Sweet & Maxwell, 1999)

GAY J, *FABLES By the late Mr. Gay. Volume the Second.* (1738), reprinted in *John Gay, Fables, Two Volumes in One* (Menston, The Scholar Press Limited, 1969)

GOEBEL L, "The role of history in copyright dilemmas", 9 *Journal of Law and Information Science* 1998, 22

GOLDSTEIN P, *Copyright's Highway. From Gutenberg to the celestial jukebox* (New York, Hill and Wang, 1994)

GOULDEN R J, *Some Chancery Lawsuits 1714–1758: An Analytical List By R J Goulden* (1982) British Library, x.205/1260

HANDOVER P M, *Printing in London. From 1476 to Modern Times* (London, George Allen & Unwin Ltd., 1960)

HANSON L, *Government and the Press 1695–1763* (Oxford, Clarendon Press, 1932)

HARGRAVE F, *An Argument in Defence of Literary Property* (London, Otridge, 1774), reprinted in Parks (ed.), *Four Tracts on Freedom of the Press, 1790–1821.*

HARRIS M, *London Newspapers in the Age of Walpole: A Study of the Origins of the Modern English Press* (London and Toronto, Associated University Press, 1987)

—— "Scratching the surface: engravers, printsellers and the London book trade in the mid-18th century", in Hunt A/G Mandelbrote/A Shell (eds.), *The Book Trade and its Customers, 1450–1900: historical essays for Robin Myers* (Wincester, St Paul's Bibliographies, 1990)

HARRISON F M, "Nathaniel Ponder: The Publisher of the Pilgrim's Progress", 15 *The Library* 1934–35, 257

HAYTON D W, *The House of Commons 1690–1715*, vol.1 (Cambridge, Cambridge University Press, 2002)

HEALEY G H, *The Letters of Daniel Defoe* (Oxford, Clarendon Press, 1955)

HESSE C, *Publishing and Cultural Politics in Revolutionary France* (Berkeley, University of California Press, 1991)

HEWARD E, *LORD MANSFIELD* (Chichester and London, Barry Rose Ltd., 1979)

HOLMES G, *British Politics in the Age of Anne* (London, MacMillan, 1967)

—— *The Trial of Doctor Sacheverell* (London, Eyre Methuen, 1973)

—— *The Making of a Great Power, Late Stuart and early Georgian Britain, 1660–1722* (London and New York, Longman, 1993)

HOLMES G, and SZECHI D, *The Age of Oligarchy: Pre-Industrial Britain 1722–1783* (London and New York, Longman, 1993)

HOLMES G, and SPECK W A (eds.), *The Divided Society, Party Conflict in England 1694–1716* (London, Edward Arnold, 1967)

HOLYOAK J, and TORREMANS P, *Intellectual Property Law* (London, Dublin and Edinburgh, Butterworths, 1995)

HOME H, *Remarkable Decisions of the Court of Sessions, From the year 1730 to the year 1752* (Edinburgh, A Kincaid and J Bell, 1766)

HOPPITT J (ed.), *Failed Legislation 1660–1800: Extracted from the Commons and Lords Journals* (London, The Hambledon Press, 1997)

HORWITZ H, *Chancery Equity Records and Proceedings 1600–1800: A Guide to Documents in the Public Records Office* (London, HMSO, 1995)

HUNT A/G MANDLEBROTE/A SHELL (eds.), *The Book Trade and its Customers, 1450–1900: historical essays for Robin Myers* (Winchester, St. Paul's Bibliographies, 1990)

HUNTER D, "POPE v BICKHAM: An Infringement of An Essay On Man Alleged", 9 *The Library* 1987, 268

—— "Copyright Protection for Engravings and Maps in Eighteenth-Century Britain", 9 *The Library* 1987, 128

IBSEN H, *PEER GYNT* (London, Penguin Books, 1970)

KAPLAN B, *An Unhurried View of Copyright* (New York & London, Columbia University Press, 1967)

KAYMAN M A, "Lawful Writing: Common Law, Statute and the Properties of Literature", 27 *New Literary History* 1996, 761

KEETON G W, *Sheridan, Equity*, 2nd ed. (London, Professional Books Limited, 1976)

KENYON J P, *Stuart England* (London, Penguin Books, 1978)

KERNAN A, *SAMUEL JOHNSON and the Impact of Print* (New Jersey, Princeton University Press, 1987)

KERR W W, *A Treatise on the Law and Practice of Injunctions in Equity* (London, William Maxwell & Son, 1867)

KHAN B Z, *Intellectual Property and Economic Development: Lessons from American and European History* (London, Commission on Intellectual Property Rights, 2002)

KING LORD P, *The Life of John Locke, with Extracts from his Correspondence, Journals and Common Place Books*, vol.1 (London, Henry Colburn & Richard Bently, 1830)

KISHLANSKY M, *A Monarchy Transformed, Britain 1603–1714* (London, Penguin Books, 1997)

LADDIE H/P PRESCOTT/M VITORIA/A SPECK/L LANE (eds.), *LADDIE PRESCOTT and VITORIA, The Modern Law of Copyright and Designs*, 3rd ed., vol.1 (London, Butterworths, 2000)

LATHAM R (tr.), *The Travels of Marco Polo* (London, Folio Society, 1968)

LAW E, *Observations Occasioned by the Contest about Literary Property* (Cambridge University, 1770)

LEVACK B P, *The Formation of the British State: England, Scotland, and the Union 1603–1707* (Oxford, Clarendon Press, 1987)

LIEBERMAN D, *The Province of Legislation Determined, Legal Theory in eighteenth-century Britain* (Cambridge, Cambridge University press, 1989)

LOCKE J, *The Second Treatise of Government* (Gough J W (ed.)) (Oxford, Blackwell, 1966)

LOEWENSTEIN J, *The Author's Due: Printing and the Prehistory of Copyright* (Chicago, University of Chicago Press, 2002)

—— *BEN JONSON and Possessive Authorship* (Cambridge, Cambridge University Press, 2002)

LOWNDES J J, *An Historical Sketch of the Law of Copyright* (London, Sanders and Benning, 1840)

MCCLEAN D/K SCHUBERT (eds.), *Dear Images: Art, Copyright and Culture* (London, Institute of Contemporary Arts, 2002)

MCDOUGALL W, "Copyright Litigation in the Court of Session, 1738–1749, and the Rise of the Scottish Book Trade", 5 *Transactions* 1988, 2

—— "Scottish books for America in the mid 18th Century", in Myers R/M Harris (eds.), *Spreading the Word: The Distribution Networks of Print, 1550–1850* (Winchester, St Pauls Bibliographies, 1990)

MACFIE R A, *Copyright and Patents for Inventions* (Edinburgh, T&T Clark, 1879)

MCKETTERICK D, *A History of Cambridge University Press, Volume Two, Scholarship and Commerce, 1698–1872* (Cambridge, Cambridge University Press, 1998)

MCKENZIE D F, *Making Meaning: "Printers of the Mind" and other Essays*, McDonald P D/M F Suarez (eds.) (Amherst, University of Massachusetts Press, 2002)

MacLaurin J, *Considerations on the Nature and Origins of Literary Property* (1768), Bodleian Library, Johnson e.386

—— *On the Origin and Progress of Literary Property* (1798), reprinted in Macfie R A, *Copyright and Patents for Inventions* (Edinburgh, T&T Clark, 1879)

McLaverty J, "The first printing and publication of Pope's Letters", 2 *The Library* 1980, 264

MacLean A J, "The 1707 Union: Scots Law and the House of Lords", 4 *Journal of Legal History* 1983, 50

Maclehose J, *The Glasgow University Press 1638–1931* (Glasgow, Glasgow University Press, 1931)

MacQueen J, *The Appellate Jurisdiction of the House of Lords and Privy Council* (London, 1824)

Manchester A H, *A Modern Legal History of England and Wales 1750–1950* (London, Butterworths, 1980)

Mann A, *The Scottish Book Trade 1500–1720, Print Commerce and Print Control in Early Modern Scotland* (East Lothian, Tuckwell Press, 2000)

Martin J E, Hanbury & Martin, *Modern Equity*, 16th ed., (London, Sweet & Maxwell, 2001)

Matthews B, *Books and Playbooks* (London, Osgood, McIlvaine & Co., 1895)

Maugham R, *A Treatise on the Laws of Literary Property* (London, Longman, 1828)

May T E, *May's Parliamentary Practice*, 6th ed. (London, Butterworths, 1868)

Meston M C/W D H Sellar/The Rt. Hon. Lord Cooper, *The Scottish Legal Tradition, New Enlarged Edition* (Edinburgh, The Saltire Society & The Stair Society, 1991)

Millhauser S, *In the Penny Arcade* (London, Phoenix, 1999)

Milne A A, *Winnie-The-Pooh* (London, Methuen & Co., 1926)

M'Millan A R G, *The Evolution of the Scottish Judiciary* (Edinburgh, W Green and Son, Limited, 1941)

Montefiore J, *The Law of Copyright* (London 1802)

Morison W M, *The Decisions of the Court of Session from its institution until the Separation of the court into 2 Divisions in the Year 1808, Vol.39–40, Synopsis, Vol.1–2* (Edinburgh 1811)

Mumby F A, *Publishing and Bookselling: From the Earliest Times to 1870*, 5th ed. (London, Jonathon Cape, 1974)

Murray A L, "Administration and the Law", in RAE T I (ed.), *The Union of 1707: Its Impact in Scotland* (Edinburgh, Blackie & Son Limited, 1974)

Myers R/M Harris (eds.), *Spreading the Word: The Distribution Networks of Print, 1550–1850* (Winchester, St. Paul's Bibliographies, 1990)

Nichol D W, *Pope's Literary Legacy: The Book-Trade Correspondence of William Warbuton and John Knapton with other letters and documents, 1744–1780* (Oxford, The Oxford Bibliographical Society, 1992)

Nichols J, *Biographical Anecdotes of William Hogarth*, 2nd ed., (London, 1782)

Orwell G, *Nineteen Eighty-Four* (London, Secker & Warburg, 1999)

Parks S (ed.), *Four tracts on Freedom of the Press, 1790–1821* (New York and London, Garland, 1974)

Parks S (ed.), *Horace Walpole's Political Tracts 1747–1748 with Two by William Warburton on Literary Property, 1747 and 1762* (New York and London, Garland, 1974)

PARKS S (ed.), *The Literary Property Debate: Eight Tracts 1774–1775* (New York and London, Garland, 1974)

—— (ed.), *English Publishing, the Struggle for Copyright, and the Freedom of the Press: Thirteen Tracts, 1666–1774* (New York and London, Garland, 1975)

—— (ed.), *The Literary Property Debate: Six Tracts 1764–1774* (New York and London, Garland, 1975)

—— (ed.), *Freedom of the Press and the Literary Property Debate: Six Tracts 1755–1770* (New York and London, Garland, 1975)

PARSONS I, "Copyright and Society", in Briggs A (ed.), *Essays in the History of Publishing, in celebration of the 250th anniversary of the House of Longman* (London, Longman, 1974)

PATERSON J M, *Kerr on Injunctions*, 6th ed. (London, Sweet & Maxwell, 1927)

PATTERSON L R, *Copyright in Historical Perspective* (Nashville, Vanderbilt University press, 1968)

PAULSON R, *Hogarth's Graphic Works*, vol.1 (New Haven and London, Yale University Press, 1965)

—— *Hogarth: His Life, Art, and Times*, vol.I (New Haven and London, Yale University Press, 1971)

PAYNE W L (ed.), *The Best of Defoe's Review, An Anthology* (New York, Columbia University Press, 1951)

PLOMER H R, *A Dictionary of Booksellers and Printers who Were at Work in England, Scotland and Ireland from 1668 to 1725*, Esdaile, A (ed.) (London, 1922)

PLUMB J H, *England in the Eighteenth Century* (London, Penguin Books, 1950)

POLLARD M, *Dublin's Trade in Books, 1550–1800* (Oxford, Clarendon Press, 1989)

RAE T I (ed.), *The Union of 1707: Its Impact in Scotland* (Edinburgh, Blackie & Son Limited, 1974)

RAND B, *The Correspondence of John Locke and Edward Clarke* (Oxford, Clarendon Press, 1927)

RANSOM H, *The First Copyright Statute: An Essay on An Act for the Encouragement of Learning, 1710* (Austin, University of Texas, 1956)

—— "The Personal Letter as Literary Property", 30 *Studies in English* 1951, 116

REES A J, *The Practice and Procedure of the House of Lords 1714–1784*, Unpublished Doctoral Thesis (University of Wales, Aberystweth, April 1987)

ROBINSON A, "The Evolution of Copyright, 1476–1776", 67 *Cambrian Law Review* 1991, 67

ROGERS S, "The Use of Royal Licences for Printing in England, 1695–1760: A Bibliography", *The Library* 2000, 133

ROSE M, "The Author in Court: *Pope v Curll* (1741)" 10 *Cardozo Arts and Entertainment Law Review* 1992, 475

—— "Authority and Authenticity: Scribbling Authors and the Genius of Print in Eighteenth-Century England", 10 *Cardozo Arts and Entertainment Law Review* 1992, 495

—— *Authors and Owners. The Invention of Copyright* (London, Harvard University Press, 1993)

—— "The Author as Proprietor: *Donaldson v Becket* and the Genealogy of Modern Authorship", in Sherman B/A Strowel (eds.), *Of Authors and Origins: Essays on Copyright Law* (Oxford, Clarendon Press, 1994)

ROSS T, "Copyright and the Invention of Tradition", 26 *Eighteenth Century Studies* 1992–93, 1

SACHS C, *World History of Dance* (New York, W W Norton & Company Inc, 1963)

SAUNDERS D, "Copyright, Obscenity and Literary History", 57 *Journal of English Literary History* 1990, 431

—— "Approaches to the Historical Relations of the Legal and the Aesthetic", 23 *New Literary History* 1992, 505

—— *Authorship and Copyright* (London, Routledge 1992)

SEBALD W G, *Vertigo* (London, Harvill Press, 1999)

SHERBURN G (ed), *Correspondence of Alexander Pope*, vol III (Oxford, Clarendon Press, 1956)

SHERMAN B/A STROWEL (eds.), *Of Authors and Origins: Essays on Copyright Law* (Oxford, Clarendon Press, 1994)

SHERMAN B/L BENTLY, *The Making of Modern Intellectual Property Law, The British Experience, 1760–1911* (Cambridge, Cambridge University Press, 1999)

SIEBERT F S, *Freedom of the Press in England, 1476–1776* (Urbana, University of Illinois Press, 1965)

SIMPSON A W B (ed), *Biographical Dictionary of the Common Law* (London, Butterworths, 1984)

SMITH H A, *The Principles of Equity* (London, Stevens and Sons, 1856)

—— *A Practical Exposition of The Principles of Equity*, 5th edn (London, Stevens and Sons, 1914)

SNYDER H L, "The Circulation of Newspapers in the Reign of Queen Anne", 23 *The Library* 1968, 206

SPRY I C F, *The Principles of Equitable Remedies*, 4th ed. (London, Sweet & Maxwell, 1990)

STEVENS R, *Law and Politics. The House of Lords as a Judicial Body, 1800–1976* (London, Weidenfeld and Nicholson, 1979)

STOLJAR S J, "The Transformations of Account", 80 *LQR* 1964, 220

SUTHERLAND J R, "The Circulation of Newspapers and Literary Periodicals, 1700–30", 15 *The Library* 1934–35, 110

—— "The Dunciad of 1729", 31 *Modern Language Review* 1936, 347

THOMAS P D G, *The House of Commons in the Eighteenth Century* (Oxford, Clarendon Press, 1971)

TOMPSON R S, "Scottish Judges and the Birth of British Copyright", 18 *Juridicial Review* 1992, 18

TORRINGTON F W (ed), *Lords Papers 1739 to 1743–44* (New York, Oceana Publications, 1978)

TURBERVILLE A S, *The House of Lords in the reign of William III* (Oxford, Clarendon Press, 1913)

—— *The House of Lords in the Eighteenth Century* (Oxford, Clarendon Press, 1927)

—— *The House of Lords in the Age of Reform, 1784–1837* (London, Faber & Faber, 1958)

TURNER S, *An Epitome of the Practice on the Equity Side of the Court of Exchequer* (London, W Clarke & Sons, 1806)

VEEDER V V, "The English Reports, 1537–1865", in *Select Essays in Anglo-American Legal History, Volume II*, (Cambridge, Cambridge University Press, 1908)

VON RANKE L, *A History of England*, vol 5 (Oxford, Clarendon Press, 1875)

WHICHER J, "The Ghost of Donaldson v Beckett: An Inquiry into the Constitutional Distribution of Powers over the Law of Literary Property in the United States — Part 1", 9 *Copyright Society of the USA* 1961–2, 102

WILLIAMS H (ed.), *The Correspondence of Jonathan Swift, Volume IV 1732–1736* (Oxford, Clarendon Press, 1965)

WITTKE C, *The History of Parliamentary Privilege* (New York, Da Capo Press, 1970)

WOODMANSEE M, "The Genius and the Copyright: Economic and Legal Conditions of the Emergence of the 'Author'", 17 *Eighteenth Century Studies* 1983–84, 425

YALE D E C (ed.), *Lord Nottingham's "Manual of Chancery Practice" and "Prolegomena of Chancery and Equity"* (Cambridge, Cambridge University Press, 1965)

Index

CPSIA information can be obtained at www.ICGtesting.com
Printed in the USA
236624LV00003B/1/P

9 781841 133751